Systems Theory for
Organization Development

WILEY SERIES ON
INDIVIDUALS, GROUPS AND ORGANIZATIONS

Series Editor
Cary Cooper,
Department of Management Sciences,
University of Manchester Institute of
Science & Technology,
Manchester

Associate Editor
Eric J. Miller,

Tavistock Institute of
Human Relations,
London

Theories of Group Processes
Edited by Cary Cooper,
University of Manchester Institute of Science & Technology

Task and Organization
Edited by Eric J. Miller,
The Tavistock Institute of Human Relations

Creating a Community of Inquiry: Conflict,
Collaboration, Transformation
William R. Torbert,
Graduate School of Education,
Harvard University

Organizational Careers: Some New Perspectives
Edited by John Van Maanen,
Sloan School of Management
Massachusetts Institute of Technology

Interactions and Interventions in Organizations
Iain Mangham,
Centre for the Study of Organizational Change and Development,
University of Bath

Exploring Individual and Organizational Boundaries
A Tavistock Open Systems Approach
Edited by W. Gordon Lawrence
Tavistock Institute of Human Relations

Systems Theory for Organization Development
Edited by Thomas G. Cummings,
University of Southern California

Systems Theory for Organization Development

Edited by

Thomas G. Cummings
University of Southern California

JOHN WILEY & SONS

Chichester · New York · Brisbane · Toronto

British Library Cataloguing in Publication Data:
Systems theory for organization development. –
  (Wiley series on individuals, groups and
  organizations).
  1. Organizational change 2. System theory
  I. Cummings, Thomas G.
  658.4'06   HD58.8   79-42906

ISBN 0 471 27691 X

Typeset by Pintail Studios Ltd., Ringwood, Hampshire
Printed in Great Britain by The Pitman Press, Bath, Avon.

Contributors

MICHAEL BEER	*Harvard University*
JOHN D. BIGELOW	*Oregon State University*
L. DAVE BROWN	*Case-Western Reserve University*
W. WARNER BURKE	*Columbia University*
TERRY CONNOLLY	*Georgia Institute of Technology*
THOMAS G. CUMMINGS	*University of Southern California*
CARSON K. EOYANG	*Naval Postgraduate School*
ROGER EVERED	*Naval Postgraduate School*
WARREN R. FLYNN	*Idaho State University*
LARRY E. GREINER	*University of Southern California*
ANNE SIGISMUND HUFF	*University of Illinois*
CRAIG C. LUNDBERG	*State University of New York at Binghamton*
FRED MASSARIK	*University of California at Los Angeles*
WILL MCWHINNEY	*Los Angeles, California*
LOUIS R. PONDY	*University of Illinois*
PETER REASON	*University of Bath*
WILLIAM E. STRATTON	*Idaho State University*
NOEL TICHY	*Columbia University*

v

Contents

PART III. SYSTEMS APPLICATIONS TO ORGANIZATION DEVELOPMENT PRACTICE

PART IV. BEYOND SYSTEMS: EXPANDING THE BOUNDARIES OF ORGANIZATION DEVELOPMENT

Editorial Foreword

Over the last decade, there has been an enormous growth of interest in the social and psychological aspects of institutional and organizational life. This has been reflected in a substantial upsurge in research and training in the field of organizational behaviour particularly in Institutes of Higher Education and Research throughout the Western World. Attention in this development has focused on the interrelationship between the individual, the variety of groups to which he belongs and the organizational environment within which he and his group operate.

The purpose of this series is to examine the social and psychological processes of these interrelationships, that is the nexus of individual/personal development, group processes and organizational behaviour and change. Within this context, a wide range of topics will be covered. These will include: the individual, his role and the organization; multiple roles and role conflict; the impact of group processes on personal and organizational development; strategies for 'humanizing' the organizational environment to meeting individual and group needs; and the influence of technical and economic factors on organizational life.

The series will attempt to draw together the main schools of organizational behaviour including, for example, the American behavioural science tradition as reflected by Harvard, UCLA and National Training Laboratories, and the British socio-technical and open systems approaches of the Tavistock Institute of Human Relations. It is hoped that this will add significantly to understanding the distinctive characteristics of the various approaches and also provide a link between them through which individual, group and organizational behaviour can be seen in fuller perspective.

CARY COOPER
ERIC MILLER

Foreword

Organization development and systems theory are odd bedfellows. Both have grown up in an aura of mysticism fed by zealous advocates. Each has matured from a fad to become fashionable, and probably the organizational sciences owe their rescue from classical malaise solely to these two movements. They appeal to ideologues and realists alike – emphasizing interrelationships and interactions over simple one-way causal inferences, reaching out to encompass a holistic set of variables, speaking to audiences in a new language that provokes insights, and sounding as if their approach is a panacea for making sense out of a confused world.

Yet there are striking differences that cause one to wonder if these two goliaths will ever be on speaking terms. A factor analysis of their jargon could easily place them in opposing quadrants. Although oversimplified, consider these likely polarities:

Systems Theory	*Organization Development*
Abstract	Concrete
Cognitive	Behavioural
Formal	Informal
Closed	Open
Knowledge	Skill
Stability	Change
Impersonal	Personal
Rational	Emotional
Ideas	Feelings
Descriptive	Normative
Left brain	Right brain

All of which makes this book a possible *tour de force*, or flop – take your pick after reading how the various authors bring them together. Critics have long said that OD is a movement in search of a good theory. Has it found one in systems theory? I doubt it because of their distinctly different intellectual roots. But perhaps they can provide a mirror for each other: to show what is significant, what is missing, and what needs to be done next.

For example, every time that OD has failed me, I have retreated to systems theory to show that organizations are too interwound for changes to occur so easily. Or those nasty unintended consequences of OD always seem to flow from some overlooked and interrelated variables.

But already I am falling into a trap that I hope this book escapes – that of critiquing OD while deifying systems theory. Perhaps OD even has some messages for systems theory, which can appear so lifeless on a piece of paper cluttered with boxes, arrows, and feedback loops. Are organizations so 'systemy', or are they more diffuse and diconnected? Can we objectively identify all the relevant variables and their interconnections, or are organizations more elusive and subjectively determined by human action and meaning?

A book devoted solely to systems theory or to OD would be hard enough to assemble, while a comparison between them invites oversimplification. In reality there are no two 'things' called systems theory and OD; there are as many definitions as there are authors. I rarely meet two OD scholars who share the same bandwagon, and when they do, they often confuse their shared model with reality. The same goes for systems theorists.

But at least this book promotes a metaphorical communication between two worlds that seldom have been bridged. It is a welcome step to compare and connect conceptual paradigms in a scholarly world that has become usurped by questionnaires and statistical tests. The empiricists continue to hope that the 'truth' will be found after turning over a hundred rocks. Yet my reading of scientific history suggests that the problems of discovery are often rooted in conceptual blindness. The angle of view may be more important than what is under the rock.

LARRY E. GREINER
University of Southern California

Preface

At several times during the past decade I have wanted to write a book applying systems theory (ST) to organization development (OD). The underlying motivation came from the realization that OD often espoused a systems perspective, yet rarely practised it. This apparent gap, between theory and action, seemed at first an unfortunate oversight; over time, however, it appeared more attributable to the difficulty of translating the abstract concepts of ST into specific applications appropriate to planned organization change. Indeed, the few published attempts to bridge the gap, such as socio-technical systems design and open systems planning, seemed strained and somewhat abstruse.

My fantasy was to rectify this problem. I would write a book about ST for the OD practitioner. It would admonish OD consultants for their naïve use of ST and their tendency to apply it metaphorically. It would clear up this abuse by explicating the foundations of ST and its relevant concepts and by showing how this general knowledge provides a practical foundation for planned change. The only thing separating fantasy from fact was the actual writing of the book.

As months stretched into years and years into a decade, it became obvious that the task was more formidable than I had imagined or dared to admit. In retrospect, I realize that I invented a number of useful rationalizations for postponing it. Foremost among these was the 'sheer magnitude of the task' excuse. Variants of this argument went something like this: How could I reasonably discuss ST, given the diversity of approaches and subdisciplines included under the systems banner, such as von Bertalanffy's 'open systems', Miller's 'living systems', Buckley's 'socio-cultural systems', and Shannon and Weaver's 'information systems'? How could I translate ST into a coherent view of organizations, given the different ways organizations could be conceived systemically, such as Katz and Kahn's 'role system', Galbraith's 'information processing system', Trist's 'socio-technical system', and Pfeffer's 'political system'? How could I translate organizations *qua* systems into OD practice, given the multitude of techniques loosely associated with OD, such as 'team building', 'survey feedback', 'job design', 'behaviour modification', and 'process consultation'? Although this is only a partial list of my magnitude-of-the-task rationalizations, suffice it to say that the perceived inability to choose in the face of many alternatives was a good excuse for procrastinating.

My second rationale for not writing the book derived directly from the first: If the magnitude of the task was so great, perhaps more reading and experience were needed before undertaking it? This was undoubtedly the easiest excuse to perpetrate because it gave both significant others (e.g. my department chairman, family, close colleagues, etc.) and me the distinct impression that something relevant was being accomplished even if it was not writing. Thus, starting in about 1970, I read books, monographs, articles, and unpublished manuscripts related to open systems theory, organizational systems theory, systems introductions to OD, and systems theory applied to such diverse phenomena as individual personality, work groups, stress reduction, city management, hospital administration, modes of inquiry, and national development. As might be expected, each new increment of knowledge only showed how much more I really needed to know, hence reinforcing the excuse to read further. Concurrent with the reading was a series of OD projects intended to give experience in applying ST to actual organizational problems. The rationale here, of course, was to round out the book learning with on-the-job training. Among these excursions into the real world were two long-term socio-technical systems experiments, a number of open systems planning workshops with such clients as a school district, a chemical processing plant, a manufacturing division of a large company, and a family planning council, and several systems analyses including a hospital emergency room, a city court, a college cafeteria, and an assembly line for manufacturing the cardboard roll around which aluminium foil is wound. Like the reading, each new project pointed to the need for further experience.

The final excuse for not writing the book was really a compromise solution: If the task was so formidable and the necessary knowledge and experience so great, why not have others write the book and simply edit their efforts myself? I must admit that editing a book had crossed my mind on several occasions, but on each I had dismissed the idea for two major reasons. First, there were not enough published articles linking ST with OD to comprise a book. Second, the task of assembling original contributions seemed too uncertain and difficult – i.e. a variant of the magnitude-of-the-task excuse. Things would probably have remained in limbo had I not met Cary Cooper during the 1976–77 academic year. During this time he was visiting our faculty at the University of Southern California, and he and I became close friends. At one of our many informal luncheons, he suggested an alternative to my fantasy book, an edited book of original contributions. Moreover, he offered to help me to find a suitable publisher and prodded me to write a preliminary proposal. Having little to lose, I wrote the proposal, submitted it to John Wiley & Sons, and subsequently signed a contract. Now all I had to do was find appropriate and willing contributors, edit their material if necessary, and organize the book. These tasks proved to be more difficult than Cooper had led me to believe.

Finding contributors for the book turned out to be rather fortuitous. The initial recruits included participants in a symposium, 'Uses and Abuses of the Systems Paradigm in Organization Development', held at the Academy of Management

Annual Meeting in Kissimmee, Florida, in August 1977. At the time the symposium was formulated, the possibility that I might edit a book was mentioned and the participants were asked if they would like to contribute their papers if a contract developed. All agreed and the initial contributors included: Dave Brown (Case Western Reserve University), Warner Burke (Columbia University), Terry Connolly (Georgia Institute of Technology), Roger Evered (Naval Postgraduate School), and Louis Pondy (University of Illinois). The next set of contributors came from a list of individuals who I felt understood both ST and OD and had something important to say about the topic. Fortunately, seven persons from this list agreed to write a chapter: Michael Beer (Harvard University), Carson Eoyang (Naval Postgraduate School), Craig Lundberg (State University of New York at Binghamton), Fred Massarik (University of California at Los Angeles), Will McWhinney (private consultant), Peter Reason (University of Bath, England), and Noel Tichy (Columbia University). The final contributors included members from a symposium, 'Alternative Theories for Organization Development', held at the Western Academy of Management Annual Meeting in Sacramento, California, in March 1978. Interestingly, the alternative theories turned out to be extensions of current systems thinking, hence the participants were asked if they would like to add their papers to the book. Each agreed and the final contributors included John Bigelow (Oregon State University), Anne Huff (University of Illinois), William Stratton and Warren Flynn (Idaho State University), and myself.

Given the necessary contributors, the tasks of editing the material and organizing the book proceeded. Since my informal contract with the authors included the promise that they could write whatever they desired so long as they applied ST to OD, I had some misgivings about what actually would be covered in the chapters. Specifically, I worried that the contributions would be either somewhat redundant, focusing on essentially the same issues, or too heterogeneous, comprising a hodgepodge of unconnected ideas and approaches; either too abstract, having little connection with the realities of planned change, or too concrete, losing the general applicability of ST; either too pessimistic, suggesting that the ST and OD linkage was futile, or too optimistic, making claims that could not possibly be justified. As the manuscripts trickled in during the past year, these concerns were dissipated.

The authors generally believe that the abstract nature of ST is a major impediment to its use in OD. Rather than dwell on the problems inherent in translating theory into practice, they take great pains to explain systems concepts and link them to specific organization change phenomena. Hence, theoretical discussions tend to be tempered by pragmatic concerns for the realities of planned change. Concrete examples and worthwhile case studies are used extensively to clarify theory and develop appropriate OD practice. In short, the authors attempt to provide a mid-perspective bridging the gap between the higher-level constructs of ST and the practical concerns of OD.

The contributions cover a broad range of systems concepts and OD applications. Yet despite this diversity, they share a common underlying premise. The authors treat organizations as 'open systems' maintaining relatively steady states while exchanging matter/energy and information with their environments. Open systems, in contrast to the 'closed systems' of classical physics, tend towards higher states of order and complexity. They achieve this feat by virtue of their systemic properties. Specifically, open systems are:

(1) *Hierarchical* – i.e. they are both an independent framework for organizing lower-level parts and a dependent member of a higher-level system.
(2) *Negentropic* – i.e. they can replenish themselves by importing energy from their environment, transforming it into products or services, and exporting the products back to the environment.
(3) *Partially bounded* – i.e. they selectively relate to their environment maintaining necessary exchanges while excluding others.
(4) *Self-regulating* – i.e. they maintain their internal integrity and environmental exchanges by using information about the consequences of their behaviour to control future behaviour.
(5) Equifinal – i.e. they can reach a final state from differing initial conditions and in different ways, hence they can change to match emerging conditions.

The authors employ the open system construct in a number of ways. Some use it primarily as an organizing framework to categorize and arrange relevant variables and concepts and to explore pattern relationships among them. Others focus on the empirical properties of organizations *qua* open systems and derive implications for planned change. Still others use the construct mainly as an infrastructure for addressing broader issues of systems thinking and OD. The variety of approaches provides a relatively robust mapping of ST onto OD. At this state of development, such eclecticism seems preferable to more parochial views offering coherence at the expense of comprehensiveness.

A major problem in editing a book of diverse contributions, however, is finding organizing principles for arranging the chapters in some meaningful manner, especially troublesome in this case given the authors' wide discretion in choosing material. Rather than simply order the chapters alphabetically (or by date of completion, etc.), a concerted effort was made to group related contributions around common themes. Fortunately, the chapters fell roughly into four conceptually distinct and informative sections:

(1) *Conceptual foundations for systems thinking in OD* – i.e. the epistemological consequences of applying ST to organization change.
(2) *System-theoretic frameworks for OD* – i.e. systemic models of organizations and their implications for planned change.
(3) *Systems applications to OD practice* – i.e. systemic approaches to organization diagnosis, intervention, and design.

(4) *Beyond systems: expanding the boundaries of OD* – i.e. extensions of system thinking and their meaning for planned change.

I have tried in this introduction to depict the history, development, and nature of this volume. Although much of the discussion has focused on my dilemmas and editorial role, the real substance of the book rests on the dedication and skills of the contributing authors. They have done their work well. They provide a compelling argument for viewing organizations as open systems and developing them accordingly. Their contributions should provide the reader with a clearer path towards this goal.

THOMAS G. CUMMINGS

Conceptual Foundations for Systems Thinking in Organization Development

Introduction

The four chapters in Part I provide a conceptual base for applying systems theory to organization development. The authors discuss the basic assumptions underlying the systems approach, address its promises and pitfalls, and clarify the need to understand and manage organizational change systemically.

Evered outlines the meaning and origins of systems thinking and shows how it differs from the traditional model of positivistic science. He argues that organizational development requires an epistemological base that goes beyond one-way causality to include mutual interaction of elements in an organized whole. Evered identifies both positive and negative consequences of systems thinking, and suggests the need to expand its focus from technical-rational to social-phenomenal realities. He points to several areas where this development is likely to prove fruitful for the organizational sciences.

Connolly and Pondy employ a unique and effective format for exploring the ST and OD interface – a dialectical exchange between two concerned yet reactive protagonists, Alpha and Beta. The authors anchor the debate to a shared concern for improving the professional eminence of their academic departments. This provides a common reference for the discussion and underscores the difficulties of comprehending and changing organizational behaviour. Throughout much of the exchange, Alpha takes a pessimistic stance towards understanding and improving systems where almost everything is connected to everything else. Beta tempers this Iron Law of Systems Pessimism by suggesting alternative ways of understanding systems through such methods as analogical-metaphorical descriptions which account for internal rather than external sources of system change. The debate provides a balanced and insightful view of the benefits and problems of applying systems theory to planned change; it explicates the difficulties inherent in understanding and developing organizations and provides new directions for knowledge and practice in organization development. Equally important, the dialectical mode compels the reader to engage in a similar internal debate, providing the intellectual tension necessary for new integrations and learning.

Application of systems theory to organization development invariably rests on a research methodology for organizing relevant experience and drawing inferences for future action. Peter Reason provides a promising path for social systems research, a strategy accounting for the dynamic interplay between human action

3

and reflection. Like Evered, Reason argues that positivistic science is unsuited to understanding and changing social systems. He presents a more holistic and non-alienating alternative to traditional social science method, a process where individuals explore their interactions and develop personal knowledge in the service of action and change. Reason shows how this research–action learning programme can be used to diagnose and develop role systems in organizations.

The final chapter in this section provides a unique linkage between systems theory and phenomenology. Massarik integrates these separate fields through the construct of 'mental systems' – i.e. personal definitions of the system, its salient features and desired outcomes. He argues that systems attain meaning from human processes of perception and valuation; such phenomenal constructions define what is real and valuable to organizational members. Massarik shows how this self-structuring process can be used to develop projective descriptions of organizational functioning, providing a deeper alternative to standard diagnostic techniques.

Systems Theory for Organization Development
Edited by T. G. Cummings
© 1980 John Wiley & Sons Ltd.

Chapter **1**

Consequences of and Prospects for Systems Thinking in Organizational Change

Roger Evered

The purpose of this chapter is to examine some of the features of systems thinking that relate to understanding the management of change in organizations. Before discussing the unique features of the systems viewpoint and the relevant fallout from several decades of systems thinking, it may be useful to look briefly at the meaning and origins of the notion of system.

The Oxford English Dictionary defines 'system' as 'a set or assemblage of things connected to form a complex unity: a whole composed of parts in orderly arrangement'. The concept has a long history. The word seems to have entered the English language in the early 1600s to mean 'an organized whole, as with a body of men'. It derives from the Greek work *systēma* meaning 'to bring, stand or combine together in an organized whole'. Thus we read in Hobbes's *Leviathan* (1651) – surely one of the great treatises of human organization – the following: 'by systemes I understand any number of men joined in one common interest or business'.[1]

In addition to governmental systems, the notion later became used in a variety of other fields, most notably in the natural sciences (e.g. solar system, Copernican system, Linnaean system, digestive system), in philosophy (e.g. formal logic systems, systems of thought), and in the applied or technological sciences (e.g. railway system, telephone system, distribution system).

By the late nineteenth century we find increasing interest in 'systems' and in the study of coherent, functionally differentiated wholes. Herbert Spencer, for example, spent some 20 years producing a 'system of unified knowledge', part of which included an elaborate organic theory of the societal system.[2] Spencer draws an analogy between the social system and an organic biological system, replete with three functional subsystems: sustaining, distributing, and regulation (adumbrating the views of Katz and Kahn).[3] He also proposed that a societal organism (society) has six types of organs (institutions): industrial, political, professional, ceremonial, ecclesiastical, and domestic (adumbrating the views of Lasswell).[4]

Interest in organic wholes was taken up by a number of other sociologists and psychologists: most notably, Dilthey, James, Dewey, Ehrenfels, Stumpf and the four gestaltists, Wertheimer, Koehler, Koffka, and Lewin. During the 1920s we find the basic elements of wholes or systems articulated by the psychologists Koehler, Lewin, and Goldstein; by the biologists, Lotka, Canon, and von Bertalanffy; and by the philosophers Whitehead, Dewey, and Smuts. Subsequent developments in systems thinking were made, most noticeably, by Boulding, Parsons, and Miller.[5]

Von Bertalanffy became the primary articulator for the 'general systems theory' viewpoint, principally perhaps because he appreciated more than most the limitations of traditional science *and* saw the need to generate a revised science. He described general systems theory as the science concerned with complexly organized wholes.

Concepts like those of organization, wholeness, directiveness, teleology and differentiation (all attributes of a system) are alien to conventional (physical) sciences. However, they pop up everywhere in the biological, behavioral and social sciences, and are, in fact, indispensable for dealing with living organisms or social groups. . . . Thus, a basic problem posed to modern science is a general theory of organization.[6]

Initially, von Bertalanffy defined a 'system' simply as an organized, cohesive complex of elements standing in interaction. Subsequently greater emphasis came to be placed on 'interdependences' and 'environmental interactions'. A standard definition of system in the late 1960s, for example, stated that a system was 'a concept that refers both to a complex of interdependencies between parts, components and processes that involves discernible regularities of relationships, and to a similar type of interdependency between such a complex and its surrounding environments'.[7]

To conceptualize an organization and its environment in holistic system terms, as a complex of interrelating, mutually interdependent parts, and as a field of interdependencies, is a fundamentally different world view from that of a set of antecedent factors that subsequently cause changes. The 'bio-sphere' of Angyal, the 'life-space' and 'field' of Lewin, and the 'open systems' of von Bertalanffy and of Katz and Kahn are radically different foundations from the traditional causal model (the 'efficient cause' of Aristotle). They challenge the epistemological base of traditional causal, reductionistic, positivistic science itself. Systems causality, or field causality, explanations of change seem more feasible, more realistic and more amenable to authentic inquiry than the cause–effect explanations we grew up with.

The problem of organizational change from the systems viewpoint

All organizations are in continuous change, whether from the subtle processes of environmental infusion, or by the intentional design of the powerful within the organization, or by the collective will of organizational participants whose destiny is linked in some basic way to the changes. Knowing how to manage change is fast becoming one of the more urgent functions of management, especially corporate-level management. At the same time, it remains one of the most difficult and least understood of all the management functions. And as the environment of an organization becomes increasingly complex and fluid, the need for understanding change-management becomes both more necessary and more urgent.

Theories of change-management are far from adequate. We do a relatively poor job of explaining the phenomena of institutional change, and do still less towards providing action guides for organizational participants and managers. This statement remains true whether we are talking about strategic management at the corporate level or change interventions at the task level. Whether we are dealing with long-range planning, strategic marketing, policy formulation, or entrepreneurial behaviour, our understanding and representations of the process of change are still quite primitive.

Traditional causal thinking which underlies much of modern science has not proved adequate for the task of understanding change, and increasingly one senses that it never can. The assumption of an *independent*, *external*, and *antecedent* factor, a set of factors, that 'causes' changes seems far too simplistic for comprehending the phenomena of societal and organizational change. As von Bertalanffy puts it: 'We may state as characteristic of modern science that this scheme of isolable units acting in one-way causality has proved to be insufficient. Hence the appearance, in all fields of science, of notions like wholeness, holistic, organismic, gestalt, etc., which all signify that, in the last resort, we must think in terms of systems of elements in mutual interaction.'[8]

Realization of limitations of 'normal' causal thinking, and the need for the development of a fundamentally different kind of thinking that can grasp the essential wholeness of organized complexity, is to be found in most of the early 'systems' writers. We find Emery, for example, writing 'that there are gestalten qualities of living organizations that are unlikely to be revealed by the ordinary modes of scientific analysis'.[9] Likewise Angyal once wrote: 'Causal thinking has been used in science for such a long time and, in certain fields, with such success that it is almost generally considered as *the* scientific thinking, although it may well be only a subvariety of it. . . . the transition to systems thinking is at least as difficult as the transition from a three-dimensional to a four-dimensional geometry.'[10]

Until quite recently the prevailing view of science (what Kuhn calls 'normal science')[11] incorporated a bias towards generic, past-oriented, antecedent explanation. In the past two or three decades, however, the culturally infectious influences of existentialism, phenomenology, gestalt psychology and systems thinking have influenced science towards a more present-oriented, interactive and perceptual view of science – at least in some areas of the social sciences. While our culture is probably less entrenched in the past than most other cultures, it is still probably true that we have a definite proclivity towards the past as a source of explanation and understanding, in contrast to either the present or the future.[12]

Since our theoretical frameworks are ways of perceiving and making sense of our experiences, over-adherence to frameworks based on past events prevents us from experiencing or recognizing the emergent reality of the present. Explanations based on past events are devices to ensure that the unborn future will look like the past. What is being emphasized here is that theories based on the past (i.e. knowing how it was) may be fundamentally inappropriate for even learning about change phenomena (i.e. knowing how it differs from what it was).

Much of our understanding of the process of change stems less from the logico-causal thinking of traditional science than from the whole-organization systems thinking of the newly emerging science.

The fallout from systems thinking

Let me try to identify some of the fallout from approximately two decades of systems thinking. What are some of the consequences of systems thinking for those who are striving to improve the organizations that we work in? First, what may be called the beneficial fallout.

(1) Systems thinking has enabled us to think about organizations at a *higher level of abstraction* than was previously possible. Instead of thinking about particular organizations, and similarities between particular organizations, systems thinking requires that we think more in terms of the general characteristics of the organization itself – such as cohesion, interdependence, stability, etc. Systems thinking is a conceptualization of a higher order configuration than traditional science has previously considered. Moreover, systems thinking transcends the various branches of science.

(2) Systems thinking has provided us with a *language* for describing organizational phenomena. Such notions as boundary, boundary spanning, interface, feedback, homeostasis, network, control system, organization goals, input, throughput and output, differentiation and integration were all catalysed by systems thinking. Most major advances in human thought are characterized by the introduction of new language (e.g. Freud's psychoanalytic theory, Lewin's field theory).

(3) Systems thinking has enabled us to think in *relational* terms rather than in terms of things. To see organizational phenomena in terms of relationships between entities (whether persons or things) is potentially more enriching than merely aggregating the persons and things. This has led to more process-oriented, and contextual views of organizations.

(4) Systems thinking has stimulated our *holistic* appreciation. It has enabled us to think in terms of the wholeness properties of an organization such as organizational personality, climate, cohesion, and integration. There is now widespread conceptual recognition that the total relevant environment of an organization is a major determinant of corporate choices.

(5) As already discussed, systems thinking has necessitated that we *modify our*

science, away from analytical, reductionistic, causal, future neglecting positivism and towards a science that is more synthesizing, transactive, contextual, emergent, future incorporating, phenomenal and participative. To view the world, and indeed science itself, as cogenerative, transactively determined, and continuously in process is necessarily to reject (or at least radically modify) the present character of science.[13]

(6) Systems thinking has led us to a realization that there are two kinds of explanation and meaning. The first type of meaning is the traditional deductive explanation derived from logical analysis. And the second, which systems thinking has stimulated, is the meaning that derives from pattern recognition and from the gestalt processes of the human mind. These two types correspond presumably to the left-brain/right-brain functions of the human brain as described by Ornstein and others.[14]

(7) Systems thinking has given us the potential for *world-defining* by the organizational participants themselves. Boulding[15] and Lewin have described ways in which an individual can locate him/herself in the total system in which he/she is embedded – in terms of the spatio-temporal gestalt, the field of personal relationships, the world technical properties, the domain of intrapsychic feelings and sentiments, the context of events, and the pervasive pool of linguo-cultural-mythic symbols. Every individual in an organization has his/her own unique phenomenal world (or image of the world), giving rise to the necessary variety and differentiation that enables organizations to function. And when these individual 'worlds' become synthesized within an organization, we can think of the system's image of the world that characterizes that particular system, or firm. It is now believed that these system generated images – what are sometimes termed core metaphors – play an important role in energizing and guiding the system.

In addition to the above, rather impressive, benefits of systems thinking, several negative features need to be noted. They represent what might be called the negative fallout from systems thinking.

(1) Systems thinking has been used primarily for systems of tangible, physical *objects*. The design of engineering hardware systems constitutes the paramount example of systems thinking. Other areas, most notably human organizations, have been relatively neglected.

(2) Even in the field of engineering hardware systems, the emphasis has been on design control and operation. Systems *thinking* has been converted to systems *analysis*, sacrificing some of the holistic, synthesizing power of systems thinking. Consequently many of the hardware systems often seem to take on a synergistic life of their own beyond the cognizance of the systems analyst.

(3) Systems thinking has also been widely used for model building, as in the case of computerized simulation models. A representational system, comprised of variables and relationships between variables, is set up to explore the overall properties of the model. The danger has been that sometimes the assumptive structure of the model becomes forgotten and *reification* sets in. The model gets

confused with the reality or, as Korzybski says, 'the map is not the territory'. Reification constitutes a constant threat in the use of rational models.

(4) Successes with systems thinking in the realm of hardware systems and rational model-building has lead to a *false sense of certainty and control*, and to a belief in some quarters that human organizational systems can be dealt with just as easily or in similar fashion. The belief that human organizations are basically social engineering problems is likely to produce some costly large-scale disasters.

In Figure 1, I have tried to present some of the varieties of systems thinking that have been, and are being, developed. The figure is split into two broad domains, the 'socio' and the 'techno'. The point I wish to stress is that systems thinking has been far less used in the 'socio' domains than in the 'techno', undoubtedly because the 'techno' is relatively easier to deal with. The 'socio' domain has some inherent subtleties, complexities, and problems that we are only now beginning to come to grips with. We need to do more creative work on the 'socio' arenas instead of merely applying techniques developed in the 'techno' arenas.

It is interesting to note that quite the opposite criticism has been repeatedly raised against organization development (OD): namely that OD has focused almost exclusively on the 'socio' domain (the so-called soft science) and has ignored the benefits of 'techno' thinking (the so-called hard science).[16] Both technical systems thinking (such as systems design and analysis) and social systems thinking (such as OD) are in reality complementary and have much to offer each other. The issue is one of interfacing between two essentially different domains.

Future prospects for systems thinking

I should like to end this essay by identifying a number of areas (on the 'socio' side of Figure 1) that are in need of systems thinking development. The organizational sciences would benefit considerably if any of the following systems could be developed beyond our present level of understanding.

(1) Inquiry systems for generating knowledge and intelligibility.
(2) Support systems for individuals in organizational settings; the development of eupsychian systems.
(3) System interface phenomena: e.g. socio/techno interfaces, left-brain/right-brain interfaces, individual/organization interfaces, etc.
(4) The system of values within organizations, including the processes by which values become synthesized and changed.
(5) Adaptive systems within organizations, how the adaptive system is integrated with the rest of the organization and how it manages environmental changes.
(6) A systems theory of organizational change that is not a social engineering model and that can incorporate the phenomenal realities of the organizational participants.

	'TECHNO' DOMAIN			'SOCIO' DOMAIN		
	Physical world	Technological world	Rational world	Phenomenal world	Organic world	Culturo–Mythic world
PART	Atom, element	Component	Variable	Functional constituents	Individual	Value, belief
WHOLE	Object, thing	Hardware system	Model	Thematic unity	Organization	Culture

Figure 1 Varieties of systems thinking

Conclusions

In this essay I have traced some of the origins of systems thinking in order to delineate its essential features. I have tried to point out some of the fallout, both beneficial and adverse, from several decades of systems thinking. I have noted some of the dangers and prospects of systems thinking. A major implication of systems thinking is the necessity to revise or broaden our view of what constitutes 'science'. The 'normal' science of our time is in the process of change, partly due to the influence of systems thinking.

In conclusion, I wish to affirm my belief that systems thinking, as discussed in this paper, offers a real prospect for understanding and managing change in organizations. A systems-oriented theory of change must recognize the importance of incorporating: (1) the organizational participants' view of the situation, particularly their expected futures, (2) the limitations and costs of exclusively rational design approaches, (3) the process of mutual causality in contrast to traditional causal thinking, and (4) the developmental processes of system generated metaphors.

It therefore follows that organization development should consist essentially of these four processes: (1) facilitating a definition of the situation as experienced by the organizational participants themselves, (2) balancing our dysfunctional emphasis on the rational and technological with the experiential and social, (3) developing conditions and processes of mutual causation, and (4) finding ways of enabling the system's participants to modify their own core metaphors.

Acknowledgements

I would like to express appreciation to my colleague, Meryl Louis, for her insightful comments on preliminary drafts of this paper, and the Naval Postgraduate School Research Fund for financial assistance in preparing the chapter.

Notes

1. Hobbes, Thomas (original 1651), *Leviathan 2*, 12, p. 115, as cited in *The Oxford English Dictionary*.
2. Spencer, Herbert (1876–1896) *Principles of Sociology*, 3 vols.
3. Katz, Daniel, and Kahn, Robert L. (1966) *The Social Psychology of Organizations*, New York: Wiley.
4. Lasswell, Harold, and Kaplan, Abraham (1950) *Power and Society*, vol. 2, New Haven, Conn.: Yale University Press.
5. For the most recent and perhaps the most comprehensive statement of systems theory, see Miller, James G. (1978) *Living Systems*, New York: McGraw-Hill.
6. Bertalanffy, Ludwig von (1955) 'General systems theory', *Main Currents in Modern Thought*, 11 (4), 76.
7. *International Encyclopedia of the Social Sciences* (1968), New York: Macmillan, 15, 458.
8. Bertalanffy, op. cit., 80.

9. Emery, Frederick E. (1969) *Systems Thinking*, Harmondsworth, Middx: Penguin, 8.
10. Anygyal, Andras (1941) *Foundations for a Science of Personality*, Cambridge, Mass.: Harvard University Press.
11. Kuhn, Thomas S. (1970) *The Structure of Scientific Revolutions*, University of Chicago Press, 10.
12. Evered, Roger (1976) 'A typology of explicative models', *Technological Forecasting and Social Change*, **9** (3), 259–277; and Watzlawick, Paul, Weakland, John, and Fisch, Richard (1974) *Change: Principles of Problem Formation and Problem Resolution*, New York: Norton, Chapter 7.
13. See Maruyama, Magoroh (1978) 'The epistemological revolution', *Futures*, **10** (3), 240–242; and 'The post industrial logic', In *The Next 25 Years: Crisis and Opportunity*, Andrew A. Spekke (ed.) (1975) New York: World Future Society, 43–50.
14. Ornstein, Robert E. (1972) *The Psychology of Consciousness*, San Francisco: Freeman.
15. Boulding, Kenneth E. (1961) *The Image*, Ann Arbor, Mich.: The University of Michigan Press.
16. Friedlander, Frank, and Brown, David (1974) 'Organizational development', *Annual Review of Psychology*.

Systems Theory for Organization Development
Edited by T. G. Cummings
© 1980 John Wiley & Sons Ltd.

Chapter 2

General Systems Theory and Organization Development: A Dialectical Inquiry

Terry Connolly

and

Louis R. Pondy

Introductory notes

Neither general systems theory (GST) nor organization development (OD) is a well-developed, tightly integrated body of knowledge and technique. Rather, each represents a loosely articulated set of diverse theory and practice, with adherents trained in a wide range of disciplines, oriented to a wide range of methods, and attacking a wide range of problems. Any attempt to explore the relationships between the two disciplines, then, faces some rather severe difficulties.

This chapter attempts such an exploration, taking the form of a dialogue between two individuals, Alpha and Beta. As with real dialogue, the argument proceeds in various non-linear ways, as one participant reacts to the other's arguments, is diverted from, or returns to, earlier points, shifts from one set of images to another, and so on. The reader is visualized not as a passive consumer of a pre-structured argument, but as an active participant in an on-going, open-ended debate. The aim is not to supply the reader with a set of pre-packaged truths, but to lure him or her into a truth seeking process.

By way of context, Alpha and Beta are career academics of eclectic background. Their 'real world' is that of the university, and their major concern is with the process of moving the academic departments in which they are employed to a position of professional eminence. They are, then, in the organization development business, though the organizational world from which they draw their examples is most commonly the university (in which they live) rather than the business or governmental organization (in which they consult and research). The issues raised in the debate are, however, not specific to the university; they are intended to exemplify issues which arise in any large and complex organization.

A final introductory note: no particular one-to-one equivalence should be imagined between the authors of the paper and the protagonists in the debate; nor should the institutional examples be imagined as factual reports of experiences at either of the institutions with which we are affiliated. Alpha and Beta are two imaginary professors, working at two imaginary universities. Their debate is to be seen but as a broad attempt to draw together the insights of general systems theory as they relate to the immensely difficult problem of bringing about change in complex organizations.

ALPHA: It has been common among students of organizational behaviour to greet general systems theory with a certain elation – here, at last, is the conceptual framework which, when applied, will allow us to move to more exciting research on, and more confident interventions in, organizational phenomena. I, on the contrary, find the insight a discouraging one: the more I am convinced that organizations exhibit systems characteristics, the less confident I am that I can change their behaviour in ways I see as desirable. General systems theory tells us not how to change systems, but why systems are inherently difficult to change. It provides us not with a guide to action, but with a rationale for pessimism.

One way of stating this pessimism is simply to say that we do not have very powerful analytic techniques for dealing with systems of high complexity, with tightly coupled variables and complex cyclical interactions. To the extent that organizations are of this sort, we know only that we do not know enough to control them; or, to paraphase Barry Commoner, the First Law of Systems is that everything is connected to everything else. Given our well-documented cognitive limitations, we cannot possibly consider 'everything'. Thus, we cannot consider 'enough' to make predictions about the outcomes of our actions with confidence. So the first discouraging theorem to flow from the application of systems theory to organizational change is that every attempt at change will carry with it some unpredictable consequences that are remote in both time and location from the locus of the intervention. And those consequences may never become known to the original interventionist nor perhaps traced, or traceable, to the intervention, even if the effect is detected. Thus, the author of change is partially blind; he cannot choose a change rationally on the grounds of all its consequences. The choice process is not merely bounded; it is bounded in unknown ways.

For example, if you were to attempt to upgrade the scholarly output of the professors at your university by basing promotion and salary decisions on the number of papers published in refereed journals, you would set in motion not only more effort devoted to research, but perhaps also the creation of new journals to serve as outlets for the resulting papers, leading perhaps (assuming that other universities had to follow suite to keep pace with your increased prestige) to a shortage of space in the libraries of the world, a shortage of paper on which to print and reproduce the papers (to say nothing of the paper required to process articles submitted to journals for publication), increased specialization of scholarly pursuits because no scholar could keep abreast of the outpouring of ideas in his entire field, and so forth. I am confident that I could go on listing possible consequences of this single decision for many minutes. I am equally confident that such a change is typically undertaken without considering any but the most immediate effects. Systems theory makes us aware of the inadequacy of our analytical techniques for predicting the effects of organizational change, but does not help us to estimate the degree of our inadequacy.

There is a second way of stating this pessimism. As we learn more about systems, we come to realize the difficulty of bringing about even consciously desired changes. We learn, for example, that the extensive interconnection is not just a matter of multiple impacts flowing from the change of one variable, in the manner of trying to take one paper clip from a jumbled box. Our focal variable is likely to be embedded in complex, active feedback loops, whose effect is to maintain various dynamically stable system characteristics. Thus, the attempt to base rewards on publication in referred journals will be likely to be resisted by some segments of the academic community. For example, certain of the performing arts – music, theatre, dance – do not necessarily leave written traces of their scholarly output and so their practitioners will resist the imposition of a single, uniform criterion of worth that is not appropriate to their fields of specialization. If the change is weakly proposed, it is likely to be defeated or diluted by the system's reactionary response, a response aimed at conserving the *status quo*. If the change is strongly proposed and overrides these immediate objections, other chains of causation suggested above are likely to be set in motion.

To state the dilemma more generally, if our intervention is weak, it is unlikely to offset the stabilizing effects of interconnectedness, so that we have no net effect. If our intervention technology is sufficiently powerful to overcome these forces, we may expect extensive changes in many aspects of the system. These changes are unpredictable (given our lack of powerful analysis) and there is no good reason to expect them to be generally beneficial. Knowing just a little about the stabilizing mechanisms to be expected in complex systems, we are faced with either impotence or widespread and unpredictable consequences. Neither encourages costly intervention.

BETA: It seems to me that you have a tight and general argument for doing nothing. In essence, all you are saying is: 'We can't predict everything that might happen if we do something, so let's not do anything, and even if we did do something, it would be resisted and defeated by vested interests.' I'm sure you're not that opposed to action; in fact, by the same logic, we would never get out of bed each morning! Actually, of course, both you and I are committed to, and rather active in, transforming our respective academic departments in directions we think of as 'closer to excellence'. Are you suggesting that we abandon these efforts just because we either cannot, in principle, predict the consequences of implementing them or could not successfully implement them anyway because of conservative forces?

ALPHA: I'm only a little embarrassed to be caught (yet again) with a wide gap between my preachments and my practices. I am, as you know, something of an activist in practical terms. But it does somewhat bother me that I can't find solid intellectual grounds to support such activism. Indeed, some very smart people argue against the naïve activism I practice. Take, for example, Bateson's argument (1972) against activism in the context of physical ecosystems: for humankind to exercise dominion over the earth, as the Bible commands, is to destroy the ecological harmony that sustains it. By the same argument, for me to fight for the dominance of the social causes I espouse would be to destroy the social harmony that sustains the society that nurtures me. And yet I persist in my activism.

Bateson, of course, is typically concerned with high-power interventions having distant critical consequences (e.g. the DDT horror stories familiar to all eco-freaks). The usual response to the discovery of a new set of unanticipated and undesired consequences is to identify an evil-doer and demand more care – that is, to demand more knowledge (and thus allow avoidance) of remote impacts. Bateson rejects the possibility of such knowledge in general, arguing instead that ecological disasters are the product of a mistaken purposiveness in acting on systems, together with the powerful physical technologies with which we write our ignorance large. The fundamental requirement, he argues, is that we abandon our notions of purposiveness, learn humility, and find ways to live in harmony with the complex systems of which we are a part.

BETA: A word about Bateson's concept of purpose: do you recall the story of the man who was offered three wishes? After he wished for $1000, an insurance adjuster arrived at his house with a $1000 payment in compensation for his son's unexpected death. His error was in not specifying his wish completely enough. Even if he had said, 'I wish for $1000 *and* for my son's continued good health', some other unspecified event could have occurred. The difficulty with statements of purpose is that they never specify the desired state of the system completely enough. We typically do not say: 'I wish to control insects, *and* I wish to keep the DDT level in mothers' milk at a tolerable level, *and* I wish to maintain the bird population that feeds off insects, *and* ....' Systems theory, in Bateson's hands, does not merely point out the difficulty of purposive change; it reveals how misguided purposive change can be, even for the welfare of the changer, unless overall system purposes are considered. But how can we describe system purposes completely?

A statement of goals for an OD intervention in one of our universities may be quite specific about some purposes ('We wish to increase teaching effectiveness, communicate more openly, and publish more articles') but it cannot possibly state purposes or acceptable levels for all the areas which might be impacted by the intervention (' ... *and* reduce the incidence of stomach ulcers associated with our professors' skipping lunches, *and* minimize environmental damage caused by additional commuting to work at weekends, *and* . . .'). In both examples, the impossibility of stating our purposes completely is essentially the impossibility of describing systems completely. Is there some way that we can modify the concept of 'purpose' so as to avoid this difficulty?

ALPHA: Since organizations (even universities!) are quintessentially purposive entities, your question can be recast as asking how we might modify our concepts of organization and organization change to reflect the difficulties associated with system complexity. We have, I think, grasped the lesson of the impotence of simple-minded changes – for example, the ineffectiveness of using a powerful individual-change technology such as a T-group, when changed behaviour is 'corrected' by the individual's return to his previous working environment. It is not clear whether similar mechanisms will, in a longer term, 'correct' the changes brought about by T-grouping intact work groups. It is worth considering here the experiments on reduction of absenteeism: suitable participation has been found to produce fairly strong change in the behaviour of work crews, but the lack of *managerial* participation appears, in a follow-up study, to have led to a return to previous practice. The 'corrective' mechanisms may not be obvious, or work swiftly, but their existence cannot be doubted. Again, the interventionist's quandary: supposing that I have overcome the short-term stability forces sufficiently to bring about some manifest changes, it must be assumed as likely that the passage of time will either (a) reveal the activity of stabilizing mechanisms which will undo my work, or (b) reveal distant and unanticipated changes in other parts of the system, which I have no reason to expect will be benign. Indeed, I may have addicted the system to my interventions, with Change 1 the 'cure' for Problem 1, generating Problems 2, 3, etc., which I 'solve' with appropriate changes, which themselves lead to further problems in further settings, and so on. A remunerative career, but hardly a reassurance that one is doing anything good.

It is possible to argue that organizations are not really all that 'systemy', and that the gloomy comments above are not true, or only rarely so. This seems to be an empirically open question, particularly since we have only very recently attempted to examine organizations as systems, or at least as systems of more than a very simple type. Further, it appears that we are only just starting to develop change technologies of real power (i.e. capable of overcoming short-term stabilization forces). It seems reasonable to expect both that we will increase our understanding of how complex are the systemic couplings within organizations and between organizations and their environments, and that we will develop more powerful change technologies. The prospect, then, is that even if the message of gloom presented here is not now compelling, it will become more so.

Actually, though I find myself largely convinced by this line of thought, I find myself also rather optimistic about the prospects of doing something useful about organizational change. Perhaps the Iron Law of Systems Pessimism can be acknowledged as true without stopping us from muddling along in a more or less satisfactory way. I can imagine a number of specific areas in which optimism seems supportable – a patchwork of exceptions to the Iron Law. Like quilts of the same kind, it may provide adequate coverage for all practical purposes.

BETA: It seems to me that your Iron Law has two parts:
(1) Systems (The System, if one takes complete interconnection seriously) are too interconnected in too contingent a way and therefore too complex for us ever to understand. Furthermore, since all of the system describers are necessarily a part of the system, and so are their models of the system, then the more they try to describe the system, the more there is to describe, and the larger the system becomes. It is a self-defeating process. I call this the Law of Increasing Ignorance: the more one tries to understand a system, the more there is to be understood; the process of inquiry itself enlarges the system. In any case, a complex system can be defined as one that can never be completely understood; it is always capable of surprise. And virtually all of the systems that we (social scientists) work with are complex in that sense.
(2) Even if we could understand systems completely, their tendencies towards equilibrium are so strong relative to the strength of our interventions that the best we can do is to nudge the system away from equilibrium temporarily. But we cannot create a new equilibrium and move the system to it.

I have two qualifications to offer to your Iron Law. On part (1), it seems to me that complete understanding is impossible only in a left-brained, analytical sense. But if one were to accept right-brained, analogical metaphorical descriptions of the system as legitimate, then I am less sure. If it *were* true that analogical descriptions are higher in potential variety than digital, analytical ones, then systems theory ought to be making more use of metaphorical descriptions, e.g. novels, poetry, music, etc. In fact, the widespread emphasis in OD on *direct experience* of phenomena, rather than on analytic cognitive descriptions of them, suggests that OD practitioners already understand the inadequacy of merely analytic descriptions.

I am not suggesting that we abandon the power of analytical models of systems to make precise and detailed statements. But I *am* suggesting that we need to supplement them with analogical descriptions that capture the system-wide properties of system behaviour. Still, my best guess is that we cannot escape the Law of Increasing Ignorance. The system will still surprise us but perhaps surprise us less frequently and with less intensity, unless of course our greater knowledge emboldens us to undertake even stronger interventions.

As to part (2), here I have more reservations about the truth of your Iron Law. Aren't you overlooking the greatest source of power to change the system – the system itself? The metaphor I have in mind is judo, where the defender uses the attacker's own momentum to repel him. Or gardening, where the gardener merely facilitates or releases the natural growth inherent in the plants but does not *cause* the growth. In terms of Lewin's force field analysis, one makes use of forces that are *already* there, by redirecting them, or by reducing or removing opposing forces. But the change agent does not need to supply the forces for change from outside the system. There are plenty of forces active within the system that can be used. In fact, this is what produces what you have called 'widespread and unpredictable consequences' of an intervention; you have released forces that you did not know about and that you are powerless to counteract, except by redirecting the system's own natural forces. So my reaction to your Iron Law is that it holds only for cases of external application of the forces of change. But if one thinks of a system as consisting of opposing forces in balance, then one can change the system by applying minimal force from outside to release those internal forces. Systems will develop and change under their own power if only we will let them, or nudge them in certain directions. If we try to supply all the power from outside, by ourselves, then we are doomed by your Iron Law.

Perhaps I can clarify these ideas by applying them once again to our continuing example of changing the academic reward system. Presumably our aim is to upgrade the quality of scholarly activity within the university. Counting publications is merely one quantitative description of the system, and a very incomplete description at that. But there are also qualitative descriptions of the system or of desired states of the system, and these qualitative descriptions attempt to capture the system as a whole. Records of publication are, after all, descriptions of individual output that do not reflect the university as a *community* of scholars. Indeed, the metaphor 'community' may come closer to describing what we mean by academic excellence than a count of publications can. More to the point, a *complete* description of where we are and where we would like to be requires both the analytical description (e.g. more publications) and the analogical description (e.g. the university as a community). The metaphor of 'community' serves to synthesize the parts of the university disengaged by analytical measures of individual performance.

Thus, metaphor provides a symbolic, system-wide description. Symbolism also plays a role in the use of internal forces for change of academic standards. Within the university are already scholars who exemplify the values of research culminating in publication or performance in peer-evaluated media. By elevating these persons to positions of prominence, the university sets them up as role models for others to follow. They are presented as symbols of the desired performance. This is in direct contrast to representing the desired performance analytically by stating abstract quantitative measures. And it provides a mechanism of change by using natural forces already present within the system, the forces of emulation of a member of the faculty itself. By using these natural exemplars and natural imitative forces, we are more likely to effect change than by imposing change from what the faculty would regard as 'outside'.

It seems to be that these are insights that flow from 'systems thinking' which is not limited to a mechanical view of systems as richly interconnected machines.

This thought leads me to propose one other amendment to your Iron Law, drawing on Boulding's hierarchy of complexity. You recall that Boulding suggests that systems may be classified in terms of a nine-level hierarchy, moving from the least complex (frameworks, clockworks, and thermostats) through more complex (cells, plants, and animals) and finally to the most complex (humans, societies, and ultimately the unlimited 'transcendental systems'). As one moves up the hierarchy, the systems show quite new (or 'emergent') properties not found in lower levels. This emergence of wholly new properties is what he means by increasing complexity. Thus, complexity means more than just richness of interconnection. For example, level 3 systems (thermostats) achieve equilibrium by information processing, which level 2 systems (clockworks) do not; level 4 systems (cells) show the critical open system property of self-maintenance in the face of throughput, which level 3 systems do not; and so on.

This emergence of new properties as one moves up the hierarchy seems especially significant for our present effort to apply systems thinking to higher-level systems — organizations are, clearly, level 8 creatures, though most of our research to date has treated them at much lower levels (see Pondy and Mitroff, 1979). Let me suggest that in order to bring about change in an nth-level system, one needs to intervene at at least the $(n + 1)$th level. For example, in order to adjust a clock (level 2), one needs an information processing, error detecting intervention (level 3) — one imagines a human clock adjuster. Similarly, in order to train an animal (level 6), one needs an intervention at the level of self-conscious purpose, a symbol processor — that is, a level 7 intervention. I don't know if the $(n + 1)$ rule is universal, but it surely seems plausible.

Now, return to OD interventions and your Iron Law. Perhaps the law is limited to the case where the intervention and the desired change are at the same level of complexity, and doesn't hold for $(n+1)$ interventions. For example, in order to bring about a change in how people think about themselves, what their self-image is (level 7), one needs to interject new myths and metaphors into the system (level 8). One cannot change someone's self-image simply by offering a new alternative to consider. In order for the intervention to be strong enough to unfreeze the system, it has to be at a higher level of complexity than the level at which unfreezing is desired. Put the other way, I am suggesting that systems are generally very resistant to change strategies at the same level of complexity, but may be much more susceptible to higher-level interventions. (Is this why poets and novelists are regarded as such threats in totalitarian societies? By encouraging metaphoric thought in the populace they make it impossible for the authorities to make effective use of bureaucratic controls — the bureaucratic control system stresses lower-level system properties, level 6 at best, and is vulnerable to level 8 interventions such as metaphor making.)

In OD terms, this speculation suggests two rules (or, really, two alternative forms of the same rule). If one wants change at some particular level, one needs an intervention at a higher level; and if one has a given intervention, the best one can hope for is change at levels below that of the intervention. Thus, I suspect that the key to a behaviour modification approach to OD is to realize that behaviour modification is (and thus treats individuals as) level 6, while the critical element of the intervention is the self-conscious purpose which guides the selection of behaviours to be modified. Such purposes are, of course, level 7 properties, so the $(n+1)$ idea pops up again. I have already suggested that level 7 changes, such as changes of individual self-image, require level 8 interventions in the form of new myths and metaphors. I find this an insight into what T-groups actually do: they provide new metaphors which allow the individual to reassess his or her self-image (as well as providing some forces which may actually bring about the change). This process leaves open the possibility that certain interventions can be effective at bringing about changes at a lower level of complexity even if they are ineffective at the same level as the change attempt. For example, T-groups as methods of changing *group*-level functioning may be ineffective because of the Iron Law forces you suggest, but they may still be highly effective at the $(n - 1)$ level, the individual; behaviour modification strategies will run into Iron Law problems at the level of the purposeful human, though they may be very effective if one is prepared to treat organizational members as lower-level systems (it sounds harsh to say 'as animals', but I do mean 'as level 6 systems' here). The ultimate challenge, then, is for us to devise interventions at level 9, the transcendental level, so that we can get some leverage on our level 8 target, the organization itself. I can't say I have anything very solid here, as yet.

The application of this $(n+1)$ principle to our university change example seems clear. We cannot change how faculty members spend their time simply by urging them to spend it differently or even by rewarding them for spending it differently. In order to bring about a change at that level, we must effect a change at a higher level. In this case, we must change their image of the university; we must change their frame of reference within which alternative behaviours are chosen and evaluated. Once the frame is changed from the university as an 'input–output machine' to the university as a 'community of scholars', devoting effort to scholarly output will be seen as a natural consequence. The irony is that by directly rewarding publication with promotion and salary increase, the system runs the risk of reinforcing the machine metaphor and making a more fundamental shift in metaphor or frame more difficult.

In short, there seem to me to be a number of glimmers of light in the wide shadow cast by your Iron Law. First, the law seems to be clearest for analytic modes of understanding systems, and may be less true if we allow softer, richer, more metaphorical modes of understanding. Second, effecting change by outside forces (with the impotence-or-ignorance trap this seems to imply) is very different from using internal system forces to bring about change. The latter model seems much closer to what OD actually does, and, I think, may not inevitably follow the Iron Law. Finally, we must bear in mind that 'complexity' is much more than lots of variables and lots of interconnectedness; it has more to do with the emergence of higher-level properties such as the use of language and the capacity of self-awareness or of metaphoric thought. As we start to take these higher-level properties of organizations seriously, we can see all sorts of change strategies which place OD outside the gloomy limits of the Iron Law.

ALPHA: The essence of my argument thus far has been that organizations are systems too complex for our understanding to be adequate for our purposes in trying to change or 'develop' them. You have suggested several exceptions to the Iron Law. But I would like to argue that what you have called exceptions can more usefully be thought of as routes of escape. I have classified the options differently (and more systematically!) than you. Specifically, the Iron Law allows three possibilities of escape:

(1) reduce the complexity of the systems so as to bring them more nearly within our understanding;
(2) improve our understanding of systems, both generally and of organizational systems specifically; and
(3) devise ways in which we can achieve our purposes in the face of inadequate understanding.

All three strategies show promise, and I will discuss candidates of each kind.

Are organizational systems now, or can they be made to be, sufficiently simple that the Iron Law does not apply? The fact that organizations are man-made, artificial systems, whose design appears to allow some discretion to the designer, certainly suggests that some simplification is possible. The core strategy here is subsystem decoupling, reducing the amount of interconnectedness between one organizational element and another. Clearly, all organizations of any size are much less coupled than they could be: individuals communicate, either formally or informally, with only a tiny subset of other members; divisions, departments, work groups, and so on have more intense internal coupling than external coupling; budget cycles, dead-lines, accounting periods, etc., serve to limit the time-span of information flows; reduction of complex information vectors to scalar measures (e.g. performance evaluation expressed as a cash rise; product characteristics expressed as a price; effectiveness measures expressed as profits) reduce the necessary transfer of information, and so on. Such decoupling mechanisms seem essential if normal mortals are to bring about purposive activity in the systems (i.e. if the systems are to be manageable). The dilemma, clearly, is to allow sufficient decoupling that subsystems are reasonably manageable (i.e. simple enough to understand, more or less) while at the same time maintaining sufficient coupling to preserve total systems functioning. Thus, a university can be thought of as a collection of very loosely coupled academic departments that can be managed more or less independently.

It is clear that ODers have discovered the value of decoupling their change targets from the overall system. T-groups (either individual focused or intact work groups) require physical removal from normal workplaces. New work processes are tried out in 'test cells' isolated from the rest of the plant, or in entirely new plants physically separate from existing practices. The socio-technical systems approach stresses the development of *semi-autonomous* work groups. Team building approaches emphasize strong in-group interaction and identification, presumably reducing external coupling. In short, OD has discovered (as systems theory predicts) that change is more readily achieved when the target is decoupled from the rest of the system.

Three follow-on questions occur to me here: Is there available (or can we construct) a taxonomy of different techniques for bringing about decoupling? What do we know about the relative ease of achieving decoupling by these different methods, and about their costs? And, most importantly, is decoupling a temporary thing, used just for the change period, or are we trying to design organizations which are loosely coupled on an on-going basis?

BETA: To your tripartite question, a tripartite answer: 'No', 'Very little', and 'That's too big a question'. That is, I *don't* know of a good taxonomy of decoupling strategies for OD; indeed, I had not previously thought of the various techniques you list as sharing this theme. As a result, we know very little about their relative costs and benefits, though it would clearly be very valuable if we did. And, on the loose coupling/tight coupling issue, I think that serious consideration of this huge issue would take us too far afield from our current concerns.

However, I don't want to sound totally negative here, so let me share one specific idea triggered by your point about the advantages of the semi-autonomous work group approach to system simplification: you will be interested to know that Hal Leavitt has recently suggested that we 'take groups seriously'. By this he means that our organizations should hire and fire groups, not individuals; reward and promote groups, not individuals; in short make groups, not individuals, the basic building block of organizations. By absolving ourselves of the responsibility for what happens inside groups, we could certainly simplify the description of organizational systems.

My university has done something like this recently by delegating to the departments partial control of the definition of graduate standing for the faculty. The criterion for graduate faculty status has been made group-specific so that the Graduate College need not apply a universal criterion to every single faculty member. The Graduate College's control problem has been reduced from developing an adequate universal criterion to simply approving departments' proposals for particularistic criteria. It seems to me to be a lovely illustration of simplification through decoupling.

ALPHA: But isn't the simplification illusory? Would not Leavitt's suggestion hide the complexity *within* the groups? The decouple-for-change strategy and the decouple-for-manageability strategy face the same dilemma – that decoupling moves an element away from full integration into the larger system. We claim, after all, to be in the *organizational* development business, and it is far from clear that successful change at the level of the individual or subgroup will have a beneficial impact on the systemic character of the organization. As Katz and Kahn (1966) comment: 'to approach institutional change solely in individual terms involves an impressive and discouraging series of assumptions, [a chain whose] ... weaknesses become apparent as soon as its many links are enumerated'. Further, 'the difficulty with many attempts at organizational change is that the changers have not clearly distinguished their targets and have assumed that the individual or group-level target was the same as the social-structure target'. As suggested earlier, the quandary is to leave the target decoupled (and thus little integrated with the system) or to return it to the system, with the accompanying likelihood of 'stabilizing' forces vitiating the changes.

As with the general discussion of the Iron Law, we find ourselves more optimistic about the decoupling strategy than this analysis suggests. It may well be that, for practical purposes, subsystem change is made possible by this approach, and that sufficient integration may be achieved to generate net system gains. It may not be *organizational* development, but the possibility of doing good exists in many cases. Indeed, astute follow-up of streams of changes and opportunities may result in significant changes in overall organization performance.

BETA: Decoupling can also help in an unexpected way, by facilitating the process of diagnosis. In the case of a university, each department may be falling short of academic excellence for different reasons. The biology department may lack senior faculty leadership; the sociology department may be wracked with ideological conflict between faculty factions; the whole college of education may be suffering lack of hope and confidence because of poor prospects for the future of the entire field. By decoupling the system into nearly independent parts, distinctive (and therefore more accurate) diagnoses are made possible. Creating a more carefully distinguished set of organizational ills and cures may be the secret to progress in OD. As Drucker (1979) has observed about medicine:

The fundamental step from quackery to medicine was taken around 1700 when Boerhaave in Holland and Sydenham in England abstained from global theory and taught that diseases are specific, with specific causes and specific symptoms and specific cures. The great triumph of bacteriology ... was precisely that each infection was shown to be caused by a specific bacterium, spread by unique carriers ... and that each infection acts in its own specific way on specific tissue.

To decouple any system is to facilitate this kind of discriminating approach to diagnosis and the development of tailor-made techniques of change.

ALPHA: Your point about specialized diagnosis is well taken, but it does not deal with the problem of integrating or reintegrating the parts into a system. Let me try to come at this more systematically, and see if I can be clearer as to what I'm unclear about. I'm persuaded that large and complex organizations are composed of loosely interconnected, differentiated, semi-autonomous subsystems which are internally coupled relatively tightly; intra-subsystem coupling is typically tight, while inter-subsystem coupling is looser. I'll give you three supporting arguments. First, we would expect large organizations to be made up of highly differentiated 'organs' (subsystems) having specialized functions. Second, present organizational forms are largely imitated from successful survivors of evolutionary processes, and these survivors are likely to have emerged by creation or acquisition of stable subsystems, rather than by creating their complexity full-blown. Third, people just won't put up with membership in systems of undifferentiated complexity, with being small cogs in large and unintelligible machines. Our loyalties and identifications are with our subgroups (subsystems), and our feelings (and probably our realities) of being coupled tightly into the larger system are much more tenuous. Thus, to pick up Leavitt's point again, groups are the central reality for most organization members.

The densest coupling, then, is at the group or subsystem level, so these couplings are the most obvious to the OD practitioner – he or she must deal with them to get anything done at all. On the other hand, the between-subsystem couplings, though not particularly dense, are likely to be in terms of variables which are in some way 'critical'. A single bodily organ may be nearly autonomous – but the blood supply and nerve connections are surely critical. My dealings with the president of my university are extremely few – but those I have affect my work life significantly. What his criteria are for my promotion is a prime example. I'm sure you have your own favourite examples of these remote-but-critical couplings.

The couplings issue thus appears in two forms for the OD practitioner. At the local or subsystem level, we expect couplings to be very dense, and the OD intervention must take this into account to achieve any significant change at all. The obvious example of a technique which takes account of this is T-grouping intact work groups. At the whole system level – that is, at the level of attempting *organization* development – the couplings are likely to be more subtle, but highly critical to the functioning of the overall system. Perhaps the critical link in a university is promotions – an individual may be part of a highly effective subgroup, an OD triumph, but if the university still looks for individual records of publication and teaching for promotions, he or she may still be concerned that individual efforts are going to be recognized. These remote-but-critical couplings are, I think, not at all well understood. As ODers, we may be doing well at the subsystem level but generating all sorts of long-term difficulties for the system as a whole. Back to the Iron Law again: on these remote couplings, we don't know the consequences of our interventions; can we assume they will be positive?

BETA: And don't forget that your argument also reinforces the other half of the Iron Law, that subsystem equilibrium mechanisms will tend to slough off changes.

One irony of your suggestion for hierarchical growth as a way of making complex systems more understandable is that it produces, or rather builds on, *stable* subsystems, and thus incorporates resistance to change in its very essence! It seems that understandability and changeability are incompatible within your approach.

ALPHA: Leaving, for the moment, the first strategy for coping with complexity, simplifying the target system, let us consider briefly the prospects for the second strategy – improving our understanding so as to encompass irreducibly complex systems, including our two universities. What I have in mind here is simply improving our understanding to a *workable* level, not to a level of perfect description. The latter is not necessary if all we wish to do is to *improve* the system beyond what we have now. Remember that our aim is only to upgrade the quality of faculty scholarship (in our continuing example), not to perfect it. For this purpose, imperfect descriptions of the various processes are likely to be adequate. And for the moment I would like to restrict myself to analytical descriptions in which the content of specific performance and evaluation processes are spelled out.

One method for gaining analytical leverage is represented by the socio-technical systems approach. The central postulate of this approach is that an analysis of either the technical or the social system of an organization is insufficient, since the two are so intimately intertwined in many work settings. In presenting the basic idea of socio-technical systems, Cooper and Foster (1971) note that they use a type of mapping familiar to industrial engineers', stressing as it does work elements, material flows, machine interconnections, and so on. It is precisely this familiarity to industrial engineers that makes the system amenable to their tools for the analysis of physical manufacturing systems. Cooper and Foster further argue that 'both the plant layout and the handling system determine to a large extent the social system'. Thus, the general (and exceedingly difficult) problem of analysing a socio-technical system is greatly eased by the assumption that the effects of the physical (technological) system are predominant. Such systems are relatively easy to specify, and are analytically tractable by available tools. Computer simulations may be promising in technologically dominated settings, although I know of no situation in which a simulation was built in parallel with an OD effort, as a way of predicting system impacts, even where simulations approach feasibility.

Socio-tech, then, looks highly promising for understanding and modifying situations in which work technology predominates and causes psychological and sociological phenomena. Such situations may, in fact, be widespread in manufacturing and extraction industries. It is not clear that the approach will be as powerful for situations in which technological dominance is less obvious. Since a university tends to be dominated by thought processes and by collegial interchange, the socio-technical systems approach would seem less applicable there. With the growing influence of the computer, even in the humanities, social science, music, and architectural design, this may, however, be changing. Nevertheless, I think it is unlikely that we will soon achieve the level of detailed analytical descriptions of universities which is available, say, from a cybernetic analysis of an automatic steering system for a spacecraft. In the latter case, the detailed relationship between each system element can be specified with considerable precision, and the structure of the interconnections is unambiguously known – and even then, practical cases quickly get outside the range of the formal analytical techniques. As organizational analysts, we frequently do not even know what control loops exist, let alone their exact performance characteristics.

Although adequate simulation requires a rather high level of prior understanding of how the system performs, the work associated with feedback dynamics may nevertheless be of relevance here. A major element of this approach is the belief that the most critical determinants of system performance are the feedback loops it contains, with less concern for exact parameter values of relationships. Note that this is a different level of description than spelling out the analytical content of each of the constituent processes of the whole organization. Mapping the feedback loops requires only an understanding of the structure of relationships among processes; it does not require a detailed understanding of the internal workings of each process. Thus, even though we may not understand how a faculty member creates a new idea, or how his creative output is evaluated by his peers, we may be able to say how those two processes are connected to and influence one another. Such 'feedback structure' models are thus much less data-hungry than full-scale detailed simulations, and may be more feasible than they are for development as part of an OD effort. In particular, since one widely used OD technique involves exactly the modification of feedback loops (the survey feedback approach), it seems entirely appropriate that feedback dynamic models be used in parallel with such interventions, to give greater insight into the likely systemic consequences of using the technique.

BETA: That's an interesting insight on the socio-technical systems approach – perhaps we should call it the 'technico-(social) systems' approach, since, as you point out, the systemic part of the analysis turns heavily on the technical system, rhetoric on the coequal treatment of both technical and social aspects notwithstanding. I would comment only that understandable technique is not limited to hardware-based technology but includes, for example, bureaucratic procedures that are rooted in the system of shared knowledge amongst organization members. Thus, the analytical distinction you make between technical and social systems seems more blurred than you would have us believe. The real problem is *not* modelling systems composed of both technological and human components; it is instead modelling systems that have both routine, describable components and non-routine, indescribable components, especially where the latter dominate the system. In universities, the non-routine functions of faculty scholarship dominate the routine functions of the physical plant and business office, and thus I would

agree with you that socio-tech has limited usefulness for the purpose of intervening to upgrade academic excellence, even though it might be useful for improving
the efficiency of support functions.

I'm also intrigued by your suggestion of a marriage between survey feedback
interventions and feedback dynamics modelling. Two comments are in order.
First, note that survey feedback not only models the feedback loops in the
organization, but it changes them as well. It not only represents the organization
to itself, but it alters the channels of communication and influence. It does not
seem to me that the survey feedback people have taken adequate note of the
impact of their efforts on the feedback loop structure of the organization. In our
terms, there is an important difference between doing survey feedback once and
making it a permanent part of the system.

Second, you claim to be elaborating the second of your escapes from the Iron
Law, to wit that we can increase our understanding of irreducibly complex
systems through techniques of computer simulation and so forth. But it seems to
me that you are also dealing with your *third* escape from the Iron Law,
specifically that we can devise ways of systems control in the face of inadequate
understanding. You seem to be equating 'adequate' with 'complete'. But I would
argue that knowing the feedback loop structure is perfectly adequate for some
purposes of control although inadequate for the purpose of complete analytic
description of a system's functioning. Thus, I would argue that you have merged
your second and third escapes from the Iron Law in your prior discussion. My
next point also relates to the issue of adequacy of understanding, and was stirred
by some unspoken assumptions you made.

You say that we should improve our understanding of systems. But you do not
say who 'we' are, nor do you specify what kind of understanding or knowing you
have in mind. I presume that I can dispose of the latter point by emphasizing
(again!) intuitive forms of knowing as a supplement to analytical ways of
knowing. Is it necessary to have an explicit understanding of the system; is not a
tacit understanding sufficient for working within it?

As to the former point, 'we' may be either systems scientists who insist on completely understanding the system for purposes of scientific (i.e. logical analytical)
descriptions; *or* practising interventionists who may be willing to proceed with less
than complete knowledge and hope that they learn enough as they go along to
bring about some practical benefits; *or* the members of the system themselves. In
the last case, the nature of the intervention may be to enable the system to learn
by building in a capacity for learning how to learn (Argyris and Schon, 1978). My
guess is that our best chance to improve understanding is to improve the intuitive
understanding by the system members themselves, and our worst chance is to
improve the analytical understanding of systems by systems scientists. But that
suggests that system improvement should ultimately be in the hands of system
members and casts doubt on whether we should insist that the only legitimate
description is an analytic one, does it not?

I am not sure that I agree that organizations are artificial, man-made systems, as you suggested earlier. I prefer to think that they evolve from the inside out. External agents may be able to influence the course and pace of their natural development, but I would hardly describe organizations as a whole as artificial. Shaped, perhaps, but not artificial. Now, one of the things that can develop naturally is the system's own images of itself, the metaphors used for making sense of their own experience. An interventionist can help in that process by providing new metaphors, or even by legitimizing the use of metaphors as organizing devices. This takes us back to the argument that to influence a system at a certain level of complexity you need to intervene at the (n+l)th level of complexity. What is true for change is equally true for understanding. By supplying a university with new metaphors, you can help to make its more concrete circumstances understandable to its members. For twenty-five years, universities have been operating with a *growth* metaphor, but the fat days are over. It is no longer possible to have both new programmes and increasing faculty salaries. That impossibility is more easily understood within the metaphor of a *stable state*. But note that understanding here is achieved not by more complete and detailed description, but by properly framing the facts in a new context. If you restrict yourself to analytical descriptions, the only way open to you to make the system understandable is to simplify it down to the level of analytical descriptions. But another way to improve understanding is to admit new forms of description, more poetic than analytic.

ALPHA: You have given me much to respond to. Thank you for elaborating (and thereby buttressing!) my insights about socio-tech and survey feedback. And I in turn agree that my second and third escapes from the Iron Law of Systems Pessimism merge *if* one considers poetic levels of understanding to be equal in scientific seriousness to analytical description. But surely you can't be serious when you equate poetry and science!

The core of your rebuttal seems to be that in ill-structured systems, ill-structured understanding by the system members is adequate — indeed necessary — to bring about change. But note that you still give a controlling role to the interventionist in that he or she is expected to supply the required ill-structured metaphors. And in order for the interventionist to know which metaphors will work and which won't, he or she still needs a precise analytical description of the system in order to predict the effects of the metaphor. What you are saying implies that system members can get away with incomplete understanding, but the interventionist cannot. You distort my position! I admit that if a systems scientist knows only the structure of the feedback loops in a system, he understands the system incompletely. But I also agree that this incomplete understanding is nevertheless adequate for bringing about rough, qualitative changes in the system. It seems that we are confusing incomplete knowledge at the concrete level of system couplings with a softer, more gestalt-like knowledge of the system as a whole.

This debate seems endless. Perhaps it is time for me to summarize my own position on the contribution that general systems theory has made, or potentially could make, to OD. I must admit that my own reading of the literature has not left me very optimistic on this score. To successful practitioners, systems theory seems to occupy the role of either sacred cow or medicine bottle; when things go well, systems theory receives a nod at the write-up stage, to dignify the report; when things go badly, one reaches for the systems bottle for a more dignified description of one's failures. Your attempt to redefine GST to include poetry seems a perfect example of both sacred cow and medicine bottle.

To this point, GST (your attempted redefinition of it notwithstanding) has urged only that important couplings are important, and may be worth minimizing if one wants to bring about subsystem change. It seems likely that ODers either knew about this already, or quickly discovered it when their early change attempts failed. Identification of *which* connections are important in any particular setting still requires good insight into that setting, unguided by GST. On this score, it is hard to claim any special virtue for GST over practical wisdom and experience.

At this stage, I find myself pessimistic about the prospect that GST will soon provide a general theory for OD. There are some islands of encouragement – the promise of a particular analytic technique, the potential of a particularly analysable setting – but the general impression is that systemic analysis is grossly short of the level of sophistication required for confident understanding of organizations, or of attempts to change them. There are, however, a number of ways in which even weak theory contributes to action – notably, by providing a language into which empirically proven techniques can be integrated to their mutual benefit; and by suggesting the general form of novel techniques which can be tried out in practice – even though weak theory does not provide us with complete descriptions.

BETA: I agree with you that weak theory can contribute to action. To attempt to put this into your very technically-oriented language, there are many types of system coupling ranging from physical, hard-wired couplings in simple, primitive systems to much softer couplings of language and shared meanings in more advanced systems. And revolutionary changes at the hard coupling level can be brought about by small changes at the soft coupling level. For example, the American self-image as a motor car society surely was a necessary prerequisite to the creation of the interstate highway system. But that has been one of my central points all along.

Perhaps it is unnecessary that such insights arise from GST, so long as they are available. What seems important to me is not the techniques of GST, but the point of view, that there is a unity to events, that one creates one's own environment, and that complete analytic knowledge is not necessary for the adequate control of complex systems. GST's existence theorems are as important as its analytical procedures.

If you think back over our comments, yours have a recurring flavour of the inadequacy of our rational, analytic methods of knowing (and thus acting on) complex systems such as organizations. My recurring theme has been to agree, but to suggest other methods of knowing and acting that might help. I could attempt to reargue my case here, as you have yours.

But perhaps I should resort to a different kind of language to express what I believe about the search for understanding, about how ultimately it circles back to understanding of self in the *simplest* of terms. T. S. Eliot, in closing *The Four Quartets*, said it as powerfully as it can be said:

We shall not cease from exploration
And the end of all our exploring
Will be to arrive at where we started
And know the place for the first time.
Through the unknown, remembered gate
When the last of earth left to discover
Is that which was the beginning,
At the source of the longest river
The voice of the hidden waterfall
And the children in the apple-tree
Not known, because not looked for
But heard, half-heard, in the stillness
Between two waves of the sea.
Quick now, here, now, always –
A condition of complete simplicity
(Costing not less than everything)
And all shall be well and
All manner of things shall be well
When the tongues of flame are in-folded
Into the crowned knot of fire
And the fire and the rose are one.

Poetry, although not science, is a powerful mode of inquiry.

ALPHA: Must you always have the last word?

References

Argyris, Chris, and Schon, Donald A. (1978) *Organizational Learning: A Theory of Action Perspective*, Reading, Mass.: Addison-Wesley.

Bateson, Gregory (1972) *Steps to an Ecology of Mind*, New York: Ballantine.

Cooper, R., and Foster, M. (1971) Sociotechnical systems, *American Psychologist*, **26**, 467–474.

Drucker, Peter F. (1979) What Freud forgot, *Human Nature*, **2**, (3), 40–47.

Katz, Daniel, and Kahn, Robert L. (1966) *The Social Psychology of Organizations*, New
    York: Wiley.
Pondy, Louis R., and Mitroff, Ian I. (1979) Beyond open system models of organization.
    In Barry, Staw (ed.) *Research in Organizational Behavior*, vol. 1, Greenwich, Con.:
    JAI Press, 3–39.

Systems Theory for Organization Development
Edited by T. G. Cummings
© 1980 John Wiley & Sons Ltd.

Chapter 3

New Approaches to Research for Systems Theory and Organization Development

Peter Reason

Systems theory is often hailed as the grand new approach to the study of human social behaviour, and in particular to behaviour in organizations. It is seen as a major advance over the approaches of traditional science. While traditional science studies phenomena by reduction to the interplay of elementary units which can be investigated in isolation, systems theory offers a general science of wholes, and is concerned with the interrelation of parts and the impact of the whole on the behaviour of parts; while traditional approaches can cope with situations in which there are only a small number of variables, systems approaches hold out the possibility of dealing with the interaction of a complex of elements; while traditional approaches can only deal with complexity through statistical reduction, systems theory can deal with organized complexity; and while traditional approaches can only deal with closed systems, systems theory offers ways of understanding an open system in interaction with its environment.

The need to understand and act in complex, whole situations of human interaction has long been recognized by various students and practitioners in the field of human behaviour; it has been particularly important for those who wish to act in and make changes to human behaviour in a variety of fields. The attempt to understand wholes is not solely the province of the systems theorist or practitioner, but has been the concern of many students who take what Diesing (1972) calls the holist standpoint to the human situation:

The holist standpoint includes the belief that human systems tend to develop a characteristic wholeness or integrity. They are not simply a loose collection of traits or reflexes or variables of any sort; they have a unity that manifests itself in every part. Their unity may be that of a basic spirit or set of values that expresses itself throughout the system ... or it may be that of a basic mode of production and distribution that more or less conditions everything else ... or perhaps that of a basic personality that shapes all cultural institutions to its own needs and drives. Or the unity may not have any focal point, but may consist merely of myriad interweavings of themes and subsystems in a complex pattern. . . . This means that the characteristics of a part are largely determined by the whole to which it belongs and by its particular location in the whole system. (pp. 137–138)

The argument of this chapter is that the system, or holist, viewpoint, if it is to advance and fulfil its promise, requires a suitable research methodology. Research, in this context, is to be taken in its widest meaning: not as solely the work of academic theorists in the pursuit of abstract and generalizable laws of human behaviour, but as an activity which aims to develop possibilities for understanding and choiceful action in specific human situations. One of the roots of this view of research lies in the 'laboratory' approach to human relations training (Benne et al., 1975), as in the now classic T-group, in which people attempt to learn from their experience of the unfolding and development of human action in a small group context: here understanding of the processes of group development is closely linked with the growth of skills to act as a group member. This suggests that we might view research almost as a life-style of exploration and participant observation in the service of self-directed action; this chapter explores some possibilities for the development and systematization of this view of research.

Research methodology in the social sciences has been under heavy criticism for a number of years, and there are widespread doubts as to whether the traditional positivist approach does justice to the human condition. These doubts have been coming both from established figures in the field and from fringe groups, yet their criticisms have been significantly consistent: traditional approaches are seen as *alienating*, reducing the status of those people studied to 'things' (Heather, 1976; Rowan, 1976); as *reductionist*, looking at discrete variables rather than whole phenomena (Koestler and Smythies, 1969; Friedlander, 1977); they often ignore the significance of the *interaction* between researcher and subject (Friedlander, 1968; Cooper, 1967); and because they are often experienced as *invading* the personal space of the subjects, they have to rely on information that is captured by various devious research devices rather than given freely through a process of self-discovery and self-revelation (Maslow, 1966; Jourard, 1971).

One of the fullest critiques of traditional research methods from within the social science establishment is put forward by Harre and Secord (1972). They argue that social psychological research, based as it is on a mechanistic model of man, causal laws and a naïve determinism, and a logical positivist methodology, is 'restricted to simple manipulations of independent variables, themselves allegedly simple components of behaviour', usually in laboratory studies. They doubt whether this approach will yield reliable scientific knowledge, argue that the positivistic approach leads only to an 'illusion of objectivity', and point to the study of *meanings* and the *agency* of people as the major, and neglected, phenomena of social psychology. In suggesting a remedy for these problems, Harre and Secord suggest 'that human social behaviour cannot be made intelligible under the mechanistic, causal paradigm'; that human beings must be treated as 'agents acting according to rule'; that social behaviour must be 'conceived of as actions mediated by meanings'; and that 'lay explanations of behaviour provide the best model of psychological theory' (pp. 27–29).

Harre and Secord suggest one path towards a new research methodology; there are others which are explored more fully below. My view is that if we do not develop new approaches to research which are holistic and non-alienating we are, quite simply, stuck. If traditional, positivist approaches to research in the human sciences fail to do justice to the human social condition, they also tend to be irrelevant to the practice of OD consultants and the helping professions generally. Yet, if we do not pay attention to what we take for knowledge in our profession – and this implies the ability to use a relevant research methodology – we will remain simply technicians or, worse, organization 'tinkers' to use Mangham's (1978) felicitous phrase:

the tinker is fundamentally a botcher, a patcher and, in the pejorative sense of the word, an amateur. His approach is that of trial-and-error, suck-it-and-see. His tools are simple, his techniques crude and clumsy, his familiarity and understanding of his raw material relatively slight. To tinker with something is not to know what you are doing with it. By contrast the master of his trade, the craftsman ... is a professional, a confident, competent master of his tools, his techniques and his materials. ... Few Organisation Development consultants are craftsmen (p. xiv).

Before we can come to grips with the development of a new approach to research methodology, we need first to consider at least briefly the nature of knowledge in human affiars and its relationship to action; this is the task of the next section. Following this, we can trace a number of lines of thought which lead towards a new paradigm for research, and develop this into a specific methodology that can be applied in an organizational development context. Finally, we can explore the consequences of these ideas for the practice of consultancy.-

Reflections on the nature of knowledge and research

We are accustomed to the view that knowledge starts from reflection, from the Cartesian perspective, 'Cogito, ergo sum'. We are also accustomed to the view that there is an essential theoretical reference to practical activities – if this were not so our reflection would be meaningless, simply an exercise of fantasy. And while we may assert the Lewinian maxim that there is nothing so practical as a good theory, we are often troubled by the seeming irrelevance of various theories to our own practice, and by our inability to develop theories which are appealing and useful to our organizational clients.

Macmurray (1957) argues that this dualism of theory and practice is inevitable in any philosophy which takes *cogito* as its starting-point and centre of reference: 'If we make the "I think" the primary postulate of philosophy, then not merely do we institute a dualism between theoretical and practical experience, but we make action logically inconceivable. . . . However far we carry the process of thought it can never *become* an action or spontaneously *generate* an action' (p. 73).

Thus, Macmurray argues that if we are to overcome this split between knowledge and action, between theory and practice, we must 'substitute the "I do" for the "I think" . . . and do our thinking from the standpoint of action': 'Action . . . is a full concrete activity of the self in which all our capacities are employed: while thought is constituted by the exclusion of some of our powers and a withdrawal into all activity which is less concrete and less complete' (p. 86).

We can only *think* about what we already *know*; what we know arises from our action as agents in the world.

These philosophical considerations lead us to the view that research in the human sciences must be a process which starts from and is fundamentally rooted in the action of people in the situations in which they live and work; a process which only involves reflection divorced from action cannot lead to valid knowledge. Now, the integration of understanding with action has long been the goal of action-research, but has presented problems because in practice the action-researcher nearly always seems to be captured by the *action* or by the *research*: rarely is there an integration. Action-research is only possible when one's aim is holistic, when one needs the understanding in order to act in a situation in which one is embedded: in these circumstances the action-research becomes a whole in itself – research in the service of action – and is no longer torn between the two poles. Conversely, true action-research becomes impossible when the research aims become fragmented and disassociated from the situation – i.e. 'theoretical' or 'academic'.

The notion of praxis may provide a central guide for a holistic research process, one which is itself an integrated whole, and which is suitable for exploring whole human situations. By praxis I mean action which is informed by and based in systematic exploration of and reflection on the situation in which it is to take place. Action without awareness can become pointless, empty activism, informed not by awareness and choice but by habit and prejudice; on the other hand, reflection without action is ultimately sterile verbalism or intellectuallism, having no point of contact with reality, and no implications for action in the real world. The notion of praxis points up the essential interrelation between action and reflection: action requires reflection to give it purpose, choice, and direction; reflection requires action to give it a reality base and meaning. In any situation we need to find the appropriate and dynamic interplay between the two.

The fundamental issue is that of *personal action*, albeit personal action within the context of a social system and in relation to other people. There has over past years been a change of emphasis in the practice of the applied behavioural sciences from working with individuals to working with larger social systems: thus we have *organization* development, *team* building, *family* therapy, and so on, all of which are based on the premise that individual change is impossible unless it is accompanied by change in the larger social system. While recognizing that individuals act within a social context and that the individual's capacity to act may be constrained by that context, every human being is fundamentally capable of self-direction (Heron, 1971). One of the dangers of systems theory is that it has tempted practitioners to reify organizations, so that they are seen as entities – mechanisms or organisms – in their own right, rather than as complex patterns of individual choice made in pursuit of meaningful ends. The basic unit of experience and action is the individual working in the nexus of relationships which is his life; so it is the person, not a reified phantom such as 'the organization', 'the team', or 'the community', with whom we need to start, and through whom we may reach the wider social system of which he is part.

A basic assumption behind all this is that as people in relation to others we create our own reality, both in the conservative sense of supporing the present state of affairs by acting without reflection in a world-taken-for-granted, and in a radical sense of building a new reality from the building blocks we have available to us. For example, Huckaby (1975), writing from the perspective of the Women's Movement, has argued that the 'most powerful tool for maintaining any particular social form or relationship is the power to define reality'; thus the most powerful interventions into human affairs are those which *redefine* reality. She argues that in sexist societies 'male is defined as good, healthy, mature etc., and female is defined as bad, unhealthy, immature etc.'. To the extent that the Women's Movement is successful in developing the power to redefine this reality, it will have radical consequences for our society. In a similar vein, Freire (1971) has pointed out that people may learn to '*emerge* from their *submersion* and acquire the ability to *intervene* in reality' (p. 100). Yet this capacity to intervene is counterposed by a fear of freedom; Reich was one of the first to recognize a widespread incapacity for freedom and a fear of too much responsibility, although he also recognized that this capacity is itself a result of social conditions and hence is alterable (Boadella, 1974).

Thus, a fundamental question is, what are the processes through which people may learn to reflect critically on their experience, link it with their action, and through this transform their world? I take the view that persons in relation have the capacity to do this, although they manifestly do not do so for a large amount of their lives: most people, most of the time, are submerged in an objectified/reified social environment which they do not experience as in any sense their own creation. A basic agenda for research in the human sciences is, I suggest, to explore ways in which people may cease to be submerged and may learn to act creatively – to be self-directing.

While this is an important question for research, it is also an important issue for the practice of organization development, since it implies that through an action-based, holistic research approach we can help people become their own agents of change. If we can develop a methodology through which people can explore their situation as members of an organization, be they managers, supervisors, shop stewards, consultants, etc., critically review that situation, and develop plans to change and develop it, we will have a powerful tool for creating change which is based firmly in the reality of organization members' experience. The importance of diagnosis before action has long been recognized in the practice of organization development – at least in theory; my argument is that we must regard diagnosis as a fundamental research process concerning the development of knowledge in the service of action. This approach, if systematized and developed, can supplement and often replace traditional research processes, add enormously to our understanding of human life in organizations, and provide a solid grounding for the practice of organization development.

Pathways towards a new research methodology

There are a number of lines of thought which suggest ways towards such a research methodology – a methodology in which knowledge is developed in the service of action and change. These ideas come from anthropologists and anti-psychiatrists, philosophers and humanistic psychologists, as well as from students of organizations, yet they are all pathways which lead in a similar direction.

First of all, if we are to take the notion of praxis seriously, and argue that people can be their own change agents, we must develop a research process which is concerned with eliciting the meaning of events to those actually participating in them. This reflects Schutz's (1967) opinion that we need to go beyond the view of an outside observer who simply sees physical acts, and discover what actors themselves mean by their actions.

Second, if people are to engage in self-directed action, they must be able to examine their experience and confront the limitations of their current world view. Thus our approach must be 'critical' in the sense that Berstein (1976) quotes Horkeimer: 'Critical theory aspires to bring the subjects themselves to full consciousness of the contradictions implicit in their material existence, to penetrate the ideological mystifications and forms of false consciousness that distort the meaning of existing social conditions' (p. 182).

Mangham (1975) has made a very similar comment about the practice of organization development:

If we want to know how order is sustained within an organization we must consider the organization as seen by its members; if we want to effect change, we must influence definitions and bring about a reconstruing, a renegotiation of the world-taken-for-granted by the actors concerned. From this perspective, Organization Development becomes less a matter of values and styles of management and much more a process of helping individuals and groups examine their processes of interaction in order to accelerate or facilitate changes which are in any case an intrinsic if atrophied attribute of the process of organization itself (p. 7).

Third, if we are to develop an approach to the study of personal action, we need to engage with others in personal – authentic and non-alienating – relations. Thus we must work from Laing's (1965) premise that 'the science of persons is the study of human beings that begins from a relationship with the other as person and proceeds to an account of the other still as person. . . . The other as person is seen by me as responsible, as capable of choice, in short, as a self-acting agent' (pp. 21–22).

Fourth, as I have already argued, since the human situation consists of whole systems of experience and action, we need to approach it from a holistic stance. This means that as well as exploring the 'whole' quality of human situations, we must attempt to capture some of 'the unique characteristics, the distinctive qualities and patterns that differentiate this system from others' (Diesing, 1972). Diesing argues that it is at this point that the holist may part company from many social scientists, since he believes that his subject-matter is more important than the canons of 'science': 'The holist believes in the primacy of subject matter; he believes that whatever else a method may be, it should at least be adequate to the particular thing described and should not distort it. This belief in the primacy of the subject matter is perhaps the most striking characteristic of the holist standpoint. (p. 140).

Finally, since we take the view that knowledge of the human situation arises in the context of action, we need to develop what Torbert (1976) calls an action science in contrast to a reflective science: 'a science useful to the actor at the moment of action rather than to a disembodied thinker at the moment of reflection' (p. 167).

These views about taking the actor's point of view, about being critical, about authentic non-alienating relationships, about developing a whole view, and about being action-oriented, all represent paths towards a new research methodology. This methodology can be developed more precisely through the ideas of John Heron and John Rowan, and through the development of earlier work of my own.

The experiential method

Heron (1971) has developed an approach to research of the human situations which he refers to as the 'experiential method'. He argues that there is an implied assumption in traditional research approaches that human behaviour is absolutely determined by antecedent conditions – it is behaviour we engage in 'precisely because we cannot know in advance what particular form it will take'. Heron argues that research behaviour and other original creative activity can only be explained in a model which has at its centre the 'notion of intelligent agency . . . the notion of a self-directing person' (p. 2). Thus human actors must be seen as *relatively* determined, and any piece of social behaviour may be explained in terms of three levels of explanation which are distinct yet interrelated: 'There is a causal explanation in terms of relatively determining conditions of inner needs and environmental factors; there is a conventional explanation in terms of tacit com-mitment to prevailing social norms; and there is autonomous explanation in terms of fully explicit self-directed commitment to certain social purposes and principles' (p. 4).

It is this last level of explanation, the autonomous, which is most relevant for the research approach I am developing here. Heron suggests that this viewpoint leads to two major questions for psychological inquiry: '1) How does the capacity for human self-direction become constrained, blocked, inhibited, suppressed, or distorted? . . . 2) How can the human potential for self-direction be actualised?' (p. 5).

This second question is, of course, almost identical to my own earlier one about the development of praxis – action which is guided by and informed by awareness. Heron argues that, while the question may to some extent be answered in terms of external agencies, in the end it 'must necessarily be answered in terms of the agent himself'. It is to answer this question that he has developed the experiential method, which he regards as the 'central and crucial method for *systematically* exploring how human potential for self-direction can be actualised. In the experiential method, the agent himself engages systematically in a self-directed exploration of his own experience and behaviour and attends fully to the experience and behaviour of other agents who are similarly engaged in interaction with him' (p. 7).

Heron has contrasted the traditional and experiential approaches to research in the following manner. In the traditional approach the experimenter (E) investigates the behaviour of the subject (S) as indicated in Figure 1. The relationship is unidirectional, and the experimenter is in control of the research. In contrast to this, the experiential method may be portrayed as in Figure 2, and is about six times more complex. There is a dyadic and coequal relationship between two persons which is reversible so that both engage as experimenter and as subject; they engage in a mutually accepting and supportive relationship with each other, taking facilitative initiatives, giving feedback, and sharing experiences. They share a minimal but explicit theory which describes a process of learning

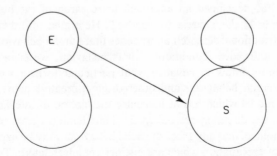

Figure 1   Adapted from Heron (in preparation)

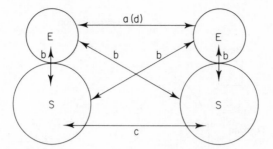

Figure 2   Adapted from Heron (in preparation)

and change, and which sets out techniques of methods for such change ('a' in Figure 2). On the basis of this theory and method they engage in a systematic and self-directed exploration of their experience and behaviour both individually and jointly ('b' in Figure 2). At times in the process they may become so involved in the experience that they lose sight of the theory and become totally immersed in the subjective experience of the process of discovery ('c' in Figure 2). After a period of such mutual systematic exploration, they step back from the exploration and review critically and revise the theory and method in the light of their experience ('d' in Figure 2), thus completing the cycle.

Clearly there are disadvantages in the experiential method: the basic concepts and theory tend to be phenomenological, and their full significance can only be grasped experientially by 'living through', and thus you cannot fully accept and grasp the theory until you have made a commitment to its practical implications; there is a danger of 'consensus collusion', since the commitment involved to the approach may lead to a tacit norm to overlook some areas of experience which would raise questions about the initial theory; the experiential method cannot lead readily to quantification and thus there is a danger that 'excess emphasis on the experiential method could lead to a development of emotional and interpersonal competence at the expense of critical discrimination, intellectual rigour and competence' (Heron, 1971, p. 16).

However, the advantages of the method are clear too: it allows access to areas of experience and behaviour not available to traditional positivist methods, and provides the possibility of gathering rich qualitative information about the development of self-directed behaviour.

The research cycle

John Rowan (1976) has developed what he calls a 'new paradigm in research', based on a dialectical research cycle (Figure 3). In a traditional research project, each stage of the cycle carries on smoothly from the former: when the researcher identifies an arena for research, he first spends his time thinking about it and

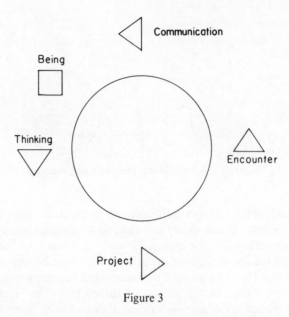

Figure 3

reviewing the literature; once this stage is complete, he moves on to design his research approach (Project) and from there into an engagement with his subjects in data gathering (Encounter); when this is completed, he disengages, returns to his desk, analyses the data and writes up his results (Communication); that finished, he returns to rest until another issue engages his attention.

If, however, we regard research as part of a life-style, in which people as actors are seeking to understand and act effectively and creatively in particular social situations, this research cycle must be seen as a *dialectical* cycle, in which each stage contradicts the previous one:

One starts by resting in one's own experience. But at a certain point existing practices seem to be inadequate – one becomes dissatisfied. So the first negation arises; one turns *against* the old ways of doing things. A real problem has arisen.

So one moves into a phase of needing new thinking. Perhaps one starts by finding out what others already know – gathering information about alternative possibilities. Often little can be learnt from this, and again one becomes dissatisfied. At a certain point gathering more and more information is *abandoned*.

Thinking is *not* enough. One must make a definite decision as to what to aim for. What is the major contradiction? That is what we need to attack. Philosophising any further would be sterile and useless. Some action plan has to come into being. This may require some daring, some risk-taking, some breaking of bounds.

But again, at a certain point, plans are *not* the point. Action itself is the thing to get into. In action I am fully present, here now, Plans are a mere distraction from the past, and can only hamper and impede. I must be ready to improvise if unexpected reactions occur.

But at a certain point, after I have been immersed in this for some time, I begin to get dissatisfied. Action is *not* enough. I must withdraw and find out what it all *means*. How can I *understand* what I have been through? What have I actually accomplished and achieved? Can I explain it to someone else? Can others learn from my mistakes and false starts? From my successes?

But at a certain point, I do *not* want to turn in to communicator, I want to get back to some real work. Now that I know what to do, I can go happily into my field of work and continue practising there what I have learnt. Until. . . . (Rowan, 1976)

Rowan argues that there exist a wide range of styles of research, depending on the nature of the journey round the research cycle, and the relationship between the various persons involved in the research endeavour. At one extreme is pure basic research, in which the nature of the project is entirely in the hands of the researcher in the traditional sense, and in which he makes contact with the 'subjects' only briefly at the point of encounter. At the other extreme are forms of research such as Heron's experiential method, in which 'researchers' and 'subjects' jointly engage in all stages of the endeavour. Rowan is arguing for a much broader view of research than the traditional.

Rowan also argues that there is a much wider range of questions which people engaged in a research project need to consider than is traditionally accepted. Traditional research, based in positivistic thinking, tends to concentrate on what Rowan calls 'efficiency questions': is the experimenter familiar with the field and its literature; can he marshal and correlate information to bring the problem to focus; is a proper experimental design set up; and so on? But in addition to these questions (please note *in addition*, not instead of) are a whole range of other questions about authenticity (is the experimenter aware of his motives?), alienation (does the research tend to turn the subject into an object?), politics (whose interests does this research serve?), patriarchy (is the research sexist, racist, reinforcing patriarchal patterns of domination?), and dialectics (does the research honour the conflicts and contradictions of the situation?). These questions are just as important as the efficiency questions, and at times some of them may be paramount.

Holistic research

Finally, I have developed and used a holistic approach to research (Reason, 1976, 1977), the methodology of which is reflected throughout the underlying orientation of this chapter. I have argued above that the research process needs to be fundamentally rooted in action, and that the notion of praxis can be a guide for such research. My view is that many people in both private and organizational settings seem to be incapable of effective action, not because they lack boldness or have no will to act, but because they lack effective means of gathering information about their situation and understanding it so that their action may be choiceful. The holistic approach aims to facilitate the exploration of a situation by those actually involved in it. Thus, the actors become researchers, the researcher becomes a facilitator of the total research process, and they engage together in exploration based on a variety of theoretical viewpoints and experiential exercises.

In traditional research, the actors in a situation are the objects of an outsider's investigation. Holistic research rests on the view that the best researchers of a situation are those who are actually involved in it: they are the ones who have to integrate understanding and action, who use ideas and information as a basis for intelligent action; they are the ones who have the most direct access to data about themselves and their situation. The extent and manner in which actors can become their own researchers is open to empirical investigation. Conventional wisdom suggests that it is impossible to see the whole of a situation from inside: one needs to be outside and therefore more 'objective'. On the other hand, to be outside means to be separate and detached and therefore unable to see the whole situation. There must be an iteration and dialogue between the necessarily partial views of internal and external perspectives.

This dialogue can be facilitated through the development of collaborative and multiple roles: as the actor becomes actor-researcher, so the researcher, who in traditional research stands outside the situation under study, becomes researcher-actor. His role changes from becoming primarily responsible for the outcome of the research towards being a facilitator of the actors' research process and an expert in the development of inquiry systems. Thus, he might work with the actors to determine the various points of view from which the study might be made; help them design means of gathering information; help them explore ways in which they typically deal with information; and so on. This collaborative and mutually facilitative aspect of holistic research can be enhanced if it is conducted in the context of a supportive group of people involved in similar research ventures – a peer learning community – in which it is relatively safe for people to explore their situation in new ways, yet where they may be confronted by others about the shortfalls of their explorations.

Those involved in a holistic research venture will need to use a variety of theoretical orientations to guide their explorations. The traditional approach to research uses theory to generate hypotheses which can be tested through the research process with the aim of testing the theory; the theory is in the hands of the researcher and is used to control the research process. In a holistic, action-oriented research process, the role of theory is primarily as a guide to action by the actor-researchers in what Torbert (1977) calls 'experiments in action'. Thus, there is a difference between theory in positivist research, which is used in the service of unilateral control and is therefore oppressive in the sense of not enhancing – even suppressing – possibilities for aware action, and theory in an action science, which as a guide to self-directed action is liberating (Torbert, 1977).

Theory in this latter kind of research has a number of meanings. First, different theories of personal and social action can be used as a guide for participant researchers as they undertake their explorations; this is the same use of theory as in Heron's experiential method. Second, we can expect that these explorations will lead to more or less explicit theories of the particular situations in which participants are engaged and which will be guides to their action in those situations. Third, we may use theory to mean the process theories concerning the development of social praxis which guide the development of programmes.

The selection of theory as a guide for participant researchers presents some interesting issues. We need to select theory which provides a window or perspective on the situation to be explored, and one which leads to manageable techniques for exploration. Since the construction of theory involves in some way the simplification of 'reality' – it is a map rather than the territory – we need ideally to draw on theories which we may expect will illuminate different aspects of the world, draw attention to different things, and thus help develop a more complete picture. The interaction *between* theories or perspectives is likely to lead to better understandings of human situations; to put it loosely, the 'reality' of a situation may fall between the gaps left by various academic theories, and the judicious choice of contrasting perspectives may help to narrow this gap.

One approach to choosing such contrasting perspectives is to use Geertz's (1975) suggestion that there are three interdependent aspects of a completely concrete system of social action: culture, social structure, and personality. Culture is 'the fabric of meaning in terms of which human beings interpret their experience and guide their action'; social structure is 'the form that action takes, the actually existing network of social relations'; personality is 'the pattern of motivational integration within the individual'.

Each of the three must be considered to be an independent focus of the organisation of the elements of the action system in the sense that no one of them is theoretically reducible to terms of one or a combination of the other two. Each is indispensable to the other two in the sense that without personalities and culture there would be no social system and so on around the roster of logical possibilities. But this interdependence and interpenetration is a very different matter from reducibility, which would mean that the important properties and processes of one class of system could be theoretically derived from our theoretical knowledge of one or both of the other two. (Sorokin, 1937, quoted by Geertz, 1975, p. 145.)

This suggests that in selecting theories as perspectives for understanding a concrete human situation, we must attempt to select theories which provide a window from each of these three viewpoints: theories which will illuminate the person, the social structure in which he is embedded, and the wider culture.

Problems in the new methodology

The three approaches to research outlined here – Heron's experiential method, Rowan's new paradigm, and my own holistic approach – have much in common. In particular, they all lead away from traditional concepts of 'science': abstraction, objectivity, generalization are challenged, and we move towards a form of consciousness raising. A strange view of scientific research, some might say. Clearly it is important not to throw the baby of science out with the bathwater of scientism (by which I mean the over-use of classical science procedures so that behavioural science no longer describes the human condition). If these new research procedures are to be adopted, they must proceed with the traditional caution and scepticism for which science has always stood, and which has always been the foundation of the scientific method.

No research method can be perfect. In traditional research, there are always numerous threats to internal and external validity which need to be managed but which can never be totally removed; similarly, we will never be able to invent an alternative to traditional research which cannot be challenged. Doubtless as we use these new approaches we will be better able to consider the practical and theoretical issues arising from them; however, some important issues can be identified already:

(1) The quality of the data   The problem of consensus collusion has already been mentioned: participant researchers may collude to overlook certain areas of experience which do not fit their world view. This is part of a larger issue concerning the validity of data which may be qualitative, fleeting, and at times frankly impressionistic. Diesing (1972) argues that the researcher must seek 'contextual validity' for his data: 'First, the validity of a piece of evidence can be assessed by comparing it with other kinds of evidence on the same point. Each kind . . . has its own characteristic ambiguities and shortcomings and distortions, which are unlikely to agree with those of another kind. . . . The second form . . . is to evaluate a source of evidence . . . to locate the characteristic pattern of distortion' (pp. 147–148).

The question here is whether we can trust people to be honest with us and with themselves in the exploration and reporting of their situation. I would suggest that we *can* trust people much more than is assumed in traditional research processes, and that we can take data as given unless there appear to be clear reasons why we should not do so. In practical terms, it is usually possible to see when a person is engaged in a genuine exploration, and when his incongruent behaviour suggests that we should be more sceptical.

(2) Data collection   This is a major problem in the 'craft' of the new research methodologies. It would appear that the best way to obtain rich data from people involved in self-directed research is to be present with them, really listening to what they have to say in a supportive relationship. This, of course, demands enormous amounts of time and energy, not only in the gathering of data but in sorting them afterwards. There is certainly no easy way through this problem, and much work will have to be done experimenting with ways of contracting with people to use tapes, diaries, letters, interviews, etc. Our basic stance must be that those

directly involved in the project are in control of the data and of the methods of collection.

(3) Contracting   The involvement of time and energy demanded by this kind of methodology is enormous: ideally we will be working with people as they explore and take action in central aspects of their lives. This raises major questions about how we explain the process to them at the beginning so that they may freely choose to join in, and also questions about how to review and if necessary revise contracts throughout the process. At this stage we can only say that much atten- tion must be paid to the problems of contracting and recontracting, and that we will know more about the problems involved as we engage in these processes.

(4) Use of authority   The kinds of process outlined here for action and research are in a sense paradoxical: we are inviting people to join together in their own action-research process and to be self-directing, yet at the same time, we are saying that we know quite a lot about how to do this. We cannot escape this paradox: we must accept that we are setting ourselves up as authorities in the development of peer learning and self-direction, and that in the early stages a peer learning community may require considerable leadership. Again, there are no easy answers to this problem, but there are possible directions: first, we can include our authority as part of the contract by being as explicit as possible about how we see our behaviour as facilitators of the research process; second, we can expect to move from more directive styles of leadership in the early stages of the process and to more facilitative styles in the later stages (see Heron, 1977, for a discussion of dimensions of facilitator style); third, we can attempt to match our leadership style to the development of the group of people involved in the research process so that our leadership facilitates the emergence of an interdependent and self- directing group (for recent discussions of the stages of group development see Srivastva *et al.*, 1977, and Southgate and Randall, 1977).

(5) Generalization   This discussion leads to another problem for alternative methodologies, that of generalization. Traditional approaches suggest that the ideal goal for research in the social sciences is to be 'able to construct universally true statements about relationships between variables' (Festinger and Katz, 1953). Maslow (1966) points out that while this may be the main business of classical science, 'if I want to know a person in those aspects of his personhood most important to me, I must approach [him] as an individual unique and particular, the sole member of his class'. Slater (1974) points out that the conceptualization of systems, and a concern for the general rather than the unique, cuts us off from a more direct understanding of phenomena so that we follow our maps rather than reality. Vickers (personal communication, 1978) argues that social scientists need to face the 'intense particularity of situations in the social world'. Torbert

(1977) suggests that the only valid form of generalization is generalization to other aspects of the researcher's life.

Thus, there are many doubts about the issue of generalization in scientific inquiry which demand a much fuller exploration than is possible here. For the present, I simply wish to assert that the primary aim of the research processes described here is to describe and understand unique situations, so that participant researchers may act with awareness in them. If in addition we can richly describe these situations, providing what Geertz calls a 'thick' description, this may have the effect of holding up a 'mirror' in which other people may find illuminated their own reality. Finally, I take the view that tentative generalizations may be possible about process issues concerning the nature of the research process itself.

(6) Reporting and communication   The last issue for the new methodology which we will consider here is that of communication to a wider audience than those directly involved. It is important to recognize that at the stage of communication in the research cycle the purposes of the actor-researchers and the more academic researcher must inevitably begin to separate: while the actors may be interested in communication in order to influence others within their world of action, the academic is interested in informing his professional colleagues about his work. There are at this stage likely to be considerable problems arising from this separation of interests. First, who owns information that is likely to be personally and politically sensitive? Who has the right to tell what to whom? What are the consequences of revelation? Second, how do you report the idiosyncratic and capture the flavour of unique events? How do you stop a living process of exploration without taking all meaning from it? Management of the first problem will involve the most careful negotiation and contracting. The second can be partially resolved if we portray our research almost in the form of novels, plays, and other sensitive means of expression.

Role review: a research–learning–action programme

How then can these ideas for a research methodology be used in the context of an organization development intervention? One approach is through a role-review and development programme, consisting of a series of workshop events in which participants are invited to research their own situation and in which the staff act as facilitators of the research process. Such workshops would provide a peer learning community in which people might step back from everyday reality, learn theories and methods that will help them illuminate their life situation, and plan how to use these when away from the workshop. These workshops would be interspersed with periods when the participants would return to their everyday life and work to test the ideas and methods and put into practice plans they had developed at the workshops. Such a programme would have to be designed, of course, to suit particular groups of participants in particular situations, and also designed in collaboration with the participants. However, some of the issues of designing such a programme are explored here, and a broad outline suggested.

The *role* of an individual organization member is typically taken to refer to the responsibilities which attach to his *position*: that is to say, the body of expectations which other organization members, and the role holder himself, entertain of someone because he occupies a particular position in the organization. In classical organization theory, the roles of a well-designed organization were expected to be clear and consistent, since role ambiguity and role conflict were seen as sources of stress and inefficiency.

Modern organization theory, in particular the contingency theories of writers such as Galbraith (1973) and Lawrence and Lorsch (1967), have challenged this notion of clear and consistent roles: they have pointed to the increasing complexity of organization life, and to the turbulence of organizational environments, and argued that *complex* and *ambiguous* roles may be required if an organization is to manage this complexity and turbulence in the most adaptive manner. Everyday experience as a member of a large modern organization, and as a consultant, will confirm this suggestion: there are now many organization positions in which the occupant is subjected to conflicting expectations from different members of his role set; to the need to manage a complex political situation; to the requirement to work without clear rules and guidelines; and to make decisions in the face of great uncertainty.

The role-review programme is addressed to the problems of managing such complex roles. It is useful to managers who are faced with complex boundary management problems; to those in 'integrating' roles who are expected to help reconcile the differences between widely differentiated groups; to those on special assignments who have to work outside the formal organization structure; to those who are in the process of moving into a new role; in short, to managers whose task and position require high social and political skills as well as technical competence.

Since this programme is designed so that it may be tailored to the individual needs of different participants, it is not possible to describe in detail the outcomes which may be expected; these will vary from participant to participant. However, each participant should leave the programme with a much clearer idea of the nature of his role, its problems and opportunities; with a clear plan for the development of the role which he has tested and begun to put into action, and with skills to implement it; and with a set of supportive relationships with other participants such that he will be able to call on them for support and advice on a continuing basis.

Elements of programme design

In designing a role-review programme for such complex roles, we are faced with two major problems: first, how to make the programme fully relevant to those joining it; and second, how to ensure that there is a transfer of whatever learning takes place on the programme to the work situation. These are ever-present problems for those who use training programmes as an organization intervention; they are of particular importance for this role-review programme.

These problems of programme design can be met by using the ideas for a research methodology as the basis for the programme. This means that the programme is not regarded as a training situation, in which a course is designed by 'experts' and managers attend as students, but rather as a learning community in which each participant is helped by staff and other participants to develop his own personal research, learning, and action project. The programme is guided by the notion of praxis, so that action plans are developed which are informed by and based in a prior systematic exploration of and reflection on the concrete situation in which it is to take place. Time is initially devoted to a systematic exploration of the work situation in which each participant is working, an exploration which is guided by the use of theoretical orientations, experiential learning exercises, and the development of a personal research project. This period of exploration and reflection leads to a phase of action which is guided and assisted by the development and testing of a concrete action plan, and by building and using support systems and relationships. These elements of the programme are discussed in more detail in the next few paragraphs.

Theory Participants in the programme need to gain familiarity with a framework which will guide their personal research and action plans; such a framework will enable them to look at and gain an understanding of their situation from a number of different perspectives. As has been suggested above, three such perspectives are appropriate: (a) the individual and his styles of behaviour; (b) his role in the organization and the other social structures of which he is a part; and (c) the overall organization culture (norms, values, meaning, and belief systems). These three perspectives are closely interrelated, and together should provide a fairly complete view of the total situation; they are portrayed in Figure 4. There

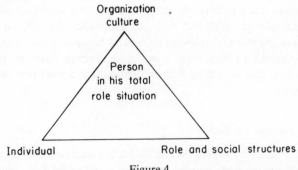

Figure 4

are many ways in which these three perspectives might be used, the choice of which are detailed design decisions which do not need consideration here.

These theoretical approaches enable each participant to gain a fuller appreciation of his total situation, to understand some of its dilemmas and contradictions, and to see some of the opportunities for change and development. They should provide a cognitive basis for making sense of the experiential exercises and provide assistance for the development of plans to review a participant's role situation in a personal research project as described below.

Experiential learning   Theory alone is arid, and does not inform action; it is not possible to apply theory to practice without developing the capacity to be aware of one's own experience, the behaviour of self and others, to be able to reflect on these as participant-observer, and to act appropriately on the basis of these observations and reflections. Thus this programme is heavily experiential, drawing particularly on psycho- and socio-dramatic approaches to experiential learning, as these seem most suitable to a programme which emphasizes linking learning with action.

Personal research project   This is a core feature of the role-review programme. It is essential for participants to review and research their role situation systematically before making any attempt to make changes to it; this belief is based in part on the old adage, 'No diagnosis without action, no action without diagnosis', and partly on the view held by gestalt therapists that change is made by becoming what one fully is, working with rather than against reality. The theoretical perspectives and the experiential exercises should provide each participant with an opportunity to return to his workplace and take a fresh look at his role and at the pattern of interaction in which he typically engages; it is on the basis of this careful personal research that later development plans can be firmly rooted. Participants will be able to make some initial reviews of their role while in the workshops, and this will provide the basis for developing a plan for further research in the work situation. This research will almost certainly involve interviewing critical members of their role set, keeping a diary of significant interactions, and generally using the theoretical perspectives as a guide for decision making. The details of each project would depend on the problems and opportunities of each role situation.

Support systems   As has been pointed out above, the transfer of learning from training situations to real life is often problematic, since social pressures and personal habits tend to force people to revert to old patterns of behaviour. The importance of developing and actively using relationships of support, advice, and encouragement is clear; it is otherwise a lonely task to take new ideas and behaviours and apply them for the first time. Thus we emphasize the development of relations of support within the participant group, and also the importance of helping each participant develop and actively use relations of support with boss, colleague, spouse, friends, etc., in the 'real life' situation. The explicit negotiation of support is likely to be difficult, and may in fact be the first event in the transfer process. Since these relationships of support will be of critical importance for the implementation of plans for the change and development of roles, it is important that these support relations are not simply planned for but actively used during the early phases of the programme, so that they are readily available at critical times later on.

Action plans   In addition to the development of support systems, the transfer of learning from workshop situations is facilitated by the choice of challenging but manageable problems to solve, and the development of concrete action plans. The early elements of the programme – theory, experiential learning, and research project – will all contribute to the development of a specific action plan for each participant, in which he will indicate the ways he wishes to change and develop his management of his role situation, and how he proposes to go about it. Staff and other participants will provide help in the development of the plan, in testing its feasibility, and practising parts of it through, for example, psychodrama.

The role-review programme

The elements of the programme outlined above are arranged in six phases of workshop and application activity which follow in general terms the stages of Rowan's research cycle; each phase builds on earlier phases and leads into later phases. They lead the participant from reflection on the present situation, through learning from theory and experience, and active personal research, to the construction of a plan for the development of his role situation; this is followed by the opportunity to carry out the project, and finally to a review and consolidation.

Phase 1: Introduction and contract setting   It is likely that we will engage with people as they begin to be dissatisfied with the present state of affairs, and to look for a means of change. It is at this stage that the contract between the prospective participant, the facilitator, and the group as a whole must be set, so that as far as possible relationships, scope, theories and methods can be agreed. It is, of course naïve to think that a totally firm contract for this kind of exploration can be set at this stage; it *is*, however, possible to devise an outline, and to work out the patterns of future negotiation (Heron, 1977).

Phase 2: Three-day residential workshop
    To build a supportive learning community.
    To gain familiarity with theoretical frameworks.
    To start the personal research project and build a research plan.

This phase is an intensive residential session, building the group, putting energy into launching the project, learning and beginning to use some theoretical frameworks, and ending up with a design of a personal research project which will enable each participant to conduct a systematic review of his work situation.

Phase 3: Several weeks of on-the-job activity
  To gather information directly from the role situation.
  To test ideas and the potential of the situation.
  To build back-home support systems.

The work in Phase 1 will provide each participant with an agenda of activities. Each participant will have done as much as he can to review his situation away from his workplace; he should be clear about the issues he wishes to address, the information he needs to gather, the people whose support he needs to engage and maybe confront. He will have made some fairly detailed plans about this activity; Phase 3 will be his opportunity to carry them out.

Phase 4: Three-day residential workshop
  To review the information gathered about the present state of each role situation.
  To identify a direction for development.
  To draw up a detailed plan for the development of each role.

By this stage, each participant will have accumulated a large amount of information about his role situation; he should know how he is seen by other members of his role set, their expectations, hopes, fears, irritations, etc. He should have a good idea of the major tensions that exist at present, of the possible avenues for development, and the kind of choices with which he is confronted. Phase 4 is an opportunity for each participant, in the light of all this information, to review where he is and make explicit plans for the development of his position. In addition, much of the groundwork, in the form of support systems and entry points, will have been developed. Thus Phase 4 will involve *choice* of direction, the generation of plans for the development of each role, and the testing and practising of each plan.

Phase 5: Several months of on-the-job activity
  To implement plans made in Phase 4.

This phase is in many ways similar to Phase 3, in that the same considerations apply: specific plans that are challenging but achievable have to be implemented, with a support system available. On the other hand, one must assume that the implementation of plans to change a role is more hazardous than simply gathering information about that role, and by this stage the range of issues in the group of participants will be broad. Thus, it is critical at this stage that the support available to participants is flexible, and that it is experienced as fully available.

Phase 6: Two-day residential workshop
   To continue as appropriate.
   To review successes and failures.

This final stage is an opportunity, once again, to stand back from action and, as Rowan puts it, 'withdraw and find out what it all *means*'. The role-review process will have set in motion a large number of activities. Hopefully, the participants will have been able to change and develop at least a portion of their roles; hopefully, they will experience themselves as more in charge of their situation and personally stronger than before, and will have established the means and support to continue their work of developing their roles. This final session will serve, on the one hand, to continue the processes set up in the earlier phases, and, on the other, to review the whole process of role review through its six phases and to bring the whole project to a sensible conclusion: an activity which is finished yet integrated into everyday life.

New research methods and the practice of organization development

I began this chapter with the assertion that systems theory and the holist stance require a new approach to research. I have argued that such an approach would be concerned with the development of knowledge specific to particular situations, and that it would be firmly rooted in the actions of participants of those situations. This can be done through inviting the actors in a situation to become their own researchers and agents of change, and seeing the consultant as a facilitator of these personal research and action projects within the context of a peer learning group. I have also described a role-review programme as one specific way in which these ideas can be used in practice.

   I hope that in doing this I am not understood as simply putting forward another piece of technology for organization development, since this field has an abundance of techniques and a lack of integrated theory and practice. My view is that the effective practice of OD does not simply consist of the use of particular theories or practices or techniques, but must be primarily concerned with the development of systems of inquiry and exploration so that self-directed action by organization members can be enhanced. More colloquially, I am arguing for research as a life-style – and thus a style of management and of consultancy.

   There are several important problems in the design and management of modern organizations to which this research approach could be fruitfully applied; these are problems that require much more fundamental knowledge before we can pretend to know how to deal with them effectively. The first of these, which I have already mentioned, lies in the management of complex cross-functional and 'integrator' roles: it is apparent that this kind of role is becoming more common with the increasing complexity of business and the turbulence of organizational environments, yet very little solid information is available about the problems of these roles and how they might be effectively managed. A second problem is that of the role of supervisors: for years it has been recognized that they are in an invidious position as the 'men in the middle' between top management and the employees, and a lot of concern has been expressed about their situation, yet their problems remain with us. Here again, a research process along the lines I have suggested would be invaluable in exploring the problems and opportunities of the supervisors' position and learning how to manage and develop these roles. A third and larger problem is the management of joint decision making between management and trades union representatives, which is likely to become increasingly important, certainly in the UK, as the pressure for industrial democracy increases. There is a fundamental danger that political pressures will lead to the adoption of formal systems of industrial democracy without consideration of how these systems can be implemented by those actually involved in them. My own initial research in this area indicates that there are major problems of role conflict, skill development, communication, and the management of boundaries between the formal and informal systems which require very careful exploration before they can be effectively managed. Again, these problems could be best investigated through the new research processes.

These are some of the directions in which my own research is proceeding. I would like to leave the reader with one question: how can your own practice of OD be developed so that it is truly a research process, so that interventions are in the control of the actors and firmly rooted in knowledge about the particular organization situation? Only if OD is seen in terms of the development of effective systems of inquiry can our practice be developed.

References

Benne, K. D., Bradford, L. P., Gibb, J. R., and Lippitt, R. O. (eds) (1975) *The Laboratory Method of Changing and Learning: Theory and Application*. Palo Alto, Calif.: Science and Behavior Books.

Bernstein, R. J. (1976) *The Restructuring of Social and Political Thought*. Oxford: Blackwell.

Boadella, D. (1974) *Willhelm Reich: The Evolution of His Work*. New York: Vision Press.

Cooper, D. (1967). *Psychiatry and Anti-psychiatry*. London: Tavistock.

Diesing, P. (1972) *Patterns of Discovery in the Social Sciences*. London: Routledge & Kegan Paul.

Festinger, L., and Katz, D. (1953) *Research Methods in the Behavioral Sciences*. New York: Holt, Rinehart & Winston.

Freire, P. (1971) *Pedagogy of the Oppressed*. New York: Seabury Press.

Friedlander, F. (1969) Behavioral research as a transactional process. *Human Organization*, **27** (4), Winter.

Friedlander, F. (1977) Alternative modes of inquiry. Paper presented at American Psychological Association Symposium 'Toward a Reconceptualization of Research', August.

Galbraith, J. (1973) *Designing Complex Organizations*. Reading, Mass.: Addison-Wesley.

Geertz, C. (1975) *Interpretation of Cultures*. London: Hutchinson.

Harre, R., and Secord, P. F. (1972) *The Explanation of Social Behaviour*. Oxford: Blackwell.

Heather, N. (1976) *Radical Perspectives in Psychology*. London: Methuen.

Heron, J. (1971) *Experience and Method*. Human Potential Research Project, University of Surrey.

Heron, J. (1977) *Dimensions of Facilitator Style*. London: British Postgraduate Medical Federation.

Heron, J. (in preparation) Experiential research methodology, in P. W. Reason and J. Rowan (eds), *Human Inquiry: A Sourcebook of New Paradigm Research*. London: John Wiley (in preparation).

Huckaby, M. A. (1975) Toward a theory of selfhood for women. Unpublished qualifying paper, Department of Organizational Behavior, Case Western Reserve University, Cleveland, Ohio.

Jourard, S. (1971) *The Transparent Self*. Princeton, N.J.: Van Nostrand.

Koestler, A., and Smythies J. (eds) (1969) *Beyond Reductionism: New Perspectives in the Life Sciences*. London: Macmillan.

Laing, R. D. (1975) *The Divided Self*. Hamondsworth, Middx.: Penguin Books.

Lawrence, P. R., and Lorsch, J. W. (1967) *Organization and Environment*. Cambridge, Mass.: Harvard University Press.

Macmurray, J. (1957) *The Self as Agent*. London: Faber.

Mangham, I. L. (1975) Negotiating reality: Notes towards a model of order and change within organisations. Working Paper, Centre for the Study of Organizational Change and Development, University of Bath.

Mangham, I. L. (1978) *Interactions and Interventions in Organizations*. London: Wiley.

Maslow, A. (1966) *The Psychology of Science*. New York: Harper & Row.

Reason, P. W. (1976) Explorations in the dialectics of interpersonal relationship. Doctoral dissertation, Case Western Reserve University, Cleveland, Ohio.

Reason, P. W. (1977) Holistic research and social system change. Working paper, Centre for the Study of Organizational Change and Development, University of Bath.

Rowan, J. (1976) The new paradigm in research, in P. W. Reason and J. Rowan (eds), *Human Inquiry: A Sourcebook of New Paradigm Research*. London: John Wiley (in preparation). See also: A dialectical paradigm for research (abstract), *Bulletin of the British Psychological Society* **31**, (1978) 28.

Schutz, A. (1967) *The Phenomenology of the Social World*. Evanston, Ill.: Northwestern University Press.

Slater, P. (1974) *Earthwalk*. New York: Anchor Press/Doubleday.

Southgate, J., and Randall, R. (1977). Creative and pathological processes in the self managing work group. Loughborough University of Technology, Department of Management Studies.

Srivastva, S., Obert, S. L., and Neilsen, E. E. (1977) Organisational analysis through group processes: A theoretical perspective on Organization Development. In C. Cooper, (ed.) *Organization Development in the UK and USA: A Joint Evaluation*. London: Macmillan.

Torbert, W. R. (1976) *Creating a Community of Inquiry: Conflict, Collaboration, Transformation*. London: Wiley.

Torbert, W. R. (1977) Why educational research has been so uneducational: the case for a new model of social science based on collaborative enquiry. Paper presented at the American Psychological Association Symposium 'Toward a Reconceptualization of Research, August.

Systems Theory for Organization Development
Edited by T. G. Cummings
© 1980 John Wiley & Sons Ltd.

Chapter 4

'Mental Systems': Towards a Practical Agenda for a Phenomenology of Systems[1]

Fred Massarik

The scholarly literature on systems persistently provides models and constructs that might be characterized as essentially 'mechanistic and concatenated'. Within a range of schemata from simple 'input/output' frameworks to complex cybernetic formulations, systems normally are regarded as 'hard', rigorously and, if possible, quantitatively expressing dynamic interrelations among cogent variables. On the other hand, the term 'phenomenology' (to the extent that it is at all understood) calls forth in the minds of some an image of the fuzzy anti-scientific and surely 'soft'. There is little evidence that, at this stage, systems thinking and phenomenological conceptualization have found much common meeting ground. Beyond C. P. Snow's view of Two Cultures, denoting the schism between science and the humanities, an increasing convergence between apparent opposites may be in order, and indeed may prove mutually enriching. In this vein, it is proposed that the time is right for the development of a practical agenda for a 'phenomenology of systems'.

Some starting-points for a phenomenology of systems

At the outset, we need to consider some epistemological assumptions variously relating to systems theorizing and phenomenology. In its classic sense, the term 'systems' – as, for example, in the sense of Galilean or Newtonian 'world systems' or cosmologies – is, of course, concerned with regularities and discernible *systematic* interrelations among the earth, other heavenly bodies, and associated astronomic considerations. In a more recent but still remote sense, with special relevance to the field of managerial thought, the term 'system' denotes practical approaches to the management of (primarily industrial) enterprise. For instance, it is instructive to scan the journal *System*, published in the early years of this century, subtitled 'A Monthly Magazine for the Man of Affairs'. For instance, some issues published in 1906 consider, among other things, topics such as 'Accounting Systems for Waterworks', 'Systems for the Professional Man', 'Storage and Warehouse Systems', and the like. Throughout, the approach is pragmatic, shirt-sleeves, on occasion military ('The Conquerors of Business', 'Ammunition for the Salesman', etc.). In the present context, it is not necessary to recite the plethora of references characteristic of the contemporary fundamental and applied systems literature. One may note, however, that in its evolution, 'system' owes something both to grand cosmology and to 'hands-on' administration. The common link, perhaps, might be epitomized by focus on *regular (or regularized) interrelationships among salient variables.*

In the cosmological sense, unless one wishes to adduce the presence of a regularizing deity (possibly an anthropomorphic, rewarding and punishing God), the interrelationships among the variables may be viewed as constituting *natural* regularities which, at least at the stage of discovery, proceed without specific human intervention. The human observer, of course, necessarily enters the picture and in this sense becomes an *active* participant in the drama. Yet, this is a quite different role from that encountered in the search for *purposeful* regularities. It is the latter – carrying the concept of regularity to associated goals such as 'efficiency' – that identifies the philosophy of journals such as the post-industrial revolution *System*, with its thrust of purposefulness – 'of making it happen' to bring about desired objectives.

It is the emergence of *intentionality* that provides an appropriate linking point between the classic systems view and the precepts of phenomenology. If one wishes directly to affect the results (outputs?) of a system, it becomes necessary to develop, by aprioristic assumption and by *a posteriori* knowledge, *images of alternative interrelationships* that, given specified sets and characteristics of salient variables, may be so designed and operated that the desired results will come about. It is this process, specifically in *purposive systems*, that necessarily requires a construction of *mental systems* to define it all, and eventually to guide and operate the functioning system itself.

In turn, the creation of mental systems (and it is indeed a *creative* act) inevitably calls for *salient perceptual patterns*, exploring hypothetically or *in situ* the system's components and consequences. In this sense, the system is necessarily a 'gestalt'. This attribute of (if one may indulge in an awkward neologism) 'gestalting' functions at two interrelated levels: (1) from the standpoint of the creator or observer of the system and (2), in a formal analytic sense, conceptualizing the system as though it functioned entirely in terms of its mechanical and mathematical properties.

In both contexts (1) and (2), the notion of gestalt is instructive. For the creator or observer of the system, meaning is derived by a process of perceptual highlighting and subordination of variables and interaction patterns. Were it not for this approach, involving purposeful differentiation, 'all would be alike', and it would be impossible to provide significant statements as to the system's actual or hypothetical operation. The requirement of selectivity, and for differentiated allocation of emphasis, focusing on, not all, but specifically *strategic* variables and their interrelations is fundamental. To provide the necessary contrasts, translated into purposeful meaning attributions, *figure* and *ground* are distinguished, and relative *salience* is noted. Sudden organizing insights by the system's creator or observer are not uncommon and the 'aha' phenomenon is not unheard of. Perceptual shifts, specifying what is and what is not important (in relative if not necessarily in absolute terms), characterize from time to time the process of systems design and analysis, as delineated by the human agent who makes it all happen.

In conceptualizing the system in formal/mathematical terms the problem is not as different as one might suspect. Let us postulate a purely mathematical description of a system, consisting of a set of equations and related formal propositions bearing on the system's properties. These statements, of course, derive as well from the operations of a conceptualizer whose ultimate source is necessarily human. This holds even if any number of rigorous models and computational algorithms have intervened. All these evidently emerge from human process, however disciplined and formally circumscribed.

In the light of this framework, we shall note two procedures for the delineation of 'mental systems' in organizational contexts that may be helpful in systematically explicating the phenomenal structures of organizations. Here, much as in various projective techniques (and, indeed, empirical phenomenology necessarily shares some of the latter's risk), the emphasis is placed on the individual's self-structuring encounter with an 'external reality' which, however, itself is constituted in its *meanings* by people's definitions and valuations. This is not to deny, of course, (as a hypothetical solipsist purportedly might) that a solid economic and technological world manifestly exists; nevertheless a world of this kind is, *ipso facto*, devoid of meaning, unless *human beings* provide such meaning.

The phenomenology of organization charts

It is evident that *any* organization chart represents a phenomenal construction, based on certain meaning attributions, presumably related to the dynamics of this organization. On this basis, as many a practical consultant is well aware, organization charts as published and 'officially' specified provide – within the bounds of the observer's conceptual frame – significant insights into that organization's processes, going beyond a simple structural analysis.

Perhaps of still greater interest are *phenomenological projections of organization charts*. Variously used by OD specialists, small-group trainers, and others concerned with the elucidation of meaning in formal systems, this procedure partakes of the following general characteristics:

(1) The observer is asked to reflect on the nature of a specified organization of

which he is a member. (The OD specialist, trainer, etc., serves as the phenomenologist, in the context of a mutual exploration of the organization's significance.) The observer is asked to consider a subjective *organization chart*.

(2) The phenomenologist may, on the assumption that some conceptual meanings are shared, further ask the observer to focus on (a) the form, shape, or structure of the organization; or (b) simply on the organization as a whole, with no parameters specified.

(3) The observer then proceeds, in accordance with the phenomenologist's inquiry, *to draw a picture* of the organization chart as it is conceived by the observer. The basic phenomenological projection of the organization, as reflected in the drawing, provides an opportunity for the observer to add such detail as he/she chooses. Below, we shall consider major rubrics of such detail.

(4) The phenomenologist, by individual interaction with the observer or by group process including two or more observers, elicits from the observer(s) an exploration of the various meanings attributed to the organization, as a unit and in its internal differentiations. At this stage, the relationship–trust dimension linking phenomenologist and observer is crucial. In an extension of the conventional 'rapport' notion, deeper and committed trust is of heightened importance if the examination of the chart(s) provided is to extend beyond the typical rhetoric concerning organization structure.

The resulting *cogito* representing the mutually examined meaning patterns, as based on the phenomenological projections of organization charts and interaction with the phenomenologist, serves to provide a graphic and substantive 'mental system' permitting, if all has gone well, an enhanced view of salient and significant aspects of the organization under consideration. This synergic joint product, resulting variously from independent projections of a number of observers and ultimately from a shared examination of similar and different meanings, may well provide understandings beyond those often obtained by disparate survey questionnaires or conventional open-ended interviews.

While certain fairly obvious elements contained in phenomenological projections of organization charts are easily discerned (e.g. number of positions shown, number levels indicated, relative size of various 'boxes', etc.), repeated exploratory use of the method suggests that meanings are elicited typically within a set of interrelated and not always exclusive categories, as follows:

(1) The observer's self-referent position, indicating his/her 'location' within the phenomenal organization, focusing particularly on issues of perceived power and/or powerlessness *vis-à-vis* other focal points in the organization as perceived.

(2) Macro-power/influence centres, indicating those 'locations' in the perceived organization from which major career impacts on the observer may be generated. In some instances this simply may refer to the immediate 'boss',

while in others reference may be made to personnel departments, to particular individuals in top management, or to external economic forces.

(3) Micro-power/influence centres, referring to those 'locations' in the organization from which daily, relatively on-going task impacts emanate. These may include one or more of the 'locations' noted in item (2) above, as well as colleagues at peer and horizontally associated levels, people at levels above or below, etc. It should be clear that in this kind of analysis, it is not the *nominal status* that has much relevance, while the often less obvious perceptual linkages tell the tale.

(4) Analogous to (2), that concept's converse: macro-impact 'locations', identifying those persons and/or units which the observer significantly impacts in major respects, actually or potentially.

(5) Analogous to (3), that concept's converse: micro-impact 'locations', denoting those persons and/or units on which the observer has impact in relatively on-going day-by-day functions, actually or potentially.

(6) Support 'locations' in the organization, indicating the observer's affective and/or task aides and allies, however defined.

(7) Disturbance 'locations', denoting 'trouble spots' in the organization, for the observer or with more widely diffused consequences.

(8) Activity 'locations', indicating those focal points in the organization at which major current important 'things' are happening. (These, of course, may be overlapping or interrelated with support and disturbance 'locations', as above, but also may be constituted primarily by significant task-oriented functions, representing heavy personal and technological energy commitments.)

(9) Nominal presences identify those 'locations' which 'exist', representing the observer's descriptive posture with regard to other persons and units in the organization. For these 'nominal presences', affect appears generally subsidiary to the very *fact* of their existence. One surmises that these 'locations' provide little aware 'emotional charge' for the observer though, of course, still more deeply probing analysis might reveal their further, substantially more significant, connotations. (In initial analysis, a fair amount of the revealed material falls in this category, but inquiry may lead to major redefinition and shift to emphasis associated with other categories, as above.)

Considering the category set as heuristically derived from exploratory phenomenological inquiry, this set is conceptualized principally in terms of *power/influence flows*, *support/disturbance flows*, *activity/energy flows*, and *direct description* of relationships. As is conventionally known, these include upward-vertical, downward-vertical, horizontal and diagonal linkages.

The analytic neatness implied by these several categorizations is, of course, itself 'constructed' from a welter of interlocking and sometimes fuzzy data. At the manifest level, the forms of expression are familiar; they include among others (1) the familiar (and perhaps too ubiquitous) 'boxes', conventionally drawn in formal organizational charts, and their various solid and dotted connecting lines; (2) stick figures, indicating various individuals and, in combination, groups of individuals; (3) 'happy faces' and 'sad faces', indicating once again individuals and attributed affect; (4) various irregular shapes (circles, surfaces with erratic boundaries, etc.) indicating specific organization units or other entities; (5) visual representations of structures (such as buildings associated with the organization, and representations of other technological elements, e.g. pipelines, computer installations, headquarters offices, etc.); and (6) symbols representing aspects of the organization's environment, e.g. customers, suppliers, governmental agencies, and the like.

A description of these symbolic entities, while superficially interesting in terms of a rather mechanistic review of the phenomenological projections, necessarily skirts the issue of *Eidos*, the pure apprehension seeking underlying essential truths that may be elicited on the basis of the empirically projected version of the organization. Whether one wishes to adduce the concept of *Noesis*, with its implication of harbouring meaning, or whether one wishes to consider directly the term 'meaning' in its more popular sense, it is the concern with the interrelated totality, focusing on the organization as fundamentally perceived by the observer, that constitutes the primary and appropriate focus of the phenomenal analysis. It is in this quest that the phenomenologist, hand in hand (but more properly eye in eye) with the observer, utilizes the projective drawing as starting-point for deeply probing review.

We now turn to a somewhat different 'mental system'.

A Lewinian revisitation

It is useful to recall the common intellectual heritage reaching to Brentano that in direct lineage led to the work of Husserl and, by way of Stumpf, to the efforts of Kurt Lewin. However one wishes to trace the appropriate history of ideas, it is clear that Lewin's accomplishments, particularly those relating to 'practical theory' in psychology and thence to organization study, draw strength from a core of concern with *immediate* experience.

Especially germane to the understanding of mental systems in organizational contexts (as indeed in many other situations concerned with charting the person's present and future-oriented conception of self) is the notion of *life space*. Foreshadowed in Lewin's earliest work (a paper concerned with 'the landscape of war', *Kriegslandschaft*), the 'life space' idea finds ready analogous reflection in Husserl's *Lebenswelt*. Lewin, going beyond philosophic abstraction, provides operational frameworks for the concept's explication. It is with regard to this potential for visualization of complex psychodynamics in social environments that the 'life space' idea proves promising once again in present consideration.

In various writings in which the life space concept is treated, Lewin's usage is not totally consistent. To simplify discourse, and to maintain focus on central positions, this paper will proceed with some simplification of these several slightly varied frameworks.

The well-known, even tautological starting-point, 'the person in the situation', establishes a two-fold initial schema:

(1) 'The present region': focus on the self, as *now* positioned and as experiencing 'the world as it is'. In other terms, the present region may be likened to 'the existential moment'.

(2) 'The boundary': focus on the present *range* of awareness or conscious concern. The boundary establishes a perimeter within which further definitions of the person's reality may proceed.

Sequentially, this concurrent duality of 'here I am' plus 'there is something out there that matters' necessarily precedes a purposive (or inadvertent) process of *structuring* the life space. In fact, a given life space construction, in the sense that it can be viewed as a meaningful system, cannot be fully simultaneous; a number of 'mental operations' need to be performed, beginning with the bracketed self boundary to provide essential starting positions for a time-extensive process in which various behaviour possibilities are identified and differentially valued. In these terms, the life space, though sometimes regarded as a single immediately current construct, necessarily partakes of a set of mental *moves*, vicariously testing, examining, rejecting, projecting, and the like. The raw material of these processes is composed of *various behaviour possibilities*, or in Lewin's terms, of *regions*.

The specific pattern in which regions are arrayed with respect to one another constitutes the structure of life space 'at a given time', or more properly 'within a given time sequence'. The relevant psychological problem now is defined in terms such as these: 'Being myself in this situation, what do I want to do/what can I do to reach some goal(s)?' The concept of *valence* is now necessary, denoting the various attraction/repulsion powers of various regions and positive/negative goal states. In turn, *barriers to locomotion* are evidently manifest, restraining the person from going in some directions rather than others. With these variables at hand, we can trace vicarious and, eventually, actual paths describing purposeful human behaviour.

Viewed from the standpoint of phenomenology, various aspects of the process of life space structuring may be regarded as the *cogitatio*, focusing on aspects of conscious experience, while others resemble the *cogito*, emphasizing directed perception, and an immanent 'glancing towards' events concerning the observer. One may argue that Lewin's approach to life space analysis stops too soon, if one wishes to pursue the goals of an empirical phenomenology. While it considers the experience of 'physical things' and of ourselves (variously *Erfahrung* (retrospective experience) and *Tatsächligkeit* (factuality)), it does not move towards an 'inseeing of essences' or an 'apodeictic' next step. The events of the self defining his/her experience and projected world may be handled lucidly by life space analysis. As such, the stage is set for the examination of the more deeply recessed meanings which the events described hold for the person.

Various strategies may be opened in this connection. Evidently, the person himself/herself, in assessing the differential feasibility of various paths, involving locomotion through a specified set of regions, may profit by the institution of 'phenomenological abstention', the *epokhe* as variously considered by Husserl and others. Here the person, as by the process of *bracketing*, recognizes his/her own reality, while instituting a condition of disconnection and constructive doubt by means of which he/she may assess the substantive meaning and alternative consequences of his/her present and projected actions. Further, the life space diagram, created by the observer, establishes a suitable basis for a mutual examination of meanings by observer and phenomenologist. This process may be analogous to that considered above relating to the joint examination of the phenomenal projection of the organization chart.

In the context of study of organizational systems, the life space approach may be productively rediscovered and applied. As combined with supplemental phenomenological approaches, it can provide insight into the perception by the person of the direct working environment, of the specific job and its consequences, including such issues as job simplification/job enlargement, participation, etc., and career planning, to mention but a sampling.

Towards the rediscovery of mental systems

Not too farfetched is the parable that 'people *invent* their organizations'. While surely any existing organization reflects complexly its human, technological, and economic heritage, and the history of its interaction with its environments, so does the maintenance and development of organizations proceed by an iterative process of invention and reinvention. This process is based significantly on the creation of new, and the examination of existing mental systems, in the sense of the organization charts and the life spaces considered in this chapter. By way of empirical approach, relevant realities are initially sketched or otherwise expressed in visual fashion. These expressions, eliciting salient aspects of the person's experienced world, or of worlds anticipated, then provide further opportunity for observer and phenomenologist to consider in requisite depth (as, for instance, by means of the 'phenomenal interview') the central meanings of events and their significance for the people who move in frequently fragile balance between their unique psychological worlds and relevant organization systems and their pervasive requirements.

Note

1. Information on organization chart/organization projective drawings, antecedents to empirical phenomenology, and phenomenologic reanalysis of Lewin's concepts may be obtained from the author, c/o GSM, UCLA, Los Angeles, CA, 90024.

PART II

System-theoretic Frameworks for Organization Development

Introduction

There are innumerable ways to conceive of organizations as systems. Among the system-theoretic models currently in vogue are organizations as: political systems, information-processing systems, role systems, socio-technical systems, and economic systems. Part II of this book comprises four distinct yet complementary approaches to conceptualizing and developing organizations as systems. Each chapter presents a comprehensive framework for understanding the systemic properties of organizations and for managing planned change. The different perspectives underscore the complexity of organizational phenomena and suggest that no single theory is appropriate for all situations or purposes. The contributions challenge the reader to assess where and when the different approaches are most appropriate, a necessary step towards developing a contingency theory of OD.

Beer introduces Part II with a social systems model of organizations. He synthesizes a diverse body of theory, research, and OD practice in terms of major organizational components and their interrelationships. Beer's framework begins with the important interaction between people and organizational structures which results in specific organizational behaviours and processes; these in turn affect human and organizational outcomes in the context of the organization's culture, external environment, and dominant coalition. Beer identifies the significant variables in these components and explores relationships among the variables and between the different components. He offers strategies for organizational diagnosis and change consistent with the social systems framework.

Tichy undertakes the ambitious task of integrating the three dominant traditions for understanding and changing organizations into a meta-theory of OD – rational-economic, political, and normative prespectives. He uses social network theory to describe organizations in respect of the three traditions and suggests that organizational effectiveness rests on how well the parts of the organization fit each other rationally, politically, and normatively. Tichy develops separate submodels for explaining rational, political, and normative processes in organizations and uses the models to describe OD change processes from a social network perspective. He ties the theoretical discussion to relevant case studies which highlight the meta-model and show its application to organizational diagnosis and intervention.

Huff views organizations as political systems where power-based conflicts underlie important decisions. She reviews five major political theories and shows

71

how each raises distinct and different issues for organizational diagnosis and planned change. Huff's political perspective is a significant counterpoint to traditional OD theories and assumptions; it questions the humanistic bias so prevalent in the discipline.

Brown raises the important issue of whether current OD methods are appropriate to systems which are underorganized – i.e. where system behaviour is only loosely constrained by regulatory mechanisms. He suggests that the degree to which a system is organized (varying from underorganized to overorganized) is critical to understanding and changing organizations. He explains degree of organization in terms of the organization's use of human energy, flow of information, management of differences, task activity, response to novelty, and external boundaries. Brown contrasts OD in overorganized and underorganized systems and suggests that the latter require a change strategy, change process, and client/change agent relationship quite different from traditional OD. He offers two case studies to illustrate his ideas and to show their application to planned change in underorganized systems.

Systems Theory for Organization Development
Edited by T. G. Cummings
© 1980 John Wiley & Sons Ltd.

Chapter 5

A Social Systems Model for Organization Development[1]

Michael Beer

Organizations are formed to achieve purposes which individuals alone cannot achieve. Individuals join organizations to achieve personal goals they cannot attain on their own or which are better met through membership in organizations. Thus organizations are social inventions designed to achieve certain purposes and at the same time to fulfil members' needs. In effect organizations are social structures (formal arrangements of people and groups) and processes (behaviours and interactions between people and groups). The goodness of the invention or the effectiveness of the organization can best be determined by the extent to which its social structures and processes facilitate the achievement of the purposes (economic and others) for which they were designed and the extent to which they provide fulfilment of members' needs and goals.

Even a cursory survey of contemporary organizations would indicate that there is an on-going struggle to meet members' needs and to achieve economic purposes. Absenteeism, turnover, and labour strife are just a few of the symptoms which indicate that the relationship between individuals and organizations is a dynamic one. Individuals look to meet their needs and expectations by finding new organizations which are better equipped to meet them than their current ones or they attempt to force changes in management and organization in their current organization. Similarly, productivity problems, declining market shares, lowered profitability and, at the extreme, bankruptcies and/or mergers indicate that the relationship between an organization and its environment is also dynamic. Organizational strategies which may have been successful in the past may no longer work as effectively because new competitors have entered the market or a new technology has emerged. Thus organizations find themselves in a continuous struggle to define and redefine their relationship with their environment through changes in strategy, structure, and process.

The picture of organizations which emerges is a dynamic one. They are adaptive coping systems (Schein, 1970) that take on structures and processes required to fulfil members' needs and expectations and to achieve organizational goals, to survive, and to grow. In effect organizations are continually changing to develop and maintain congruence or fit between several major social system components:

People: Members' needs, abilities, values, and expectations.
Process: The behaviours, attitudes, and interactions that occur within the organiza-
                 tion at the individual, group, and intergroup level.
Structures: The formal mechanisms and systems of the organization that are designed
                 to channel behaviour towards organizational goals and fulfil members'
                 needs.
Environment: The external conditions with which the organization must deal include its
                 markets, technology, and government environment.

There is growing evidence that organizational effectiveness, an organization's capacity to achieve its goals and to fulfil members' needs, is a function of the congruence or fit between people, process, structure and environment (Friedlander, 1971; Lorsch, 1975; Miles and Snow, 1978). Thus, developing organizational effectiveness requires on-going diagnosis of the fit between the organization's major social system components, and managerial action to change one or more of these components when better fit is required. This sounds a lot simpler than it really is. In effect, each of the major social system components subsumes many dimensions and the cause and effect relationships between the components are often circular. In order to improve the effectiveness of organizations one must fully understand their complexity.

Some of the most frequent causes of failure in organizational change efforts come from an incomplete understanding of the multiple causes of a problem. A superficial and incomplete diagnosis of the problem then leads to an incomplete action plan in which only a few of the critical organizational dimensions which influence behaviour and results are targeted for change. Just as often, an inadequate diagnosis leads to organizational arrangements or management practice that causes unanticipated secondary problems. Two examples will help clarify the importance of understanding the complexity of organizations.

(1) A small electronics firm experienced a high rate of turnover in its engineering department, which was key to the company's success. The turnover occurred immediately after the vice-president of engineering had departed and was attributed by the president to the strong personal relationships this VP had established with the engineers.

A closer analysis of the problem indicated, however, that many more fundamental problems caused the turnover. The company's business had evolved over a number of years from small R&D contracts, which one or two engineers could complete, to larger-scale production run contracts in which many engineers, purchasing, and production people were involved. The turnover of engineers was a function of their frustration in getting things done in this new environment. They could no longer design the system alone. A manufacturing function had now created rules and procedures which engineers needed to take into account. A manufacturing manager who was autocratic enforced these procedures arbitrarily, making life difficult for the engineers who had been employed to be creative.

Thus the changes in business and subsequent changes in tasks had violated the engineers' needs and expectations. Furthermore, no structural mechanism or procedure existed to facilitate the new coordination required within engineering and between engineering and other functions.

The VP of engineering had held the effort together through his relationships with engineers and other functions. When he left no other organizational forces were in place to facilitate the complex coordination required. The president of the company was busy on new acquisitions and had not actively provided leadership for the functions. The new engineering manager lacked the unique leadership and management skills held by the old VP. So-called engineering project leaders did not understand their roles nor did other engineers or manufacturing people accept their influence. The measurement systems encouraged manufacturing to emphasize efficiency, making them less receptive to the many on-going design changes that were required.

A plan to find a new VP of engineering would have been totally inadequate in dealing with the problems. A clarification of roles and a reorganization of engineering along project lines in addition to the existing functional structure was needed. Project leaders needed clarification of their roles and new skills to act as coordinators. A control system that allowed for tradeoffs between the efficiency orientation of manufacturing and the design interests of engineering were needed. Similarly, the president needed to become more involved in the day-to-day affairs of the company, while the manufacturing VP needed to modify his arbitrary style.

(2) Changes in the organization of work on a production floor of a plant resulted in each worker assembling a whole product. These changes were aimed at increasing the involvement, motivation, and satisfaction of these employees. While these changes had the desired effects on motivation and satisfaction, a new set of unanticipated problems arose.

Supervisors, who had been used to traditional assembly line jobs, found that the new way of organizing work gave far more initiative to workers than before which diminished their previous authority. Supervisors were now required to facilitate more than direct. Some of these supervisors had difficulty adjusting; while some might adjust with the help of education others would probably have to be replaced. Workers who now had new responsibilities wanted to be paid more but the job evaluation system of the company prevented this because the elements of decision making and initiative now required in the jobs were not weighed sufficiently. When stocks were too high company policy called for layoffs based on seniority.

Unless these problems could be solved the organizational improvements would be jeopardized by workers who felt underpaid for new responsibilities, by supervisors who might undermine the changes, or by worker insecurity.

Organizational improvement efforts which do not identify the root causes of the problem or which do not anticipate the consequences of planned organizational changes fail to develop credibility among organizational members. Apathy or resistance develop, the momentum of change is lost, and the organization may ultimately regress to earlier states. Unanticipated consequences, failure to achieve the desired momentum of change, and repeated attempts to change followed by regressions are indications that the change agent has not fully understood and acted upon the organization as a system.

But what is meant when organizations are referred to as systems, and how does understanding that help in planning a change effort? This chapter will deal with the nature of organizations, present a systems model of organisations and its conceptual underpinnings, and discuss how such a model might help, indeed how it is essential, in planned organizational improvements.

A systems view of organizations

A strong argument has been made for viewing organizations as dynamic entities continually interacting with their environment, changing and adapting to develop congruence between people, process, structures, and external environment. This dynamic view helps explain why bureaucratic organizations, the dominant form of organization when the environment was stable, are under stress and new organizational forms are evolving. It also provides a historical and developmental perspective for any one organization and aids in diagnosing the current state and problems within that organization.

Healthy organizations sense changes in the environment and make adaptations in the way they function to accommodate new environmental demands. They may also elect to interact with only parts of a larger environment based on assessment of their capacity to respond. Finally, they can try to influence their environment to be consistent with organizational arrangements and dominant managerial practices (Starbuck, 1976).

Systems theory applied to organizations

Systems theory, the ideas that help explain the dynamic interrelationship of several parts of a larger whole as it interacts with its environment, has in the last several decades been applied to organizational theory (Kast and Rosenzweig, 1970; Katz and Kahn, 1978; Lawrence and Lorsch, 1967; Stogdill, 1959; Roethlisberger and Dickson, 1939). Even more recently systems theory has found its way into organization development where it has helped in organizational diagnosis and intervention strategies (French and Bell, 1978; Kotter, 1978; Beer, 1976; Huse, 1975; Beer and Huse, 1972). Applying systems theory to organizations leads to the following list of general characteristics.

(1) Organizations are composed of several components or parts which are in interaction with one another while at the same time part of an identifiable whole. These components may be subunits or they may be dimensions such as people, process, structure, and culture.
(2) Organizations, having more or less permeable boundaries, interact with an external environment from which they obtain energy/matter or information as inputs and to which they export a product or service as outputs. (By energy/matter is meant people, electricity, money, materials, etc.)
(3) Organizations are a network of people, structures, and technical operations

that transform the raw materials, such as energy or people, into a product or service desired by users in the environment.

(4) Organizations have feedback mechanisms that allow its various parts or components to adjust to its other parts and components. Similarly there is information flow between the organization and its environment that allows it to adapt and influence. Market research departments are examples of external sensing functions, while various interdepartmental meetings are examples of internal feedback mechanisms.

(5) Entropy, or a running down of the system, will occur to the extent that energy is not continuously imported and converted into valued outputs that allow reinvestment and further development. For social systems, the most important maintenance source is human effort and motivation. Thus the motivation of people in the organization becomes just as important a source of energy as financial and other energy/matter resources.

A social systems model of organizations

The idea that organizations convert inputs such as energy/matter and information from their environment into outputs that are usable by the environment can be translated into a social systems model of organizations. This model is presented in Figure 1. It synthesizes a diverse body of research, theory, and OD practice in a large multinational corporation over an eleven-year period.[2]

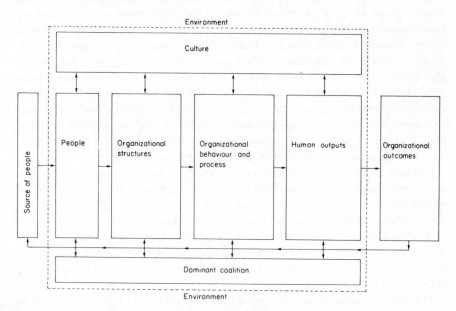

Figure 1   A social systems model of organizations

The model specifies the relationships between the major organizational components which have to fit or be congruent in order for an organization to be effective. These are:

(1) People
(2) Organizational structures
(3) Organizational behaviour and process
(4) Human outputs
(5) Culture
(6) Dominant coalition
(7) Environment
(8) Organizational outcomes.

The model specifies a flow of events beginning with the qualities that people bring with them (*people*) and ending with the attitudes and psychological states of organizational members (human outputs) after they have lived and worked in the organization for some period of time. The organization's *structures* (reward systems, policies, control and evaluation systems, etc.) signal to organizational members what behaviour is desired and reinforce (reward or punish) actual behaviour. Thus, structures shape *organizational behaviour and process*. Structures and process together mediate the relationship between people's needs, expectations, and capacities when they enter the organization and the attitudes and capacities developed as a result of living and working in the organization. Organization *culture*, commonly held beliefs about how the organization is and should be operating, is formed by all four of the components just described but also influences and shapes them. Similarly the *dominant coalition*, a small number of key decision makers, impact all of the aforementioned organizational components through their position of power and influence in the organization, but are also influenced by their experience in the organization with all of the components listed. Economic indicators, such as profit, and quality of work life indicators, such as turnover, reflect the organization's performance (*organizational outcomes*) in its market, social environment, and technological environment. They are a function of all the components of the social system working in concert but are particularly well predicted by the organization's human outputs.

It should be clear, however, that while this way of describing an organization is a convenient way of thinking about the flow of a social system, any part of the system can affect any other part. For example, levels and kinds of satisfaction will affect people's needs; culture will affect employee expectations; the behaviour of people will affect the required structures; attitudinal outputs affect behaviour, and the organization's environment and economic performance can directly affect several components of the system. The feedback loops in the model illustrate these and other interdependencies.

The social systems model does not explicitly recognize tangible assets such as buildings, stock, money, and materials as organizational inputs. The reason for this is not that they are unimportant but rather that the model provides a framework for understanding organizations as social systems in which these other inputs, though equally important, are not in the centre of the stage.

Indeed, an organization with financial resources or technology superior to its competitors can probably operate successfully for longer periods of time with relatively low human output and quality of work life outcomes. Sooner or later, however, entropy in the social system (inability to attract, keep, motivate, and influence talented people) will lead to reduced profit and thus reduced financial and technological resources. Organizational specialists and managers must keep this tradeoff in mind in estimating the return on investments in organization development. They must keep in mind that investment in organization development can itself lead to an increase in tangible assets of the corporation over the long term.

Practical value of a social systems model

As we saw in the two cases presented at the beginning of this chapter, the planning and implementation of organizational improvements requires an understanding of the complexity inherent in social systems. A manager or organizational specialist can adopt the model presented here or develop his own, but he *must* internalize a social systems perspective if he is to be successful in managing organizational effectiveness for the following reasons:

(1) A model provides a taxonomy of key organizational dimensions that guide data collection and diagnosis, without which the latter becomes confusing and difficult.
(2) Some sense of the complex relationship between key organizational dimensions is useful in diagnosing the causes of a given problem and appreciating the circularity of causes and effects.
(3) A model can be useful in categorizing intervention methods by the components or dimensions of the organization to which they apply. This allows a more systematic, efficient use of change methods.
(4) A model forces managers to be quite specific about the outcomes (economic, attitudinal, and behavioural) they desire and how organizational changes are intended to effect these outcomes. Without a model organization changes are often based on what other managers are doing, what is faddish, or the manager's own values.

The case examples in the beginning of this chapter illustrate the model's applicability quite clearly. Turnover among engineers and its potential effects on profits (organizational outcome) was related to changes in the business (environment), which caused organizational structure, personnel, policy, roles, measurement systems (structures), and expectations by engineers (people) to become outdated. These structures and inappropriate leadership practices by the president (dominant coalition) prevented the organization from developing required coordination between functions (organizational behaviour and process).

As the social systems model is discussed in more depth its capacity to provide a convenient shorthand method of diagnosing organizational problems and planning improvements will become evident. Someone else, perhaps the reader, might draw such an organizational model quite differently. Kotter (1978) has developed a somewhat different model, but one that contains many of the same components and relationships. The similarity of his model, developed quite independently of the present model, suggests that the components and relationships presented in Figure 1 would also appear, though perhaps in somewhat different form, in models developed by other organizational specialists.

The components of the social systems model

This section will deal with each component of the model presented in Figure 1, describing more fully what kinds of organizational phenomena are subsumed under it and how it relates to other components. The components will be discussed in the order in which a typical diagnostic process might proceed. The first component discussed is organization environment. This is followed in turn by discussions of organization outcomes and human outputs; of organizational behaviour and processes which produce these outcomes; and of structures, people, and culture, the major driving forces of behaviour.

The sequence of this discussion demonstrates certain biases in approaching organizational diagnosis. Perhaps the most obvious is the concern for understanding the environment. The functionality of organizational attitudes and behaviour can only be evaluated in relation to the organization's environment and the task which the organization faces if it is to succeed in its environment. Finally, organizational structures, people, and culture can only be evaluated in the light of behaviours observed or desired. The reader is cautioned to remember, however, that in systems thinking everything is connected to everything else and another sequence of diagnosis may work just as well as long as it encompasses *all* the relevant components.

A social system interacts with its environment

Organizations interact with their environment by importing people, and using their energy to make products or provide services that are exported into the environment. The relationship between a social system and its environment is much more complex than that of a technical system. For one thing it is difficult to define what the boundaries of an organization are. Where does the organization leave off and the environment start? For example, employees are hired by the organization and are physically and mentally inside the organization much of their lives. But they are also members of a society, are influenced continually by society, and continually transmit social concerns and changing values to the organization.

Similarly, management practices, corporate strategy, policies, structure, and other means the organization uses to convert people's energy into performance outcomes are directly and continually influenced by the environment through legislation, market forces, new knowledge, and so on. This interaction has led to the conception of social organizations as open systems as opposed to more closed technical systems (Katz and Kahn, 1978).

What aspects of the environment are relevant for an organization? Is it society as a whole, the political and governmental system, other companies in the same market, the financial community, the technology of the organization, or the local community in which the organization finds itself? Clearly all comprise an organization's environment to the extent that they place demands on the organization and there is an interaction, but several aspects of an organization's environment are particularly relevant to its structures and management practice:

(1) *Market environment* This is defined by the type of product or service which an organization provides, the type of customers it serves, and/or the industry of which it is a part. Some markets are complex and competitive while others are less so, thus placing differing demands on the organization for market sensing, decision making, and responsiveness to customers and competitors. In general, successful organizations can be separated from unsuccessful ones by the appropriateness of their structural form and management process to their environment (Burns and Stalker, 1961; Lawrence and Lorsch, 1967).

(2) *Technological environment* Each organization operates within a different product technology and uses different technologies to make a product or deliver a service. The rate of technological change and innovation will define the task of the organization. For example, how much the organization must stay in touch with the basic sciences that support its technology defines how extensive its R&D operations need to be, and how closely these must be linked with other parts of the organization that use the technology. Also the technology for making the product and delivering the service also affects the nature of jobs at the working level, and the opportunities for providing people with motivating tasks. The importance of technology in influencing the structure of organizations (Woodward, 1967) and the behaviour and attitudes of people (Davis, 1966; Hackman, 1977) has been widely documented. Indeed, it has led to the concept of an organization as a socio-technical system in which behaviour and attitudes are influenced by technology and these in turn affect decisions about the way technology is applied to jobs (Trist *et al.*, 1963).

(3) *Social environment* The social environment in which an organization operates may be defined by the values and culture of the society. These affect organizations directly through legislation and government regulations and indirectly through the expectations and values of its employees. An organization

must be sensitive to the values of society to avoid being sanctioned for management practices which violate these values. Recent revelations about illegal corporate political contributions and payoff practices in foreign countries illustrate this point. The changing values of Swedish workers fostered by higher levels of education and social legislation influenced Volvo's decision to experiment with more attractive and interesting alternatives to assembly line jobs (Gyllenhammer, 1977).

An organization's environmental complexity and degree of uncertainty are particularly important dimensions to assess (Thompson, 1967; Lawrence and Lorsch, 1967; Galbraith, 1973). By these is meant the extent to which there are numerous forces acting on the organization and the extent to which the environment is changing unpredictably. Uncertain and complex environments place very difficult information-processing and decision-making demands on organizations. They must be able to sense change rapidly, bring people together who have the latest information for problem solving, and make decisions responsive to the most recent environmental trends. Such organizations require new and different managerial processes, structures, and information handling systems (Galbraith, 1973). For the moment, the reader should note that examining the environment is important in understanding the task of the organization and its required structures and management process. This organization/environment perspective is a central part of what is meant by a systems view of organizations. Below is a list of the important environmental dimensions to be considered:

Organization environment

> Markets
> Competitive position
> Technology
> National and local government legislation
> Social culture
> Uncertainty
> Complexity

A social system has multiple purposes and performance outcomes

On a very long-term basis an organization's survival is dependent on how well it has been exchanging with its environment. If a business organization delivers a valued service or product at lower cost than its selling price – it survives. The effectiveness of this exchange can be measured by the *amount of profit* the organization returns since this determines how much can be reinvested to maintain current operations or develop new business opportunities. Thus profit, return on investment, and other financial indicators are the most frequently stated purposes and criteria of organizational performance.

There are other criteria and purposes, however. An organization must fulfil the needs of its members for a secure job, equitable monetary compensation, meaningful work, and a compatible social environment at work. In a word, the organization must provide for a satisfactory quality of work life, or will ultimately be unable to attract, keep, motivate, and influence employees.

These criteria of performance create conflicting demands. Managers are often forced to trade off one objective against another. They may reduce profits to pay workers more or they may pay a dividend while firing people to reduce costs. How they trade off between these organizational outcomes will be determined by the costs to the organization of low quality of work life. Unfortunately, these costs cannot always be assessed with the same precision, ease, and frequency as more tangible costs. Perceptions of quality of work life are quite subjective and its behavioural and economic consequences quite variable. Moreover, objective measures like absenteeism and employee turnover are difficult to attribute to specific events or actions by managers and their exact costs to the organization are not always immediately apparent. Despite these difficulties in measurement, experience and research suggest that the impact of quality of work life outcomes does have an intermediate to long-term impact on economic performance of the organization. In many countries (particularly in Western Europe) social welfare legislation and legislation which makes firing employees extremely difficult is increasing the cost to organizations of low quality of work life by preventing these costs from being passed off to the individual and society. For example, making it more difficult to fire employees whose performance has deteriorated forces management to search for conditions which may be demotivating employees. Thus, despite difficulties in assessing the economic value of quality of work life outcomes (difficulties that promise to be reduced by new developments such as human asset accounting), managers must weigh the impact of their decisions on both sets of outcomes and balance them appropriately.

In summary, the ultimate outcomes by which an organization may judge how favourably it is exchanging with its environment are:

Outcomes
Economic measures
 Profit
 Return on investment
 Rate of growth
 Etc.

Quality of work life measures
 Turnover
 Absenteeism
 Ability to attract good people
 Etc.

The economic and quality of work life outcomes listed above are a result, among other things, of the attitudes people have about themselves, their jobs, their management, and the organization. The next section deals with these attitudes under the heading of human outputs.

Attitudes and psychological states are the human outputs of social systems

One of the characteristics of systems, particularly social ones, is that there is a considerable time lag between the ultimate non-achievement of goals and indicators within the system that provide early warnings that goals will not be achieved. The research of Rensis Likert and his associates has shown that employee attitudes and psychological states, such as satisfaction, commitment and motivation, will predict declines in profits several years hence (Likert, 1967). Recently employee attitude measures have been directly linked to costs in a bank (Mirvis and Lawler, 1977), a bank's service image (Schneider, *et al.*, undated), and unionization activity (Hamner and Smith, 1978). These and other studies demonstrate the link between the condition of an organization's human assets and performance. Thus the way an organization is managed (the functioning of its social systems), affects employee attitudes and competence and these can help predict the *ultimate* capacity of the organization to perform in its environment. Some of the human outputs that research and OD practice have shown to be important are:

Human outputs

Clarity of goals
Clarity of roles
Feelings that the organization is effective
Motivation and energy level
Commitment
Feelings of personal growth and competence
Competence of employees
Extrinsic satisfaction
Intrinsic satisfaction
Willingness to collaborate
Willingness to risk new ideas
Trust and supportiveness
Awareness of personal and organizational realities

In saying that human outputs are predictors of organizational performance there is no attempt to imply that all of them are equally important to all organizations or that they are independent of each other. One organization may require extremely high levels of commitment and risk taking while another may require only a moderate or even a low level. The level required will depend on the benefit that a given human output provides in comparison with the cost and difficulty of obtaining it. For example, an organization that manufactures complex electronic equipment may require substantial amounts of collaboration or risk taking with new ideas while a company that makes bottles in a relatively simple and stable environment will not.[3] Similarly, the types of people employed by the organization, their needs and expectations, will determine the kinds and amounts of satisfactions the organization must provide to attract, keep and motivate them.

By analysing the task or environment, a manager can rank the relative importance of various human outputs. This rank ordering can be compared with a diagnosis of actual attitudes in the organization. Discrepancies and a diagnosis of their causes can lead to a clearer understanding of which managerial and structuring approaches are most appropriate and which types of people might be employed. Much of organization development practice involves collecting attitudinal data that reflect human outputs and helping managers diagnose their implications for organizational change.

Numerous *diagnostic interventions* have been developed to facilitate this process (Beer (1976) provides a description of these). One class of diagnostic interventions utilizes survey methods in which attitude data are collected by means of questionnaires and/or interviews and fed back to groups that can take action on them. These methods typically rely on organizational consultants to collect the data and to help in their feedback and interpretation. A second class of diagnostic intervention involves members of the organization more fully in generating information and diagnosing problems. Various meeting formats have been developed in which people in the organization whose attitudes are of interest are brought together with managers who impact their attitudes. Direct communication is expected to influence their behaviour directly and lead to changes in structure and process.

We now turn to an examination of those parts of the organization that affect human outputs.

In social system things get done through behaviour and process

The behaviour of people and the process by which they interact are the means by which goods are sold, products manufactured, work coordinated, and budgets and plants developed. Behaviours and interactions are the means by which potential energy and motivation are converted into results. The more congruent the behaviours and interactions are with the organization's purpose and task, the more effective the organization will be in achieving its performance goals. From this perspective the job of managing an organization is the job of managing and guiding behaviour.

The human processes in an organization are dynamic and transitory. Thus they are often difficult to observe and measure. Managers are usually so immersed in the content of their transactions – the technical problems, the financial decisions, the marketing strategy – that they miss the process by which the content is dealt with. Yet, research and experience point to the fact that when process is consciously examined and managed by organizational members, they perceive improvement in the quality of decisions, coordination and effectiveness, clarity of goals and strategy, involvement and motivation, and satisfaction among other processes (Friedlander, 1967; Dyer, 1977; Hackman, 1976).

A good deal of organization development work is helping individuals and groups to examine their process and their behaviours so that these can come under their control. These *process interventions* usually involve a consultant who provides or facilitates the feedback of information to individuals or groups (Beer (1976) provides a description of these). For example, team building, one of the most frequently used methods, starts with a consultant interviewing members of a group about their perception of each other and the group's effectiveness. Their comments are organized by the consultant and are discussed in depth in an off-site meeting. The discussion is aimed at helping individuals and groups gain insight into their own behaviour so that they might change those behaviours that block effectiveness. Similar methods are used to help two groups examine their relationships. Sometimes the consultant will sit in on an actual meeting and help managers examine their behaviour during the meeting. While a consultant is needed by groups who have not been through this type of process before, more sophisticated managers can manage their own process interventions. In all these interventions, the objective is self-understanding and behaviour change.

Many behaviours and interactions are required to manage and run an organization. Below are listed those processes that research and practice have found important in understanding and improving organizations. The list is not exhaustive nor are these categories independent of each other:

Organizational behaviour and process

Leadership and supervision
Communication – quantity and quality
Intergroup relation and integration
Conflict management
Decision making process
Problem solving
Planning and goal setting
Group and meeting process
Interpersonal relations
Evaluation and control processes
Critique and renewal processes

There is no prescription implied by these categories about what is the 'right' process for managing an organization. Research about what behaviour constitutes effective management has shown that it depends on a variety of situational factors, such as the needs and expectations of the people involved, their loyalty and commitment to the organization, the task, the information available, and who has the information (Vroom and Yetton, 1973; Galbraith, 1973; Fiedler, 1967; Morse and Lorsch, 1970).

There has been considerable controversy in the field of organizational behaviour between advocates of *contingency theories* on one hand and *normative theories* on the other. Contingency theories of management suggest that the kind and amount of behaviour desired (leadership, integration, conflict management) depends on the organization's environment and/or the characteristics of its members. Normative theories suggest that all organizations need to approach certain ideals like openness, participation, or confrontation of conflict.

This controversy is still largely unresolved due to the fact that advocates of these different viewpoints implicitly assign different values to various organizational outcomes and measure these outcomes on different time horizons. For this reason, the question of whether organizations should strive for high levels of participation, open communication and planning, to mention only a few processes, is best answered by looking at what the costs are compared with the benefits.

All processes and behaviours take time and money to develop and perform (i.e. whether planning or good interpersonal relations) and must compete with other investments of time and energy. The systems view of organizations suggests that the degree to which each process is adequately developed must depend on environmental and task demands on the one hand and employee needs and desires on the other. For each process dimension at least some knowledge exists that can help managers to make decisions about the behaviours appropriate for their organization, though space limitations do not allow a discussion of this body of knowledge.

Perhaps even more important than this knowledge, however, is the capacity of managers and workers to examine how they are working together so that inappropriate processes can be corrected based on first-hand knowledge of the task and people's needs. This, of course, is the essence of organization development.

Historically, OD has been almost exclusively concerned with improving organizations through intervention methods aimed at changing process or behaviour directly (Leavitt, 1965). But laboratory training methods and other interventions aimed at helping people and groups to examine their behaviour have been found to have only short-lived effects. Thus attention has increasingly shifted to the examination of structures within organizations which guide and shape behaviour. We now turn to a discussion of these structures.

In social systems behaviour is influenced through structures

Structures are the formal aspects of an organization. They signal to people that certain behaviour is desirable and that rewards are likely to result if they practice it. In designing an organization to obtain desired behaviour and results, managers typically use the following structures or design tools:

Structural dimensions and design tools

Departmentalization and formal reporting relationships
Job design or structure
Types and frequency of formal meetings
Personnel policies and systems
      Rewards and compensation system
      Management development and promotion system
      Labour relations policy
      Performance evaluation and development system
      Recruitment, selection, and transfer policies
      Etc.
Control and measurement systems
      Management information systems
      Accounting systems
      Budgeting systems
      Etc.
Geographical location and physical layout

There are many examples of how structures are used by management to obtain desired behaviour. For example, pay systems, particularly bonus systems, are designed to obtain high levels of motivation and goal accomplishment from senior executives. Piece rate incentive systems are designed to obtain high levels of effort from production employees. The assembly line with its specialized jobs is designed to control closely the behaviour of workers and reduce undesired deviations in work practices. Financial budgets and control systems are aimed at getting functional managers to emphasize certain goals deemed important for the organization. The structure of the organization which has functional managers reporting to a common general manager is aimed at ensuring that inevitable conflicts between functional goals will be resolved in the best interests of the organization.

Unfortunately, research and experience indicate that these structures do not always induce desired behaviours and sometimes cause undesired or dysfunctional behaviours. For example, managers may budget sales or profits at lower levels than they expect to achieve for fear of negative consequences if they miss their targets (Lawler and Rhode, 1976). Functional goals without proper balancing of integrative goals can cause undesired competition and conflict between groups (Walton and Dutton, 1969), or incentive systems can reduce worker receptivity to technological changes (Whyte, 1955). Still other structures, like pay systems, job design or office layout, can cause frustration and dissatisfaction if they are not consistent with employee expectations or if they block task accomplishment.

Because structures that stimulate and reinforce desired behaviour and reduce as much as possible undesired behaviour are so important, the long-range decisions managers make concerning the design of the organization's structures are very important. Organization development must, therefore, include a diagnosis of the impact of structures on behaviour, attitudes, and task accomplishment and help in the design of alternative structures.

If structures influence organizational behaviour, and behaviours must be consistent with the organization's environment, then the structures appropriate for any given organization must be consistent with its particular environment. In recent years, so-called contingency theories of organization have articulated this viewpoint (Lawrence and Lorsch, 1967; Burns and Stalker, 1961; Galbraith, 1973; Miles and Snow, 1978). Research supporting these theories has shown that successful organizations in uncertain and dynamic environments use structures and control systems which are quite different from those of unsuccessful organizations in the same environment and successful organizations in less dynamic environments. Thus, structures and environment or strategy (the organization's selected environment) must fit if an organization is to be successful. The electronics firm described at the beginning of this chapter is an excellent example of a firm whose performance suffered as a result of not adapting its structures to a new business environment.

Unfortunately, not all organizations approximate the adaptive capacity of the theoretical social system. The structures of organizations are often determined by long-held values, personal experience of success, and beliefs of managers about the 'right' way to organize rather than more flexible and contingent viewpoints. An example of this can be seen in new managers who restructure an organization they have just taken over to resemble the organization they have left. The blockade of Cuba ordered by John F. Kennedy in 1961 is cited by Weick (1973) as an example that organizations are not naturally adaptive systems. A blockade of Cuba was ordered at a 50-mile perimeter for specific strategic reasons; but naval regulations and tradition specified a 200-mile perimeter and that is where the Navy placed the blockade. Apparently the Navy could not change its regulations (structure) when confronted with a new environment and task.

In summary, organizations approximate social systems to the extent that structures do seem to differ with different environments and different types of people. Generally, more rigid and 'mechanistic' structures are found in stable environments, loose and 'organic' structures in dynamic environments (Burns and Stalker, 1961). But organizations are far from perfect social systems and there are many examples of maladaptive structures that shape inappropriate behaviour.

There are numerous *structural interventions* available for diagnosing the impact of structures on behaviour and attitudes just as there are *structural inventions* which are available as alternatives to traditional structures (Beer (1976) provides a description of these). These methods can facilitate the adaptation of organizations by providing a means for the rational analysis of structures. For example, methods have been developed for diagnosing the impact of job design on motivation, and principles for restructuring jobs which are motivationally inadequate have been developed (Hackman, 1977). Similarly, conceptual frameworks for diagnosing the fit of organizational structure with environment or strategy and choosing alternatives have been developed (Lawrence and Lorsch, 1969; Miles and Snow, 1978). In addition an impressive array of alternative structures such as new pay systems, personnel systems, and matrix structures have been developed in the last two decades and offer managers new design solutions for old problems (Beer, 1976).

People are the raw material of social systems

Organizations recruit and select people on the basis of their estimated potential to achieve certain desired levels of performance. Industrial psychologists have for years attempted to predict the performance of individuals by identifying and then assessing those individual characteristics which best predict performance on the job. While these attempts have been somewhat successful, the correlation between individual characteristics and performance criteria have at best been moderate, while the relationship between individual characteristics and ultimate organizational performance criteria is often nonexistent (Schneider, 1976).

One reason for this is that individual characteristics comprise a potential only. There is some evidence that low correlations between individual characteristics and performance criteria are a function of inappropriate organizational arrangements, such as job design, organization structure, and management process. Thus organization design and process play an important role in unleashing people's potential. For example, organizations have been shown to realize more motivation when job structure and management style fit the needs, expectations, and abilities of organizational members (Hackman and Lawler, 1971; Turner and Lawrence, 1965; Morse and Lorsch, 1970; Vroom, 1960). The importance of organizational arrangements in eliciting full human potential probably increases with the complexity of the task and required coordination.

A mismatch between the organization and the characteristics of people in it often occurs because the structures and managerial processes are based on certain invalid assumptions about people. Douglas McGregor (1960), Robert Blake and Jane Mouton (1964) and Chris Argyris (1962) have pointed out that a manager's implicit assumptions about people's needs, values, abilities, and expectations will be revealed in the way he manages. They have argued persuasively that the behaviour of many managers and the assumptions underlying the design of many organizations are inconsistent with what is known about people. Changes in education, society, and social policy within the more industrialized countries of the world are probably increasing this gap between people and organizations.

But for this notion of individual/organization fit to be operationally useful, a social systems model of organizations must at least specify which individual characteristics are important for a manager to examine and take into account in attempts to improve organizations.

It is often useful to distinguish between the 'can do' or ability components of performance and the 'will do' or motivational components of performance. Some managers tend to emphasize one component to the exclusion of the other, thus missing the fact that performance is a function of an interaction between abilities and motivation. The relationship has been conceptualized (McGregor, 1967) as follows:

$$P = M \times A$$

where P = performance, M = motivation, A = abilities.

We now turn to a discussion of ability and motivation as important components in total performance. However, to this list must be added expectations, or what people perceive will happen when they behave or perform in certain ways.

Individual's skills and abilities   Historically, the field of organization development has been heavily influenced by the values and belief systems of the human potential movement which developed in the 1950s and 1960s. People in this movement and many OD people adopted the view that almost anyone had the potential to grow and develop into what they wanted to become. If there were problems in performance, they were a function of the organizational climate and supervision.

Thus ability was perceived to be less of a constraint on human performance in organizations than was motivation. This relative inattention to ability came from the inability of OD specialists to deal with the problems of intervening in the competence question. If a manager is trying to develop trust and collaboration, how can he fire people without destroying trust? Or, how can a consultant discuss the competence of an organizational member with management without destroying his relationship of trust with organizational members?

It seems clear that individuals do differ in abilities and skills and that these differences limit their capacity to respond to various situations. Differences in ability seem to fall into three primary categories: physical abilities, mental abilities, and interpersonal skills. Obviously, the required mix of these three dimensions and their various subcomponents, together with experience and education, will differ for each job.

Engineers may require more technical knowledge, a mental ability, than interpersonal skills; managers may require high mental ability and interpersonal skills; production workers may require primarily physical and mental skills. However, as the organization's arrangements change, the skills required of individuals are constantly changing.

Enormous amounts of research have been conducted by psychologists on the relationship between abilities and performance. At least a moderate relationship can be found in many instances (Schneider, 1976). Errors in prediction have probably been due both to the motivational component in performance and to errrors in measurement. It should be noted that most of the attempts to predict performance from ability have concentrated on the more measurable mental and physical abilities. However, in the last ten years assessment centres (Bray, Campbell, and Grant, 1974) and various clinical methods have been used successfully to assess interpersonal skills required in management. It is rare in OD practice to find organizational outcomes affected by inadequate technical competence and much more frequent that interpersonal competence is lacking. Not that technical competence is unimportant, but society and organizations are far more sophisticated in selecting, developing, and maintaining technical skills than they are in selecting and developing interpersonal ones.

A gap between an organization's current and desired skill and ability mix can only be understood in the context of the organization's recruitment, selection, promotion, and development systems and strategies. The relative importance of selection *v.* development as strategies for human resource development will depend, of course, on the deficiencies discovered, a realistic assessment of whether they are developable or not, and the relative costs and benefits of replacement and selection strategies.

Individual needs Need is commonly acknowledged to be the springboard of motivation. Needs are an internal state in a person that cause objects or outcomes to become attractive. Needs range from basic physical needs, such as hunger, to so-called higher-order needs, such as esteem or achievement. Unless a person has needs he will not behave. The need he has will determine his desired outcomes, as well as the rewards the organization must provide to stimulate motivation. Thus in efforts to improve social systems effectiveness, it becomes extremely important to have a framework for analysing the need structure of organizational members.

Many frameworks and lists of needs have been put forward (Maslow, 1954; Murray, 1938), but research and OD practices have shown that a relatively short list, based on Abraham Maslow's work, is sufficient (Lawler and Rhode, 1976). They are:

(1) existence needs such as hunger, thirst, and oxygen;
(2) security needs;
(3) social needs for belonging, companionship, support, love, etc.;

(4) needs for esteem, status, and reputation;
(5) needs for self-control, influence, and independence;
(6) needs for competence, achievement, and self-realization.

It is generally agreed that these needs are arranged in a two-level hierarchy with existence and security needs at a lower level and esteem, autonomy, and self-realization at a higher level, and that a person is likely to experience them all simultaneously. Furthermore, there is evidence that higher-level needs appear only when lower-level needs are reasonably well satisfied, and are reduced in strength when lower-level need satisfaction is threatened. Only lower-level needs are likely to become less important as they are satisfied. Higher-order needs are likely to stay high and even increase in strength as they are satisfied. Thus the only continuous source of energy for a social system is higher-order needs. For example, the more money is used as a reward, the less powerful it becomes as a motivator to the extent that it satisfies needs for security and physical well-being. This is not the case with a reward such as completing a meaningful task which is likely to arouse even a higher need to achieve.

A process of organization development should lead to a social system designed to attract, keep, and motivate people with a variety of needs, as well as to accommodate the general societal shifts in individual needs whereby people move from lower-order to higher-order ones.

Individual expectations People in organizations do not just react to organizational forces. They develop, at the very least, some general plans aimed at meeting their needs. For example, they purposely choose to work more or less or to take certain career routes. These plans are often not detailed nor are the various options always fully investigated. Indeed these plans are often not conscious. People do, however, develop at least generalized ideas about what they want and how they would like to be treated by the organization. The organization in turn sends many signals that indicate what it is reasonable for people to expect.

For example, an individual may expect pay, promotion, and job security if he acts in certain ways, exerts a certain amount of effort, or performs well. These expectations are a function of his need structure, the larger society of which he is a part, what the organization signals is reasonable to expect, and what other organizations offer.

Expectations are part of the individual's 'psychological contract' with the organization (Schein, 1970). That is, the individual expects certain rewards in return for meeting the organization's expectations. When the psychological contract is violated by the organization, the person becomes dissatisfied and frustrated which leads to new behaviours – perhaps less effort or a decision to leave the organization (Kotter, 1973).

As with needs, expectations are developed and later met or frustrated through an interaction between the individual and the organization. A manager who desires to maintain a viable psychological contract between the organization and its employees must understand what expectations are created or met by personnel policies, management practices, and organizational arrangements, and how changes in these may affect the fulfilment of these expectations (Thomas, 1974). The OD process often generates data about people's expectations and the extent to which they are being met or frustrated.

The individual and the organization: A motivational framework   The idea that employee motivation is a function of their needs and expectations in interaction with the organization has been formalized by some psychologists in what has come to be known as expectancy theory (Vroom, 1964; Porter and Lawler, 1968; Lawler, 1973). This theory states that motivation to behave in a given way is a function of: (1) people's expectancies or beliefs about what outcomes or rewards are likely to result from their behaviour, and (2) the valence or attractiveness individuals attach to the outcomes or rewards as they estimate the outcomes' ability to satisfy their needs (Lawler and Rhode, 1976).

In symbols:

$$M = (E \times V)$$

where M = motivation, E = expectancy, and V = valence of an outcome.

For example, a manager's effort to achieve certain budgeted performance goals in his unit will be related to his expectations about what positive or negative outcomes, for instance a bonus or a promotion, are likely to occur as a result of achieving these goals. Of course, how much he values these outcomes will also determine the choice he makes about the amount of effort to exert. If a bonus is highly probable, but he does not need the additional compensation, the bonus will have little effect on his behaviour. On the other hand, if the probability of saving his marriage by doing less at work is low, but saving it is very important, he may still reduce his effort.

The expectancy model suggests that individuals are rational decision makers in making choices about their behaviour. This is, of course, not totally true. People do not fully understand their needs or their expectations. Furthermore, they are not capable of processing all the information required to weigh outcomes, their probability of occurring, or their desirability. To do this would take too much time and energy. It is also known that people are content to satisfy their needs at some acceptable level rather than exert additional effort to optimize outcomes (March and Simon, 1958). Finally, people perceive the same situation differently and therefore may see the rewards available to them quite differently in terms of value or the probability that they will be obtained.

Despite arguments about specific elements, the expectancy model provides a useful framework for conceptualizing how social systems and people's needs and expectations interact to create certain behaviours and processes. There is evidence that organizational processes like leadership (House, 1971), structures such as jobs and pay (Lawler, 1971, 1977; Hackman, 1977), and culture (Wakeley, Frost, and Ruh, 1974) affect motivation. They do this to the extent that they provide valued outcomes (those that people want) and to the extent to which they shape expectations about the relationship between effort, successful performance, and rewards (James *et al.*, 1977).

Managers who want to understand the behaviour of people in the organization must learn as much as possible about people's needs and how organizational policies and managerial practices shape their expectations. Only then can managers take positive action to reshape expectations as appropriate.

People are adaptive   We would not want the reader to conclude that changes in organizational arrangements should always follow an assessment of members' needs and abilities. Quite the opposite sequence is possible. Organization development can begin with changes in organization design and process or with educational methods aimed at individual growth in needs, expectations, and abilities. If people are given more freedom of action and influence over their goals and/or if they are taught to set goals appropriately, could it be that their need for achievement might increase?

There is evidence that such changes can and do occur (McClelland, 1965, 1969). Apparently, people's needs and expectations are learned and are subject to influence by their environment (Porter, Lawler, and Hackman, 1975). The adaptive nature of people can provide significant adaptive opportunities for organizations when a dynamic rather than static view is taken.

Such optimism, while well founded, must be balanced with the realistic view that not all individuals are equally adaptive nor are they unlimited in their capacity to grow. Even when organizational changes are made with the understanding that individuals who cannot adapt or grow will leave, this strategy is limited by the rate at which the organization can manage an orderly turnover from less capable to more capable people.

There are numerous individual selection and development methods which have been developed to help organizations facilitate the process of individual adaptation (Beer, 1976, 1979). For example, laboratory training methods have been used to help individuals to improve their interpersonal competence and increase their orientation towards collaboration. Similarly, training in achievement motivation has been shown to increase the need to achieve. Career development laboratories have been used to help individuals gain a better understanding of their career goals so that they might make better and more explicit career choices. Finally, assessment centres have been used to help organizations to make more effective promotional decisions and to help individuals to learn about their potential managerial strengths and weaknesses. When these methods are coordinated with structural and process changes, they are likely to facilitate individual adaptation in the direction of planned organizational change and/or to help individuals and the organization to make more conscious and better decisions about individual/organization fit as the organization changes.

Social systems have cultures

So far, a number of organizational components crucial to the understanding of organizations as social systems have been specified. But our description of organizations as social systems would fall far short of its mark if we did not introduce the concept of *organization culture*. In recent years researchers (e.g. Halpin and Croft, 1963; Litwin and Stringer, 1968; Tagiuri and Litwin, 1968; Schneider and Bartlett, 1968) and OD practitioners (Steel and Jenks, 1977) have been devoting increasing attention to this concept because much of individual and group behaviour can be accounted for by the culture of the organization. Yet despite its importance, culture – or climate, as it is sometimes called – is a dangerously elusive organizational phenomenon difficult to define and measure. Nevertheless, this section will attempt to do so.

What is culture? One of the reasons culture is difficult to define is its phenomenological nature. That is, it is a characteristic of the day-to-day environment as seen and felt by those who work in it. It is to organizations as personality or self-concept are to the individual. It is determined by all of the components of the organization (structures, people, process, and environment) described in previous sections, yet it is more than their sum.

As individuals in organizations work with others, are supervised, and are affected by policies and procedures, they develop a composite perception of their environment, which is often expressed by adjectives or short phrases such as 'open', 'risk taking', 'warm', 'tough', 'soft', 'impersonal', 'informal', 'rigid', etc. A summary of what the organization is like, and, therefore, what behaviours and individual values are acceptable within the organization, is developed. These shared beliefs and feelings which form an informal set of ground rules about what is expected and what will be rewarded (formally or socially) are the culture of the organization (Margulies and Raia, 1978).

Harrison (1972) has referred to culture as an organizational ideology which provides an important organizing theme for behaviour. The more beliefs and values are shared about how to do things, the 'stronger' the culture of the organization and the more influence it exerts on individual and group behaviour. According to Harrison, culture performs the following functions:

(1) 'Specifies the goals and values toward which an organization should be directed and by which success and worth should be measured,'
(2) 'Prescribes the appropriate relationships between individuals and the organization (i.e., "the psychological contract" that legislates what the organization should be able to expect from its peopls and vice versa).'
(3) 'Indicates how behaviour should be controlled in the organization and what kinds of controls are legitimate and illegitimate.'

(4) 'Depicts which qualities and characteristics of organization members should be valued or vilified; as well as how these should be rewarded or punished.'
(5) 'Shows members how they should treat one another – competitively or collaboratively, honestly or dishonestly, closely or distantly.'
(6) 'Establishes appropriate methods of dealing with the external environment – aggressive exploitation, responsible negotiation, proactive exploration.'

While the list of behaviours and activities influenced by culture is not exhaustive, it is suggestive of the pervasive impact of culture, which the following example illustrates:

In one large corporation a widely held belief system existed that customer relations and a strong selling orientation were key to business success. This belief system was translated into a variety of practices, including the promotion to senior executive positions of sales people who spent much of their time in customer relations activity. It resulted in values which emphasized smooth relations (common to sales functions) and eschewed disagreement, supported loyalty and discouraged firing people. It resulted in an emphasis on growth in volume to the exclusion of sufficient concern for manufacturing efficiency. Thus top management created policies and made decisions which favoured new product development projects over cost reduction and the development of manufacturing technology. Predictably, manufacturing people were not valued and did not generally rise to the top. Not surprisingly, most key executives had the same image. They dressed extremely well and had excellent interpersonal and verbal skills. They spent most of their time outside the company and little in managing it internally.

This pattern of values and beliefs prevailed over a period of fifteen to twenty years while the corporation grew significantly in size. But market shares declined by 20 per cent, and profitability dropped significantly, because the business environment, which increasingly was becoming more cost competitive, rewarded low cost and efficient producers.

Thus culture represents the organization's cumulative learning, as reflected in many promotion, reward, and structural decisions, which tends to perpetuate beliefs and behaviour, sometimes beyond the point where they are functional and when there are clear signals from the environment that change is needed. It is this phenomenon that caused Blake and Mouton (1969) to coin the term 'culture drag'.

It is important to note that large and complex organizations do not typically exhibit single homogeneous belief systems or patterns of behaviour. That is, there may be more than one culture in an organization. For one thing, there are the differences between the formal culture, which consists of idealized statements of what beliefs and behaviour *should be*, and the informal culture, which consists of *actual* beliefs and behaviour (Margulies and Raia, 1978). There are also likely to be different cultures in various functional groups in the organization, such as R&D or manufacturing, as there are likely to be differences between blue-collar, white-collar, and management levels. That is, whenever the task requirements have resulted in a unique combination of people, structures, and behaviour the confluence of these forces will create a unique culture.

In addition, the larger organization, of which these subgroups are a part, may also have a culture that is distinguishable from other large systems. Sometimes, as in the example above, the culture of the larger systems is influenced by one group which has gained power and influence. In any case even large and relatively heterogeneous corporations, such as IBM or ITT, are known to have unique cultures. The functionality of a strong culture for a large corporation will depend on the heterogeneity of its market environment and people.

Culture as a mechanism for socialization   The discussion above points to the desirability of thinking about organizations as *social learning systems* where certain beliefs and behaviours are acquired, maintained, eliminated, or avoided (Margulies & Raia, 1978). It is commonly recognized that the shared values and beliefs that constitute culture are transmitted to new members through a process of *socialization*. That is, individuals change and modify their behaviour as a consequence of membership in an organization. There are several mechanisms by which organizational culture is transmitted over time. Margulies and Raia (1978) list the following:

(1) *Reinforcement* Learning theorists (Hilgard and Bower, 1966) have long pointed to the importance of rewards in shaping behaviour. Behaviour that is so reinforced is likely to be continued. Organizations provide many desired outcomes which can reinforce behaviour. Among these are money, promotion, intrinsic satisfaction, recognition, and peer approval. Indeed, the structures, people, and organizational process and behaviour in the organization are the mechanisms of reinforcement that, as stated earlier, determine culture.

(2) *Social modelling* Much learning in organizations occurs from imitating the behaviour of high-status individuals. As in other forms of social learning, organizational members can be expected to adopt behaviours and values of others when they see these leading to valued outcomes (Bandura and Walters, 1963). Thus key managers may be expected to have an important influence on beliefs and behaviours.

(3) *Social interaction and influence* The direct interaction of high-status social models (managers, experienced hands) with organizational members through mechanisms such as performance appraisal, coaching, and meetings of various kinds is an important socializing process. The interaction provides the means for social reinforcement of behaviours consistent with the culture.

(4) *Selection and training* While selection systems and training are examples of structures which provide reinforcements for culturally consistent behaviour, these mechanisms are sufficiently important to receive separate mention. Selection of new people and replacement of employees who do not conform to cultural values is an obvious means by which culture is maintained. To this must be added self-selection in and out of an organization, as people learn that they can and cannot receive desired outcomes. Training programmes also act to transmit cultural

values. They often signal what is expected and what will be reinforced. They also teach desired behaviour.

Culture and organizational change If organizational culture has such a profound effect on behaviour, then the management of change requires an understanding of organizations as social learning systems. Indeed, OD is unique as a change strategy in that it explicitly recognizes change as a 'normative reeducative' process (Bennis, Benne, and Chin, 1961). That is, behavioural change cannot occur without an explicit effort to reeducate people to adopt new values and norms. In most organizational changes, such explicit account of culture is not taken. Changes may be announced with little planning for changing the socialization mechanisms described in the previous sections. If these mechanisms do work to support the change, it is often by accident.

To avoid culture drag, change agents must explicitly plan reinforcements (incentive systems, performance appraisal systems and measurements, and control systems), social modelling (leadership by example), social interactions (communication about change, coaching, performance appraisal interviews, the development of group norms), and selection and training interventions (replacement of key people and educational programmes) to support new behaviours.

Unfortunately, the adoption of supportive mechanisms depends on a proper diagnosis of present ones, which does not always occur. To confront the culture explicitly can be threatening to managers as they recognize their own values in the process. Also managers may shy away from planned changes in these mechanisms on the false assumption that to plan change is somehow unethical or wrong. There is no question that such planned changes in socialization mechanisms constitutes planned manipulations. However, these mechanisms are a fact of organizational life and affect behaviour anyway, often guided by the unconscious motives of managers towards behavioural ends about which they are not clear and to which they would be opposed if they were. Thus cultures sometimes develop that demand conformity, dishonesty, distortion of communication, and other behaviours that have negative effects on organizational effectiveness and quality of work life. Recent revelations about corporate political contributions and payoff practices in foreign countries indicate how culture that is not explicitly examined and shaped can reinforce unethical behaviour.

The natural evolution of organizations is accompanied by changes in culture. Thus organization development requires planned changes in culture and periodic assessments of progress in shifting value and belief systems of the organization. Beer (1971) has argued that a major indicator that an organizational change has 'taken' and indeed may have some permanence is what he calls 'climate emergence'. This is the point at which people inside the organization begin to characterize the organization in new terms and become aware that a change has occurred. It is the point at which people with traditional values (those from other parts of the larger system) coming into the organization feel upset and lost in their first few months in the new culture, or the point at which those with long tenure who cannot adapt leave the organization. The following example illustrates this phenomenon:

A plant of a large company changed over a period of several years the structure of jobs and the way decisions were made. Workers were given more responsibility for the total job; supervisors' roles changed and the plant's management adopted a more participative management style. The change effort spanned a period of several years. By the end of three years, new people coming into the organization reported feeling lost and uncertain about how to manage. They exhibited hostility towards the plant's management whom they characterized as weak and indecisive. They viewed the plant as out of control. They felt, at least until they had been in the plant for several months, at odds with the 'management philosophy' of the plant. Similarly, a number of individuals sought to leave the plant, feeling that the plant was not being managed well.

The importance of viewing organizations from a cultural perspective cannot be overemphasized. It is not sufficient to see only structures, process, behaviour, and environment. While each of these is important in its own right, complete understanding of an organization cannot occur without the holistic perspective that the concept of culture provides. For this reason organizational diagnosis and change require that managers and change agents find ways to visualize culture and verbalize it. It is important that events during the process of change, such as the ones described in the example above, be used to gain an understanding of how culture is changing and where it is evolving.

To date there are few good measures of culture, and so its assessment must be primarily clinical in nature. In forming these judgements, important sources of data are the reaction of people coming into an organization and of those leaving, as well as who is promoted and what is rewarded. Perhaps the skills required to assess culture are best summarized by an applied behavioural scientist who has studied organizational climate and has attempted to measure it by questionnaires: 'the best way I know how to assess culture is to put up my antenna'.

The influence of the dominant coalition

The dominant coalition is *a group of key decision makers whose influence on the system is greatest* (Miles and Snow, 1978; Kotter, 1978). As we saw in the example of the sales dominated company described in the previous section, this group has an enormous influence on all components of the social system and therefore on its culture. Thus, the fit between their values and beliefs and the culture required by the organization to be effective becomes an important question in any organizational diagnosis.

The job experiences, skills, cognitive orientation, personality, and values of these key people predispose them to perceive certain aspects of their environment and not others, and thus to define the environment and the organization's strategy in a way that is consistent with who they are as individuals, with their own self-concepts. Similarly, they are likely to model and reinforce behaviour consistent with their own self-concept just as they are likely to select and promote people like themselves. The tendency for people to selectively perceive the environment according to their own motives and to reinforce behaviour and values consistent with their own have been amply documented in social psychological literature.

All of this suggests that one cannot understand a social system without knowing who the dominant coalition is (they may not always be the obvious people in the organization chart), what their background and experience has been, and what their personality and values are like. The importance of the dominant coalition also suggests that any major attempt to help organizations to adapt to changes in people and environment must include helping the dominant coalition to understand how their own predispositions and behaviours have shaped the social system in functional or dysfunctional ways.

Major organizational transitions invariably involve some fairly profound self-examination and change by the dominant coalition or it involves their replacement. One of the more important roles for external organization development consultants is to help the dominant coalition through this process. The board of directors can play an important role in stimulating this process or, for that matter, becoming directly involved in it provided they are able to be objective in their assessment of the organization's needs and the dominant coalition's characteristics.

The social system model and organizational improvement

The social system model presented in Figure 1 has been reproduced in Figure 2 with all of the dimensions listed in the previous sections included. The full model provides a useful framework for collecting data and systematically examining the causes for poor organizational performance and quality of work life outcomes.

The model does not specify explicit linkages between various dimensions, partly because of the large number and partly because of the circular cause and effect relationships between them. Also, we simply do not fully understand the relationship between all these dimensions and are unable to specify all the circumstances that moderate these relationships. Nevertheless, this model and others like it can be used by managers or change agents as a tool in *open system planning* (Beckhard and Harris, 1977).

Open system planning is a process by which managers distance themselves from their organization and systematically examine the relationship between their organization and its environment. Following a definition of the environment and their strategy in it, managers can specify the demands of the environment and its implications for the kind of human outputs, people, structures, culture, organizational process and behaviour required. By comparing the actual state of

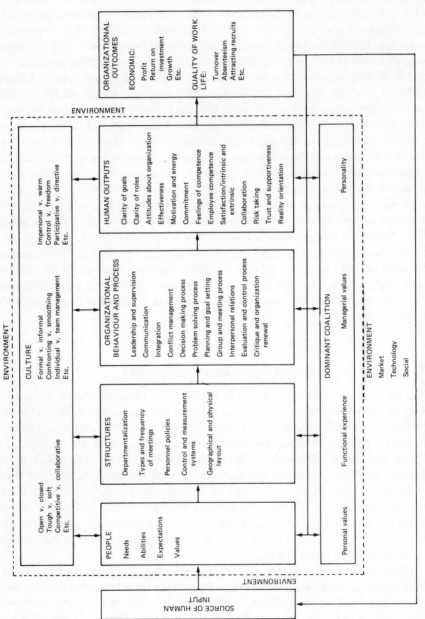

Figure 2   A social systems model of organizations

the social system with the required state, a plan for organizational improvement can be developed. A consultant's diagnosis can follow the same pattern.

For example, an organization operating in a highly turbulent market environment in which the highest priority is on new product development will have to develop a willingness to take risks with new ideas and with collaboration between functional groups. If these human outputs are assessed (through data collection and diagnosis) to be lower than desired, a strategy will have to be developed for changing the social system of the organization.

Due to the interdependence of the many components and dimensions of a social system, managers contemplating permanent improvements in the human outputs of collaboration and risk taking will have to plan multiple changes in the social system. To identify the dimensions in each social system component needing change, an assessment of each and its potential affect on risk taking and collaboration will have to be performed. Then action plans for making changes in certain components and dimensions must be developed.

Two examples of how managers have used the model to improve their organization may be helpful in understanding how a social system model can aid in organizational improvement efforts.

(1) A plant manager and his staff were presented with the model at an off-site meeting. With the model posted on the wall, they diagnosed an employee turnover problem the plant was experiencing. They agreed that concern for job security (human output) was causing turnover. They discovered to their surprise that the recent introduction of a management by objective (MBO) system and training programme (structures) were probably causing the insecurity. The MBO system had been introduced during a time when the plant was experiencing a slowdown in business (environment). Better and more structured measurement of performance at a time when everyone was having difficulty meeting performance goals was causing the insecurity and the turnover.

(2) The top management team of a $100 million company commissioned an internal OD consultant to assess organizational effectiveness. He developed a questionnaire which asked salaried employees to rate the extent to which they perceived problems in each dimension of the model and to provide illustrative examples. An analysis of the questionnaires was performed and six dimensions of the model were identified which were rated as presenting the most problems. In a feedback meeting to management, the consultant presented findings and his diagnosis of the cause and effect linkages between these problem dimensions. The top management group appointed six task forces to investigate these problem areas in more depth and to recommend changes in management practice and organization which might alleviate them.

The process of diagnosis and open system planning using a model such as the one presented in Figure 2 can have a number of important affects on the *dominant coalition* undergoing such an experience:

(1) They become aware of the complexity and dynamics of social systems and the multiplicity of 'levers' to be pulled in order to create change.

(2) They can gain an appreciation of the time and energy that will have to be

invested to create needed changes. This will be particularly evident as they target dimensions of the organization for change and develop action plans to support change goals.

(3) They will be clearer on the outcomes to be achieved by an organizational improvement effort and the tradeoffs between alternative strategies. For example, if changes needed to increase collaboration and risk taking require more change and upheaval than is acceptable to them, they will be forced to confront the alternative of changing their strategy to compete in less dynamic parts of the market where collaboration and risk taking are not required. A system framework helps force informed choices about what the organization should be.

(4) They may become more aware of how their own predispositions have affected the social system. This awareness will be sharpened if they openly acknowledge that they are an important influence and accept data about the effects of their influence.

It is generally accepted that it can be several years before a decline in human outputs, such as motivation, satisfaction or innovation, is followed by a decline in profits or an increase in employee turnover (Likert, 1967). The larger, more complex, and financially or technically endowed the organization is, the longer this time lag is likely to be. For this reason some organizations make routine assessments of organizational health using some kind of a social system model as a framework. Since large numbers of employees are often involved, questionnaires are used as in the example above. But interviews and various group meetings can also be used. IBM, one of the largest companies employing a routine assessment of its social system, surveys 250 000 employees a year (Dunnington, 1978).

Assessing system level functioning

Inherent in a systems view of organizations is a contingent view of management. That is, the right organizational design, the qualities of the right person, or the right management style *depends* on the desired outcomes for the social system and the characteristics of the various interdependent parts of the system. This means, of course, that managers must decide (with influence from other stakeholders) what outcomes they want from the organization and only then, together with the assessment of the current situation, will the appropriate way to organize and manage emerge.

This contingent view of organizations makes it difficult to assess the effectiveness of a given managerial approach or social system. Any number of fit combinations between the various components of the social system may be equally good depending on the outcomes desired. Leaving the question of the manager's own values and inclinations aside for the moment, a systems approach means that the manager is put in the unhappy situation of having to make frequent assessments about how to manage. The fit or systems perspective takes away the easier route of looking to management principles as guides for whether the organization is being managed right. It makes earlier sound choices about organizational design and management style obsolete as organization strategy, people, or environment change.

Nevertheless, the concept of fit does allow the use of broader *meta-criteria* which can be useful in determining whether a social system is functioning well over a longer period of time (5 to 25 years). These criteria are (1) *efficiency*,[4] (2) *effectiveness*, and (3) *health*. No specific organizational outcomes such as profitability or satisfaction are implied by these criteria. Rather, these are systems-level criteria which allow an assessment of the extent to which the organization has adapted to internal and external changes and the extent to which it has the capacity to adapt and cope with future internal and external changes.

Efficiency

This criterion may be defined as 'the extent of fit between and among the internal components of the social system'. The more congruity exists between these components, the more the organization will function smoothly with relatively little dissatisfaction on the part of members with the organization. That is, there is likely to be relatively little interpersonal or intergroup conflict between various constituencies, such as supervisors and subordinates or union and management. Furthermore, individuals are likely to view the organization as meeting their expectations and are likely to be motivated and committed to the organization. To the extent that motivation and commitment affect individual and organizational performance – that is, there are no overriding outside influences – these will also be high.

Thus in an efficient organization, relatively little energy would have to be spent in social maintenance activities to keep people happy and to keep them from leaving or unionizing. Quality of work life outcomes such as turnover, grievances, or absenteeism would be positive (low).[5]

Effectiveness

Effectiveness may be defined as 'the extent of fit between the organization's environment and all the internal components of the social system'. The more congruity exists between the internal social system components and the environment, the more the organization is likely to exchange favourably with its environment. That is, organizational performance indicators, such as customer or client satisfaction, profitability, market share or growth in volume, are likely to be positive (high). Furthermore, people in the organization are likely to feel a greater sense of competence as they experience task accomplishment and success from their efforts.[6]

Recent research by Miles and Snow (1978) indicates that the most rapid and effective organizational adjustments, ones that result in the least losses in organizational effectiveness, were ones which were preceded by appropriate changes in structure and process. That is, it was not sufficient for an organization to change its strategy by developing a new product/marketing thrust and/or by developing new technology to produce the new product or service. Unless they translated this trust into a new conceptualization of organizational structures and management process and implemented these new structures and processes early, financial loses and ultimate failure in the new strategy (ineffectiveness) were likely to result.

Organizational health

As we said, an adaptive organization is one which can sense problems resulting from a lack of congruence between various social systems components, respond to this information with changes, yet continue to test reality for changes that might be required in the future. Thus organizational health, the third meta-level criterion for assessing the state of a social system, may be defined as 'the capacity of an organization to engage in on-going self-examination aimed at identifying incongruities between social systems components and to develop plans for change in strategy (environment), structure, process, people, culture, and the dominant coalition responsive to data obtained in the process of self-examination'. Such a healthy organization is likely to maintain organizational efficiency and effectiveness in the long term.

In recent research, Miles and Snow (1978) studied the adaptive process of a large number of companies in four industries and concluded that organizational adaptation is a function of some more or less active process of examination and change. They call this process the *strategic choice* approach (Child, 1972). They argue that neither *natural selection*, a more or less chance process by which social components develop or do not develop congruity, nor *rational selection*, a completely conscious process of developing congruity, are at work.

Rather, the strategic choice view of organizational adaptation argues that organizational structure is only partly determined by environmental conditions beyond the control of managers, and that top-level decision makers (the dominant coalition), who are typically in a position to know what is going on in the environment, make continual choices about structure and process when necessary. In addition the dominant coalition attempts to manipulate the environment itself in order to bring it into alignment with the organization. For example, recently companies in the electronics industry in the USA successfully influenced legislation and public policy on Japanese imports which were cutting into their business.

The cumulation of many decisions about strategy, structure, process, people, and culture results in a strategic choice about how the organization will adapt. However conscious this process may be, it is often imperfect. The factors that prevent an organization from adapting to its environment and their implications for organizational health are:

(1) *Delegation by top management* Top management may become too involved in day-to-day operations to appreciate or understand the longer-range needs of their organization (Chandler, 1962). This suggests that a healthy organization is one in which decisions are delegated to the lowest level consistent with knowledge, information, and competence (Beckhard, 1969), thus freeing the top to take a longer-range view.

(2) *Valid data and diagnosis* There may be limited valid data available about the environment or internal organizational problems. Limited data about the environment may be a function of environmental uncertainty and complexity, but it may also be a function of the ambitions of those who prepare data and recommendations for key decision makers. Similarly, the backgrounds and experience of the dominant coalition may cause them to diagnose data to fit their own predispositions. In both cases, personal motivation may distort the data gathering and interpreting processes. Finally, top management may not have valid data about internal organizational problems. Information about these problems is often distorted on the way up or never gets there at all.

This suggests that a healthy organization is one which has a competent environmental sensing function (market research, technological assessment) and an on-going process for collecting data about internal functioning. Not only must these processes be on-going but they must provide valid data.

(3) *Top managers' adaptability* Chandler (1962) has argued that needed organizational changes may not occur if they threaten management's personal position, power, or psychological security (Miles and Snow, 1978). A culture that stresses collaboration rather than competition will probably reduce these threats. Similarly, managers who have a broad range of competence and see career options outside their organization or current career track are less likely to feel threatened by new strategic choices.

This suggests that healthy organizations will have an on-going process of performance evaluation and career development in which managers are given valid data about themselves to increase the range of their managerial skills and values. Cross-functional and divisional transfers as well as management education are used by healthy organizations to accomplish this. Such organizations also actively assess performance and potential, promoting the most adaptive managers and replacing those who cannot adapt.

(4) *The management of change* One of the factors that frequently prevents adaptation is the ineffective management of change. Resistance develops because people are inadequately involved or committed. This occurs because the implications of the change for people have not been fully understood by management.

This suggests that managers in a healthy organization have a good conceptual understanding of how to manage change, have the personal skills required to do so, and know or have available to them up-to-date methods for managing change.

The characteristics of a healthy organization listed above have not yet been fully documented by research, but the known barriers to adaptation clearly point to them. In addition, OD practitioners entering inefficient or ineffective organizations often find that barriers to the exchange of valid information, insufficient delegation, or limits in the adaptiveness of key managers are barriers that have prevented adaptation. Indeed, the emergence of the field of OD itself is some evidence that the process of collecting valid data and acting on the social systems in accordance with a diagnosis is needed by organizations to maintain efficiency and effectiveness in a rapidly changing environment.

Relationships between criteria

An organization may or may not be high on all of these system-level performance criteria at any one time. For example, an organization can be very efficient if it has people with low needs for responsibility managed with a highly directive management style. There would be little frustration or dissatisfaction. But the organization would not necessarily be effective. This would depend on the demands of its environment. In a rapidly changing market environment the organization would be ineffective, but in a more stable environment it would be quite effective.

On the other hand, an organization that has introduced a matrix structure to deal with a dynamic environment would be quite effective but, until behaviour and other practices become consistent with the structure, it would be inefficient.[7] Either of these organizations could be unhealthy if an on-going process of self-examination is not institutionalized.

An organization could be efficient and effective but not healthy if it has historically operated in a stable environment. Such an organization could be subject to a major upset should society, people or its business change rapidly and unexpectedly. This would be so because the hierarchical structures, directive management practices, dependent people, and closed culture typically found in an efficient and effective operation in a stable environment do not foster, indeed discourage, the processes we have said are needed for an organization to be healthy.

In such an environment managers will find that they have sufficient information and knowledge to make most of the decisions and thus, unlike managers in more uncertain environments, will *not* be forced to learn how to delegate decisions to lower levels. Similarly, such organizations are not likely to be employing young knowledge workers (Drucker, 1969) who are likely to demand more responsibility for decisions and more open communication. There are simply no pressures for such organizations to develop the dimensions enjoyed by a healthy organization.

Perhaps the best example of this dilemma is the steel industry. Recent foreign competition has shown steel companies in the USA to be both ineffective and unhealthy. It is clear that in recent years they have not examined their situation and acted to improve their capacity to compete. Thus while they have been efficient and, until recently, more or less effective, they have not been capable of self-renewal.

The apparent contradiction between organizational arrangements that seem to exist and work in stable environments and the managerial processes needed for adaptation present a dilemma for organizations in such environments. Can they or should they develop the characteristics of a healthy organization while still retaining the more hierarchical and top-down approach that seems to work in stable environments? Indeed, can they develop such characteristics without undermining the efficiency of their routine operations? New organizational forms, such as collateral or parallel organizations in which (Zand, 1974; Carlson, undated) overlay structures are developed for sensing, planning, and renewal activities, may provide the solution to this dilemma. We may also find that more participative approaches to management typically found in organizations which operate in dynamic environments may be applicable, in somewhat different form, to organizations in more stable environments (Miles and Snow, 1978; Blake and Mouton, 1978).

It is highly unlikely that the reverse condition, a healthy but inefficient and ineffective organization, is likely to exist for very long. The renewal processes in a healthy organization would stimulate efforts by management to make changes needed to align the various social systems components with each other and with the environment, thus achieving efficiency and effectiveness fairly rapidly.

The systems perspective and OD values

The field of organization development has historically been associated with a number of humanistic, optimistic, and developmental assumptions and values (French and Bell, 1978). For example:

(1) organizations should provide personal growth and development for people;
(2) organizations should encourage openness and collaboration;
(3) organizations should encourage the expression of feelings.

Inherent in these and other normative positions about what organizations should be like are implicit assumptions and values about what organizational outcomes are desirable. The social system perspective, on the other hand, holds that congruity is the only criterion by which organizations can be judged and that there are many organizational arrangements that can result in congruity.

What structures, processes, and culture an organization develops will depend on what people and strategy the organization chooses and vice versa. Of course, implicit in these strategic choices about the way an organization ought to adapt are values. The social systems perspective of organization development assumes that managers and other stakeholders, not OD practitioners or OD theory, need to decide about personal and organizational outcomes (value judgements). Thus organization development is a process of clarifying these choices based on a diagnosis of the current state of fit between social system components and the outcomes to be expected with alternative strategic choices.

Organization development theory need not and should not take a normative position about how organizations ought to function. This suggests that a development effort may take an organization in a direction opposite to traditionally stated OD values so long as the outcomes of such an effort have been clarified. Whether a change agent wants to help an organization move in such a direction is a matter of personal values and choice.

The reader will recognize a certain similarity between some of the OD values (openness, collaboration, etc.) and what were described earlier in this chapter as the probable characteristics of healthy or adaptive organizations. This is not surprising, since many OD practitioners implicitly assume that an organization should be adaptive and that this is a desirable outcome for all organizations.

It is likely that as the rate of change in the environment accelerates, organizations will need and want to become more adaptive. It can be argued, however, that this too is a strategic choice for which costs and benefits can be assessed. For example, should a management that expects to operate in a stable environment for the foreseeable future invest in developing an adaptive organization? This would depend, of course, on the costs of doing so, the importance they attach to survival, the resources the organization has to invest in this process, and their managerial values.

Organization development cannot specify what management should do, but it can help to clarify the choices. If this is done, it is much more likely that decisions to invest in organization development will be made with more commitment and will result in longer-term organization development efforts.

Given this social system perspective, the only values that need to be associated with organization development are those of informed choice. That is:

(1) organization development must help organizations to generate valid data about the state of the organization in relation to its environment;
(2) organization development must help organizational stake holders to clarify desired outcomes;
(3) organization development must help organizations to make strategic choices based on a diagnosis of the current state and desired outcomes.

This is not to say, of course, that change agents do not or should not have values. They clearly do. It does say that change agents or consultants should be clear and open about their values. Only then can they be helpful to organizations in making informed choices.

Notes

1. This chapter is taken with only slight modification from a recently published book by Michael Beer entitled *Organization Change and Development: A Systems View*. Santa Monica, Calif.: Goodyear Publishing, 1980.

2. The writer is indebted to the management of Corning Glass Works for providing an environment which allowed the development of OD and this conceptual framework. Thanks are also due to numerous members of Corning's OD department. In particular I would like to acknowledge the contribution of Dr Alan Hundert.
3. The differential impact of organization environment on required human outputs is nicely illustrated by two cases – Higgins Equipment Co. (B), and Empire Glass (B) – in Lawrence, P., Barnes, L., and Lorsch, J. (eds.), *Organizational Behavior and Administration*. Homewood, Ill.: Irwin, 1976.
4. The concepts of efficiency and effectiveness were first formulated by Chester Barnard (1938).
5. There is substantial research evidence to support this general proposition. Specifically research suggests that satisfaction, motivation, individual performance and/or organizational performance are highest when reward systems are consistent with the needs and expectations of employees (Porter and Lawler, 1968), job design is consistent with the needs of employees (Hackman and Lawler, 1971; Hackman, 1977), organization structure is consistent with the needs of employees (Morse and Lorsch, 1970), performance evaluation procedures are consistent with organizational values (Miner, 1968), supervisor style fits subordinate needs (Vroom, 1960), and there is fit between the individual and the climate of the organization (Schneider, 1972).
6. Evidence for this proposition comes from research which suggests that when organizational structure, culture, and/or process are consistent with the environment and task organizational performance is higher than when they are not consistent with the environment and task (Miles and Snow, 1978; Lawrence and Lorsch, 1967; Woodward, 1967; Burns and Stalker, 1961; Schneider *et al.*, undated). The research of Morse and Lorsch (1970) suggests that when organization structure and management process fit the task unit performance and people's feelings of personal competence are higher than when there is a poor fit between these components. For example, a poorly performing R&D laboratory was structured and managed quite similarly to a high-performing plant, but quite differently from a high-performing R&D laboratory.
7. Matrix structures are structures in which people within different functions are joined by horizontal structures such as programme teams or business teams. They work for two bosses, a functional manager and programme or business manager.

Bibliography

Argyris, C. (1962) *Interpersonal Competence and Organizational Effectiveness.* Homewood, Ill.: Dorsey.

Bandura, A., and Walters, R. H. (1963) *Social Learning and Personality Development.* New York: Holt.

Barnard, C. I. (1938) *The Functions of the Executive.* Cambridge, Mass.: Harvard University Press.

Beckhard, R. (1969) *Organization Development: Strategies and Models.* Reading, Mass.: Addison-Wesley.

Beckhard, R., and Harris, R. T. (1977) *Organizational Transitions: Managing Complex Change.* Reading, Mass.: Addison-Wesley.

Beer, Michael (1971) Organizational climate: A viewpoint from the change agent, in B. Schneider, *Organizational Climate* a symposium at American Psychological Association Convention, Washington, DC.

Beer, Michael (1976) The technology of organization development. In M. D. Dunnette (ed.) *Handbook of Industrial and Organizational Psychology*. Chicago: Rand McNally.

Beer, Michael (1980) *Organization Change and Development: A Systems View*. Santa Monica, Calif.: Goodyear.

Beer, Michael, and Huse, E. F. (1972) A systems approach to organization development. *Journal of Applied Behavioral Science*, **8** (1), 79–101.

Bennis, W. G., Benne, K. D., and Chin, R. (1961) *The Planning of Change*. New York: Holt, Rinehart & Winston.

Blake, R. R., and Mouton, J. S. (1964) *The Managerial Grid*. Houston, Texas: Gulf.

Blake, R. R., and Mouton, J. S. (1969) *Building a Dynamic Corporation through GRID Organization Development*. Reading, Mass.: Addison-Wesley.

Blake, R. R., and Mouton, J. S. (1978) *The New Managerial Grid*. Houston, Texas: Gulf.

Bray, D. W., Campbell, R. J., and Grant, D. L. (1974) *Formative Years in Business, A Long Term AT & T Study of Managerial Lives*. New York: Wiley.

Burns, T. and Stalker, G. M. (1961) *The Management of Innovation*. London: Tavistock.

Carlson, H. (undated) Central Foundry Division parallel business planning organization, Unpublished paper. General Motors Corporation.

Chandler, A. (1962) *Strategy and Structure*. Cambridge, Mass.: MIT Press.

Child, John (1972) Organizational structure, environment, and performance – The role of strategic choice, *Sociology*, **6**, 1–22.

Davis, L. E. (1966) The design of jobs. *Industrial Relations*, **6**, 21–45.

Drucker, P. F. (1969) *The Age of Discontinuity*. New York: Harper & Row.

Dunnington, Richard (1978) Personal communication.

Dyer, W. G. (1977) *Team Building: Issues and Alternatives*. Reading, Mass.: Addison-Wesley.

Fiedler, F. E. (1967) *A Theory of Leadership Effectiveness*. New York: McGraw-Hill.

French, W. L., and Bell, C. H. (1978) *Organization Development: Behavioral Science Interventions for Organization Improvement*. Englewood Cliffs, NJ: Prentice-Hall.

Friedlander, F. (1967) The impact of organizational training laboratories upon the effectiveness and interaction of ongoing work groups, *Personnel Psychology*, **20**, 289–307.

Friedlander, F. (1971) Congruence in organization development. *Academy of Management Proceedings*, Atlanta, G., 15–18 August.

Galbraith, J. (1973) *Designing Complex Organizations*. Reading, Mass.: Addison-Wesley.

Gyllenhammer, P. G. (1977) *People at Work*. Reading, Mass.: Addison-Wesley.

Hackman, J. R. (1976) Group influence on individuals in organizations. In M. D. Dunnette (ed.) *Handbook of Industrial and Organizational Psychology*. Chicago: Rand McNally.

Hackman, J. R. (1977) Work design. In R. J. Hackman and L. J. Suttle, *Improving Life at Work: Behavioral Science Approaches to Organizational Change*. Santa Monica, Calif.: Goodyear.

Hackman, J. R. and Lawler, E. E. (1971) Employee reactions to job characteristics. *Journal of Applied Psychology*, **55**, 259–286.

Halpin, A. W., and Croft, D. B. (1963) The organizational climate of schools. *Administrators' Notebook*, **11**, 4 pages.

Hamner, C. W., and Smith, F. J. (1978) Work attitudes as predictors of unionization activity. *Journal of Applied Psychology*, **63** (4), 415–421.

Harrison, R. (1972) Understanding your organization's character. *Harvard Business Review*, May–June.

Hilgard, E. R., and Bower, G. H. (1966) *Theories of Learning* (3rd ed.). New York: Appleton-Century-Crofts.

House, R. J. (1971) A path goal theory of leader effectiveness. *Administrative Science Quarterly*, **2**, 321–339.

Huse, E. F. (1975) *Organization Development and Change*. St Paul, Minn.: West Publishing.

James, L. R., Hartman, E. A., Stebbins, M. W., and Jones, A. P. (1977) Relationships between psychological climate and VIE model for work motivation. *Personnel Psychology*, **30** (2), 229–254.

Kast, F. S., and Rosenzweig, J. E. (1970) *Organization and Management: A Systems Approach*. New York: McGraw-Hill.

Katz, D., and Kahn, R. (1978) *The Social Psychology of Organizations*. New York: Wiley.

Kotter, J. P. (1973) The psychological contract: Managing the joining-up process. *California Management Review*, **15** (3), 91–99.

Kotter, J. P. (1978) *Organizational Dynamics: Diagnosis and Intervention*. Reading, Mass.: Addison-Wesley.

Lawler, E. E. (1971) *Pay and Organizational Effectiveness, A Psychological View*. New York: McGraw-Hill.

Lawler, E. E. (1973) *Motivation in Work Organizations*. Monterey, Calif.: Brooks/Cole.

Lawler, E. E. (1977) Reward systems. In R. J. Hackman and L. J. Suttle, *Improving Life at Work: Behavioral Science Approaches to Organizational Change*. Santa Monica, Calif.: Goodyear.

Lawler, E. E., and Rhode, J. G. (1976) *Information and Control in Organizations*. Santa Monica, Calif.: Goodyear.

Lawrence, P. L., and Lorsch, J. W. (1967) *Organization and Environment*. Division of Research, Graduate School of Business Administration, Harvard University, Boston, Mass.

Lawrence, P. L., and Lorsch, J. W. (1969) *Developing Organizations: Diagnosis and Actions*. Reading, Mass.: Addison-Wesley.

Leavitt, H. J. (1965) Applied organizational change in industry: Structural, technological and humanistic approaches. In J. G. March (ed.) *Handbook of Organizations*. Chicago: Rand McNally.

Litwin, G. H., and Stringer, R. A., jun. (1968) *Motivation and Organizational Climate*. Graduate School of Business Administration, Harvard University, Boston, Mass.

Likert, R. (1967) *The Human Organization*. New York: McGraw-Hill.

Lorsch, J. W. (1975) A note on organization design. Graduate School of Business Administration, Havard University, Boston, Mass.

McClelland, D. C. (1965) Toward a theory of motive acquisition. *American Psychologist*, **20**, 321–333.

McClelland, D. C., and Winter, D. G. (1969) *Motivating Economic Achievement*. New York: Free Press.

McGregor, D. (1960) *The Human Side of Enterprise*. New York: McGraw-Hill.

McGregor, D. (1967) *The Professional Manager*. New York: McGraw-Hill.

March, J. G., and Simon, H. A. (1958) *Organizations*. New York: Wiley.

Margulies, N., and Raia, A. P. (1978) *Conceptual Foundations of Organizational Development*. New York: McGraw-Hill.

Maslow, A. H. (1954) *Motivation and Personality*. New York: Harper.

Miles, R. E., and Snow C. (1978) *Organization Strategy Structure and Process*. New York: McGraw-Hill.

Miner, J. B. (1968) Bridging the gulf in organizational performance. *Harvard Business Review*, July/August.

Mirvis, P. H., and Lawler, E. E. (1977) Measuring the financial impact of employee attitudes. *Journal of Applied Psychology*, **62** (1), 1–8.

Morse, J. J., and Lorsch, J. W. (1970) Beyond Theory Y. *Harvard Business Review*, **48** (3), 61–68.

Murray, H. A. (1938) *Exploration in Personality*. New York: Oxford University Press.

Porter, L. W., and Lawler, E. E. (1968) *Managerial Attitudes and Performance*. Homewood, Ill.: Irwin-Dorsey.

Porter, L. W., Lawler, E. E., and Hackman, R. J. (1975) *Behavior in Organizations*. New York: McGraw-Hill.

Roethlisberger, F. J., and Dickson, W. J. (1939) *Management and the Worker: An Account of a Research Program Conducted by Western Electric Company, Hawthorne Works, Cambridge*. Cambridge, Mass.: Harvard University Press.

Schein, E. H. (1970) *Organizational Psychology* (2nd ed.). Englewood Cliffs, NJ: Prentice-Hall.

Schneider, B. (1972) Organizational climate: individual preferences and organizational realities. *Journal of Applied Psychology*, **56**, 211–217.

Schneider, B. (1976) *Staffing Organizations*. Santa Monica, Calif.: Goodyear.

Schneider, B., and Bartlett, C. J. (1968) Individual differences and organizaational climate: I. The research plan and questionnaire development. *Personnel Psychology*, **21**, 323–333.

Schneider, B., Parkington, J. J., and Buxton, V. E. (undated) The climate for service in banks: A study in organizational climate, Mimeographed report. College Park Maryland, University of Maryland.

Starbuck, W. H. (1976) Organizations and their environments. In M. D. Dunnette (ed.) *Handbook of Industrial and Organizational Psychology*. Chicago: Rand McNally, 1069–1124.

Steele, F., and Jenks, S. (1977) *The Feel of the Work Place: Understanding and Improving Organization Climate*. Reading, Mass.: Addison-Wesley.

Stogdill, R. M. (1959) *Individual Behavior and Group Achievement*. New York: Oxford University Press.

Tagiuri, R., and Litwin, G. H. (1968) *Organizational Climate: Explorations of a Concept*. Graduate School of Business Administration, Harvard University, Boston, Mass.

Thomas, R. R. (1974) Managing the psychological contract. Graduate School of Business Administration, Harvard University, Boston, Mass.

Thompson, J. D. (1967) *Organizations in Action*. New York: McGraw-Hill.

Trist, E. E., Higgins, G. W., Murray, H., and Pollock, A. B. (1963) *Organizational Choice*. London: Tavistock.

Turner, A. N., and Lawrence, P. R. (1965) *Industrial Jobs and the Worker*. Graduate School of Business Administration, Harvard University, Boston, Mass.

Vroom, V. H. (1960) *Some Personality Determinants of the Effects of Participation*. Englewood Cliffs, NJ: Prentice-Hall.

Vroom, V. H. (1964) *Work and Motivation*. New York: Wiley.

Vroom, V. H., and Yetton, P. W. (1973) *Leadership and Decision Making*. Pittsburgh, Pa.: University of Pittsburgh Press.

Wakeley, J. H., Frost, C. F., and Ruh, R. H. (1974) *The Scanlon Plan for Organization Development: Identity, Participation and Equity*. East Lansing, Mich.: Michigan State University Press.

Walton, R. E., and Dutton, J. M. (1969) The Management of Interdepartmental Conflict: A Model and Review. *Administrative Science Quarterly*, **14**, 522–542.

Weick, K. (1973) 'Systems Theory and Organizational Research', a symposium, Eastern Academy of Management, Philadelphia, Pa.

Whyte, W. F. (1955) *Money and Motivation*. New York: Harper.

Woodward, J. (1967) *Industrial Organization: Theory and Practice*. London: Oxford University Press.

Zand, D. (1974) Collateral organizations: A new change strategy. *Journal of Applied Behavioral Science*, **10** (1).

Systems Theory for Organization Development
Edited by T. G. Cummings
© 1980 John Wiley & Sons Ltd.

Chapter 6

A Social Network Perspective for Organization Development

Noel Tichy

Introduction

Organization development (OD) has a limited future unless a more comprehensive model of organizations and hence of managed change is adopted. In the opinion of this author, contemporary OD is limited for two major reasons: (1) practitioners tend not to focus attention on some of the major organizational leverage points for change, such as strategy and organization design; and (2) practitioners tend to over-rely on change strategies which are normative to the exclusion of political and rational strategies.

Below is a list of change problems which are increasingly demanding attention:

(1) *External interface* As the environment becomes more complex and turbulent, the task of identifying and predicting pressures becomes more difficult. The development of new environmental scanning and information processing capabilities is often required.

(2) *Mission* In times of relative environmental stability and surplus resources, it is possible for organizations to function quite effectively with nebulous, shifting goals and priorities. As the economic, political, and social pressures mount, so does the need for clear statements of organizational mission to guide the organization in strategic decisions.

(3) *Strategy* This requires the development of a strategic plan with operational objectives at many levels in the organization. Installing such a plan requires a set of management techniques and processes.

(4) *Managing organizational mission/strategy processes* As planning and decision making become more complex it will be necessary to develop more sophisticated processes which realistically engage the relevant interest groups.

(5) *Task* A shift in strategy may entail the introduction of new tasks and technologies to the organization. This requirement may result in the introduction of new professionals into the organization, or the training and development of existing staff.

(6) *Prescribed networks* Adjustments are required in the networks of communication and authority to deal with new tasks and/or technologies. The introduction of a new task requires management to plan or prescribe the necessary network of communication, who talks to whom about what, as well as who reports to whom.

(7) *Organizational process–communication, problem solving, and decision-making* Increasingly post-industrial organizations have multiple managerial/professional splits, matrix splits, etc. Therefore, clear lines of decision making authority become blurred, making it imperative that managers understand and utilize consensual decision making approaches as well as conflict bargaining procedures.

(8) *People* Any organizational change entails altering individual behaviour. Thus, an explicit focus on motivating people becomes part of the managed change process.

(9) *Emergent networks* A major part of an organizational change process is to manage the informal communication and influence networks which exist throughout the organization. Coalitions and cliques in these networks can facilitate or hinder the change effort and thus need explicit attention.

Where does OD stand on these points?

OD has traditionally emphasized the last three of these problems. This is reflected in the OD literature on diagnosis and intervention (Huse, 1975; Friedlander, 1976; Bowers, 1973; French and Bell, 1977; Beckhard and Harris, 1977). The result is that, often, OD ends up tinkering at the non-critical margins of organizations rather than working with strategic levers for change. For example, many OD practitioners talk about implementing and trying to operate effectively matrix structures. This is done, however, after a strategic decision was made at the top of the organization to go with a matrix structure. Yet the critical matter is to help top management to determine whether its total structure is appropriate to the organization's strategy rather than to implement a matrix. This is an arena in which few OD practitioners are currently equipped to operate. Other examples of OD's characteristic follow-up, 'keep the gears greased' role are: helping with the introduction of new pay systems rather than designing them; helping to plan for a new plant opening rather than helping to decide whether to open such a plant or not; working on interdepartmental conflicts rather than examining overall departmental structures. If OD is to become more viable and useful in dealing with strategic management problems, it must broaden its concern to other strategic organizational components.

In addition to focusing on a limited set of change levers, OD has limited itself in the use of change strategies. The field has yet to address Bennis's challenge (1969) of a decade ago:

Organization development practitioners rely exclusively on two sources of influence: truth and love. Somehow the hope prevails that man is reasonable and caring, and that valid data, coupled with an environment of trust (and love) will bring about the desired change. . . . Organization Development seems most appropriate under conditions of trust, truth, love and collaboration . . . there seems to be a fundamental deficiency in models of change associated with organization development. It systematically avoids the problem of power, or the politics of change . . . unless models can be developed that include the dimensions of power conflict in addition to truth-love, organization development will find fewer and narrower institutional avenues to its influence. And in so doing, it will slowly and successfully decay. (pp. 77–78).

The need for new models

This chapter proposes means to broaden the role of OD to be concerned with all types of planned change in complex work organizations. The chapter builds on the notion that three dominant traditions have guided thinking about organizations and the practice of change and that these traditions should be brought together in order to provide managers of change with the requisite set of strategies and tools.

One tradition views organizations and change from a rational-economic or technical perspective and prescribes change strategies based on empiricism and enlightened self-interests. As Arygris and Schon (1978) point out: 'The viewpoint is instrumental and rational . . . the focus is upon the acquisition and application of knowledge useful for effective performance of organization tasks, and the organizational world is conceived as fundamentally knowable through scientific method. . . .' (p. 323)

The second tradition views organizations as political entities which can only be changed by the exercise of power by the dominant group over those with less power or by bargaining among powerful groups.

The third tradition views organizations as cultural systems of values with shared symbols, shared cognitive schemes which tie people together and form a common organizational culture. Change comes about by altering the norms and cognitive schemes of the members of the organization.

Practising managers, students of organizations, and change theorists tend to think in terms of only one of the above traditions to the exclusion of others (Tichy, 1974; Bennis, 1969). The result of such unidimensional thinking often leads to unanticipated negative consequences.

Management scientists and production engineers frequently view work and organization design as essentially a technical engineering problem. This can lead to problems. An example of the dysfunctional consequences of such an over-reliance on this perspective was the General Motors Lordstown, Ohio, plant built to produce Vegas. The plant was billed by GM as the most modern engineered and technically efficient motor car assembly plant in the world. The actual performance, however, fell below the expectations of management, the production engineers, and plant designers. There was high absenteeism, low-quality control, productivity was below target, and eventually there was a wild cat strike. My analysis of the events at Lordstown – where the workers in 1972 struck because they were rebelling against the 'system', unchallenging tasks, and speed-up attempts by management – concludes that psychological and sociological factors were ignored in the design. The plant was not congruent with the normative culture of the young workers who did not fit the purely rational view of the production engineers. The GM Lordstown experience can be contrasted with the new Volvo production plant built in Kalmar, Sweden, at about the same time. The Volvo plant was built with a strong normative cultural orientation as well as a strong technical perspective (Tichy, 1976).

A purely political orientation to organizational life and change is also likely to be dysfunctional. It can lead to low levels of trust, cynicism, and a view that all interactions are win/lose bargaining situations. Many large public agencies, such as the Department of Health, Education, and Welfare (HEW) are dominated by this orientation. For example, at HEW it would not be unusual for internal programme staff to cynically bargain 'save the hungry children in Appalachia programmes' for 'inner city adolescent programmes'. In the bargaining the substance of the programmes would be irrelevant to the power brokering of who controls how much of what budgets. The dysfunction is that the potential for cooperative links is greatly reduced. The goal is to win, to keep your budget and staff as big as possible. The ultimate goals of the organization are lost in the day-to-day political brokering.

Cultural orientations can also be overdone as has occurred with some OD enthusiasts. As pointed out earlier in the quote from Bennis (1969), OD's reliance on truth, love, and collaboration avoids the problem of power and the politics of change. Many OD practitioners' overreliance on a normative orientation has limited their use of a wider range of rational change approaches, especially those derived from the organization design and management fields (Tichy, 1978).

This tendency to subscribe to one dominant mode of change strategy is assumed to be a major reason for the current view among many researchers and managers that we know little about how to manage change. We in fact know quite a bit if we can break down the barriers between these traditions and promote integration.

An example of a more complex integrated view of organizations is Zaleznik's (1970):

Whatever else organizations may be, problem solving instruments, sociotechnical systems, reward systems and so on, they are political structures. This means that organizations operate by distributing authority and setting the stage for the exercise of power. . . .

Organizations provide a power base for individuals. From a purely economic standpoint, organizations exist to create surplus of income over costs by meeting needs in the market-place. But organizations are also political structures which provide platforms for expressions of individual interests and motives. The development of careers, particularly at high managerial and professional levels depends on the accumulation of power as the vehicle for transforming individual interests into activities which influence other people. (p. 48)

In addition to the political and technical view there is the cultural view. Organizations exist to perpetuate values and ideologies. They are normative vehicles for reinforcing certain value orientations. Thus, an integrated view of organizations includes all three perspectives.

The usefulness of this integration will be to increase the competence of those faced with the difficult task of managing change. Through the use of a mix of the above orientations to develop change strategies (the orientations are summarized in Table 1), managers of change can more effectively deal with such tradeoffs or extremes as balancing the advantages and disadvantages of explicit strategic plans against simply muddling through; being excessively flexible in organization design as against being too rigid; attending to quality of output *v.* attending to quantity of output; investing in the growth and development of people *v.* investing in system development; encouraging conformity of behaviour *v.* dissent. Managing change involves making technical, political, and cultural decisions about desired new organization states, weighting the tradeoffs and then acting on them.

Figure 1 depicts the process of managed change. Change is triggered by a threat and/or opportunity which is of sufficient magnitude so that organizational

Table 1   Three perspectives on organizations

1. *Technical assumptions:* 'An organization is the rational coordination of the activities of a number of people for the achievement of some common explicit purpose or goal, through division of labor and function, and through a hierarchy of authority and responsibility'. (Schein, 1970). These assumptions have guided the work of Lawrence and Lorsch (1967); Thompson (1967); Galbraith (1977); Kwandwalla (1977); and Nadler and Tushman (1978), all of whom have contributed to a contingency, information processing approach to organization design. That is, the design at the organization is effective to the extent that its information processing capacity matches the level of uncertainty facing the organization.

2. *Political economy assumptions:* organizations are 'coalitions with ill-defined and inconsistent preferences ... with the critical questions not how well are we doing? but to whom and for whom are we doing it? Governance, control and political processes are related to issues of structure' (Pfeffer, 1977, p. 8). Cyert and March (1963) developed this view initially. Pfeffer (1977) argues that 'coalition participants must receive inducements from belonging greater than the contributions they are required to make. Coalition members, then, are continually calculating whether they might fare better if they altered their participation. In addition to the allocation of resources, policies and policy commitments are important, and they are the objectives of bargaining as well' (p. 5).

3. *Cultural system assumptions:* organizations are held together by people's beliefs in a set of norms which make up the organization's culture. Organizational and individual effectiveness is enhanced when the organization ensures 'a maximum probability that in all interactions and in all relationships within the organization, each member, in the light of his background, values, desires, and expectations will view the experience as supportive and one which builds and maintains his/her sense of personal worth and importance' (Likert, 1961). OD is concerned with a normative orientation to organizations which leads to prescriptions for change.

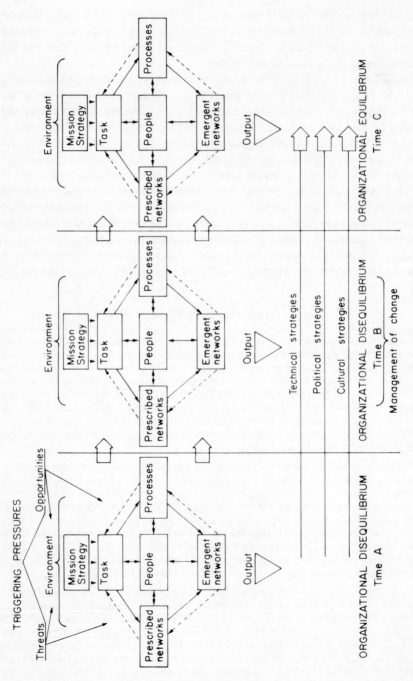

Figure 1   Strategic change management

members cannot ignore it. This occurs at time A. This is followed by the organization entering a time of disequilibrium at time B. Time B is the period during which change towards some new desired state occurs. This view of the change process derives from Beckhart and Harris's (1977) transition-management approach.

The purpose of this chapter is to show how the management of change can be guided through the disequilibrium phase, time B, towards a new equilibrium at time point C.

Figure 1 indicates three strategies which can concurrently move an organization towards a new equilibrium. As mentioned previously, each of these strategies is grounded in a theoretical orientation to organizations. Successful change must rely on the ability to channel and guide all three strategies. This means that at times the change manager will be a political builder of coalitions, a power broker and manipulator of influence. At other times he/she will be solving problems technically, relying on 'scientific' data and principles. At other times, he/she will be facilitating the development of new attitudes, beliefs, and norms about openness, honesty, and trust. Or he/she may be doing all three simultaneously. Therein lies the paradox, and the need for the OD professional to adapt a new organization and change model.

The model

The use of an organizational model to guide organization development action has been a basic cornerstone of the field with the rallying slogan being Kurt Lewin's 'there is nothing so practical as a good theory'. Thus, there is no need for an argument for the use of a model, rather for the use of a more comprehensive and adequate model. The criteria for such a model are:

(1) that the model integrate political, technical, and cultural orientations to organizations;
(2) that the model lead to pragmatic diagnostic questions;
(3) that the model lead to intervention strategies and technologies in the political, technical, and cultural areas.

The social network view

The model developed here is largely based on a social network perspective on organizations. The network model views a social system as composed of social objects (people, groups, organizations) joined by a variety of relationships. All pairs of objects are not directly joined, and others are joined by multiple relationships. Network analysis is concerned with the patterning of these relationships and seeks to identify both their causes and consequences (Tichy *et al.*, 1979).

Organizations are conceived of as clusters of people joined by a variety of links which transmit goods and services, information, influence, and affect. These clusters of people are both formal (prescribed), such as departments and work groups, and informal (emergent), such as coalitions and cliques. Prescribed networks are typically represented in organization charts. Clear distinctions are made here between prescribed and emergent networks to emphasize the point that within organizations there exist a multiplicity of social structures which arise out of many possible types of social relationships. Only a portion of the organization structure is prescribed. Thus, unplanned structures and behaviour patterns will always emerge.

These emergent structures and behaviour patterns have been misleadingly labelled the 'informal organization', and often assumed to be something undesirable. They are neutral and take on desirable or undesirable characteristics, depending on how they are managed.

This chapter briefly overviews the network perspective and presents a set of network concepts and measures which are applicable to organizational diagnosis and improvement strategies. Figure 2 is presented to convey some of the salient features of a network approach to organizations:

(1) The traditional formal organization chart is still in evidence as one of the networks in the organization.

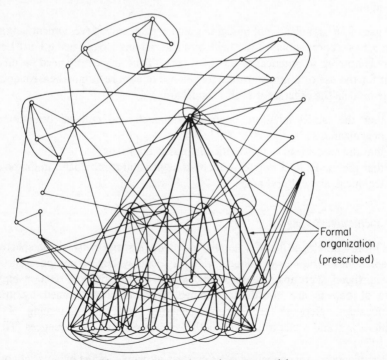

Formal
organization
(prescribed)

Figure 2   Network contingency model

(2) The organization is embedded in larger social networks with individuals having varying boundary spanning links to the external environment.

(3) Influence, information, and affect are each potential modes of exchange between nodes (individuals). Thus, lines in Figure 2 can be further specified to identify the transactional content (affect, influence, information).

(4) Clusters within the network are identified by who is linked to whom (clique members, for example, are all directly linked to each other via affect links).

(5) The links in Figure 2 represent a simplification of the actual number found in most organizational settings. Thus, there is clear need for concepts and methods for summarizing important aspects of networks.

Network analysis facilitates the integration of the three orientations to organizations and change by highlighting the explicit analysis of what flows through the networks – influence, information, and/or affect. With a model such as that figuratively portrayed in Figure 2, it becomes relatively easy to analyse chains of influence by finding out who influences whom. Also, a network analysis identifies coalitions and can help foster the analysis of how they operate through the identification of subgroups which have come together to exert influence.

A technical approach to organizations, such as the contingency and information processing organization design orientation (Galbraith, 1977; Nadler and Tushman, 1978), is also very compatible with the network perspective. The prescribed networks can be adjusted to match the level of task and environmental uncertainty with the appropriate level of information processing capacity. Finally, the cultural processes in organizations can also be analysed using a network approach; this is because values and beliefs are built into a social fabric via interactions among people. The network perspective specifically focuses on such interactions.

Network perspective is not new

The network perspective is not new. Its origins derive from three schools of thought:

(1) Structural-functional theory (Merton, 1968; Parsons, 1956) focuses on the underlying determinants of recurring social relations. This approach forces the analyst to consider both formal and informal aspects of organizations.

(2) Exchange theory (Blau, 1964; Ekeh, 1974) deals with the content of the relationships joining individuals: under what conditions will bonds exist between social actors, and what will the evolution of these bonds be over time (Homans, 1961; Blau and Scott, 1962).

(3) Role theory (Katz and Kahn, 1966) defines organizations as role systems; it views organizations as 'fish nets' of interrelated offices. While role systems imply network concepts, the literature on role analysis has been limited to first-order, zone role sets (that is, people directly linked to a focal role) rather than more extensive sets (networks of people) (Kahn *et al.*, 1964; Gross *et al.*, 1958).

Table 2   Network properties

Property	*Explanation*
A. Transactional content	Four types of exchange:
	(a) expression of affect
	(b) influence attempt,
	(c) exchange of information,
	(d) exchange of goods and services.
B. Nature of the links	
1. Intensity	The strength of the relation between individuals.
2. Reciprocity	The degree to which a relation is commonly perceived and agreed upon by all parties to the relation (i.e. the degree of symmetry).
3. Clarity of expectations	The degree to which every pair of individuals has clearly defined expectations about each other's behaviour in the relation.
4. Multiplexity	The degree to which pairs of individuals are linked by multiple relations.
C. Structural characteristics	
1. Size	The number of individuals participating in the network.
2. Density (connectedness)	The number of actual links in the network as a ratio of the number of possible links.
3. Clustering	The number of dense regions in the network.
4. Openness	The number of external links of a social unit as a ratio of the number of possible external links.
5. Stability	The degree to which a network pattern changes over time.
6. Reachability	The average number of links between any two individuals in the network.
7. Centrality	The degree to which relations are guided by the formal hierarchy.
8. Star	The individual with the highest number of nominations.
9. Liaison	An individual who is not a member of a cluster but links two or more clusters.
10. Bridge	An individual who is a member of multiple clusters in the network (linking pin).
11. Gatekeeper	A star who also links the social unit with external domains.
12. Isolate	An individual who has uncoupled from the network.

Empirically, network analysis represents convergence of work from several fields. Using anthropological methods, Whyte (1955) and Chapple and Sayles (1961) were some of the earliest organizational researchers to systematically employ network concepts. Homans (1961) and Blau (1964) further developed exchange theory from a set of network studies. Leavitt (1951) and Bavelas (1951) used network ideas in their study of group structure, while the literature on voting behaviour (Katz and Lazersfeld, 1955) and the diffusion of innovations subsumed network concepts (Katz and Lazarsfeld, 1955; Coleman *et al.*, 1957; Rogers and Shoemaker, 1971). Finally, network approaches have had a long tradition in the community power studies (Dahl, 1961; Lauman and Pappi, 1975), rural anthropology (Mitchell, 1969), and in the R & D management literature (Allen, 1977). In short, while the interest in networks is clear, and methods exist, what has yet to emerge is a comprehensive organizational model based on network thinking.

Table 2 lists the elementary network terminology which will be used in this chapter. The intent is not to confuse readers with jargon but to familiarize them with a common set of tools for application. The major properties of networks are discussed more fully below.

Transactional content

Four types of relations can be distinguished in organizational contexts: (1) exchange of goods or services, (2) exchange of affect (liking, friendship), (3) exchange of influence (power), (4) exchange of information. As Kadushin (1978) points out, exchange theorists have systematically considered these aspects of network flow without explicitly using network terminology.

By recognizing each set of relations as a distinct network, we are able to investigate research questions relating multiple networks within the same organizations (prescribed and emergent of influence, affect, or information). We can examine the relationships between people by type of exchange and begin to address such issues as whether a relationship which exchanges both information and influence is a stronger tie than one with only one type of exchange.

Nature of the links

The links between pairs of individuals in the network can be analysed in terms of:

(1) Multiplexity Individuals have multiple statuses such as worker, husband, father, club member, community member. Multiplexity identifies the degree to which a pair of social objects is linked by multiple statuses. The more strands linking one person to another, the stronger the tie. The strength of a tie is also enhanced by the frequency of interaction and by the qualitative character of the tie, for instance, a kinship tie.

(2) Intensity of the link The intensity of a link is the strength of the tie as indicated by the degree to which individuals will honour obligations or incur personal costs by carrying out obligations (Mitchell, 1969). Intensity has been related to multiplexity, but often, as with kinship or ethnic linkage, uniplex relationships can represent intense ties.

Network structure

Structural characteristics can be divided into four levels of analysis:

(1) Extraorganizational networks Interorganizational networks, boundary spanning networks, etc.

(2) Total network structure The anatomy of the total organizational network.

(3) Clusters within networks These refer to the characteristics of the dense regions of the network, i.e. parts of the network where people are more closely linked to each other than they are to the rest of the network (Boissevain, 1974). There are various types of clusters in networks, e.g. formally prescribed work groups, emergent coalitions, and cliques (see Table 1). A coalition is a temporary alliance of distinct parties that generally forms to increase control over a task or social agent (Thibaut and Kelley, 1959). Cliques tend to form primarily for fulfilling affective needs but can also exchange information and task instrumental material (Tichy, 1973).

(4) Individual network characteristics The sociometric characteristics of individuals in the network. For example, sociometric stars are those who receive the most nominations; bridges are those who belong to multiple clusters and provide intercluster linkages through dual membership (Tushman, 1979).

Whatever the dimensions chosen, a network approach forces the analyst to look at the multiple and interrelated aspects of networks. This approach also forces the analyst to consider several levels of analysis simultaneously (e.g. network structure, cliques within the structure, and key nodes, i.e. individuals within the clique).

Organizational model

A complete conceptual framework which combines both social network perspective and the technical, political, and cultural aspects of an organization is presented in Figure 3. The model is built on the assumption that organizational effectiveness (output) is a function of the characteristics of each of the components as well as how the components interrelate or fit together within a system. Thus, descriptions of the components as well as the interrelationships between components are necessary for analysis. Table 3 briefly defines each of the components of the organizational model included in Figure 3.

Interrelationships among components

The model portrays organizations as more than a set of static parts or components. Organizations are systems which are in dynamic interplay with their

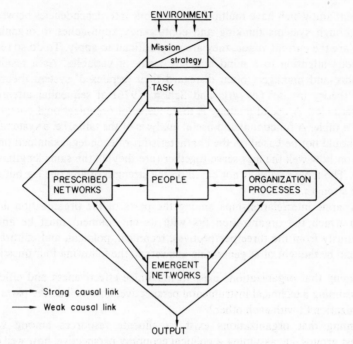

Figure 3   Organizational model

Table 3   Components of the model

Mission/strategy/objectives   This includes the organization's reason for being, its basic approach to carrying out its mission – its strategy and its criteria for effectiveness – objectives.

Task   This refers to the technology(s) by which the organization's work is accomplished.

Prescribed networks   This refers to the explicitly designed social structure of the organization. It includes the organization of subunits and communication and authority networks as well as structural mechanisms for integrating the organization.

People   This includes the members of the system, their personal characteristics, their managerial style, etc.

Organizational processes   These are the mechanisms (communication, decision making, conflict management) which enable the prescribed network to carry out the dynamics of work.

Emergent networks   These are the structures and processes which, while not planned or formally prescribed, inevitably emerge in the organization.

environment and which have multiple and dynamic interdependencies between the parts. Although systems thinking and contingency approaches to organization designing are the current vogue, they are very difficult to apply. To do so requires simultaneous attention to a mind boggling array of variables. As a result, OD practitioners and managers often disregard their 'espoused' system theory and follow a 'theory in use' (Arygris and Schon, 1976) of sequential attention to specific variables. A useful analogy is to conceive of organizational components as legs of a table. A functional and useful analysis of the table, i.e. a systems perspective, should not be based on the characteristics of each leg, examined one at a time, but on how well the legs serve together (are they all the same length, shape, size, etc.). The table's value is not based on the strength of any one leg but on the combined strength.

The dynamic interrelationships among the parts of the organization and the degree to which the organization fits with its environment must be analysed simultaneously from the three perspectives, technical, political, and cultural. The analysis can be thought of as generating answers to the following four questions:

(1) Assuming that organizations exist to maximize effectiveness and efficiency, i.e. assuming a technical-instrumental perspective, how well do the parts of the organization fit with each other?
(2) Assuming that organizations exist to allocate resources among various interest groups, i.e. assuming a political economy perspective, how well do the parts of the organization fit?
(3) Assuming that organizations exist to perpetuate and reinforce value/ideological systems, i.e. assuming a cultural perspective, how well do the parts fit?
(4) How congruent are the three perspectives – technical, political, and cultural – with each other?

Guidelines are presented for analysing each of the three types of fit as well as the relationship among the rational, political, and normative perspectives.

Technical fit

This analysis derives from the orientation that organizations are rational-instrumental tools driven towards effectiveness and efficiency. Figure 4 presents the basic outline for the technical fit analysis. The approach is drawn largely from Nadler and Tushman's (1978) information processing model of organization design. Organizations are viewed as mechanisms for processing information. The organization is effective to the extent that there is a match between the amount of uncertainty it faces and its capacity to process information for dealing with the uncertainty. The assumptions guiding the rational fit analysis are:
(1) Tasks vary in their degree of uncertainty; uncertainty is defined as the

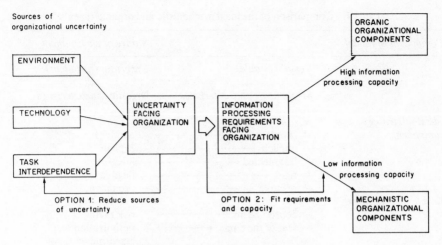

Figure 4   A model for technical fit

difference between information required to complete a task and information possessed. There are three major sources of uncertainty in organizations:

(a) *The nature of the environment* The more changing and complex the environment, the more uncertainty.

(b) *The nature of the tasks* The simple routine tasks such as manufacturing lead to very low levels of uncertainty, whereas the complex, non-routine tasks such as research and development lead to high levels of uncertainty.

(c) *The nature of the interdependence* The greater the interdependence among the tasks of an organization, the greater the uncertainty.

(2) As work related uncertainty increases (from any of the above three sources, or a combination of them) so does the need for increased amounts of information, and thus the need for increased information processing capability. For example, if the organization's environment suddenly becomes uncertain, pressures are set in motion which call for increased capacity to process information necessary to cope with and deal with such an environment. Often, this may result in such information processing approaches as marketing research departments, government affairs offices, etc.

(3) Different organizational configurations (networks, people, and processes) have varying capabilities to process information. As information processing requirements change, adjustments are called for in the components of the organization model. Table 4 presents characteristics of mechanistic organizations, those with low information processing capacity, and organic organizations, those with high information processing capacity. Note that there are variations in all of the organizational components.

(4) Organizations will be more effective and efficient from a rational instrumental

Table 4   Comparison of the ideal mechanistic and organic types

Component of model	Certain (stable) ↓ Mechanistic characteristics	Uncertain (turbulent) ↓ Organic characteristics
Nature of environment		
Mission/strategy component	– simple ⟵⟶	– complex
	– implicit ⟵⟶	– explicit
	– fragmented ⟵⟶	– integrated
	– rigid ⟵⟶	– flexible
	– reactive ⟵⟶	– proactive
People–management style	– conservatism ⟵⟶	– risk taking
	– seat of the pants ⟵⟶	– optimization of performance
	– formal authority ⟵⟶	– flexibility–situational expertise
	– power dominance ⟵⟶	– non-authoritarian
	– non-participative ⟵⟶	– participative
Socio-technical component	– simple integration mechanisms (rules and programmes, hierarchy, goal setting) ⟵⟶	– complex integration devices (vertical information system and lateral relations)
Organizational processes	– minimal communication ⟷	– open, minimal time lag, minimal distortion communication
	– conflict avoided, smoothed over or resolved by hierarchy ⟵⟶	– conflict confronted and managed openly
	– non-participative decision making ⟵⟶	– participative decision making
Emergent networks	– friendship, non-task related cliques ⟵⟶	– extensive task related networks and task coalitions

perspective when there is a match between the information processing requirements facing the organization and the information processing capacity of the organization's components. Too much capacity is as dysfunctional as too little. This is because high information processing capacity is costly and complex to manage.

(5) When there is a poor match between uncertainty and information processing capacity in the organization, there are two basic options to remedy the situation. Option 1 (see Figure 4) is to alter the uncertainty. This can be accomplished by

attempting to change the environment such as when organizations form cartels, attempt to lobby for protective legislation, or stop operating in uncertain markets. This option can also be carried out by changing the tasks of the organization or altering their interdependence. However, these are often not realistic alternatives and the organization must go to option 2 (see Figure 4) which is to adjust the fit between information processing requirements and the information processing capacity. This may entail altering many of the organizational components from the mechanistic end of the scale towards the organic end.

(6) Finally, there is a time dimension. Organizations never reach a static equilibrium, rather they reach a quasi state of equilibrium. As time passes there are changes in information processing demands. The organizational characteristics must evolve to match these new demands.

Political fit

This test of fit is based on a view of organizations as coalitions (March, 1962; Cyert and March, 1963) 'altering the purpose and domain to accommodate new interests, sloughing off parts of themselves to avoid some interests, and when necessary, being involved in activities far afield from their stated central purposes' (Pfeffer and Salancik, 1978, p. 24). The coalitional view of organizations implies that the behaviour of an organization is the outcome of a political bargaining process among individuals to see whose interests will dominate in the allocation of organizational resources. The organizational drive is for survival as contrasted with the technical-rational view which assumes that the drive is maximizing or at least optimizing effectiveness and effeciency. Survival, fed by growth, ensures that the organization can continue to provide for the allocation of resources to fulfil the interests of the dominant coalition(s). Survival and growth depend on an ongoing bargaining process among competing coalition interests both internal and external to the organization. There is a constant exchange going on among these interest groups in which individuals and groups are induced by money, prestige, and threats to contribute something to the organization's survival, such as labour, money, support, etc. The more dependent the organization is on the contribution of a member, the more power the individual (coalition) has over the allocation process (see Figure 5).

The political test of goodness of fit is similar to the technical test in that the objective is to reduce uncertainty. The difference, however, is that the uncertainty which is important is uncertainty regarding the power to allocate the resources and to decide on the organization's goals.

The assumptions guiding the political analysis of fit are:

(1) Organizations vary in their degree of political uncertainty, uncertainty being defined as the degree of stability and predictability with regard to the bargaining and exchange relations among interest groups over the allocation of resources, power, prestige, etc. Political uncertainty varies due to:

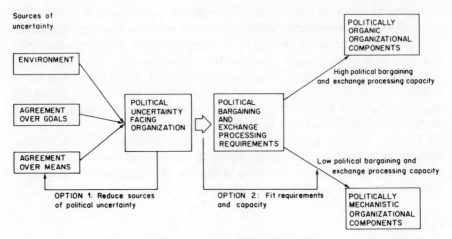

Figure 5   A model for political fit

(a) *The environment* The more changing and complex the environment, the more
    is political uncertainty likely to be found in the organization. For example, the
    Equal Employment Opportunity Commission's requirements and class action
    suits have created affirmative action uncertainty for organizations, as
    evidenced by General Electric's recent $32 million settlement. These environ-
    mental changes have altered the political position of personnel and human
    resource departments as well as the political position of women and
    minorities.
(b) *The degree of agreement over goals* Political uncertainty related to the level of
    goal agreement in the organization. Lack of goal consensus creates political
    uncertainty.
(c) *The degree of agreement over the means for achieving organizational goals*
    The less agreement there is over means, the more there is political uncertainty
    (Thompson and Tuden, 1956).

(2) As political uncertainty increases, so does the need for increased amounts of
political bargaining and exchange in order to manage the uncertainty. Hence,
there is an organizational requirement for increased bargaining and exchange
capacity to deal with the increased need.
(3) Different organizational configurations (networks, people, and processes) have
varying capabilities for facilitating bargaining and exchange processes. Table 5
contrasts the characteristics of organizations which have a low capacity for
facilitating political bargaining with those that have a high capacity. The
mechanistic/organic distinctions are used in much the same fashion as they were
for the technical fit analysis.
(4) Organizations will manage the political bargaining and exchange process and

Table 5   Politically mechanistic and organic forms of organization

Politically mechanistic

Power relations very formally prescribed.

Little capacity in the organization for managing shifts in power.

Examples: military organizations, the Catholic Church, family-owned business organizations.

Politically organic

Power relations both prescribed and emergent.

High capacity in the organization for shifting power bases (democratic mechanisms, etc.).

High capacity for managing on-going bargaining relationships (contracting mechanisms, conflict resolution mechanisms, etc.).

Rules guiding conflict and bargaining, such as:
The rules are known.
The rules are not perceived to be biased or against one's own interest.
Both parties adhere to the rules.
Violations are quickly known by significant others.
There is significant social approval for adherence and significant social disapproval for violations.
Adherence to the rules is rewarded and has been historically.
The intent is to reapply the use of rules in the future (Deutsch, 1973, pp. 379–380).

Examples: political parties, kibbutzim, democratically-managed labour unions, participationally-managed organizations.

be more effective from a political perspective to the extent that there is a match between the political bargaining and exchange requirements facing the organization and the political bargaining processing capacity of the organization's components.

(5) When there is a poor match between political uncertainty and bargaining and exchange processing capacity in the organization, there are two basic options to remedy the situation. Option 1 is to alter the uncertainty. This can be accomplished by attempting to change the environment, such as when organizations form political coalitions, use interlocking directorates to maintain control, etc. Or Option 1 can be exercised by developing goal consensus and/or means consensus. When these options are not feasible, then Option 2 must be followed which entails making adjustments in the fit between political bargaining needs and political bargaining processing capacity. This is done by making adjustments on the mechanistic organic scale for the organization as outlined in Table 5.

(6) Finally, as with the technical fit, there is a time dimension. As time passes there are changes in the political bargaining processing demands and the organization must make adjustments to meet these new demands.

Cultural fit

The cultural analysis perspective is based on a view of organizations as systems for perpetuating and reinforcing sets of values and norms. Norms are internalized rules or internalized structures which create regularities in behaviour. The culture is the organization's dominant set of beliefs and cognitions. Jay (1971) described the basic identity of the organization as its cultural tradition. Elements of the culture include the emergent network, shared concepts of appropriate behaviour, and kinds of information which are exchanged among organization members. Jay uses a term 'central faith' which he describes as follows:

Whereas the other elements take time to grow up, the central faith is there from the start. It is the belief at the root of the business, and I call it faith because it rests on a number of unproved assumptions: 'People want quality', 'If you can make a better mousetrap the world will beat a trail to your door', 'It's not the product that matters, it's how hard you sell it', 'If you want to stay in business, you've got to deliver on time'. All these expressions of commercial and industrial dogma spring from the central faith. . . . A good way to find the central faith of an organization is to get its members to see who can formulate the biggest blasphemy. . . . In the BBC: 'I admit it wasn't really true, but the Home Secretary was very keen we should say it.' In Rolls-Royce: 'It's a lousy bit of engineering but it will sell like hotcakes.' (pp. 182–183)

The culture channels perceptions and hence guides actions. As Weiland and Ullrich (1977) indicate: 'supportive behavior on the part of a superior may be interpreted as an indication of weakness in a power ridden work culture. Identical behaviour may be viewed as a sign of strength in an organization practicing Likert's System Four Management' (p. 260).

An organization and its components can be evaluated in terms of how congruent the value/cultural system is. Figure 6 portrays the basic outline for the

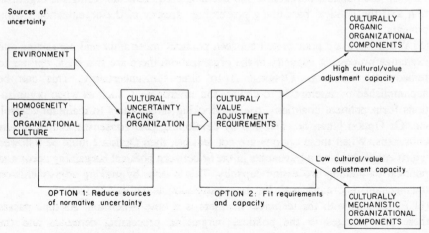

Figure 6   A model for cultural fit

cultural analysis of fit. First, the organization and the environmental value/cultural systems can be examined in terms of congruence. That is, does the organization have values similar or dissimilar to those of the wider community within which it operates? Second, the organization can be examined for the degree of homogeneity of value orientations among its members. Mixed ideologies and cultures within the same organization create uncertainty. This occurred in some organizations in the 1960s when there was widespread use of sensitivity training in organizations with a dominant culture that was power-oriented. There were often countercultures which grew up around some of the 'sensitized' managers which clashed with the older culture. Organizations are effective to the extent that value/cultural inconsistencies are matched with a capacity for making value adjustments among members.

The assumptions which guide the cultural analysis of fit are:

(1) Organizations vary in their degree of ideological congruence, congruence being defined as the degree of consistency among organizational members with regard to values and organizational culture. Congruence varies due to:

(a) *Environment* Cultural value shifts in the wider environment are reflected within the organization thus creating normative incongruence.

(b) *Diversity of backgrounds of employees* in the organization differ along such dimensions as ethnic background, education, professional identification, sex, and age, thus contributing to greater value/cultural incongruence.

(2) As organizational value/cultural incongruence increases, so does the need for increased amounts of cultural/value adjustment and hence the need for greater organizational capacity for dealing with cultural/value shifts.

(3) Different organizational configurations (networks, people, processes) have varying capabilities for facilitating cultural/value adjustments. Table 6 contrasts the components of an organization which have low cultural/value adjustment capacity with those which have a high capacity. The mechanistic *v.* organic distinctions are used for analysis of cultural fit as well.

(4) Organizations will manage the cultural/value adjustment process and be more effective from a normative perspective to the extent that there is a match between the cultural/value incongruencies facing the organization and the cultural/value adjustment capacity of the organization's components.

(5) When there is a poor match between cultural/value incongruence and the cultural/value adjustment capacity in the organization, there are two basic options for changing the situation. Option 1 is to change either the environment and the organization's relationship to the environment, or the diversity of people in the organization. This option is exercised when an organization develops selection criteria which lead to relatively homogeneous populations of workers. This can be found in a variety of industries ranging from publishing to investment banking where there are Jewish organizations, Protestant organizations, and Catholic organizations. Option 2 is to make adjustment in the fit between value/cultural

adjustment demands and the organization's value/cultural adjustment capacity. This entails making adjustment on the mechanistic to organic dimensions for the organizational compoents as outlined in Table 6.

(6) Finally, as with both the technical and political fits, there is a time dimension. Adjustments are required over time as new value/cultural incongruencies emerge.

Organizations generally have a dominant organizing perspective, that is, either technical, political, or cultural processes dominate. For example, in religious organizations cultural processes are dominant, whereas in a union or political party the political dominates; and in a business organization, the technical generally dominates. Identification of an organization's dominant focus is important for several reasons:

(1) What is explicitly presented as dominant may in fact not be dominant. For example, in July 1978, Henry Ford II fired Lido Anthony Iacocca, president of the Ford Motor Company. The dismissal was presented by Ford in technical terms, that is, to improve organizational effectiveness and efficiency. However, an examination of events leading up to the change indicate rather clearly that there were other more political processes involved. In April 1977, the Ford Motor Company created the office of the chief executive, Henry Ford II formed a three man office including Iacocca as president, Philip Caldwell as vice-chairman and himself as chairman with 'an extra vote'. A year and three months later he dismissed Mr. Iacocca after having expanded the office of the chief executive to include his younger brother, William Clay Ford.

No data have come to light indicating that Iacocca's performance was subpar, rather quite the contrary. However, there are data indicating that 'there were other

Table 6   Culturally mechanistic and organic forms of organization

---

Culturally mechanistic

Little capacity for incongruent values/ideologies.

People fear being vulnerable.

Relations are manipulative.

Defensive interpersonal relations.

Defensive norms – little helping, mistrust, lack of real risk taking, conformity, external commitment, power centred, competitive.

Culturally organic

High capacity for managing differences in values/ideologies.

People oriented towards facilitative/collaborative relations.

Minimally defensive interpersonal relations.

Learning-oriented norms – trust, individuality, open confrontation on difficult issues, risk taking, internal commitment.

---

signals of possible change, including manifestation of Ford's own sense of dynasty' (*Fortune*, 14 August 1978, p. 13). In 1976, after recovering from an angina attack, Ford said, 'I think the public wants, after I go, to see somebody called Ford somewhere right at the top of the company.' The change was therefore not in pursuit of organizational effectiveness and efficiency (technical strategy), but in pursuit of adjusting the power group, the dominant coalition, to ensure that the allocation of power and resources was acceptable to Henry Ford II and the 'family' (political strategy). The technical strategy was invoked after the political to justify the change publicly.

(2) Also, the dominant process can obfuscate the functioning of the other processes thus blinding manager(s) of change to other problems of fit. For example, if the dominant process is technical and the focus of attention is always on the rational solution to problems of how to make the organization more effective and efficient, it is likely that political processes will go undermanaged. This appears to have happened at Citibank in New York in their 'backroom' operations where they brought in a team of production managers from Ford Motor Company to turn the paper processing (cheques, etc.) into a factory operation. This was done very technically. The consequence is that some political time bombs were planted. The backroom transformation upset political balances and the traditional 'bankers' were angry with the impact the 'factory managers' were able to have on the organization; this resulted in internal power struggles, especially over the top management control of the bank. The political goodness of fit is now in need of readjustment at Citibank.

The central concern, however, is not just to achieve good fit with the dominant process, but to achieve fit among the three processes – technical, political, and cultural. The analyses should include all three and identify the one which is in most disequilibrium, and thus where the major readjustment is needed, keeping in mind that a change in any one area inevitably alters the others. The Ford Motor Company example shows that Henry Ford II's adjustment of the political fit, with seeming disregard for the expertise and experience required for effective top management functioning, resulted in a bad technical fit. Iacocca was an important component of the top management team. The political readjustment requires some technical readjustments as well.

Overall organization effectiveness

Effectiveness has been discussed in rational-instrumental terms throughout this chapter. At this point the definition will be broadened. It not only includes the organization's ability to adapt and survive. To this end, effectiveness is enhanced to the extent that there is goodness of fit in all three processes.

OD can benefit from these concepts in several ways. First, the social network perspective provides operational measures of influence, information, and affect flows as well as measures of coalitions and cliques. Second, the emphasis on simultaneous attention to technical, political, and cultural processes broadens the OD diagnostic focus as well as the repertoire of interventions.

Organization development and the social network perspective

In this section the organization model presented previously is discussed in the context of managed change. Expanding the basic model of organizations is critical because models focus attention and help to organize data into meaningful patterns. Thus, when coping with some of the problems listed at the beginning of this paper, the use of the model just presented should lead us to quite different change strategies than those traditionally associated with OD. Table 7 contrasts a traditional OD approach with that of a social network approach, both faced with the same environmental change problem. As can be noted, the diagnosis and the change strategies differ.

The object of introducing the social network perspective and applying it in

Table 7   A traditional *v.* social network OD approach

	Traditional	*Social network*
Objective	Develop a strategy for coping with changing environment including the reformulation of mission.	
Trigger event	Increased environmental uncertainty.	Increased environmental uncertainty.
Overall approach	Top management engage in open open systems planning to define the mission and map environmental pressures. Identify environmental pressures and project changes and develop organizational coping responses.	Identify who really influences the organization's missions. Identify self-interests for dominant coalitions regarding the mission(s) with focus on the extent of agreement. If high level of agreement, then follow traditional OD approach with the exception that all dominant coalition members be involved, not just top management. If disagreement, then develop political bargaining approach.
Implicit assumptions in two approaches	Top management equals the dominant coalition. The dominant coalition is committed to rationally maximizing effectiveness and efficiency. Change occurs through rational problem solving supported by norms of openness and honesty.	Top management does not necessarily equal dominant coalition. Dominant coalition has mixed motives, e.g. maintaining power bases, career aspirations, etc. Change occurs through a mix of political, rational, and normative processes. Sometimes norms of openness and honesty are facilitative.

Table 7 is not to bring Machiavellism into management one more time, but to inject a broader view of reality. It is possible and, in the opinion of this author, extremely desirable for the OD field to develop normative views of requisite organizations which foster quality of work life as well as effectiveness and efficiency. These views, however, should not be based on naïve assumptions about the nature of people and organizations which ignore power and politics. This chapter does not attempt to develop such a normative view, but one might read Elliott Jacques's *General Theory of Bureaucracy* (1976) for a solid attempt in this direction.

The discussion of the OD change process is divided into three phases: (1) the trigger for change, (2) the diagnostic phase, and (3) the strategy formation phase. OD interventions are also considered in respect of network theory.

Triggers for change

Organizations are constantly changing and evolving. These evolutionary, non-managed changes are important sources of organization flux. But the focus here is on the process of large-scale, strategic change which is reflected in an organization's attempt via decisions made by its leadership, those members who are able to control the allocation of resources and often referred to as the dominant coalition (March and Simon, 1958; Cyert and March, 1963; Thompson, 1967), to maintain control and deal with uncertainty.

The planned change process is started when problems, crises, or opportunities are recognized by means of a threshold phenomenon. 'From the plethora of data received by managers, certain unique kinds of information exceed a threshold of perception and galvanize strategic responses' (Weiland and Ullrich, 1977, p. 422).

Once the change process has been triggered by any combination of the above factors, it begins with an organizational diagnosis. Time pressures, resource limitations, and the nature of the triggering event all influence the form of the diagnosis, which can range from a quick, 'radar scan' diagnosis in which the components of the model and the fits are superficially examined to the other extreme in which a detailed, in-depth organizational assessment is carried out. The discussion of the diagnosis presented below aims to present guidelines for an in-depth assessment.

Organizational diagnosis using the social network model

At the core of a planned change process is an adequate diagnosis. An overall organizational diagnosis based on the social newtork model begins with an analysis of the organization's environment and an assessment of its history and its output. This is followed by an analysis of each of the organizational components. Table 8 summarizes some of the major diagnostic information sought for each organizational component, along with suggested methods for collecting the information.

Table 8   Diagnostic plan

I *Input*

Diagnostic focus	*Specific information sought*	*Method of data collection*
(a) History of organization	What were the critical events in the organization's history, are there identifiable phases of development?	Documents Interviews
	What is the service/product mix history of the organization? (sequence of development, relative success, and performance)	Documents Interviews
(b) Environment of organization	Who or what is the organization interdependent with for what (services, goods, information, influence)? (identify external network)	Documents Interviews
	How changing are elements in the environment? (economy, markets, competition, labour markets, etc.)	Interviews Documents
	When there is environmental change how predictable is it?	Interviews
(c) Organizational resources	What capital does the organization control?	Documents Interviews
	What is the state of the organization's technical capability?	Interviews Documents
	What are the overall people resources? (numbers, skills, etc.)	Documents

II *Mission/strategy analysis*

Questions	*Data collection methods*
(a) Mission	
(1) What is the formal view of the mission?	Documents Interviews
(2) How do members describe the mission?	Interviews
(3) How is the mission formulated? (who is involved, doing what, when)	Interviews
(b) Strategy	
(1) Is there a formal strategy? If so what is it?	Interviews Documents
(2) What do members perceive to be the strategy?	Interviews
(3) How is strategy arrived at? (who does what, when)	Interviews

Table 8   Continued

Questions	Data collection methods
(c) What are the perceived goals?	
(1) What are the goals as perceived by key staff?	Interviews
(d) Organizational process surrounding mission/strategy formation	
(1) Who are the key actors with regard to strategy formation: how do they work together to influence mission/strategy?	Interview Documents

III *Task analysis*

Questions	Data collection methods
(a) What are the basic tasks?	
(1) What are the core tasks?	Interviews Documents Job descriptions MBO documents, etc.
(2) Who performs what tasks?	Interviews Observation Documents

(3) What is the nature of the core tasks?
       – Expertise required
       – Standardization of tasks
       – Discretion of task performers
       – Task variability
	Interviews
	Documents

(b) How do the tasks interrelate?	
(1) Integration of core tasks. Who is interdependent with whom for what?	Interviews Observation

IV *Prescribed organization analysis*

Questions	Data collection method
(a) What is the overall configuration of the organization? *Differentiation*	

(1) How is the organization differentiated?
       – Vertical
       – Horizontal
       – Spatial
	Organization chart
	Documents
	Interviews

(2) What is the distribution of authority – over budgets, personnel, tasks?	Interviews Documents

Table 8   Continued

	Data collection
Questions	

(3) What are the characteristics of individual units?   Documents
      – # job titles   Interviews
      – # of tasks   Observation
      – Heterogeneity of people, skills
      – Interchangeability of roles

(b) What is the overall configuration of the organization? *Integration*

(1) Which simple integrating mechanisms are in use and how   Interviews
     effectively?   Documents
      – Rules/programmes
      – Hierarchy
      – Planning

(2) Which mid-level integrating mechanisms are in use and how   Interviews
     effectively?   Documents
      – Slack resources
      – Buffering
      – Self-contained units

(3) Which complex integrating mechanisms are in use?   Interviews
      – Vertical information systems   Documents
      – Liaison personnel
      – Task forces
      – Teams
      – Matrix structure

V *People analysis*

	Data collection
Questions	methods

(a) What are the demographic characteristics of the staff?

(1) Education and skill levels of staff?   Documents
     Questionnaire

(2) Personal characteristics – sex, age, etc.   Documents

(b) What are the managerial styles of key staff?

(1) How risk taking?   Interviews
     Observations

(2) How much use of professional management techniques?

(3) How participative?

(4) How open and flexible?

(c) What are the motivational forces driving various staff?

(1) How do staff perceive their own ability to control their   Interviews
     effectiveness?

Table 8 Continued

Questions	Data collection methods
(2) What outcomes do different staff value? (money, security, challenge, career, mobility, etc.)	Interviews
(3) What is the perceived match between what employees value and what they feel they get?	Interviews

VI *Organizational processes analysis*

Question	Data collection methods
(a) What are the characteristics of communication?	
(1) How open is communication and for what issues?	Interviews Observation
(2) Is there much distortion?	Interviews Observation
(3) What is the quantity and quality of communication relevant to task accomplishment?	Interviews Observation
(b) What are the characteristics of decision making?	
(1) Are there different modes of decision making for different issues? If so, what are they?	Interviews Observation
(2) What is the level of participation? (for what issues)	Interviews Observation
(3) Who actually makes what decisions?	Interviews
(c) What are the characteristics of control?	
(1) What are the basic information and control systems?	Interviews Documents
(2) What are the standards of control and how are they set?	Documents Interviews
(3) How are the standards monitored?	Documents Interviews
(4) When targets are not met, what happens, by whom, how timely?	Documents Interviews
(d) What are the characteristics of the way in which conflict is managed?	
(1) How is conflict handled?	Interviews (ask for critical incidents)
(2) What are the norms around conflict? (avoidance, confrontation, etc.)	Interviews Observation

Table 8   Continued

Questions	Data collection methods
VII *Emergent organization analysis*	
Questions	*Data collection method*
(a) What is the overall emergent organization?	
(1) Who shares information with whom? (types of information specified)	Interviews Observation
(2) Who influences whom around what issues?	Interviews Observation
(3) Who is friendly with whom?	Interviews Observation
(b) What are the coalitions which form?	
(1) Are there identifiable clusters of people who coordinate in order to exert influence? If so, around what issues?	Interviews Observation
(c) What are the cliques which exist?	
(1) Are there relatively durable small clusters of friends?	Interviews Observation
VIII *Output analysis*	
Questions	*Data collection methods*
(a) What is the degree of goal optimization?	
(1) Are they applying their limited resources towards the attainment of its goals or are there 'unfunded' goals and 'funded' non-goals?	*Interviews Documents (analysis by budget)*
(2) Is there a clear relationship between the amount of resources the organization spends on the various goals and the importance of the goals?	*Interviews Documents*
(3) What kind of return on investment are they getting on its resources? (return on staff time, etc.)	*Interviews Documents*
(4) Are all parts working towards at least one of the organizational goals?	*Interviews Documents*
(5) Are goals adjusted with environmental changes?	*Interviews*
(b) What are the behavioural impacts of the organization?	
(1) How satisfied are staff with their work, each other, their careers, pay, etc.?	*Interviews*

The analysis of history, environment, and output sets the stage for the remainder of the assessment. Essentially one wants to have a clear sense of how well the organization is doing in its particular environment and how it got to the state it is currently in.

The analysis of the components is carried out in a sequential fashion. Each component is described in terms of the dimensions identified in Table 8.

As noted in Table 8, there are diagnostic questions appearing in most of the components which are social network questions. Such questions have been largely absent from OD diagnostic approaches (French and Bell, 1977; Huse, 1975; Kotter, 1978).

The organizational diagnosis proposed in Table 8 can be applied at several levels of analysis in the organization. It can apply to the total organization, to divisions and/or departments of the organization. It is important, however, to specify in advance the unit of analysis and then consistently apply the diagnosis at that level.

Once data have been collected for each component in Table 8, a diagnostic summary is written for each component. These are brief summary statements of the characteristics of the component.

The next step in the diagnosis is to make an analysis of fits among the components of the model. This is carried out by taking one perspective at a time – e.g. technical, political, or cultural – and examining the relationships among components for congruence. For the technical perspective, the information processing logic is used to see if the component's information processing capacity matches the information processing requirements. For the political perspective, the political bargaining logic prevails, in which the match between political uncertainty and political bargaining capacity is examined. For the cultural perspective, the value/cultural congruence model is used. The analysis focuses on the degree of value/cultural congruence and the appropriate match with value/cultural adjustment capacity. Table 9 presents a matrix for summarizing the goodness-of-fit for each perspective.

The final step in diagnosis is the comparison of fits between the three processes. The question is asked: What is the overall fit between the technical processes in this organization and the political processes? Similar comparative questions are asked regarding technical and cultural processes and political and cultural processes. This final level of diagnosis keeps the OD practitioner aware of the point that adjustments in one area will undoubtedly result in adjustments in the other two areas.

Developing a change strategy

The diagnostic approach just presented helps us to discover what adjustments are needed. The change strategy which follows consists of two parts: (1) an image of the organization in 'good fit', that is, a desired state; and (2) a plan for moving the

Table 9   Analysis of fits

Components	Technical goodness of fit: information processing → effectiveness and efficiency	Political goodness of fit: uncertainty → allocation of resources	Cultural goodness of fit: congruence → ideology
Environment/ mission-strategy			
Mission-strategy/ task			
Mission-strategy/ prescribed networks			
Mission-strategy/ organization processes			
Mission-strategy/ people			
Mission-strategy/ emergent networks			
Prescribed networks/ people			
Prescribed networks/ organizational processes			
Prescribed networks/ emergent networks			
Organizational processes/ emergent networks			
Organizational processes/ people			
Emergent networks/ people			

organization from its current state to the desired state, a transition management plan (Beckhard and Harris, 1977). The purpose of the change strategy is to achieve a state of better fit in the organization than the current state of disequilibrium which is caused by a trigger event. The desired state image consists of the organizational components being in technical, political, and cultural fit. Thus, in the case of Henry Ford II, it includes achieving goodness of technical fit in the new management team without Iacocca; or in the Citibank case where there is technical goodness of fit, making adjustments in the political area. In another organization it might include making changes in the prescribed networks so that they are better able to integrate complex interdependent tasks, such as when a matrix structure is introduced. In both of these cases, the emphasis is on what the desired state should be, not on how to get the organization to the desired state.

The desired states are developed from the analysis of fits. Each of the Figures 4, 5, and 6, which outlined the goodness of fit logic for the three perspectives, identified two options for obtaining goodness of fit. In developing a change strategy, both options should be carefully considered. For example, an organization in which disequilibrium is triggered by a new government regulation might attempt to restore 'fit' by Option 1 – alter the environment through lobbying and changing the law – rather than through Option 2 where the internal information processing capacity is changed. Similarly, an organization faced with cultural incongruence due to a change in employment practices, which resulted in an influx of a large number of young workers with values at odds with an older workforce, might use Option 1 by reverting to the old employment practice and selecting only value congruent workers. Option 2 in this case might include the use of sensitivity training or intergroup confrontation workshops to allow the internal groups to make mutual adjustment so as to be able to manage the value incongruence.

The actual change strategy is selected after examination of both options. Where possible, Option 1 is preferred as it often results in the least resistance and is quickest to implement.

Once the desired state is specified, Beckhard and Harris (1977) argue that there is a *transition state* which should be defined as a set of conditions separate from the present or desired state. In so doing, they propose that special attention be given to the type of governance and management necessary for effective control of the change process. Several of the governance structures they propose imply the mobilization of emergent networks in the organization. This includes forming coalitions from representatives of organization constituencies, forming coalitions of natural leaders, using cliques, and developing a coalition representing a diagonal slice of the organization.

The transition plans as outlined by Beckhard and Harris include a statement of the current state based on an organizational diagnosis as outlined above; a statement of the desired state or the organization in good fit; and two types of plans for getting the organization to the desired state. The first is the *process plan*. This corresponds to the rational stream pictured in Figure 1. It is purposeful, task specific, integrated, temporal, adaptable, agreed to by the top (dominant coalition), and cost-effective.

The second is the *commitment plan*. This refers to the securing of support of those subsystems which are vital to the change effort. The commitment plan deals with the political and normative streams found in Figure 1. The plan identifies individuals and groups whose commitment is needed. This includes defining the critical mass of support needed to ensure effective implementation; developing a plan for getting commitment from the critical mass; and developing a monitoring system to assess progress.

The commitment plan is largely focused on the mobilization of the emergent networks required to effect change. Its aim is to help deal with resistance through a series of collaborative and/or bargaining processes depending on the degree of goals and/or means agreement present in the system.

In developing the transition plan, the network characteristics presented in Table 2 provide a set of conceptual and operational tools for identifying and designing appropriate change networks. The key ingredients of a change effort are information and influence. Because information and influence networks often only partially overlap, it is helpful to develop a network influence and a network information map of the organization; that is, who influences whom about what, as well as who communicates with whom. For example, the people who influence budget allocations may or may not be those who influence the selection and placement of people.

By developing these network maps, which can be derived from the diagnostic data outlined in Table 8, it will be possible to identify 'stars', 'liaisons', and 'bridge' people. These individuals can be influenced directly once they are identified. The selection of a diagonal slice which draws on specific constituencies should be based on the individual's position in the organizational networks. Generally, key representatives should be stars because of their high impact on their constituencies.

In addition, cliques and coalitions within the networks can be identified and directly approached. It is important to point out that all change involves altering some aspect of the networks (prescribed and/or emergent), that is, a modification of relationships of who influences whom about what, who communicates to whom about what, or which coalition controls what tasks or resources.

Organization development interventions in network terms

Many of the existing OD technologies are compatible with the social network perspective. For example, data feedback is only slightly modified when approaching change from a network perspective. The shift is in the type of data collected, namely, mapping of influence, information, and friendship relationships. Other OD technologies, such as confrontation meetings and responsibility charting, are also consistent. But in each case, the implications and leverage points for change are formulated in network terms. For instance, a confrontation between the top management, the dominant coalition, and other interest groups would be orchestrated so that the key power people, as determined by a network analysis, were involved. It would be assumed that such people would have maximal impact on other parts of the organization because of their linkages with wider constituencies in their networks.

Rather than review existing OD technologies in network terms, several unique social network technologies are described in Table 10. The table presents examples of network change technologies related to each of the model's categories. Those marked with asterisks are discussed in more detail below.

Table 10   Social network OD interventions

Model category	Intervention
I Environment interface	Developing boundary spanning networks. Interlocking directorates.
II Mission/strategy	Identifying and working with dominant coalition(s).
III Prescribed networks	Use of liaisons, task coalitions, teams, the matrix structure to combine multiple networks.* Use of sociometric data to form work groups.
IV People	Network awareness* and skill training. Career network planning. Boundary spanning development.
V Organizational processes	Reformulate traditional OD communication, decision making and conflict interventions into network terms.
VII Emergent networks	Transferring personnel* to build up emergent information and influence networks.

*Described in the text.

Prescribed network change to manage bargaining   In systems with high political uncertainty and hence high needs for political bargaining and exchange capacity, there are technologies which encourage open and fair coalition negotiation. Such an OD intervention was developed by Wiesbord and Lawrence using what they called a 'mixed model' which combines a traditional functional organization and a matrix organization (Weisbord, 1974).

They created a design which kept the integrity of traditional academic departments with faculty having on-going research and teaching commitments in a traditional format, while at the same time they created a matrix structure for special projects and for clinical interdisciplinary training. The structure fostered open and direct negotiation with departments and coalitions for the allocation of resources. Coalitions wanting to allocate resources had to develop explicit contracts with departments and the head of the medical centre. Thus, what in the past was most often a covert bargaining process was now brought into the open and legitimized and norms of reciprocity and fair exchange were instituted. In network terms, the dysfunctional emergent networks, covert coalitional activity to allocate resources, were channelled by the existence of new prescribed networks, the matrix structure, to foster open deals. Since the matrix structure only prescribed some of the relationships, new emergent coalitions could form at any time to initiate a new teaching, research, or service project.

Transferring for emergent network building and control   One intriguing approach to managing emergent networks is to utilize transfers as a strategy for control and coordination. Galbraith and Edstrom (1976) proposed that it is occurring unintentionally in some organizations. A strategic approach using transfers is based on the assumption that management of emergent social networks will provide an organization with a new, hitherto unused or misused integrating tool. Strategic transferring demands a response on the part of transferees to pay attention to the development of emergent networks. The integration occurs, as Galbraith and Edstrom observe, because 'transfers behave differently with respect to their information collection behaviour. That is, transferees communicate more often with colleagues in other units and have larger networks of contacts with other units' (Galbraith and Edstrom, 1976). By transferring managers – and thus widening their emergent networks of contacts – the organization can more readily afford to have different organizational arrangements and cultures at different locations without losing its ability to integrate and coordinate. This approach, however, is not likely to succeed merely by transferring people. Additionally, it requires the development of network bridging procedures. The organization strategically needs to plan transfers and to attend to problems of linking the transferees into the relevant networks. Strategic transferring of this order contrasts with much of the current practice in organizations which is intuitive and the network weaving portion is left implicit.

Individual network skills   These skills are important because it is assumed that in complex organizations they are survival skills which people currently learn through trial and error and observation of others. In order to get necessary information and exert task relevant influence, especially in organic systems, individuals need to develop networks. They can be taught to understand networks and how to build and establish needed networks. The building of network relationships can grow out of a role analysis diagnosis.

The sequence of activities in a role analysis diagnosis is as follows. (1) The individual identifies his/her current network configuration relative to the fulfilment of his/her role, that is, who is communicated with for what, how influence is exerted, etc. (2) The individual identifies areas where there is need for more information flow, more influence flow, and more affective flow, as well as where there is too much or inappropriate flow. (3) This leads to an identification of areas requiring change, including places where new network relationships are required. (4) Action plans can then be developed for altering network configurations.

Career planning can build from the role diagnosis activity described above. An individual can project the future and look at the career paths and the types of networks necessary both for getting access to certain jobs and to learn the new jobs.

Finally, an important network OD technology is facilitating the development of cosmopolitan, boundary spanning types of network formation on the part of key organizational members. This means rewarding organizational members for active involvement in professional associations. Developing employee boundary spanning can bring new input from the environment and enhance individual career mobility. As Grannovetter's (1974) work indicates, the majority of professional managers and technicians secure jobs through informal personal networks. Enhancing and encouraging such mobility on the part of some organizations works in their favour. That is, losing people to other organizations and bringing new ones in can be highly beneficial, since it widens the organization's networks as the new members link additional new networks into the organization.

Finally, individual skills are needed for effective coalitional activity. Individuals are trained with two sets of skills. One is how to organize a coalition, how to identify the necessary resources, and how to get people together. The other is effective negotiation. This includes how to develop proposals and deal with the allocation of organizational resources.

The network model in action

This section presents two case examples showing how the social network model can be applied to change efforts.

Southwest Hospital System

The organization is called Southwest Hospital System (SHS). It consists of a chain of twelve small to medium sized, non-profit making hospitals and three primary care clinics. The total operating budget for the system in the fiscal year 1976–1977 was $76 million. The chain serves a population characterized by poverty, unemployment, and dependence on welfare.

Top management of the chain is located in a central headquarters office building remote from any of the chain's hospitals. The director is a physician who was previously a private practitioner.

The system has always had financial difficulty, and during the phase discussed in this chapter it was operating at a deficit of over $2 million a year. It faced extraordinary financial pressures. One of the major employers in the area cut back its insurance benefits. The reduction, which required employees to share in health costs previously paid for by the employer, resulted in the immediate reduction of hospital utilization as well as in non-payment of bills by employees of this company. Consequently, as this case unfolded, the system was thrown into a major fiscal crisis, requiring staff cutbacks, reduction in work hours, and curtailment of services.

The social network model was used to diagnose problems of the system and to develop a strategy for long-term organizational viability. The immediate financial crisis was viewed as a severe manifestation of more serious underlying managerial and organizational problems even though the immediate problem needed to be resolved at once.

Trigger for change The triggering event was the extreme financial pressure caused by the reduction in revenues.

Diagnosis By using multiple data collection methods, each of the components of the model was analysed. The focus of the analysis was the overall management and organization design of SHS. The basic format of the diagnosis followed the outline described in Table 8. Interviews and questionnaires were completed for 40 of the SHS staff, all hospital administrators, heads of nursing, medical directors, and central headquarters management.

The major problems of fit were found to be (1) environment/mission-strategy in terms of the technical goodness-of-fit; and (2) mission-strategy/people in terms of political goodness-of-fit. There was also a series of secondary analyses of fit which required attention and will be discussed below.

Fit 1: environment/mission-strategy The SHS environment was assessed to be highly uncertain. The organization's strategy had, however, been very mechanistic, that is, simplistic, implicit, fragmented, rigid, and reactive. From an information processing perspective, a more appropriate fit to such an uncertain environment is a more organic mission and strategy. That is, one which is complex, explicit, integrated, flexible, and proactive (Khandwalla, 1977).

Fit 2: Mission-strategy/people This problem of fit is a political one. The director, at the time of the case diagnosis, had major control of the dominant coalition in the organization. His implicit, simplistic and fragmented mission/strategy had contributed to the organization's troubles. To alter the mission/strategy required altering his dominance and hence his power to influence the allocation of resources and the direction of the system. An organic mission/strategy would have required altering his managerial style to one which was less authoritarian or more participative, flexible, and less seat-of-the-pants. The alternative was to replace him with someone with a more appropriate style.

Fit 3: mission-strategy/prescribed networks Both were assessed to be mechanistic. This means that at the time they were congruent with each other but the uncertain environment called for changing the strategy to an organic one. This in turn required that the prescribed networks become more organic as well. In other words, the information processing capacity of the networks would have to be increased. This fit represents a technical goodness-of-fit, that is, how to make the organization more task efficient and effective. Such rational readjustments would have an impact on the political or cultural goodness-of-fit.

Fit 4: prescribed networks/organizational processes As indicated in the previous fit evaluation, both are currently mechanistic, and both would need to be changed if the strategy is to be adjusted to match environmental uncertainty. The technical adjustment towards more organic characteristics is likely to create political and cultural uncertainty. People's power bases will be affected.

Fit 5: prescribed networks/emergent networks/organizational processes   These three components were jointly mechanistic and required shifts to become more organic.

Developing a change strategy   Table 11 presents a summary of some of the key diagnostic findings along with implications for change. The overriding factor in the SHS case is pressure for change brought on by an unstable environment. This in turn requires major readjustments of the organization model. The lack of an organic strategy and of strategic decision making capability severely hampered the organization's ability to cope with its environment. The technical goodness-of-fit between the organization and its environment is kept that way due to the politically vested interests of the current dominant coalition.

Table 11   SHS diagnosis and implications

Diagnostic finding	Change implication
Socio-technical/process fit SHS processes are mechanistic. If the integrating mechanisms are made more complex in parts of the SHS system, then the fit between socio-technical and process will worsen.	For areas of the organization in need of more organic processes, provide training and development support for improved communication, conflict management and problem solving effectiveness.
Socio-technical/process/emergent networks fit SHS has few task supportive emergent networks. Thus, the emergent networks have low task relevant information processing capacity.	Facilitate the development of task relevant emergent networks by developing reward system for informal lateral (cross-hospital) problem solving, etc.
Environment/strategy/management style fit The SHS environment is high in uncertainty, yet has a strategy and a management style which are mechanistic.	Management development effort to alter style and/or replace managers with more organic style managers. Introduce and develop a systematic strategic planning process.
Strategy/socio-technical fit The SHS strategy ideally should be organic, requiring an organic socio-technical component. SHS has no complex, organic integrating mechanisms, and the simple mechanisms need adjustment.	Adjust simple integrating mechanisms (clarify rules and programmes, hierarchy and goals). Develop more complex lateral integrating mechanisms for specified complex interdependent tasks. Redesign management information system to meet the organization's information processing capacity, not external accounting needs.

The basics of the process plan for the SHS case are outlined in Table 11. The fully developed plan included a timetable, specification of the relationships between the various change activities and cost figures, amount of personnel's time required, and the consultant resources needed.

The commitment plan for SHS brought on a confrontation with the political base of the director whose vested interests were linked to a dysfunctional strategy. The fact that the director was an extremely powerful node in the influence network with close ties with board of trustee members and politicians in the external environment created a situation where the management of change needed to be based on careful diagnosis of the influence networks around the director. In this case, two areas within the influence network had to be analysed and mobilized. First, the influential 'stars' on the board of trustees were identified and involved in the transition. Second, influence stars within the managerial ranks were identified, some of whom had strong influence links with the board. In this particular case, the director concluded that he should resign and did so prior to the mobilization of a coalition with sufficient power to remove him.

The new director became the strategic change manager, mobilizing a sufficient coalition to implement the process plan presented in Table 11.

Texas Instruments

Texas Instruments (TI) began a major change effort in the early 1960s which was geared towards preparing itself for long-term, fast growth and survival in an increasingly turbulent environment. The company is now preparing for battle with the Japanese for dominance in the consumer electronics business of the 1980s. In 1979 TI had sales of $2.5 thousand million, compared with less than $400 million in 1964. There are 68 000 workers in 45 plants in 18 countries. The company is a fast-growing (15–20 per cent a year), high technology concern. This case provides a sharp contrast with the SHS case in which a troubled system struggled for survival. TI is a very successful system which is proactively developing itself for future growth and viability.

This is not a typical OD case in that it does not reflect the work of OD practitioners but that of managers. It is, however, a major organizational change case with important lessons for other organizations with regard to innovative, prescribed network interventions.

Trigger for change The early 1960s were a time when the semiconductor industry went through a major shake-out and TI found itself faced with the loss of some major contracts. The future looked rather bleak unless TI could manage both innovation and tight production control.

Diagnosis Each of the organizational components are briefly described as they were in the early 1960s.

History   The company began as a builder of oil exploration equipment and then moved into the electronic components business, primarily supplying to producers of end products. The growth prior to the 1960s had been steady but not spectacular. By the early 1960s, however, things were picking up and it was clear to management that they had a chance to play a major part in the high technology, fast growth electronics field.

Environment   The early 1960s found TI facing an uncertain and turbulent environment. There was increasing competition in the field and they had just lost several important government contracts.

One manager at TI described the environment which they were to face throughout the 1960s in terms of the role of obsolescence: 'At the moment when a newly designed electronic component or end product enters production for the first time, it is already obsolete.' He went on to say: 'Markets are equally explosive.'

Another factor was sales which oscillated through wide volume ranges. Finally, there was a lot of raiding among firms for experts. One way to obtain new innovations was to entice employees away from firms which were innovative so that they brought their knowledge with them. Thus, there was uncertainty regarding being able to keep key innovative people.

Mission/strategy   The major strategy of TI from the early 1960s through today has been to adhere rigidly to what is referred to as the 'learning curve theory'. Simply put, it states that 'manufacturing costs can be brought down by a fixed percentage, depending on the product, each time cumulative volume is doubled'. (*Business Week*, 18 September 1978, p. 68). The strategy involves constant redesign improvements of the product and the process so that prices can drop as fast as possible.

In the early 1960s strategy was formulated by the top management group which then attempted to implement it through the divisional structure at TI. This was a problem. Innovation was stifled. The learning curve could be implemented, but the other important strategy of TI was to keep innovating so that they would have products to which to apply the learning curve theory.

Prescribed networks   In the early 1960s TI was organized in a standard divisional structure as shown in Figure 7. This structure created decentralized Product Customer Centers (PCCs). It worked well for short-term production purposes. However, there was duplication of resources and a lack of integration for long-range projects which needed to cut across PCCs. In other words, to develop innovations for the future it was important to have a way of bridging the prescribed networks which were divided into separate PCCs.

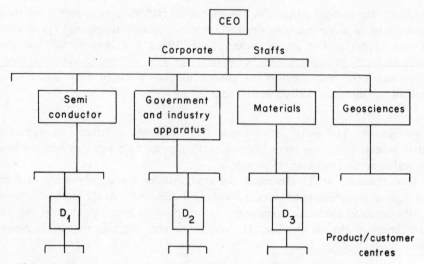

Figure 7   Texas Instruments divisionalized prescribed networks
Source: Jay Galbraith and Daniel Nathanson, *Strategy Implementation: The Role of Structure and Process*. St Paul, Minn.: West Publishing, 1978, 129

People   The organization has always had a high percentage of technical personnel. However, in the early 1960s they were not driven towards innovation as much as they are now. They focused more on short-term improvements of existing capabilities or incremental expansions.

Organizational processes   The communication, decision making, and conflict management processes were very much influenced by the prescribed PCCs which supported the production side of the organization but not the innovation and long-range planning side. Participation was low and communication was mostly from the top down on important matters.

Emergent networks   As with the SHS case, there was little use of emergent networks to foster task accomplishment, especially in the area of innovation.

Fit 1: environment/mission-strategy   The basic strategy was sound: innovation and the learning curve in the electronics field. However, the strategy formulation process and the strategy implementation process were weak.

Fit 2: mission-strategy/prescribed network   This represents the major poor fit in the case. The PCC structure supports the learning curve activity, efficient high-volume production. It works against innovation by focusing on short-run efficiency concerns. The prescribed networks needed to be adjusted to support both aspects of the organization's strategy.

Fit 3: mission-strategy/people/organizational process   Because of the need to change the prescribed network, the other two components also required readjustments. The people and the processes were only supporting the PCC prescribed network.

Fit 4: prescribed/emergent networks   The fit prior to the change effort was congruent. However, once the prescribed networks were changed to support innovation, then the emergent required modification.

Fit 5: technical/political/cultural fits   The major uncertainty facing TI in the early 1960s was in the technical domain. That is, in order for TI to become more effective and efficient, its capacity to deal with greater uncertainty had to be increased. The goodness of technical fit, Option 1 (Figure 4), changing the environment, task, or task interdependence, was not a viable option. Thus, Option 2, increasing the information processing capacity, was required. The political goodness-of-fit and the cultural goodness-of-fit were not problems. However, once TI began its change strategy and its phenomenal growth, the political and cultural fits were readjusted via such means of self-selection, strong monolithic political leadership, and a development programme which drove towards homogeneity of values.

In summary, the diagnosis of TI in the early 1960s led to identifying a need for a strategic, long-range planning process supported by an organization which closely monitored technology and market, was adaptable and flexible to product/market changes, was able to foster design of production facilities, and which reinforced major research and development efforts and encouraged creativity among its people.

Change strategy   The change strategy was developed so that TI could maintain a high growth rate (15–20 per cent) in a high technology business committed to a strategy of continually driving down its production costs, so allowing price to be the weapon by which to achieve share in growing markets. As noted above, both tightly controlled production, which TI was already managing, and innovation, which it was not, were required.

Process plan   The desired state for TI was a system which was able to formulate and implement long-range strategic plans continuously while driving its PCCs. The solution was to design a new prescribed network which was to be superimposed on the existing PCC structure. This is the Objectives, Strategy, Tactics (OST) network at TI. It was created to supplement the PCC structure which remained intact. The OST network was to be used for strategic long-range planning and supporting innovation. The same people were to be members of both networks. The company's total expenditures are divided between OST and PCCs.

The OST process operates as follows:

(1) Business objectives (nine of them) are set at the top and represent the major businesses TI will operate in for the long run.

(2) Each objective states such factors as those listed in Figure 8, percentage of market share, sales volume, and return on investment. Each objective has a manager who is also a manager in the PCC structure. Some 20 to 50 per cent of the manager's time is spent on OST work.

(3) Each objective has several strategies which are stated in terms of 5–10-year goals. Each strategy also has a manager. These managers have roles and two bosses, one for OST and one for PCC.

(4) Strategies have several tactics each of which is a 6–18-month check point and is assigned to PCCs. These are monitored on a monthly basis. This is how the strategic thinking of the OST network is tied into the production organization.

(5) These prescribed networks are supported by changes in other components of the organization:
Extensive planning process including a one-week objective when strategy is reviewed and decided upon for the future.
Budgets are integrated between the two systems.
Reward and information systems monitor and reinforce both systems.
Career development paths rotate managers through line, then staff, then line, etc., positions.

(6) Fostering of emergent networks to support innovation was also done.

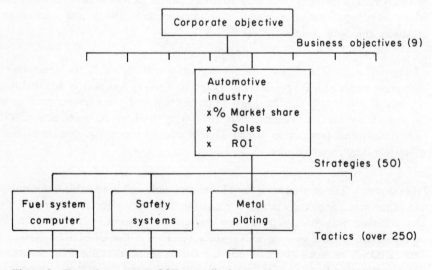

Figure 8   Texas Instruments OST prescribed networks
Source: Jay Galbraith and Daniel Nathanson, *Strategy Implementation: The Role of Structure and Process.* St Paul, Minn.: West Publishing, 1978, 129

In response to the potentially negative consequences of such a rational strategic planning system, namely that some creativity and innovation will be stifled, TI fosters emergent innovation via two mechanisms. The first is part of the formal OST process where there is a mechanism for funding some of the more speculative programmes which were originally being underfunded; the device is the 'wild hare' idea. It allows managers to rank speculative projects separately and hence give more funding to them. The emergent network innovation provides any organization member with a chance to obtain a grant from a $1 million pool to work on an innovative project. Thus, emergent coalitions form and apply for grants which they then work on. It was through this process, called IDEA, that TI developed the $19.95 digital watch.

Commitment plan   In order to move TI from its early 1960s point of equilibrium to the present day equilibrium, a great deal of transition management occurred. The previous president, Patrick Haggerty, who is credited with the decision to develop OST, views it as a 10-year process of implementation. It required development of a very tight dominant coalition in the organization. This coalition had to exercise and channel its power in one concerted effort. The politics of the change were straightforward. the people had to be socialized to manage in the new system or pushed out of the organization. Once the dominant coalition was uniformly behind OST and the supporting processes and reward systems were developed, the major commitment plan devices employed were the careful selection of managers (employment of people who would fit ideologically into TI) and the careful termination of employment of people who did not fit into the TI culture. As one researcher put it, TI's culture 'polarizes people – either you are incorporated into the culture or rejected'. 'The culture tends to reject "strange individuals".' 'The internal environment focused on intense loyalty to the company's goals and disciplines. . . .'

In summary, the TI case is an example of how an organization systematically and concertedly manages its prescribed and emergent networks in the service of a very clear and explicit strategy. The political and cultural fits are monolithically controlled, allowing the organization to make constant readjustment in the rational goodness of fit by introducing such programmes as 'wild hare' and IDEA.

Conclusion

This chapter is meant to provoke a reaction in OD practitioners and scholars. The OD practitioners of the future are likely to face problems of the magnitude of the SHS and TI cases. In order to handle such cases, there is a need for new organizational models to deal with the complexity of strategic management problems from technical, political, and cultural perspectives. Social network analysis, coupled with the political, technical, and cultural fit views of organizations, was presented as one promising avenue for OD to pursue.

These approaches focus OD practitioners' attention on sets of variables which are often missed in more traditional OD work. The future effectiveness of OD practice in large systems is felt to be dependent on whether practitioners are willing to develop and learn to use new frameworks such as those presented in this chapter. This author's recommendation is to draw upon a social network approach and combine it with the technical, political, and cultural organizational change transitions as a step towards a redefinition of OD.

References

Allen, J. (1977) *Managing the Flow of Technology*. Cambridge, Mass.: MIT Press.

Arygris, C., and Schon, D. (1976) *Theory in Practice*. San Francisco: Jossey-Bass.

Arygris, C., and Schon, D. (1978) *Organizational Learning: A Theory of Action Perspective*. Reading, Mass.: Addison-Wesley.

Bavelas, A. (1951) An experimental approach to organizational communication. *Personnel*, **27**, 366–371.

Beckhard, R. (1967) *Organization Development: Strategies and Models*. Reading, Mass.: Addison-Wesley.

Beckhard, R., and Harris, R. (1977) *Organizational Transitions: Managing Complex Change*. Reading, Mass.: Addison-Wesley.

Benne, K., Bennis, W. and Chin, R. (eds) (1969) *The Planning of Change*. New York: Holt, Rinehart, & Winston.

Bennis, W. (1969) *Organization Development: Its Nature, Origins, and Prospects*. Reading, Mass.: Addison-Wesley.

Blau, P. (1964) *Exchange and Power in Social Life*. New York: Wiley.

Blau, P., and Scott, R. (1962) *Formal Organizations*. San Francisco: Chandler.

Boissevain, J. (1974) *Friends of Friends*. New York: St Martin's Press.

Bowers, David (1973) OD techniques and their results in 23 organizations: The Michigan ICL study. *Journal of Applied Behavioral Science*, **9**, 21–43.

Chapple, E., and Sayles, L. (1961) *The Measure of Management*. New York: Macmillan.

Coleman, J., Katz, E., and Menzel, H. (1957) The diffusion of an innovation among physicians. *Sociometry*, **20**, 253–270.

Cyert, R., and March, J. (1963) *A Behavioral Theory of the Firm*. Englewood Cliffs, NJ: Prentice-Hall.

Dahl, R. (1961) *Who Governs?* New Haven, Conn.: Yale University Press.

Deutsch, M. (1973) *The Resolution of Conflict*. New Haven, Conn.: Yale University Press.

Ekeh, P. (1974) *Social Exchange Theory: The Two Traditions*. Cambridge, Mass.: Harvard University Press.

French, W., and Bell, C. (1977) *Organization Development*. Englewood Cliffs, NJ: Prentice-Hall.

Friedlander, F. (1976) OD reaches adolescence: an exploration of its underlying values. *Journal of Applied Behavioral Science*, **12**, 7–21.

Friedlander, F., and Brown, L. D. (1974) Organization development. *Annual Review of Psychology*, **25**, 313–341.

Galbraith, J. (1977) *Organization Design*. Reading, Mass.: Addison-Wesley.

Galbraith, J., and Edstrom, A. (1976) International transfer of managers: some important policy considerations. *Columbia Journal of World Business*, **11**, 100–112.

Grannovetter, M. (1974) *Getting a Job: A Study of Contacts and Careers*. Cambridge, Mass.: Harvard University Press.

Gross, N., Mason, W. and McEachern, A. (1958) *Explorations in Role Analysis*. New York: Wiley.

Homans, G. (1950) *The Human Group*. New York: Harcourt, Brace, & World.

Homans, G. (1961) *Social Behavior: Its Elementary Forms*. New York: Harcourt, Brace, & World.

Huse, E. (1975) *Organization Development and Change*. St Paul, Minn.: West.

Jacques, Elliott (1976) *A General Theory of Bureaucracy*. London: Heinemann.

Jay, A. (1971) *Corporation Man*. New York: Random House.

Kadushin, C. (1978) Introduction to macro-network analysis. Unpublished working paper. Teachers College, Columbia University, NY.

Kahn, R., Wolfe, D., Quinn, R., Snoek, R., Diedrick, J., and Rosenthal, R. (1964) *Organizational Stress: Studies in Role Conflict and Ambiguity*. New York: Wiley.

Katz, D., and Kahn, R. (1966) *The Social Psychology of Organizations*. New York: Wiley.

Katz, E., and Lazarsfeld, P. (1955) *Personal Influence*. New York: Free Press.

Khandwalla, P. (1977) *The Design of Organizations*. New York: Harcourt, Brace, Jovanovich.

Kotter, J. (1978) *Organizational Dynamics: Diagnosis and Interventions*. Reading, Mass.: Addison-Wesley.

Lauman, E., and Pappi, F. (1975) *Network of Collective Action*. New York: Academic Press.

Lawrence, P., and Lorsch, J., (1967) *Organizations and Environment*. Cambridge, Mass.: Harvard University Press.

Leavitt, H. (1951) Some effects of certain communication patterns on group performance. *Journal of Abnormal and Social Psychology*, **46**, 38–50.

Likert, R. (1961) *New Patterns in Management*. New York: McGraw-Hill.

March, J. (1962) The business firm as a political coalition. *Journal of Politics*, **24**, 662–678.

March, J., and Simon, H. (1958) *Organizations*. New York: Wiley.

Merton, R. (1968) *Social Theory and Social Structure*. New York: Free Press.

Mitchell, J. (1969) The concept and use of social networks. In J. C. Mitchell (ed.) *Social Networks in Urban Situations*. Manchester, England: University of Manchester Press.

Nadler, D., and Tushman, M. (1978) Information processing as an integrating concept in organization design. *Academy of Management Review*, **3** (4) (December).

Parsons, T. (1956) Suggestions for a sociological approach to the theory of organizations I and II. *Administrative Science Quarterly*, **1**, 63–85, 225–239.

Pfeffer, J. (1977) *Organizational Design*. Arlington Heights, Ill.: AHM Publishing Corp.

Pfeffer, J., and Salancik, G. (1978) *The External Control of Organizations: A Resources Dependence Perspective*. New York: Harper & Row.

Rogers, E. and Shoemaker, F. F. (1971) *Communication of Innovation*. New York: Free Press.

Schein, E. (1970) *Organizational Psychology*. Englewood Cliffs, NJ: Prentice-Hall.

Thibaut, J., and Kelley, H. (1959) *The Social Psychology of Groups*. New York: Wiley.

Thompson, J. (1967) *Organizations in Action: Social Science Bases of Administrative Theory*. New York: McGraw-Hill.

Thompson, J., and Tuden, A. (1956) Strategies and processes of organizational decision, in J. Thompson *et al.* (eds) *Comparative Studies in Administration.* Pittsburgh, Pa.: University of Pittsburgh Press.

Tichy, N. (1973) An analysis of clique formation and structure in organizations. *Administrative Science Quarterly*, **18**, 194–207.

Tichy, N. (1974) Agents of planned social change: Congruence of values, cognitions and actions. *Administrative Science Quarterly*, June.

Tichy, N. (1976) When does work restructuring work? Organizational innovation at Volvo and GM. *Organizational Dynamics*, **5** (1).

Tichy, N. (1978) Diagnosis for complex health care delivery systems: A model and case study. *Journal of Applied Behavioral Sciences*, **14** (3).

Tichy, N., Tushman, M., and Formburn, C. (1979) Social network analysis for organizations. *Academy of Management Review*, **4**, 507–519.

Tushman, M. (1979) Determinants of subunit communication structure: A contingency analysis. *Administrative Science Quarterly*, **24**, 82–98.

Weick, K. (1969) *The Social Psychology of Organizing.* Reading, Mass.: Addison-Wesley.

Weiland, G., and Ullrich, R. (1977) *Organizations: Behavior, Design and Change.* Homewood, Ill.: Richard D. Irwin.

Weisbord, M. (1974) A mixed model for medical centers: Changing structure and behavior. In J. D. Adams (ed.) *Theory and Method in Organization Development: An Evolutionary Process.* Arlington, Va.: NTL Institute for Applied Behavioral Science, 211–254.

Whyte, W. F. (1955) *Street Corner Society.* Chicago: University of Chicago Press.

Zaleznik, A. (1970) Power and politics in organizational life. *Harvard Business Review*, May–June, 47–60.

Systems Theory for Organization Development
Edited by T. G. Cummings
© 1980 John Wiley & Sons Ltd.

Chapter **7**

Organizations as Political Systems: Implications for Diagnosis, Change, and Stability

Anne Sigismund Huff

'Change' is a central word in the vocabulary of organization development. More specifically, the kind of change which interests practitioners and academicians in the field involves a deliberate response to organization problems. The key figure in this effort is the change 'agent' who collects and uses data from the organization in an educative attempt to alter behaviour, especially interpersonal behaviour (Marguilis and Raia, 1978; French and Bell, 1978). The roots of organization development efforts are frequently described as allegiance to humanistic values, and the methods used draw almot exclusively from psychology with secondary influences from sociology.

This chapter explores an alternative perspective on the nature of organizations and change.[1] It suggests that organizations are in part political entities (Pettigrew, 1973; Pfeffer and Salancik, 1974; Tushman, 1977; Schien, 1977). The political perspective recognizes the power-based conflicts which underlie important decisions. It leads to the conclusion that one act is often chosen over an alternative on the basis of its advocates rather than on its intrinsic merits. The timing of decisions is similarly attributed to the energy of special interests as well as to the requirements of the task.

The political perspective challenges many tenets of OD work. It concurs with Beer and Huse's (1972) findings that impactful, deliberate change can be initiated at all levels of the organization, and in particular can be exerted upwards by those with relatively little benefit from the *status quo*. It agrees with Katz and Kahn (1978), Leavitt (1965), and Lippitt, Watson, and Westley (1958) that some aspects of the organization will be more susceptible to change efforts than others. But, it provides new rationale for selecting leverage points and identifies new ways of influencing as well. Perhaps most important, the political perspective challenges at least a part of the 'humanistic', consensual, and interpersonal underpinnings of OD work in favour of a view which expects incompatible aims and rewards in organizational life and points to decisions as the important arena for investigating the effects of these incompatibilities.

Although the political perspective may not be comfortable, it deserves attention especially because it grows out of long-term observation of human behaviour by political scientists whose methods and work are rarely familiar to those in OD. Some of these political science observers have suggested that organizations have many similarities to government (Denhardt, 1971; Dahl, 1959). This chapter attempts to specify the analogy more clearly with special attention to the implications of political theory for organization change.

Political models of organization interaction

The study of politics goes beyond the direct study of power (which Dahl (1957) defines as the ability to affect valued outcomes) to encompass the setting within which power is exercised. Four key questions are particularly important to political analysis:

(1) What are the sources of power within the organization?
(2) How do critical outcomes reflect the interplay among those with power?
(3) How do new interests arise to challenge existing power relationships?
(4) How is continuity maintained as power relationships change?

Various answers to these questions have been suggested by political scientists. The plan of this chapter is to briefly outline five alternatives from the many available and then to look more closely at the answers each offers to questions 3 and 4. The intention is to contribute a beginning 'typology' of political models to the

Table 1   Five views of organization politics

	What is the primary source of power within the organization?	What do formal decisions reflect?
Structural model	Subunit jurisdiction	'Check and balance' among overlapping subunit decisions
Group model	Organized special interest groups	Compromise response to present and potential coalitions
Elites model	Informal influence divided between key individuals and middle level influentials	Elite opinion
Incremental/ bureaucratic model	Past commitments and current crises	Past decisions marginally modified by current conditions
Systems/resource model	Control over resources	Composition of external resource inputs, plus desired internal outputs

relatively small body of OD literature concerned with the politics of change efforts (e.g. Mohrman and Mohrman, 1977). As an overview, Table 1 defines the five models in terms of the political influences each model considers most important to the development of policy decisions.

The structural model

The first of the five models offers perhaps the most straightforward way of describing political entities by focusing on formal structural relationships. In government, this model is often described as central to the development of the Constitution of the United States. The emphasis of the model is on the necessary balance of powers among formal units of an interacting system. Each unit has an input to overall policy direction, and these inputs partially overlap so that one serves as a check on the others. Ostrom, a recent proponent of this model as a viable description of government, calls this necessary characteristic of the structural model 'overlapping jurisdiction' (1974, p. 77).

Figure 1 offers a diagrammatic representation of the organization as a political

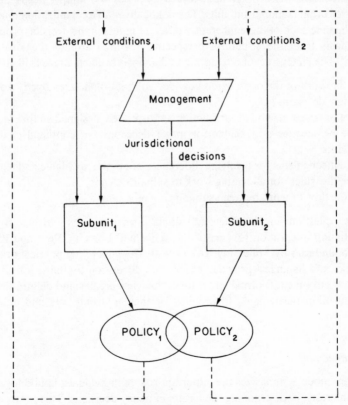

Figure 1   A structural model of intraorganizational politics

unit of formally specified subunits. Each subunit is identified with a specialized task needed to complete the work done by the organization. The initial task of organization design can be equated with the problems of the Continental Congress: (1) how to divide the work of the organization relatively evenly so that no one unit will continually dominate the work of the others; (2) how to ensure check points so that major flaws in the work of one unit will be revealed by the others.

The importance of balance is intensified by two factors which make it unlikely that different subunits will have similar views of appropriate decisions. First, just as judicial, legislative, and executive functions lead to somewhat different preoccupations of government units, so the differences between each task in the organization can be expected to create differences between subunit understanding of the work of the organization. Second, the distinction between the branches of government is also externally maintained by the different constituencies in which the house, senate, president, and courts are responsible. So, too, in organizations, each subunit is oriented towards a different aspect of the environment upon which it is dependent for the competent execution of its tasks within the organization. The existence of these differential forces amplifies the unique needs and perspectives of organizational subunits. The politically stable organization must find a way to include each of these inherently different inputs in the decision process.

Diagnosis from the structural perspective revolves around the idea of task 'domain'. The change agent attempting to diagnosis problem areas is likely to ask:

– Is the work of the organization divided so that no one area overly dominates policy decisions?
– Are overlaps in subunit jurisdiction appropriately designed so that more than one perspective is available for major decisions but continual challenge is avoided?
– Are mechanisms for resolving differences of opinion available and tested?
– Are the 'rules' for allocating work to subunits clear?
– Is the flow of work between subunits unambiguous?

These questions are somewhat similar to questions arising from the differentiation/integration scheme of Lawrence and Lorsch (1967) and the study of task boundaries by Miller and Rice (1967). The underlying political orientation of 'checks and balances' provides an internal dimension to analysis based on fit with the environment. Formal structure in this view creates and defines the ability of organization participants to provide for their own interests and affect each other.

The group model

The group model emphasizes the important role of individuals, bound together by special interests, in determining the nature of policy decisions. This perspective, as articulated by Truman (1953) and others, leads to a view of government as the mechanism for coordinating the incompatible needs of society. The coordinating process is made more difficult by the great number of demands made. 'Balanced' policy (and the democratic nature of the system) is maintained in theory by overlapping group membership and the competing demands of various groups. The policy maker is also aware that in addition to the demands currently articulated by organized interests, other 'potential coalitions' may be formed if irresponsive decisions are made.

An organizational representation of this view is outlined in Figure 2. The organization, seen as a political entity, is composed of differentiated interests which cut across the formal structure of the organization. In making demands upon the organization, these internal interests often coordinate with, or specifically oppose, external demands (Ohlin, 1960). Management responds to these groups through a range of policy decisions which are partially responsive to the variety of demands made.

The maintenance of the organization as a stable political system in the group model depends upon finding compromise decisions which will meet at least the

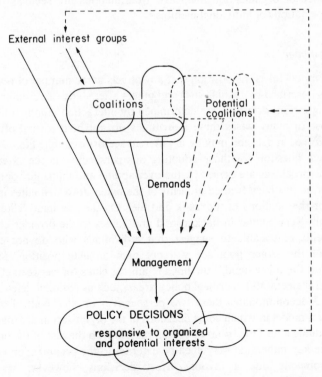

Figure 2 An interest group model of intraorganizational politics

minimal demands of groups with power, while avoiding precipitating the formation of powerful new groups with unmet demands. Political analysis from this perspective involves identifying (1) individuals with perceived common interests (often across organizational boundaries) and (2) the demands each set of interests makes on managerial decisions.

More specific questions for organizational diagnosis include:

- Does the present range of policy decisions respond to the varied interests of organization members? Or do the most visible demands dominate decisions?
- To what extent are internal interests 'skewing' organization perception of external demands?
- Are new interest groups arising around needs unmet by current decisions? Will these needs be reinforced by external/internal unmet needs?
- Are some decisions responsive to needs which are no longer current among influential interest groups?

These questions lead to an analysis of organization life that is quite similar to that proposed by Cyert and March (1963). Policy decisions are an expression of the influence of organization members. Malfunctions are seen as the result of unmet expectations of individual members.

The elites model

The elites model takes the position that a relatively small number of people control policy. As described by Dahl (1961) and others after study of community decision making, important decisions are determined by interaction among a few powerful individuals. In many cases these individuals do not hold formal office and are widely involved in decision making in different sectors of public life.

A critical quesiton for those adopting this perspective is the extent to which democratic processes are denied by the overlapping and informal control of elites. This question has been framed in terms of the extent to which elites interact with and mirror the opinions of the 'rank and file'. On the one hand, elite individuals are typically very similar in background and values to the broader constituency, and it seems reasonable to suggest that individuals who do not embody the interests of the larger populace will not gain an elite position. Mills (1956) suggests, on the other hand, little linkage among elites (or between elites and the more general electorate) in critical policy areas, such as national defence.

Figure 3 accommodates these two perspectives on elite control of policy by suggesting a model in which some decisions in the organization are made by a few key individuals after little or no direct interaction with the rest of the organization. In fact, the key individual may even be external to the organization (a mentor, a spouse, someone due a favour). Most decisions, however, are made by organizational elites who are closely linked with each other, primarily in informal ways. Most policy decisions are formed by the consensus which arises from this

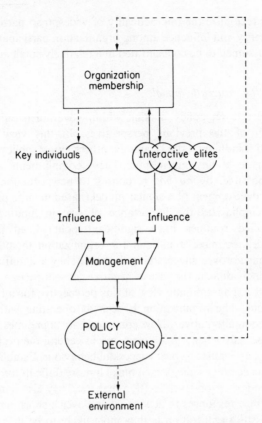

Figure 3   An elites model of intraorganizational politics

interaction. The politically stable organization, in this model, is one which can satisfy members that their interests are taken into account, in part by limiting decisions made without organization interaction.

Political analysis based on an elites model begins with an understanding of interpersonal influence. Questions of importance to the analyst include:

- Who influences each of the most important formal office holders?
- In what areas are these individuals influential?
- How do influentials gain information about the organization? Does this information reflect widely held opinion?
- How extensively do influentials interact?
- What infrastructure supports this interaction?
- Is the pattern of influence widely understood in the organization?
- Which organization members feel 'well represented' by elites?

These questions recognize the impracticality of widespread participation and the differential in energy and influence among organization participants. Power in the organization is assumed to be concentrated in a relatively small number of people.

The incremental/bureaucratic model

A fourth perspective on policy making within government challenges a basic precept of each of the previous perspectives. In this view, articulated by Braybrooke and Lindblom (1963) among others, most policy decisions have already been made at any given time. These commitments are changed, as marginally as possible, by *ad hoc* responses to new situations as they arise. Allison's (1971) development of a similar model (based in large part on Cyert and March, 1963) emphasizes the importance of size in limiting organizational flexibility. Specified routines have significant political advantages as well. Established guidelines make it difficult for organization members to influence patterns which have proved successful in the past. They also diffuse responsibility from any single individual, in the case of negative consequences.

Figure 4 offers a diagrammatic view of this perspective for intraorganizational political behaviour. The organization is seen as operating with an established 'repertoire' of action alternatives. New conditions are sometimes referred to decision makers, especially when crises occur, but in general the organization acts in ways which are very similar to past successful behaviour. Established procedures introduce confidence and rigidity which make it more difficult for specific crises to come to the attention of top-level decision makers. They also hamper the leader's ability to devise new responses to new situations over a short period of time. The politically successful organization is thus most likely to be in a setting which is characterized either by stable demands or by conditions which change so rapidly and unpredictably that immediate adaptation is not desirable.

Political analysis from the incremental/bureaucratic model involves an understanding of how past success of the organization interacts with the action required by present conditions. More specifically, analysis involves the following kinds of questions:

- How has the organization been most successful in the past?
- Which current actors reaped the benefits of past success?
- What 'signal' is the organization responding to in choosing its present course of action?
- Are conditions significantly different from the circumstances in which the present course of action was most successful?

These questions imply an interaction between the choices of organization members and the 'routines' or actions that the organization is most capable of accomplishing. The 'political' aspect of this interaction, as Cyert and March (1963) discuss, has to do with the expected reward of actions successful in the

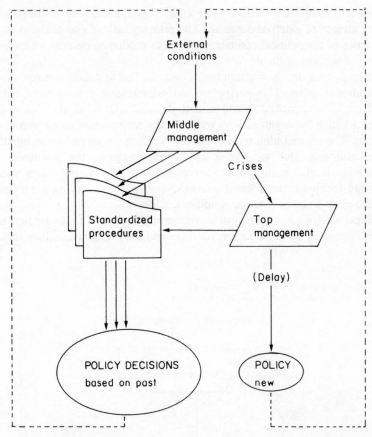

Figure 4   An incremental/bureaucratic model of intraorganizational politics

past versus the risks (to the individual as well as to the organization) of untested behaviour.

The systems/resource model

The systems view of political interaction explains policy decisions in terms of the external demands and support which flow into the system. In Easton's (1965) development of this perspective, external demands are directed towards those who have authority or governing responsibility over the system. Demands provide the information necessary for these dominant members of the system to orient themselves towards major problems. The tension such demands create in the system is likely to increase with demand volume, content complexity, or time pressure. Environmental support is important as a separate explanatory variable because it allows the political 'community' enough stability to respond to a varying stream of external demands. The primary task of authorities is to direct the activity of the political community towards producing outputs which increase the level of support available.

Figure 5 provides a diagrammatic view of the systems/resource model in organizational terms. This perspective on organization politics emphasizes the loop from environmental resource and demand inputs to the demands and resources which the organization exports to the environment as a result of policy decisions. The organization must 'balance' itself against the pattern of inputs from the environment. But as Thompson (1967) suggests, the politically stable organization is able both to make arrangements with external forces such that inputs are facilitative to internal interests, and to change its own interests and practices in response to external conditions.

Political analysis from the systems/resource perspective hinges on first tracing resource transfers between the environment and the organization, then looking at

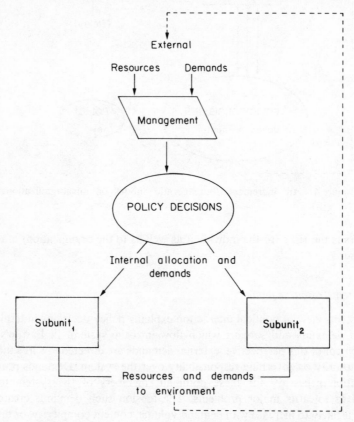

Figure 5   A systems model of intraorganizational politics

the allocation of resources within the organization. Specific questions for directing this diagnosis include:

- What are the sources and levels of external support for organizational activities?
- Are the uses of funds required by these sources consistent with other external demands placed upon the organization?
- How are resources allocated among organization subunits?
- Does internal allocation maximize resource generating environmental response? (Or, for example, does allocation represent past commitments as predicted by the incremental/bureaucratic model?)

The initial operating assumption is that power will accrue to those who supply 'outputs' which generate more external resources (Salancik and Pfeffer, 1974).

Implications for action taking

The political perspective indicates that it is important to locate the sources of power in organizations both to understand how interests can be protected and to locate 'leverage points' for change. This analysis is of concern to all actors in the organization, although the definition of what should be protected and what should change will vary depending upon the perspective.

The two issues which are of most interest can be expressed as reciprocals. On the one hand, those involved with the organization need the means to promote stability and control. When change is desired, the alternative problem is how present relationships can be rearranged or debilitated so that new power relationships can be formed. Once this is accomplished, interest reverts back to stabilizing and controlling the new arrangements.

The second half of this chapter examines the political implications for directing the two-sided process of initiating change in organizations and of protecting change efforts once introduced. It is assumed throughout, however, that the change agent is but one of several actors with a view of desirable change. Through time, if not initially, the question of introducting and stabilizing change becomes a question of thwarting (or, more benignly, 'channelling') incompatible ideas of desired change and stability which others may have. This raises value questions for the very core of OD practice which are addressed in the conclusion.

Changing the status quo

The basis for power in the organization, in the *structural* view, is through the formal subunits of the organization. The most direct way to increase power is to increase the jurisdiction of the unit. When this is not possible directly, the structural model suggests that the primary means for changing established power bases involves the creation of new entities which supplement or overlap older sub-units. Two likely functions for new units which successfully change the established political arrangement are the specialization or integration of tasks needed by the organization.

The *group* model, on the other hand, emphasizes interpersonal contacts and knowledge of participant self-interests as the source of power in organizations. The primary mechanism of influence is the established interest group with the ability to work against policy decisions if necessary. (It should be remembered that these interest groups often cut across the formal structural units of the organization.) The actor not already linked to an established interest group has the option of identifying interests not served by current groupings. Articulating dissatisfied interests may increase discontent to the point that a new group can be formed. Since some interests will always be unmet within the organization, the mere threat of interest group politicking may be sufficient to win concessions from those with a stake in the *status quo*.

The *elites* model offers a more difficult challenge to organizational change, especially in terms of major organization decisions. The primary leverage point within the existing system is through one of the relatively small number of existing elites, with potential influence or entry through those individuals to the informal contact system. Since the group with power is not identical to those holding formal positions, even identifying powerful individuals may be difficult. The model suggests a hierarchical arrangement of elites, however, which increases the number of available contact points. The revolutionary alternative to contact is destruction of the current structure of formal positions which allow expression of elite influence.

The basis for power identified by the *incremental/bureaucratic* model lies with established decisions. Those who wish to increase their power seek to institutionalize more favourable routines. Since routine decisions are not easily changed, an important strategic option for change suggested by the incremental model is to relate one's interests in some way to the past and projected future course of organization decisions. This is particularly important since past policy commitments are likely to have more impact on the direction of future policy than any deliberate efforts of individual organization members or groups. The alternative option, however, is to create or join a disturbance with enough force to be labelled a 'crisis', requiring organizational departure from established policy.

The basis for power in the *systems/resource* perspective, in contrast to the models developed previously, is command over the use of resources. Conditions can be changed by altering the allocation of resources to subunits of the organization. The primary means of capturing new resources is to alter the pattern of subunit outputs such that new demands or, even more advantageously, new resource inputs are presented to the organization from the environment.

Present power as an independent variable

Political change strategies can be arranged according to the level of power which the initiating unit currently enjoys, as summarized in Table 2. The models assume that even those with high levels of power, the top managers or key elites, will have difficulty in creating desired change. This, in fact, is the entering wedge which leads to the employment of OD professionals. Nor is relative 'level' of power always easy to determine, since it may not correlate with formally designated authority. One way in which organization members test their level of power or learn that old levels have changed is by observing the success or lack of success they experience in trying to change the system.

The left side of Table 2 suggests alternative strategies from the five models for promoting change which facilitates the interest of those in power. Two of these strategies are people-oriented. The group model suggests a coordinating strategy which involves negotiation and consensus building and thus is quite compatible with current OD practice, except that the model explicitly suggests 'grand coordination' of all interests which is highly unlikely. The elites model suggests

Table 2 Political strategies for organization change

	Actions with relatively great power		*Actions with relatively little power*
Structural model	Alter structural relationships	Expand domain	Integrate Specialize
Group model	Coordinate existing demands	Activate potential coalitions	
Elites model	Consolidate access to formal office holders	Increase coordination among middle-level elites Gain access to elite group Consolidate access to key individuals	Revolution leading to personnel and structural changes
Incremental/ bureaucratic model	Amplify past decisions		Promote or join crises
Systems/resource model	Alter resource allocation among units	Alter inputs to the organization	Align with valued output producing units

more concentrated effort on improving the top leaders' channels of influence through other office holders – each of whom must reliably respond to the change intentions of those higher up. The less coercive, more charismatic and rational of these elite strategies are also well within the bounds of current OD practice, but the study of politics suggests that more reliable means of influence involve debt and habit.

The other three models suggest change strategies that are much less interactive. The structural model requires giving primary attention to task allocation and technical domains, a more macro perspective than usually implied by the job design literature. Change from the *status quo* in this perspective also explicitly involves decreasing the relative area of influence of some units while increasing that of others. The incremental/bureaucratic model, on the other hand, looks not to tasks specifically, but to the entire roster of decisions currently in force with the notion of 'tagging on' new change ideas to current procedures. A third approach highlighted by the systems model looks to the output of various units and attempts to reallocate support or create new support which will alter the overall pattern of 'production'.

When the client has less relative power in the system, the political perspective suggests a somewhat different set of strategies. The more people-oriented strategies include the advice to activate new coalitions and to improve access to elite groups. The other models suggest expanding task domain or developing new tasks which integrate existing tasks. The systems/resource model's alternative is to increase production of outputs which will have the effect of improving the organization's position *vis-à-vis* its environment.

Finally, change efforts may also involve clients with relatively little current power in the system. Specialization is the primary advice available from the structural perspective. The elites' view of the political system suggests that a major change in the structure of formal positions will be necessary to realign the influences of elites, while a related strategy suggested by the incremental/ bureaucratic model is to create or join forces with crisis producing events.

It should be mentioned in passing that many of these strategies carry their own 'dangers' in the sense that implementing them may dilute the client's original purpose. Revolution, crisis, and even new coalitions, for example, are difficult to control once initiated. Specialization decreases flexibility to initiate or respond to change in the future. New structural relations assume a power of their own and are difficult to rescind, as constitutionalists have found, and so on. In general, the political perspective may be said to highlight change as a process involving continued alteration of systems which are rarely totally satisfactory to participants including those who gain the most.

Stabilizing change efforts

The 'continual adjustment' view of organization change emphasizes the need for change agents to give attention to the stabilization of their efforts. This topic has received relatively little attention in the OD literature to date. Notable exceptions, however, include Tannenbaum's (1976) discussion of the life and death of OD efforts and work relating planned change to the literature on innovation diffusion by Zaltman and Duncan (1977).

The necessity for stabilization in the political perspective grows directly out of the incompatibility of interests and values among diverse sets of organization participants. The client at every level of the organization can thus expect planned change, no matter how participatively developed, to be challenged by others with plans of their own. Political systems arise to contain and channel these challenges.

Table 3 suggests a series of different strategies, derived from the five models, for stabilizing planned change efforts. These strategies have as a common thread the theme of 'institutionalization' of desired change. This advice is in part a bias of the type of model chosen, but the emphasis on future control is seen as consistent with most individuals' perceived self-interest in organizational settings.

As should be expected from the previous discussion, however, the models suggest different means for stabilizing change efforts. The *structural* model proposes formalization of the subunits and tasks implied by the change effort.

Table 3   Political strategies for stabilizing change

Structural model	Specify task jurisdiction implied by the change
	Minimize oversight from other jurisdictions
	Balance oversight of others with jurisdictional overlap implied in the change effort
Group model	Regularize decisions which meet group interests
	Demonstrate group strength (when great, imply when not)
	Maintain group identifying activities
	Establish recognized and powerful representatives of group interests and contacts with management
Elites model	Identify specific influentials with change and promote their commitment
	Work through 'loyal' office holders
Incremental/ bureaucratic model	Translate decisions into 'standard operating procedure'
	Make the list of signals which invoke desired changes as broad as possible
Systems/resource model	Assure standardized resource support for new activities
	Demonstrate desirability of outputs in the most immediate terms possible

Power is maximized by limiting oversight by other units while gaining jurisdiction that provides oversight of others. The *group* model, in contrast, suggests careful review of the rewards (perhaps unintended in initial planning) of the change for interests of other organization participants. Change efforts which survive and gain power will meet some needs of others. Survival also rests upon managing the visibility of the interest group. Managerial decision makers must remain aware of the primary group most benefiting from the change, while visibility to other groups remains unobtrusive.

The *elites* model suggests identification of the change effort not with a group but with a few influentials and the formal office holders most responsive to their opinions. Change efforts survive because of continued sponsorship in the elite view. Yet sponsorship is of minimal importance in the *incremental/bureaucratic* model where stability is linked to successful experience and gradual incorporation of the change effort into widely held notions of 'the way things are done'. Socialization of new members to understand and accept the way in which these routines are activated and accomplished is particularly important.

Finally, the *systems/resource* model suggests that attention to the budget is the primary means of assuring continuity for change efforts. Continued support will be most likely if change can be linked to the provision of new resources for the organization as a whole.

It might be tempting to the change agent to implement as many of these alternatives as possible to maximize the chance of continuity. While more than one strategy may be desirable, each of the models explicitly denies the equal importance of factors highlighted by other models. Time and resource restraints also encourage selection of the political model which best fits the change situation and based on continued diagnosis.

Conclusion – the political challenge to client's and consultant's values

The political perspective on organizations and change in organizations is presented as a counterpoint to theories and practice derived from psychological and sociological origins. The alternative offered by the political perspective is in fact many perspectives, but more or less prominent is an underlying threat from each of the models presented to the humanistic tradition of OD. The basic tension arises out of the 'political' assumption that conflict – in values, interests, rewards – is an inherent attribute of human interaction. Political practices attempt to contain this conflict, they do not hope to resolve it.

When successful, political practices may well be detrimental to the preservation of individual values, however. Interaction in groups and through representatives dilutes and compromises the individual perspective. Political survival dictates abandoning individual views and accommodating uncomfortable and even opposing views. Thus, California's Governor Brown, who is opposed to capital punishment, is also reluctant to support a philosophically compatible bill sponsored by a politically active member of the opposing party. The Swedish prime minister, elected in 1976 on a platform which included stopping nuclear power production, nevertheless agreed, once in office, to continue plants already under construction in order to broaden support for his party's platform as a whole.

Political views of change also imply the triumph of some values over others. Except in the most sheltered and homogeneous situation, change requires rearrangement of existing relationships – the very existence of which indicate benefit. Thus, increasing the number of minority applicants accepted to medical schools decreases the number of positions available to other qualified applicants. Increasing student representation on university committees dilutes the influence of the faculty perspective.

The continuing tension between the means of influence and individual concerns is an important reason for knowing more about organization politics. It might be said that the individual view which does not gain support should not gain power in organized efforts. It might also be said that many individuals use 'acceptable' words like 'participation' without recognizing less acceptable attendant effects such as co-optation. The political perspective, much less devoted to the sanctity of individual opinion and the 'proper' approach to change, raises a challenge for organization development which deserves attention.

Note

1. The approach taken in this paper was first suggested by a reading of Woll (1974). Several of the models are closely linked to his descriptions of alternative explanations of public policy formation. For other descriptions of competing political models, see Dye (1975), Allison (1971), and Ostrom (1974).

References

Allison, Graham T. (1971) *Essence of Decision*. Boston: Little, Brown.
Beer, Michael, and Huse, Edgar F. (1972) A systems approach to organization development. *Journal of Applied Behavioral Science*, 8, 79–101.
Braybrooke, D., and Lindblom, Charles E. (1963) *A Strategy of Decision*. New York: Free Press.
Cyert, Richard M., and March, James G. (1963) *A Behavioral Theory of the Firm*. Englewood Cliffs, NJ: Prentice-Hall.
Dahl, Robert A. (1957) The concept of power. *Behavioral Science*, 2, 201–215.
Dahl, Robert A. (1959) Business and politics. *American Political Science Review*, 53, 1–34.
Dahl, Robert A. (1961) *Who Governs?* New Haven, Conn.: Yale University Press.
Denhardt, Robert B. (1971) The organization as a political system. *Western Political Science Quarterly*, 24, 675–686.
Dye, Thomas R. (1975) *Understanding Public Policy*, 2nd ed. Englewood Cliffs, NJ: Prentice-Hall.
Easton, David (1965) *A Systems Analysis of Political Life*. New York: Wiley.
French, Wendell L., and Bell, Cecil H., Jun. (1978) *Organization Development*. Englewood Cliffs, NJ: Prentice-Hall.

Katz, Daniel, and Kahn, Robert L. (1978) *The Social Psychology of Organizations*, 2nd ed. New York: Wiley.

Lawrence, Paul R., and Lorsch, Jay W. (1967) *Organization and Environment*. Homewood, Ill.: Irwin.

Leavitt, H. J. (1965) Applied organizational change in industry. In J. G. March (ed.), *Handbook of Organizations*. Chicago: Rand McNally, 1144–1170.

Lippitt, R., Watson, J., and Westley, B. (1958) *The Dynamics of Planned Change*. New York: Harcourt, Brace & World.

Marguiles, Newton, and Raia, Anthony P. (1978) *Conceptual Foundations of Organizational Development*. New York: McGraw-Hill.

Miller, E. J., and Rice, A. K. (1967) *Systems of Organization*. London: Tavistock.

Mills, C. Wright (1956) *The Power Elite*. New York: Oxford University Press.

Mohrman, Susan Albers, and Mohrman, Allen M., Jun. (1977) Organization policies and development: OD as politics. Unpublished paper.

Ohlin, Lloyd E. (1960) Conflicting interests in correctional objectives. In R. Clow *et al.*, *Thematic Studies in the Social Organization of the Prison*. New York: Social Science Research Council, 111–129.

Ostrom, Vincent (1974) *The Intellectual Crises in American Public Administration*. Alabama: The University of Alabama Press.

Pettigrew, Andrew M. (1973) *The Politics of Organizational Decision-Making*. London: Tavistock.

Pfeffer, Jeffrey, and Salancik, Gerald R. (1974) Organizational decision-making as a political process: The case of the university budget. *Administrative Science Quarterly*, **19**, 135–151.

Pondy, Louis R. (1967) Organization conflict: concepts and models. *Administrative Science Quarterly*, **12**, 296–320.

Salancik, Gerald R., and Pfeffer, Jeffrey (1974) The basis of use of power in organizational decision-making: The case of the university. *Administrative Science Quarterly*, **19**, 453–473.

Schein, Virginia E. (1977) Individual power and political behaviors in organizations: An inadequately explored reality. *Academy of Management Review*, **2**, 64–72.

Tannenbaum, Robert (1976) Some matters of life and death. UCLA: Human Systems Development Working Paper no. 76–2.

Thompson, James D. (1967) *Organizations in Action*. New York: McGraw-Hill.

Truman, David (1953) *The Governmental Process*. New York: Knopf.

Tushman, Michael L. (1977) A political approach to organizations: A review and rationale. *Academy of Management Review*, **2**, 206–216.

Woll, Peter (1974) *Public Policy*. Cambridge, Mass.: Winthrop.

Zaltman, Gerald, and Duncan, Robert (1977) *Strategies for Planned Change*. New York: Wiley.

Systems Theory for Organization Development
Edited by T. G. Cummings
© 1980 John Wiley & Sons Ltd.

Chapter **8**

Planned Change in Underorganized Systems[1]

L. Dave Brown

General systems theory has been the dominant theoretical underpinning for explaining organizational behaviour for at least a decade. But systems theory, like any conceptual infrastructure, emphasizes some aspects of reality at the expense of obscuring others. This chapter argues that *degree of organization* is an explanatory variable that has been neglected, in part because of the emphases of systems theory, and explores some implications of that concept for planned change in organizations.

The chapter deals first with degree of organization as a concept, and with the characteristics of tightly and loosely organized systems. On the basis of these ideas, planned change activities in overorganized and underorganized systems are compared, and two cases of the latter discussed. Finally, some general implications of the distinction between tightly and loosely organized systems are considered.

Systems theory and degree of organization

A defining characteristic of 'systems' is the organization of their components in relation to one another (Miller, 1971). Aggregates of components that are not organized, like a pile of sand, are 'heaps' rather than systems. Theoretically, each system has a distinct organizing principle for arranging its components and integrating them into a larger whole. Thus living systems, concerned with survival and growth, organize their components to perform relatively enduring cycles of input, conversion, and output transactions with their environments. Living systems must organize themselves to perform these cycles effectively, while preserving sufficient flexibility to respond to environmental changes.

Over time, living systems tend to evolve patterns of behaviour – to become more organized in the sense of developing 'mechanized' patterns of behaviour to respond to recurrent problems. Systems initially tend to preserve their steady states by 'primary regulation', in which disruptions evoke responses from the

181

system as a whole. As systems become more organized, however, they develop differentiated components and feedback loops that permit 'secondary regulation' of disruptions by more localized and preprogrammed response (Bertalanffy, 1968, p. 44). Although this mechanization allows more effective use of systemic resources, it also reduces the flexibility of the system as a whole, because the specialized components and mechanisms have sacrificed some of their potential for response (Bertalanffy, 1968, pp. 69–70). The development of the motor car assembly line, for example, offers huge increases in assembly efficiency, but only at the cost of much organizational flexibility (Schumacher, 1973).

Although degree of organization has been recognized in systems theory, most research in organizations has focused on tightly organized systems, i.e. business firms, manufacturing organizations, large bureaucracies. At least three factors have contributed to this emphasis.

First, systems theory is rooted in theoretical biology, and biological systems differ from social systems in important respects. Biological organisms develop in response to a genetic template that does not change in the course of the organism's lifetime; hence, biologically-based systems theory did not develop conceptual apparatus for examining major shifts in degrees of organization during the system's life – even though such shifts are commonplace in organizations. Biological organisms achieve a high degree of organization to qualify as living systems and their components may be organized according to a single principle, but a theory based on such organisms will not necessarily apply to social systems characterized by comparatively low degrees of organization and multiple, conflicting, or vague organizing principles. Thus the conceptual apparatus of biological systems theory tends to bias research in favour of highly organized systems.

Second, tightly organized systems also tend to be more visible and amenable to investigation by present research methodologies. The most commonly studied organizations – businesses, industrial firms, government bureaucracies, military organizations – all tend to be easily identifiable as discrete entities because they are tightly organized. The difficulty and expense involved in longitudinal studies has encouraged cross-sectional comparisons as a dominant approach (Pettigrew, 1976), and so made observation of changes in degree of organization over time unlikely. Survey research and laboratory experimentation – the currently dominant behavioural science research methodologies (Diesing, 1971) – are also most useful for research in tightly organized systems where subsystems and causal links are relatively identifiable.

Finally, many of the investigators who have applied systems theory to organizations have implicitly (or explicitly) assumed an organizing principle, like a 'primary task' (e.g. Miller and Rice, 1967; Lawrence and Lorsch, 1967; Thompson, 1967), that ignores the possibility of conflicting or vaguely defined principles. This position has been characterized as the 'managerialist perspective' by critics (e.g. Pfeffer, 1978; Benson, 1977), because it adopts the viewpoint of organization managers and neglects alternative organizational stakeholders. The need for research entrée and support from management further enhances the ideological tendency to conceive of systems as tightly organized even where alternative conceptions may be clear to outsiders.

Some social scientists have pointed out that systems can differ in degree of organization. Campbell (1958) and Buckley (1967) suggested that 'degree of entitivity' is an important aspect of social systems, and Weick (1974) argued that the systems paradigm might be over-used in an often unsystemic world. The applicability of some systems assumptions has also been brought into question by empirical work. Cohen, March, and Olsen (1972), for example, examined decision making processes in 'organized anarchies', characterized by such non-systemic attributes as ambiguous goals, vague technologies, and fluid participation. Weick (1967) has argued that educational organizations are 'loosely coupled systems', in which the interdependence among subsystems and the links between intentions and actions may be unclear or indeterminate. Alderfer *et al.* (1976) distinguish between 'underbounded' and 'overbounded' systems whose differing boundary conditions call for different strategies of organizational research and diagnosis. From a variety of conceptual and empirical perspectives, then, investigators have found that organizations are not always tightly organized, and that degree of organization may be an important variable for understanding organizational behaviour.

Loosely and tightly organized systems

Degree of organization in social systems refers to the extent to which subsystem behaviour is defined and constrained by regulatory mechanisms. For instance, tightly organized systems offer fewer degrees of freedom than loosely organized systems: stations on a motor car assembly line are more closely regulated than glassblowers creating *objects d'art*, and maximum security prisoners are presumably more regimented than elite graduate students.

Regulatory mechanisms

Organizations use a variety of mechanisms to regulate subsystem behaviour. Four primary mechanisms are: leadership, informal culture, formal structure, and technology. These mechanisms are roughly ordered by ascending degree of formalization. Leadership is less formally predetermined than informal culture; informal culture is less elaborately articulated than formal structure; formal structure less clearly specifies behavioural patterns than the demands of technology. Each mechanism is discussed below before the implications of tight and loose organization are examined in more detail.

Organizational *leadership* influences the behaviour of individuals and groups in the organization directly, through specific decisions and actions, and indirectly, by creating climates and setting examples. The reactions of individuals in leadership roles are the most immediate and flexible mechanisms for responding to novelty and the need for system control.

Leadership behaviour that closely supervises and regulates subordinate behaviour contributes to tight organization; conversely, leadership that permits subordinate discretion and autonomy contributes to loose organization. Leadership roles in tightly organized systems are likely to be well-defined and powerful; leadership roles in loosely organized systems tend to be vaguely defined or low in influence. An enormous volume of research indicates that system performance is a complex function of leadership style and situational contingencies (e.g. Fiedler, 1967; House, 1971) and the appropriate mix for leaders in roles that face high degrees of turbulence and ambiguity is not fully understood (Kotter and Lawrence, 1974; Ansoff, 1972). It does seem clear, however, that leadership is an important factor in formulating organizational strategies and design, particularly when 'right' answers are not obvious (Montanari, 1978).

The *informal culture* of the organization includes myths, rituals, languages, ideologies, and norms that govern and give meaning to behaviour of organization members. Cultural mechanisms establish tacitly what is 'appropriate' behaviour without necessarily formalizing that distinction explicitly (Pettigrew, 1976).

Cultural mechanisms may organize behaviour into consistent patterns that are difficult to change. Thus, workers in dull jobs may develop elaborate rituals legitimated by strong needs (Roy, 1960), and managers may follow implicit but powerful norms even though those norms promote ineffective decision making (Argyris, 1962). Alternative norms and expectations, on the other hand, can produce less constrained interaction (Argyris, 1962).

The *formal structure* of the organization is its vertical and horizontal differentiation into levels and departments, and its formally defined rules, procedures, and roles. The structure is a relatively durable and formalized regulatory mechanism, usually designed on rational grounds for task accomplishment.

The elaboration of structural mechanisms to specify and control behaviour may contribute to tight organization, or structures may be designed that are highly differentiated without being highly constraining of system and subsystem behaviour. Whether structural design produces a loosely or tightly organized system is contingent, as for the other control mechanisms, on a variety of factors, such as the degree of uncertainty produced by the system's environment (Lawrence and Lorsch, 1967; Burns and Stalker, 1961), the degree of uncertainty inherent in its tasks (Galbraith, 1977), and the implications of a given design for the distribution of systemic resources (Pfeffer, 1978).

The *technology* of the organization refers to the processes by which inputs are converted into outputs. Technologies vary in their susceptibility to specification and rationalization: some conversion processes, like assembly lines and stenographic pools, may be relatively easy to mechanize, while others, like basic research or artistic crafts, cannot be easily standardized (Slocum and Sims, 1978; Perrow, 1970).

Technologies that are well understood and relatively predictable can be the basis for tightly organized systems, while technologies that are either not well understood or subject to inevitable uncertainties may require a more loosely organized system (Slocum and Sims, 1978). Highly predictable technologies permit 'behavioural control' in which day-to-day activities are monitored, in contrast to 'output control' over products rather than activities (Slocum and Sims, 1978; Ouchi, 1978). The behaviour of assembly line workers is supervised, while the measure of research scientist productivity is publications and their daily round of activities remains unconstrained.

Degree of organization

The degree of organization of a given system is a complex function of multiple regulatory mechanisms, and particularly of the four discussed above. Degree of social system organization can be observed and ordered from relatively loose to relatively tight in terms of constraints on subsystem behaviour, even though it may be difficult to separate the contributions of leadership, culture, structure, and technology to those constraints. In some circumstances, mechanisms may counteract each other, as in the development of a cultural norm ('a fair day's work for a fair day's pay') that undermines a structural incentive system. But the cumulative effect of the regulatory mechanisms is to render the behaviour of the system and its subsystems more or less organized and determinate.

As a concept, degree of organization can be applied to compare different types of organizations, to examine organizational changes over time, or to describe differences within and between organizational subsystems. There are indications, for example, that different organizational sectors vary in their degree of organization. Business firms, military services, government bureaucracies, and prisons often appear to be tightly organized, while research firms, voluntary organizations, political parties, and schools appear to be loosely organized in comparison.

There is also evidence that a single system may change in degree of organization over time. An initially small and loosely organized system may become more tightly organized in the interest of growth and efficiency. The tendency to increase organization may in turn have to be reversed to cope with the rigidifying effects of size and routinization if novel challenges are posed by the environment (Chandler, 1962; Greiner, 1972). Thus, there may be oscillation over time between loose and tight organization.

Degree of organization may vary across departments within the organization, since departmental tasks call for relatively tight or loose organization (Lawrence and Lorsch, 1967). Indeed, the same department may vary in degree of organization over time as it confronts tasks with different degrees of uncertainty (Duncan, 1972). Proximity to turbulent external boundaries is associated with relatively loose organization (Miles, forthcoming) and the core technology of the organization may be carefully buffered from environmental uncertainty so it can be tightly organized (Thompson, 1967). Jobs that are forced to deal with uncertainty and change, like many management roles, must frequently be loosely organized to permit innovative and adaptive response to novel problems. In short, degree of organization may vary across organizational subsystems and levels as well as across organizations and over time.

Given that systems and subsystems vary in their degree of organization, what is desirable? When is the degree of organization too loose or too tight? A variety of criteria for evaluating organizational arrangements have been proposed, including impact on their members, impact on their environments, and ability to achieve their task goals (Ackoff, 1974). Task accomplishment dominates the organizational literature as a criterion, and so will be emphasized here more than the other two. But that is a choice of convenience rather than commitment: similar analyses could and should be made of degree of organization and its impact on organization members and organizational environments.

Different degrees of organization may be appropriate for different tasks. There is some evidence that loosely organized systems are more effective in coping with turbulent environments (Lawrence and Lorsch, 1967) or uncertain tasks (Galbraith, 1977), and that tightly organized systems are more effective in stable environments and well-understood tasks (Lawrence and Lorsch, 1967; Perrow, 1970).

Thus a system may be *overorganized* or *underorganized* in terms of its task. A degree of organization appropriate to one job (e.g. developing a marketing strategy for motor cars) may be underorganized for another, more routine task (e.g. putting together the motor cars on the assembly line) and overorganized for a job involving more uncertainty (e.g. basic research on new engine design). For the task accomplishment criterion, degree of organization needs to be matched to the demands of the task, though it should be noted that this match may not be appropriate to the interests of either organization members or the organization's environment.

Figure 1 represents the continuum of organization running from the theoretical poles of totally organized (and so entirely predetermined) systems to totally unorganized (and so non-existent) systems. All living systems can be placed on the continuum somewhere between those poles. Whether a given system falls into the problematic range of under-or-over-organization turns on the criteria used to assess it: as suggested above, for example, different degrees of organization are appropriate for different tasks. Between those problematic extremes there is for most systems a range of organization which is not problematic but which offers alternative degrees of tight and loose organization.

There are characteristic problems associated with too loose or too tight organization, some of which are summarized in Table 1. This table owes much to Alderfer *et al.'s* (1976) analysis.

Overorganized systems tend to be too tightly constrained and regulated to accomplish their tasks; they have leadership, informal cultures, formal structures,

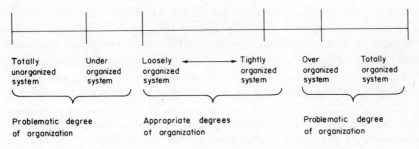

Figure 1 A continuum of organization

and technologies that are too confining for effective operation. This excessive regulation is likely to be evidenced in apathetic resignation, punctuated by outbursts of rebellious energy, on the part of organization members. Overorganization is also likely to distort or suppress the flow of information across boundaries between subsystems and levels in the organization. Potential differences between individuals and subsystems are likely to be suppressed or smoothed over in a collusive cooperation that avoids potential conflict at the expense of complete information or alternatives. Task activities are likely to be controlled by rules and caution, and response to novel situations is likely to be slow, conservative, and uninnovative. The external boundaries of the organization are likely to be clearly defined and relatively impermeable to novel inputs or outputs. Overorganized systems, in short, are subject to strangulation by their own regulatory mechanisms.

Underorganized systems, in contrast, are characterized by too little constraint and regulation for task accomplishment; they have leadership, informal cultures,

Table 1 Problems associated with extreme degrees of organization

Effects on	Overorganization	Underorganization
Human energy	Apathetic resignation; rebellious explosions	Unfocused and dissipated potentials
Flow of information	Suppression or distortion of crucial information	Relevant information not available when needed
Management of differences	Ignore differences; collusive cooperation	Withdrawal from conflict; escalated conflict
Task activity	Conservative; rule-bound; over-obedient	Inefficient; undependable; unfocused
Response to novelty	Slow; constricted; routine	Fragmented; partial
External boundaries	Rigidly defined; impermeable to novel environmental inputs or outputs	Vaguely defined; too permeable to disruptive environmental inputs or outputs

formal structures, and technologies that are not sufficiently defined or controlling to permit them to operate effectively. Human energy is likely to be diffused and dissipated by lack of adequate direction and focus by regulatory mechanisms. Since channels and responsibilities for information flows are also unclear, relevant information is often unavailable. Differences between individuals and groups in underorganized systems may result in withdrawal or escalation of conflict as a consequence of poor definition and regulation of subsystem interdependence. Task activities in underorganized systems are often characterized by low dependability and efficiency, since there are few mechanisms for regulating task behaviour. Response to novelty is likely to be fragmentary and partial, with some subsystems responding and others ignoring the issue. External boundaries are likely to be poorly defined and highly permeable to irrelevant or disruptive inputs and outputs. Underorganized systems, in short, are subject to dissolution for lack of regulatory mechanisms.

Both extremes – underorganized and overorganized – pose characteristic problems. A given organization may face problems of underorganization, over-organization, or even mixtures of the two, since different departments, levels, and situations may require different degrees or organization. The following section explores the general issue of planned change activities and their relation to degree of organization.

Degree of organization and planned change

Although the focus of this chapter is planned change in underorganized systems, change activities in overorganized systems are considered first to develop a com-parative baseline. Then some general concepts and two cases of intervention in underorganized systems are examined.

Planned change in overorganized systems

Planned change in overorganized systems involves altering the leadership, the informal culture, the formal structure, or the technology of the organization to decrease constraint on behaviour and to alleviate dysfunctional effects of those constraints. Such changes are typically designed to liberate suppressed energy, to increase the flow of relevant and accurate information, to promote constructive management of differences, to increase system capacity to innovate, and to open external boundaries to relevant environmental transactions.

A great deal has been done to respond to the characteristic problems of over-organization in business and industry under the general heading of organization development (see Friedlander and Brown, 1974; Alderfer, 1977). Organization development activities can be examined in terms of (1) characteristic *change strategies*, (2) *phases* of the change process, and (3) desired *relationships* between the client and the change agent.

Change strategies refer to the goals of planned change and the ways in which those goals have been approached. Underlying much of the work in organizational development has been the assumption that organizations are more effective if they are able to make better use of suppressed energy, information, and potentials. Thus massive efforts to create more open and participative leadership styles have been undertaken (Marrow, Bowers, and Seashore, 1967). Programmes to alter organizational culture to encourage more open communication and conflict have been developed (Alderfer and Brown, 1975). Organizational structures have been redesigned to promote more flexible response to ambiguity and changes posed by task and environment (Lawrence and Lorsch, 1969; Galbraith, 1977). Organizational technologies and their impacts on employees have been revamped to offer increased discretion and challenge (Rice, 1958; Slocum and Sims, 1978). In short, change strategies in organization development have focused on 'loosening' the constraints imposed by leadership, culture, structure, and technology to provide increased alternatives and discretion for organizational members and subsystems.

There are several *phases* of the change process in typical organization development. Although there are alternative models in the literature, there is general agreement that some versions of the following elements are included: (1) entry and contracting, (2) diagnosis and feedback, (3) planning and intervention, and (4) evaluation and follow-up (see Kolb and Frohman, 1970; Alderfer and Brown, 1975). These phases involve an iterative process of information collection and planned action that promotes valid and shared understanding of organizational problems, and joint design and implementation of solutions. During the phases and their iteration, the system hopefully becomes increasingly open to understanding and renewing itself.

The *relationship* between the organizational client system and the change agent is a critical feature of organization development activities. That relationship is potentially a microcosm of what the organization might become, and so offers the client an opportunity to test experientially what the consequences of less tightly organized interaction can be (Argyris, 1970). Thus, change agents seek to share leadership with clients, to develop norms that encourage open communications and conflict, and to create flexible structural and technological commitments in the consultation (Steele, 1975; Alderfer and Brown, 1975). Success in establishing an appropriately organized, consultant–client subsystem is good preparation for changing the larger system; failure bodes ill for the larger project.

To summarize: organization development activities have tended to derive from systems suffering from the consequences of overorganization. The resulting planned change activities are characterized by (1) strategies focused on 'loosening' the constraints imposed by organizational leadership, culture, structure, and technology; (2) phases of change that involve increasingly collaborative and penetrating cycles of entry, diagnosis, intervention, and evaluation; and (3) change agent–client relationships that are loosely organized in comparison with the larger client system.

These strategies, phases, and relationships have been developed in practice, and theoretical rationales in the literature have typically followed from that practice (Friedlander and Brown, 1974). But an internal logic can be discerned in these practice developed strategies, phases, and relationships that is concerned with 'opening up' the system in terms of choices, information, and autonomy (Argyris, 1970). The strategies, phases, and relationships in organization development are concerned in themselves with promoting increased openness at interpersonal and organizational levels of analysis. They also interact in a sequence of activities that gradually, in the ideal case, creates looser organization from the change agent–client relationship to the organization as a whole.

Planned change in underorganized systems: some contrasts

The thesis of this chapter is that the concept of degree of organization has important implications for planned change activities. This section considers planned change in underorganized systems in terms of the three catagories used to examine such activities in overorganized systems – change strategies, phases, and relationships.

Planned change in underorganized systems has fundamentally different goals from similar activities in overorganized systems. The primary concern in underorganized systems is with 'tightening' organization rather than 'loosening' it; the problems of the system have to do with *too little* regulation and constraint rather than too much. In such circumstances, the routine use of organization development strategies, created for the problems endemic to overorganized systems, can produce unexpected results. Indeed, application of such strategies may exacerbate the problems of underorganization.

Change strategies in underorganized systems should *increase* organization of the system. The role and influence of leadership may be clarified or increased through training, job definition, or selection. The impact of informal cultural mechanisms may be enlarged through the creation of new or more widely influential myths, norms, languages, or values. The regulatory effects of structure may be enhanced through new or clarified differentiations of levels, departments, roles, and procedures. The influence of technology may be expanded by clarifying, rationalizing, automating, or professionalizing the ways in which inputs are converted into outputs. In most cases, successful change activities will use a mixture of these regulating mechanisms rather than just one, but it should be clear that the thrust of change differs crucially from change in overorganized systems.

The *phases* of the change process can also be expected to vary with different extremes of organization. The phases of change in an overorganized system assume the existence of an indentifiable system that must be penetrated ('entry') to

Table 2 Planned change activities associated with extreme degree of organization

	Overorganization	*Underorganization*
Change strategies	Decrease pervasiveness and power of leadership control	Increase influence and clarify role of authorities
	Relax conformity to overconstraining cultural norms and values	Create more dependably influential norms and values
	Redesign structure for flexibility and responsiveness	Design structures to establish roles and rules
	Revise technology to promote autonomy and discretion	Rationalize technology to create predictability and regularity
Phases of the change process	*Entry:* establish expectations and contract	*Identification:* clarify nature of of system
	Diagnosis: collect and analyse data	*Convention:* bring together relevant subsystems
	Intervention: action to loosen system constraints	*Organization:* action to create control mechanisms
	Evaluation: assess intervention and plan future	*Evaluation:* assess organization and plan future
Relationship between change agent and client	Loosely organized in comparison with system as a whole: – leadership shared by consultant and client – norms for openness and flexibility – structure is loosely defined and flexible – technology is ambiguous	Tightly organized in comparison with system as a whole: – directive leadership by consultant – clear and constraining norms and values – specified roles and procedures – defined and routinized technology

gain concealed information ('diagnosis') as a prelude to opening up the system ('intervention'). But in underorganized systems, these assumptions typically do not apply. Such systems are often difficult to distinguish from their environments, and the first phase of the change process involves *identification* of the relevant system and subsystems. Once identified, work with the system as a whole requires an effort to bring relatively unconnected subsystems together, in what might be called a *convention* phase. When the relevant components of the system are in contact, an *organization* phase is possible in which new or elaborated mechanisms for regulating subsystem interaction can be created. The consequences of implementing that organization can be assessed in an *evaluation* phase, which in turn may lead to further change activities. Thus evaluation is common to change phases in both extremes of organization, but the nature of underorganized systems suggests the use of very different initial phases focused on the problems of bringing together the disparate components of the system.

The *relationship* between clients and change agents in underorganized systems may also be expected to differ from such relationships in overorganized systems. A relationship that mirrors the desired degree of organization in the larger system will be comparatively tightly organized. The change agent may develop a leadership role that is relatively well-defined and authoritative. The culture of the relationship can invoke clear and constraining norms, expectations, and languages. The formal structure of the relationship may be clearly specified in agreed-upon procedures, job descriptions, or binding rules. The ways in which the change agent and the client convert inputs into outputs, their technology, may be clearly defined and routinized. In short, client–change agent relationships, to be microcosmic models of desired changes, need to be more clearly defined and regulated in underorganized systems.

Thus, the internal logic of planned change activities in underorganized systems suggests that effective change activities will be different from those in over-organized systems. Conceptually, change strategies, phases, and relationships in underorganized systems can be expected to converge towards bringing together and tightening up the system, both alone and in their interaction. The logic of planned change in underorganized systems, it seems reasonable to expect, will be quite different from the logic relevant to changing overorganized systems. These differences in strategies, phases, and relationships are summarized in Table 2.

Planned change in underorganized systems: two case studies

Reconceptualizing an underorganized system: Ghetto Development Corporation

The Ghetto Development Corporation (GDC) was created in the wake of a major riot in the deteriorated black ghetto of a large midwestern city in the late 1960s. The explicit charge to the organization, funded by the federal government, was to promote economic development and improved housing in the area. Implicitly, the organization was expected to provide increased services to the residents and to prevent further riots. The first director of the organization was a charismatic black leader, who was able to create and maintain good relations with both the ghetto community, which was organized and militant in the late 1960s, and the urban business establishment, which had become interested in revitilizing the ghetto in the wake of the riots. GDC was instrumental in starting several small businesses and in promoting substantial new and rehabilitated housing projects in its first years of existence.

Over the ensuing decade, the city as a whole lost population to the suburbs, and the ghetto population in particular decreased by almost a third. The militant community organizations declined, and so did their vocal support for the activities of GDC. The federal funding agency, under Republican administrations, increasingly sought to promote profitable new ventures rather than provide financially draining community services. The business establishment began to lose interest in the ghetto, partly because of competing demands for resources from less deteriorated areas in the city. The controller of GDC, a man whose training and aptitudes made him adept at managing GDC's financial affairs but less skilled and interested in the 'politicking' (his word) required to maintain close ties with both the ghetto community and the business establishment, took over as the organization's director.

At the outset of the consultation, GDC was being threatened with defunding by the federal funding agency; it was essentially out of contact with the business establishment; its contact with the ghetto community was very limited; its board – composed largely of community members with a small minority of business and professional people – was a battleground for community power struggles and so unable to make decisions effectively or link the organization well to the community. The director was concerned about rumours that powerful interests planned to 'redevelop' the area by levelling present buildings and replacing them with middle-income and high-income housing developments – a suspicion fuelled by widespread discussion of 'new town' proposals that offered little room for the present low-income, black population.

Consultation with GDC began in part at the instigation of the author, who wanted to learn more about the community development corporation. The initial meetings between the author and the GDC director were unfocused and somewhat chaotic since the problems of the organization were not formulated clearly. Eventually, it became obvious that GDC did not have a clear conception of its role in the city, had no long-term strategy for implementing that role, and had little information about the various environments it faced (with the exception of the federal funding agency). It was agreed that the author and a class of doctoral students would do a preliminary diagnosis of GDC and its external environment. It was hoped that a team from the university might gain access to information and views that were not available to the organization or its director.

The consulting team interviewed GDC staff members and representatives of a number of relevant external organizations, some recommended by the director and others chosen by the team. On the basis of the interview data and a search of the literature on community development corporations, the team conceptualized GDC as a spanner of three different environments: the ghetto community, the business establishment, and the federal government. GDC's task was conceived to be coordinating or integrating these three environments to promote economic development. To accomplish this task, GDC staff members needed to establish close and cooperative relations with each environment.

But the three environments were not a tightly organized system; on the contrary, the three sectors were often unconnected or in conflict, and GDC was itself a response to riots that expressed the underorganization of the larger environment. To the extent that GDC staff established close relations with one sector (e.g. became close to the community), they were likely to come into conflict with another (e.g. the business establishment or the funding agency). Efforts to link with all three environments by GDC staff promoted internal fragmentation and underorganization to match relations among the three environments. Alternatively, GDC staff could deal with internal conflicts by avoiding close relations with sectors in conflict. There was evidence that GDC preserved close relations with the funding agency and decreased its contacts with the community and the business establishment, though GDC staff located responsibility for this development in the environment. Comments in interviews suggested more willingness to cooperate by the business establishment than was expected by GDC staff.

The information from interviews and the conceptualization of GDC as an environment spanning system were fed back to a meeting of the GDC staff. It was suggested that the conceptualization implied that (1) internal conflict in GDC might be a result of competence in relating to their environments rather than incompetence, (2) increased efforts to link with neglected but willing environmental organizations might be valuable in the future, (3) organizational structures that assigned special responsibilities for environments would be useful, and (4) future emphasis might be placed on projects that made use of existing good relations with environments (e.g. housing development).

Immediate responses from the GDC staff were very positive, particularly to the conceptualization that offered organizational explanations for problems previously explained as individual inadequacies. In subsequent months, GDC employed that framework in a crucial (and successful) proposal for further funding. They decided to increase their emphasis on housing development to take advantage of their environmental linkages. The director became much more active in 'politicking' and establishing links in the city-wide business and professional communities. In short, the brief consultation appeared to aid GDC to revise its self-concept, its associated strategy, and relevant staff behaviour.

This case illustrates graphically the difficulty of bounding underorganized systems. Although GDC was treated as the relevant system in the case, its internal problems of conflict and diffused leadership seemed in large part related to the underorganization of the larger environment with which it was intended to integrate. Ignoring the role of the environment in accounting for organizational behaviour, feasible in overorganized systems characterized by sharply defined and impermeable external boundaries, is problematic in underorganized systems, whose vaguely defined and permeable external boundaries permit catastrophic invasions by environmental factors.

The most significant elements in this consultation for changing the degree of organization in GDC appear in retrospect to have been conceptual: identification of the organization's future strategy as a problem, reconceptualizing the organization as an environment spanning system, and the implications of that framework for understanding organizational problems are cases in point. These ideas seemed to influence the organization's leadership and informal culture by suggesting new explanations for recurrent problems and implying alternative behaviours to manage them. In short, the consultation increased the self-regulative capacity of the system by offering new tools to its leadership and by influencing its cultural assumptions about task and competence.

Consistent with theoretical expectations, the identification phase of the consultation was protracted. The nature of GDC's problems and the boundaries of the relevant system were initially unclear. Indeed, the eventual conceptualization of GDC suggested that the real underorganized system was the organization's three environments. The convening phase of the project involved bringing together the staff members of GDC, who tended to be fragmented by environmental pressures; in a sense the activities of GDC itself as it tried to draw together the community, the federal government, and the business establishment are the convening phase of a larger change effort. The organizing and evaluating phases of this change were undertaken by GDC without the consulting team, though there is evidence that some new activities with organizing functions were undertaken.

The consulting team invested much effort to organize its relationship with the client system. Team members took an active role in defining the problem, designing the activities of both parties associated with the project, and clarifying the boundaries of a highly chaotic situation. Consistent with the theory of underorganized systems (but much against the 'participative' reflexes of most of the team members with experience in consulting to overorganized systems), the consulting team presented the information and their conceptualization of GDC in an authoritative fashion in the feedback meeting, with the intention of creating a conception of GDC's role that was shared across its fragmented staff. In short, the underorganized nature of the situation elicited organizing behaviour from the consulting team, even though their experience and preferences inclined them to less expert and more participative roles. The relationship between client system and consulting team became a microcosm of a system more tightly organized than GDC itself.

Regulating an interorganizational linkage: the Urban Transit Authority and the Transit Workers Union

The Urban Transit Authority (UTA) had expanded greatly over the ten years preceding the spring of 1977, in response to a large levy to support an innovative bus service. Many of the original drivers had been promoted to supervisory positions, and the force of drivers and mechanics had been drastically enlarged. Since UTA served a large university town, many of the new drivers and mechanics were ex-students of the university. In contrast to the old drivers, who were largely male, black, and lower middle class, many new drivers were white, female, well-educated, and politically radical.

The Transit Workers Union (TWU) was an independent union that had replaced a local chapter of the American Federation of State, County, and Municipal Employees several years previously. The TWU was organized and run largely by the recently appointed drivers and mechanics, who had taken over from the politically moderate leadership of the old union.

Relations between the UTA management and the TWU executive were stormy. In the contract negotiations after the election of TWU as bargaining agent, the management and union bargaining committees engaged in protracted negotiations characterized by misunderstandings, personal attacks, and activities considered to be 'dirty tricks' by both sides. The negotiations concluded with oral agreement at the eleventh hour, but misunderstandings about what had been agreed led to fourteen months of further negotiation after the contract had ostensibly been signed. Hard feelings persisted on both sides, and difficult negotiations culminating in a potentially long and bitter strike were anticipated in the forthcoming contract discussions.

Another consequence of the previous negotiations was the creation of a Quality of Work Committee, composed of union and management representatives and charged with solving a host of issues that were not negotiated at the bargaining table (e.g. redesigning some jobs and creating a new job classification). This committee had been trained and facilitated by consultants from the nearby university and its members trusted each other, in distinct contrast to union–management relations elsewhere in the organization. When it became clear that both sides expected a long and mutually costly strike, the committee proposed a 'prenegotiations workshop' for the bargaining committees. This workshop was conceived as an effort to prevent a strike based on the *process* of negotiations, rather than on disagreement about substantive issues.

After an elaborate series of negotiations between the bargaining committees, the consultants, and the Quality of Work Committee, the author was asked to interview the bargaining committees and the UTA director and to propose a workshop design on the basis of those interviews. The workshop would only be implemented if all parties agreed to the design. Financial support for the workshop was shared by the university, UTA, and TWU. The author spent a day interviewing the parties and talking to the consultants, designed a workshop for the two bargaining committees, and implemented it – with the agreement of the parties – the following day with the aid of the university consultants.

The interview data suggested that the bargaining committees were locked into a self-fulfilling pattern of relations in which negative stereotypes and mutually exploitive behaviour interacted to reinforce a cycle of escalating conflict. The interorganizational linkage between the committees was constantly in danger of dissolution as a consequence of intense conflict or withdrawal. Each party was replete with atrocity stories that featured the other as the villain and ignored its own complicity in the problem.

The workshop was designed to change the pattern of relations between the parties in three ways. First, a conceptual framework about the impersonal forces impinging on the bargaining situation was offered in brief lectures on the dynamics of intergroup conflict, its impact on group members, and means for managing conflict effectively. Second, attempts to differentiate intergroup stereotypes and increase intergroup communication were implemented by requiring the groups to list and share their perceptions of each other and the activities considered by each to be dirty tricks in negotiations. Third, near the end of the workshop the groups were offered an opportunity to negotiate ground rules for subsequent negotiations about substantive issues.

The author was careful to control the interaction between the two groups during the workshop, and to prevent escalation into personal attacks. The two committees responded by discussing each other's points of view with much interest and relatively little acrimony. Near the end of the day, as the issue of negotiating ground rules arose, the author invited the participants to decide whether they wished to go any further. To his surprise, the two groups quickly decided to try to negotiate some shared ground rules, including issues that had been major sources of contention in the previous negotiations. With comparatively little ado, the committees designed an agreement to regulate union negotiator relief time, a ground rule for contacting each other's constituencies, promises by both groups to avoid some 'dirty tricks' of the past, and commitment to meetings with the university consultants to discuss the process of negotiations as they proceeded.

Immediate reactions of both groups to the workshop were positive. As a manager put it, 'The air is cleared of a lot of stuff left over from the last negotiations.' Both groups were more optimistic about the possibility of agreement with opponents previously perceived to be ideologically and personally antagonistic.

In the longer term, there was a strike in spite of the fact that both groups kept the ground rule agreements made in the workshop. But the strike only lasted nine days, and a new contract based on the recommendations of a state appointed factfinder was accepted by both sides. Subsequent interviews with the parties indicated that the strike was a response to substantive disagreements and to the need for a test of strength rather than to the process of negotiations. Both union and management used phrases like 'reluctant respect' and 'statesmanlike' to describe the other group's behaviour in negotiations, and the quality of the negotiation process was unanimously described as greatly improved over the previous round. Management reported an unexpectedly rapid return to normal relations with the rank and file after the strike, an outcome remarkably in contrast to the poor relations after the previous negotiations when no strike occurred. In short, the workshop seems to have improved the committees' ability to regulate their interactions effectively, even though it did not prevent the strike.

In this case, it was the interorganizational system, in which the two bargaining committees were embedded, that was underorganized. The respective bargaining committees had become overorganized internally, governed by negative stereotypes and divergent views of their joint history that compelled them to fight in disregard of their interdependence. The workshop was designed to 'loosen' the degree of organization within the committees while 'tightening' the degree of organization between them. Thus, workshop lectures were intended to create a shared theory and language that emphasized the impersonal forces at work rather than the personal perfidy of individuals. Sharing perceptions and stereotypes increased between-group communications while differentiating within-group stereotypes. Negotiating shared ground rules created structures to govern inter-actions within the intersystem and to control unintended escalation. The workshop was designed, in short, to organize the interorganizational relationship – to develop regulatory mechanisms adequate to the task of negotiating complex and emotion laden issues.

The phases of the change process in this case were undertaken jointly by the Quality of Work Committee, the university consultants, and the author. The identification phase, in which the problem was defined and the parties identified, was handled by the Quality of Work Committee and the consultants. Similarly, all but the final elements of the convening phase were handled by the committee and the consultants, though the actual consummation of this phase did not occur until the author brought the two bargaining committees together in the workshop. The workshop itself involved both convening and organizing, as the parties gradually worked out cognitively and emotionally how they would work together in the future. The evaluation phase for the external parties took place several months later, in interviews about the effects of the workshop. It was clear at that time that the participants had already evaluated the experience and had invented a number of new mechanisms for interaction across the union–management gap in consequence.

The role of the consultants in this case involved a combination of loosening up overorganized bargaining committees and tightening up an underorganized intersystem between them. The Quality of Work Committee was careful explicitly to structure the steps preparatory to the workshop, so it would not become entangled with the politics of the underorganized intersystem. In interviews with parties before the workshop, the author was relatively non-directive, empathic, and open with the participants in order to develop rapport and to generate valid data about the situation. But in the workshop where the focus was on organizing the intersystem and keeping the participants from further escalating their conflict, the author was much more directive and controlling. One aspect of this role was the presentation of theoretical explanations for the previous behaviour of the parties; another was the explicit instructions about listing perceptions and sharing activities. In short, the consultant acted to promote relationships with the parties – both the committees, apart and together – that were more in keeping with the desired outcome of the consultation.

Discussion

It has been argued in this chapter that social systems exhibit varying degrees of organization, and that planned change activities must be consistent with the degree of organization of the system involved. Activities that seek to increase organization in underorganized systems are quite different from activities designed to decrease organization in overorganized systems.

The chapter so far has moved from examination of the concept of organization, through discussion of different degrees of organization and their implications for system functioning, to theory and case studies of planned change activities in overorganized and underorganized systems. It has been suggested theoretically and illustrated empirically that planned change in underorganized systems requires strategies, phases, and relationships that are fundamentally different from planned change activities in overorganized systems. In this section, more general implications of degree of organization will be considered, particularly as they relate to behavioural science consultation and research.

Inquiry in loosely organized systems may require approaches that are different from those in tightly organized systems. Such approaches may involve different underlying logics, different strategies for data collection, and different ethical issues and concerns.

A logic of inquiry for tightly organized systems has been derived from the natural sciences, particularly physics. It emphasizes the identification of variables and specification of causal relationships among them that permit explanation, prediction, and control of the system in question. But the application of that logic to complex social phenomena has been notoriously unsuccessful (Bakan, 1969; Phillips, 1973), in part because social phenomena are seldom as tightly organized as physical or even biological phenomena. A logic of inquiry appropriate to loosely organized systems must attend to the relative indeterminacy of events and relations in these systems. Sutherland (1973) has suggested that analytical modalities, or what might be called logics of inquiry, must be congruent with the degree of determinacy of the phenomenon studied. Thus he argues that positivist logic is appropriate for studying deterministic phenomena; inductive logic is appropriate for studying moderately stochastic phenomena; deductive logic is appropriate for studying severely stochastic phenomena; heuristic logic is appropriate for studying indeterminate phenomena. In this context, Sutherland's analysis suggests that deductive and heuristic logics may be required for inquiry in underorganized systems, which are likely to be less determinate than overorganized systems. Positivist or inductive logics will not be as fruitful in loosely organized systems as they have been in systems characterized by higher levels of control.

Data collection in overorganized systems must deal with the tendency for such systems to suppress the flow of valid information, particularly to outsiders. Although data collection strategies in overorganized systems have varied from creating cooperation and trust between researcher and subject (e.g. Argyris, 1970) to ferreting out information in spite of the resistance of an unwilling subject (Lehmann and Young, 1974), the dominant metaphor has been the *penetration* of relatively closed and impermeable system boundaries. The dominant problem in collecting data in underorganized systems, as Alderfer *et al.* (1976) have indicated, may be identifying appropriate boundaries and ensuring that information is collected from all relevant subsystems. The metaphorical research imperative in underorganized systems may be *inclusion*, since such systems are characterized by too little rather than too much boundary control. Penetrating the system is comparatively easy, but there is a high risk of excluding vital influences on system behaviour that are ostensibly part of its environment if too much attention is directed to the inside.

Data collection in social systems raises ethical questions concerning the potential impact of participation on research subjects. In overorganized systems, for example, the development of sophisticated methodologies for penetrating the barriers to information transfer (e.g. Webb *et al.*, 1966) poses serious issues about *violations of privacy* through misuse of information (Casell, 1978). But if underorganized systems encourage the development of methodologies that respond to their special circumstances, they may create fundamentally different risks. By definition, both information and individuals are less controlled and regulated in underorganized systems, and so both are potentially vulnerable to external influence. An ethical issue of importance in such systems may be *violations of autonomy*, in which the investigation will unduly influence respondents. For example, Brown and Tandon (1978) found that resident participation in interviews in an underorganized community resulted in increased community activism, even when the residents were randomly selected for interviews. The interview process, designed as an inquiry strategy, significantly affected respondents' behaviour six months later. The comparative lack of controls on respondent behaviour in underorganized systems may make them particularly vulnerable to influence by a data collection process, regardless of the researcher's intentions.

The need for congruence between planned change activities and degree of system organization has already been discussed in some detail. Two more pragmatic issues raised by the distinction are worth considering, however. First, work with underorganized systems raises to high salience the issue of power and how it is distributed within the system. Change activities in overorganized systems, and organization development practice in particular, have not come to grips directly with the issue of changing or preserving the distribution of power in organizations (Friedlander and Brown, 1974; Huse, 1975). This oversight is probably related to the tendency for organization development consultants to be employed by management clients, who are not interested in major changes in the distribution of power, and the tendency for overorganized systems to suppress dissent, particularly from lower levels of the hierarchy (Nord, 1978; Brown, 1976). Underorganized systems, in contrast, exhibit neither a clear power structure nor strong inhibitions on dissent. But attempts to increase organization in such systems inevitably affects whatever distribution of power exists. Change agents who work with underorganized systems must face the issues, feelings, and behaviours involved in power struggles, for they are not protected by either position in a well-structured hierarchy or controls on communications that are available in more tightly organized systems.

Second, work with underorganized systems may pose acute value dilemmas for change agents. Underorganized systems are susceptible to rapid and severe polarization around conflicts of interest, and change agents are often subject to pressure to commit themselves to one side or another. The need for change agents to take an authoritative role can interact with pressure to take controversial stands in ways that very quickly undermine their ability to work with some subsystems. Taking positions can be deadly, but so can avoiding commitment.

The combination of value dilemmas and the salience of power relations calls for special competences in change agents. Much has been written of the importance of interpersonal competence for consultants in overorganized systems (e.g. Argyris, 1970). An analogue in underorganized systems may be a *political competence* that enables the change agent to understand the distribution of power, the conflicts and concerns of interest, the dynamics of their interaction, and to manage effectively his own role and values in that interaction. Without such competence, planned change in underorganized systems is a risky proposition for both system and change agent.

Planned change in underorganized systems is a difficult challenge, and much of what is now understood about planned organizational change may be irrelevant, or worse, given its development in overorganized systems. Although the poles of the continuum of organization have been treated here, in fact most organizations exhibit varying degree of organization in different subsystems and at different times. So increased understanding of the possibilities of changing underorganized systems can be useful in most organizations. Further, many of our most pressing social issues – like the problems of social integration and development faced by the Ghetto Development Corporation, or the tensions created by conflicting interests of interdependent organizations like the Urban Transit Authority and the Transit Workers Union – can be analysed in terms of too much and too little organization. Better understanding of organization and better strategies for influencing it may well be a prerequisite to dealing effectively with such problems.

Note

1. After the first draft of this chapter was completed, the author received an early draft of Clayton Alderfer's forthcoming paper, 'Consulting to underbounded systems'. The two papers have similar conceptual roots, developed in the authors' work together, but they focus on different theoretical points. The authors cite one another's work to make quite different points, and the papers are in fact independently developed even though they have much in common.

References

Ackoff, R. L. (1974) *Redesigning the Future*. New York: Wiley.
Alderfer, C. P. (1977) Organization development. *Annual Review of Psychology*, **23**, 197–224.

202 SYSTEMS THEORY FOR ORGANIZATION DEVELOPMENT

Alderfer, C. P. (forthcoming) Consulting to underbounded systems. In C. Cooper and C. P. Alderfer (eds.) *Advances in Experiential Social Processes*, vol. II. London: Wiley.
Alderfer, C. P., and Brown, L. D. (1975) *Learning from Changing*. Beverly Hills, Calif.: Sage.
Alderfer, C. P., Meltzer, H., and Wickert, F. R. (1976) Boundary relations and organizational diagnosis. In *Humanizing Organizational Behavior*. Springfield, Ill.: C. C. Thomas.
Ansoff, I. (1972) The concept of strategic management. Working paper, Vanderbilt.
Argyris, C. (1962) *Interpersonal Competence and Organizational Effectiveness*. Homewood, Ill.: Dorsey.
Argyris, C. (1970) *Intervention Theory and Method*. Reading, Mass.: Addison-Wesley.
Bakan, D. (1969) *On Method*. San Francisco: Jossey-Bass.
Benson, J. K. (1977) Innovation and crisis in organizational analysis. In J. K. Benson, *Organizational Analysis*. Beverly Hills, Calif.: Sage.
Bertalanffy, L. von (1968) *General System Theory*. New York: Braziller.
Brown, L. D. (1976) Alternatives to the top-down approach, or If you're not a woodcutter, what are you doing with that axe? Paper for Academy of Management Symposium, Power and OD, Kansas City.
Brown, L. D., and Tandon, R. (1978) Interviews as catalysts in a community setting. *Journal of Applied Psychology*, **63**, 197–205.
Buckley, W. (1967) *Sociology and Modern Systems Theory*. Englewood Cliffs, NJ: Prentice-Hall.
Burns, T., and Stalker, C. M. (1961) *The Management of Innovation*. London: Tavistock.
Campbell, D. T. (1958) Common fate, similarity and other indices of the status of aggregates of persons as social entities. *Behavioral Science*, **3**, 14–25.
Casell, J. (1978) Risk and benefit to subjects of fieldwork. *American Sociologist*, **13** (3), 134–143.
Chandler, A. D. (1962) *Strategy and Structure*. Cambridge, Mass.: MIT.
Cohen, E. M., March, J. G., and Olsen, J. D. (1972) A garbage can model of organizational choice. *Administrative Science Quarterly*, **17**, 1–25.
Diesing, P. (1971) *Patterns of Discovery in the Social Sciences*. Chicago: Aldine Atherton.
Duncan, R. G. (1972) Characteristics of organizational environments and perceived environmental uncertainty. *Administrative Science Quarterly*, **17**, 313–327.
Fiedler, F. E. (1967) *A Theory of Leadership Effectiveness*. New York: Mc-Graw-Hill.
Friedlander, F., and Brown, L. D. (1974) Organization development. *Annual Review of Psychology*, **25**, 313–341.
Galbraith, J. (1977) *Organization Design*. Reading, Mass.: Addison-Wesley.
Greiner, L. (1972) Evolution and revolution as organizations grow. *Harvard Business Review*, **50**, 37.
House, R. J. (1971) A path–goal theory of leader effectiveness. *Administrative Science Quarterly*, **16**, 3.
Huse, E. F. (1975) *Organization Development and Change*. New York: West Publishing Co.
Kolb, D. A., and Frohman, A. (1970) An organization development approach to consulting. *Sloan Management Review*, **12**, 51–65.
Kotter, J. P., and Lawrence, P. (1974) *Mayors in Action*. New York: Wiley.
Lawrence, P., and Lorsch, J. (1967) *Organization and Environment*. Boston, Mass.: Harvard Business School.
Lawrence, P., and Lorsch, J. (1969) *Developing Organizations*. Reading, Mass.: Addison-Wesley.

Lehmann, R., and Young, T. R. (1974) From conflict theory to conflict methodology: An emerging paradigm for sociology. *Sociological Inquiry*, **44**, 15–28.

Marrow, A. J., Bowers, D. G., and Seashore, S. E. (1967) *Management by Participation*. New York: Harper & Row.

Miles, R. (forthcoming) *Macro Organizational Behavior*. Santa Monica, Calif.: Goodyear.

Miller, E. J., and Rice, A. K. (1967) *Systems of Organization*. London: Tavistock.

Miller, J. G. (1971) The nature of living systems. *Behavioral Science*, **16**, 277–301.

Montanari, J. R. (1978) Operationalizing strategic choice. In J. H. Jackson and C. P. Mill, *Organization Theory*. Englewood Cliffs, NJ: Prentice-Hall.

Nord, W. R. (1978) Dreams of humanization and the realities of power. *Academy of Management Review*, **3**, 674–679.

Ouchi, W. G. (1978) The transmission of control through the organizational hierarchy. *Academy of Management Journal*, **21**, 173–192.

Perrow, C. (1970) *Organizational Analysis: A Sociological View*. Belmont, Calif.: Brooks-Cole.

Pettigrew, A. (1976) The creation of organizational cultures. Paper presented to EIASM-Dansk Management Center Research Seminar on Entrepreneurs and the Process of Institution Building, Copenhagen.

Pfeffer, J. (1978) *Organizational Design*. Arlington Heights, Ill.: AHM.

Phillips, D. L. (1973) *Abandoning Method*. San Francisco: Jossey-Bass.

Rice, A. K. (1958) *Productivity and Social Organization: The Ahmedabad Experiment*. London: Tavistock.

Roy, D. F. (1960) 'Banana Time' – Job satisfaction and informal interaction. *Human Organization*, **18**, 158–168.

Schumacher, E. F. (1973) *Small is Beautiful: Economics as if People Mattered*. New York: Harper & Row.

Slocum, J. W., and Sims, H. P. (1978) A typology of technology and job redesign. Paper presented at AIDS meeting, St Louis.

Steele, F. I. (1975) *Consulting for Organizational Change*. Amherst: University of Massachusetts Press.

Sutherland, J. (1973) *A General Systems Philosophy for the Social and Behavioral Sciences*. New York: Braziller.

Thompson, J. A. (1967) *Organization in Action*. New York: McGraw-Hill.

Webb, E. J., Campbell, D. T., Schwartz, R. D., and Sechrest, L. (1966) Unobtrusive measures. In *Non-reactive Research in the Social Sciences*. Chicago: Rand-McNally.

Weick, K. E. (1974) Middle range theories of social systems. *Behavioral Science*, **19**, 357–367.

Weick, K. E. (1976) Educational organizations as loosely coupled systems. *Administrative Science Quarterly*, **21**, 1–19.

Systems Applications to Organization Development Practice

Introduction

In many ways organization development is a practice in search of a science. The relevant literature focuses more on specific techniques for improving organizations than on conceptual frameworks for linking the methods to explicit organizational phenomena and expected outcomes. Part III of the book bridges the gap between theory and practice. The four chapters examine different aspects of OD application and provide a systems framework for organizing OD techniques, explaining their appropriate change targets, and examining their likely consequences.

Burke presents an account of his personal experience, both positive and negative, of applying systems theory to organization development. He draws a useful parallel between systems theory and gestalt therapy, the conceptual underpinnings of his OD practice. Burke compares the two disciplines in terms of five linking dimensions: (1) open *v.* closed systems, (2) diagnosis *v.* dogma, (3) boundaries *v.* entities, (4) energy *v.* entropy, and (5) integration *v.* disintegration. He uses the concepts to elucidate OD practice and to tie systems theory and gestalt therapy to specific OD applications. Burke makes special reference to the concept of energy and suggests that both the organization and the OD practitioner must manage energy exchanges if the system is to survive and grow.

Eoyang raises the basic issue of whether organization development is really a systems approach. He presents a persuasive argument that OD tends to be narrowly focused and non-systemic in impact. Rather than belabour the point, Eoyang lays the groundwork for a systems science of OD. He develops a heuristic framework for organizing OD interventions in respect of their likely consequences for individual-, group-, and organization-level welfare. Eoyang suggests that particular OD methods may impact the three levels differentially, and that an ideal OD effort would maximize welfare at all three levels simultaneously. By linking OD interventions to multi-level outcomes, Eoyang provides a systemic approach for assessing organizational health and estimating the short- and long-term consequences of alternative OD strategies.

Lundberg, like Eoyang, focuses on organization development interventions. His point of departure is cybernetics, the application of positive and negative feedback for systems change and stability respectively. Lundberg uses cybernetics to reconceptualize OD as the creation, utilization, and extinction of feedback loops (both positive and negative); feedback processes rather than component structures are the targets of change. Based on this definition, he develops a classification of

OD interventions in terms of their change targets, intended outcomes, and feedback loop modifications. Lundberg illustrates the scheme with reference to several classical OD methods and case studies. He suggests that OD practitioners must consciously design and manage feedback loops if OD is to be a truly developmental process.

The final chapter in Part III addresses an issue often neglected in OD practice – the process of system design. McWhinney describes the premises, goals, and solutions of the two most dominant modes of system design, progressive and selective. He argues that these methods are unsuited to organizations facing complex and changing environments. He describes an alternative form of design, more responsive to these conditions – paedogenesis, or generated out of a non-mature form of the system. Paedogenic designing proceeds in four stages: (1) a disequilibrating event, (2) a retreat for a better start, (3) a founding or reassertion of identity, and (4) a return to forward designing. McWhinney describes these steps and uses concrete examples and case studies to illustrate relevant points. He offers an intriguing extension of paedogenic designing, lotal design, where one creates by allowing integrated images to rise ouf of the unconscious. McWhinney provides a comprehensive strategy for organization design: a guide for selecting from among alternative design modes a strategy appropriate to the organization, its goal, and environment.

Systems Theory for Organization Development
Edited by T. G. Cummings
© 1980 John Wiley & Sons Ltd.

Chapter **9**

Systems Theory, Gestalt Therapy, and Organization Development

W. Warner Burke

If you are a member of an organization and you've never considered yourself to be a part of a subsystem which in turn is part of a larger system which has a myriad of additional subsystems, then you've never been involved in a budget meeting. Recently I was told by one of my administrative bosses (we members of organizations called universities have difficulty in identifying our immediate superior much less *the* boss; such diffusion of responsibility and authority is characteristic of this type of system, no doubt) that if he agreed to my recruiting additional faculty, i.e. budget increase, he would be in trouble with many of his other departmental heads. The implication was that if my department were to grow other departments would have to shrink. My boss was thinking in closed system terms while I was thinking of the univeristy as an open system. I was surprised nevertheless, and a bit exasperated, to say the least. After all, I thought, we exist in an environment some aspects of which have never been tapped from a marketing standpoint. In other words, if one thinks in open system terms, it is conceivable to think about all or many departments growing as a result of a changed marketing strategy, while if one thinks in terms of closed systems, the staff of the university eats from a single pie with a limited number of slices.

Sound familiar? Of course. And am I being a bit presumptious and using hindsight to criticize my administrative boss? Probably. But as you will see later, I'm quite sensitive to the consequences of viewing an organization as a closed system. Let's set the stage first, however.

We are currently in the midst of what Ackoff (1974) has proclaimed as the Systems Age, our having passed via the Industrial Revolution from the Machine Age. That is, we not only do things differently in a technological sense – e.g. electronic data processing – but even more importantly, we think in different terms these days. We tend to see elements of our lives and work, if not our lives themselves, as being more related to and dependent on others than ever before. We are flooded with information that tells us how interconnected our society is, business with government, bank with the Federal Reserve Board, education with taxes, etc. Our society is a system which in turn, as we are being reminded more and more, is an integral part of a larger world system.

And, yes, Virginia, you should believe that the organization to which you belong is a system. It is a specific form of the more generic concept of system. An organization has multiple and interacting subsystems. Moreover, an organization consists of a systemic process of input→throughput (or transformation)→output. And depending on your favourite system thinker, an organization may be conceived as consisting of social, technical, and economic subsystems (Emery and Trist, 1960), or tasks, structure, technology, and people subsystems (Leavitt, 1965), or human, technological, organizational, and social subsystems (Seiler, 1967) or the more elaborate set of subsystems identified by Katz and Kahn (1966), namely, production or technical, supportive, maintenance, adaptive, and managerial. Apparently we are even more true believers in system theory than Virginia ever was in Santa Claus. We've been taught at school or by experience and/or we intuitively believe that when you intervene with one of these subsystems regardless of label, the process will probably have consequences, at least eventually, for all other subsystems within the total system. And as we have probably learned from organization theory if not from gestalt psychology, an organization is more than the sum of its parts – or something more than all of its subsystems. We know and believe these things, don't we? But do we, especially as consultants, act accordingly? I haven't in all of my consulting experiences, for sure. You'll see what I mean as I describe a failure or two in some case examples to follow.

Now let me explain what I am attempting to do in this chapter. I have two main purposes:

(1) In sharing what I have learned as a consultant to organizations, I hope to serve an educational purpose to other consultants. It is difficult, at best, to learn from someone else's experience. But learning occurs when experience is coupled with concepts, and if some of your experiences are similar to mine, then the concepts which I shall provide may help.

(2) As a consultant I have been stimulated by three related but different fields, general systems theory, especially as articulated by Katz and Kahn (1966) for considering organizations, organization development (OD), and gestalt therapy. I have read Katz and Kahn several times as well as related materials, I have been involved in OD for more than a dozen years, and I've been trained as a gestalt therapist. Seeing similarities, parallels, and overlap among these three areas has helped me to understand the practice of acting as consultant to organizations more thoroughly and to learn from some successes and from some rather painful failures. I shall therefore explain some of these relationships for the purpose of providing concepts which may prove useful for organizational consultants.

I shall not define or necessarily explain organization development. I shall, on the other hand, use five important dimensions which link general systems theory and gestalt therapy for the purpose of clarifying and hopefully facilitating the effective practice of OD.

To set the stage further, a general explanatory word about gestalt therapy and its relationship to general systems theory and organization development is in order.

Gestalt therapy is used for individuals and is often practised in group settings but, as such, it has not been applied to organizations. Some principles of gestalt therapy, on the other hand, have been directly applied towards the individual improvement of managers (Herman and Korenich, 1977). For the consulting process, if not for helping organizations to improve as a total system, gestalt therapy has untapped applicability. In any case, our theme is from the consultant's perspective.

Gestalt therapy, as originally developed by Fritz Perls, has its theoretical roots in gestalt psychology which was formulated by the Germans, Wertheimer, Koehler, and Koffka, and by Kurt Lewin. While there is not a literal English translation of the German word, gestalt, we know that it means something like 'meaningful organized whole'. In gestalt therapy, then, the patient is considered as a whole person but perhaps with parts which are unintegrated with that whole. The less than psychologically healthy person is one who 'uses many of his energies against himself . . .' (Perls et al., 1951, p. x). Thus, a prime goal in gestalt therapy is to mobilize the patient's energy towards integrating divided parts of this human system into a more meaningful organized whole. Joseph Zinker, an accomplished gestalt therapist, puts it this way:

Psychotherapy is a lively process of stoking the client's inner fires of awareness and contact. It involves exchanges of energy with the client – exchanges which stimulate and nourish the other person but do not deplete one's own vitality and power. In order for a person to 'work' in therapy and, consequently, to change, he needs energy. . . . Often his energy is locked in the muscular (or systemic) frigidity of his character structure, or, as most people like to see it, in his 'resistances.' (Zinker, 1977, p. 24.)

By dealing with 'unfinished business', by becoming more aware of one's suppressions (which have taken considerable and probably inappropriate energy), and by mobilizing energy towards more realistic and effective contact with the outside world, one is taking steps towards a more fully integrated and coordinated human system. And barring that unforeseen truck dashing around the corner, one has a better chance for long-term survival.

There are, therefore, obvious similarities and overlap between general systems theory and gestalt therapy. There are also parallels between the latter and OD. Whether a therapist or consultant, one emphasizes (a) the here-and-now, (b) humanistic concerns, (c) tapping unrealized potential, (d) an organic, holistic approach, and (e) experimentation, to name only a few of the many similarities and parallels.

Some linking dimensions

There are at least five important dimensions of gestalt therapy *vis-à-vis* general systems theory which help me to understand the practice of organization development more thoroughly:

(1) Open *v*. closed – viewing the organization as an open, dynamic, constantly changing system (like a human being) as opposed to a closed, static, and constantly equilibrating system, that is, everything is always in balance.

(2) Diagnosis *v*. dogma – understanding that a single subsystem is part of a larger system, and therefore that intervening in one causes ripple effects and eventual consequences for the other, helps the consultant to keep his or her focus on continuing diagnosis rather than on immediate cure. Moreover, any effect has multiple causes and to assume one cause is to move too quickly to 'corrective action'. I do not mean to imply that no action is taken or that action is unnecessarily delayed. It is more a matter of emphasis, i.e. of constantly learning about what makes this client organization tick (or not tick as the case may be). It is keeping in mind Kurt Lewin's axiom, to paraphrase: The best way to learn about an organization is to try to change it. Lewin's principle is just as applicable to one-to-one therapy.

(3) Waves *v*. particles; boundaries *v*. entities – for living systems, be they organizations or individuals, it is far more important to view the client in terms of relationships and interconnections of parts, and in terms of series of events, rather than to focus on singular bits and pieces or on specific points at particular times.

(4) Energy *v*. entropy – rechannelling energy in the organization to counteract the entropic process, a universal law of nature which states that all forms of organization move towards disorganization, that is, death.

(5) Integration *v*. disintegration – emphasizing in consultation (or therapy) the integration of all the subparts of the system for an organized effort towards a common objective. While in some instances it may be a matter of eliminating (disintegration) certain subparts which simply do not contribute or fit, the bias for consultation is more in terms of integration.

Open v. *closed*

One of my more successful efforts as an organization development consultant was with a medical school – incidentally, one of, if not the most, complex systems around. Over a period of more than three years my clients and I intervened in many aspects of the school. We changed the educational subsystem (as compared with the research and clinical subsystems) from one of teaching academic disciplines, e.g. biochemistry, to one of teaching organic subsystems, e.g. teaching the biochemistry of the endocrine system (there's that word again). This was a planned change effort directly involving more than half of the entire faculty. We also changed the structure from one of exclusively academic and clinical departments to a matrix which consisted of educational/teaching units cutting across these academic/clinical departments. We did team building with departments, we resolved intergroup conflicts, and we achieved greater goal clarity. But, while this effort was successful in the short term, it was a failure in the long run. Why? I *behaved* as if the school was a closed system even though I 'knew' it was an open one. In other words, I worked exclusively with the dean and those below him in the school's hierarchy and, for all practical purposes, ignored the fact that the school was a subsystem within a larger university. The dean had an administrative boss, the university's vice president for medical affairs, and he in turn had a boss, the president. This, of course, is administratively the case for many if not most large state university systems. The reasons I consider this case example a failure will become clear later.

What I am attempting to demonstrate concretely at this point is that change in one subsystem affects other subsystems; in this example the primary consequence was an upward one hierarchically speaking. Other examples from the same case could be provided for other directional consequences, such as within the university hospital or even across the campus at the dental school. This upward consequence, however, had dire effects.

To continue and hopefully to clarify, I must add now what may at first seem to be a tangential point. The consequences of any OD effort are frequently varied and difficult to trace. But one consequence or outcome seems clear to me. As a result of organizational members being involved in an OD effort over time, and with the outcomes of this effort being perceived as more positive than negative, these people begin to feel or experience more control over their organizational destiny.

Katz and Kahn (1966) express this point as follows: They assume that people have needs for participation and autonomy. They further assume that decision making is rewarding *per se*. When organizational members have the opportunity to make decisions this activity itself is rewarding, and people tend to repeat behaviour (or in any case have a desire to) for which they are rewarded. Thus, as organizational members become involved in decision making, especially those decisions which directly affect their area of work activity, they tend to expect and want more of these opportunities for the future. In a sense, this is a specific form of the principle of the 'rising level of expectations'. This phenomenon frequently accompanies activities which foster individual and group growth and development.

Much of OD rests on involvement techniques to accomplish growth and development. Consultants attempt to intervene so that people in organizations are directly involved in making decisions which affect them. I am no exception. I intervened in this manner many times in the medical school. When people make their own decisions, they feel more powerful, more in control. A sense of personal satisfaction is experienced by the very act of deciding something. The more this kind of opportunity occurs for organizational members, the more they feel satisfied and in control. And coupled with an increase in these feelings are rising expectations. That is, the more people experience these feelings, the more they wish to do so again in the future and probably even more often than in the past.

So, in the medical school the dean began to want more control over, among other things, his school's budget. Now it just happened that his school's budget was, in the final analysis, in the hands and at the prerogative of the university president. To make a long and complicated story short, as the dean began to put pressure on the president for more control over the medical school budget, the more the president perceived insubordination on the part of the dean. Within a matter of only a few weeks of this pressure and counter pressure, the dean finally 'lost'. He resigned and shortly thereafter joined the faculty of another medical school. Others resigned but most stayed. The OD effort, in any case, was aborted. What was especially disheartening was the fact that we had been at it for well over three years.

The subsystem ripple effect in this case was, at least in part, the desire of the dean and many of his colleagues for a more effective medical school. They had begun to move in that direction, as they perceived it, and experienced the satisfaction of positive results as a direct consequence of their own concerted efforts. With more control over their own subsystem they could do even better.

In behavioural terms, this example clearly illustrates that part of systems theory which accounts for the interactive impact of subsystems within a whole. The case example also illustrates a violation of what Katz and Kahn (1966) contend is the first step of organizational research from a systems theory frame of reference. (For our purposes here we'll substitute 'diagnosis' for their term, 'research'.) That is, 'the first step should always be to go to the next higher level of system organization, to study the dependence of the system in question upon the supersystem of which it is a part, for the supersystem sets the limits of variance of behaviour of the dependent system. (p. 58). There it was in black and white in 1966. What did I learn from this 'violation' of not acting according to systems theory?

One obvious thing I learned was to involve the boss of my client as early as possible in any OD effort. This I put into practice almost immediately. Shortly after the abortive end of my medical school consultation, another medical school dean in another part of the United States called me for consultation. I thought at the time that this second dean had obviously not heard of my previous medical school consultative experience. In any case, armed with new learning I accepted the consulting job. On my initial visit I arranged with my client dean that we visit his boss, yet another university vice president for medical affairs, to explain to him what we were planning and why. This we subsequently did and, from the standpoint of the supersystem, matters went smoothly indeed. Simply, I operated within the reality that the medical school was an open system and part of a larger organization. I made other mistakes, however, and perhaps yet other system theory violations with this medical system, but that's for another chapter at some other time and for another learning point.

Diagnosis v. dogma

General systems theory has also helped me not only to understand this medical school case more thoroughly but to be patient about eventually learning what is causing what. To see my client system as part of a larger system in terms of trying to understand what is cause and what is effect can lead to different diagnostic conclusions. Take, for example, a situation of intraorganizational conflict where everyone is blaming everyone else for the continuation of the same problem, i.e. in clinical terms, displacement abounds. In one manufacturing organization where this was occurring, I thought at first that I must be working with a peculiar breed. The predominant profession represented was engineering. They just liked to fight; putting out fires was what was fun. Never mind the cause of the fires. My second diagnosis was more clinical in that the former head of production had recently been fired and my guess was that, out of pervasive guilt, further displacement was occurring.

But subsequently I learned that the big boss from the supersystem a month earlier had told them (my client system, a division of the larger company) that unless they 'turned the division around in six months', he would close them down. It took me some amount of time to dig this piece of information out, but when I heard it, and later listened to an actual tape recording of the infamous challenge, my diagnosis was obviously much broader and clearer. In fact my intervention strategy eventually changed from one of team building and intergroup conflict resolution to suggesting changes in the reward system. With this latter move, however, I ran into a stone wall. The division general manager explained to me, rather timorously in fact, that the present reward system had been installed several years earlier by a certain individual who was now the corporate chief executive officer. My client further explained that if I wanted to change the reward system, I would have to go to the very top. I tried but never made it. The division general manager was certainly not going to climb that pyramid, at least not for that purpose.

The point is that diagnosis comes first, and a general systems theory frame of reference keeps one from moving too rapidly to inappropriate interventions. In gestalt therapy we are taught to begin each session anew regardless of how many previous sessions have occurred with the patient. With the lapse of time, the patient is never 'in the same place' as when you last left him or her, so you must begin diagnostically each time. The treatment is always diagnostically based, never assuming that the latest technique I've learned will necessarily fit the need of the patient.

Waves v. particles; boundaries v. entities

The medical school case and the manufacturing organization example have taught me the importance of working at 'connecting points' in the client system rather than exclusively with subsystems as entities. From the standpoint of the OD practitioner this means to consult at the margin, boundary, or interface of the client system with that of the larger system. This practice not only helps the consultant to diagnose behaviour within the client system more effectively but also to understand its boundaries. In other words, the practitioner is better able to clarify what the client system does, cannot do, has potential for, has prerogative for, who has authority for what, where the formal organization leaves off and the informal one begins, and linkages of communication. Also, as Margulies (1978) points out, staying at a boundary position when in a consultant role helps one to strike a more appropriate balance between content or technical, authoritative intervention and that of process consultation. Striking this balance is not easy. To use Herbert Shepard's (1975) words, 'it means living in several worlds without being swallowed up in any'. Moreover, it means to view the client organization as 'waves' of interconnecting parts rather than as static entities. In addition to describing organizations in terms of climate, one can also understand organizations as having rhythms. Some days, as with individuals, are better than others. Changes in the market, for example, often cause unsettling ripples in the organization's rhythm.

It is noteworthy to point out in this context that at least some physicists are beginning to view the invisible world of subatomic matter as 'waves of interconnections'. Prior to and during the Machine Age, physicists were some of, if not the leading, proponents of analysing matter in terms of breaking it down into its least divisible parts. Today, however, physicists tell us that matter at the subatomic level does not exist in terms of 'things' as we know them macroscopically but as 'probability waves', i.e. they only have tendencies to exist. This type of theorizing is obviously difficult to comprehend, but in a provocative article, Capra (1977), a high-energy physicist, explains, perhaps as clearly as one can to a lay reader, that protons and neutrons, those subparts of an atom, are not 'parts or particles' as we normally think of them. They are, rather, very abstract entities. Capra goes on to state:

Depending on how we look at them, they appear sometimes as particles, sometimes as waves. This dual aspect of matter was extremely puzzling. The picture of a wave that is always spread out in space is fundamentally different from the picture of a particle, which implies a sharp location.

The apparent contradiction was finally resolved in a completely unexpected way that dealt a blow to the very foundation of the mechanistic world view – the concept that matter is real. At the subatomic level, it was found, matter does not exist with certainty at definite pinpointable places but rather shows 'tendencies to exist'. These tendencies are expressed in quantum theory as probabilities, and the corresponding mathematical quantities take the form of waves; they are similar to the mathematical forms used to describe, for instance, a vibrating guitar string or sound wave. This is why particles can be waves at the same time. They are not 'real' three-dimensional waves like sound waves or water waves. They are 'probability waves', abstract mathematical quantities related to the probabilities of finding the particles at particular points in space and at particular times.

At the atomic level, then, the solid-material objects of classical physics dissolve into wavelike patterns of probabilities. These patterns, furthermore, do not represent probabilities of things, but rather probabilities of inter-connections. (p. 22)

Thus, according to Capra, in atomic physics you do not end up with 'things' but with 'a complicated web of relations between the various parts of a unified whole' (p. 23). And perhaps more fascinating is Capra's pointing to the remarkable similarities between current theoretical atomic physics and Eastern mysticism, that is, viewing the universe in terms of events (not things) which 'are woven into an inseparable net of endless, mutually conditioned relations' (Capra quoting a Tibetan Buddhist, Lama Govinda; p. 23).

Taking as evidence this type of work from the world of atomic physics, the proliferation of theory and application in areas such as operations research and system analysis, and this book itself, then Ackoff (1974) is accurate in his declaring recent years and the present to be the System Age.

So, systems theory has been highly useful in helping me (a) to understand some of my experiences as a consultant, and (b) to try to be a more effective consultant in the future. By way of summary at this point, systems theory has provided a frame of reference for remembering that even though I can only intervene in one part of a system at a time, that act may eventually have a consequence or start into motion a set of outcomes which will have an impact upon the entire system. Moreover, by concentrating my efforts at marginal or boundary points which exist between and *connect* subparts of a system I am more likely to keep the total system in mind, and I am more likely to provide a balance between content and process interventions.

But this usefulness of systems theory for me has been in retrospect. It's a little like being a Monday morning quarterback. Systems theory has seemed so lifeless to me, and being of and within the humanist current, I suppose for this reason I have ignored much of what I could have learned and thereby been more adequately forearmed as a consultant. Thus, gestalt therapy, a total system approach, but with life and a humanistic bias, has added to my consultative practice and provided a new perspective on general systems theory as well.

The final two dimensions come more from my experience with gestalt therapy than from general systems theory but the relationships and similarities are quite evident.

Energy v. *entropy*

A fundamental facet of von Bertalanffy's (1956) general systems theory is that of the energic input–output system. Katz and Kahn (1966) have applied this line of thinking to their conceptualization of an organization. For them, 'the two basic criteria for identifying social systems and determining their functions are (1) tracing the pattern of energy exchange or activity of people as it results in some output and (2) ascertaining how the output is translated into energy which reactivates the pattern' (p. 18). Open systems import energy, e.g. raw materials, money, etc., of some kind from their external environment. This energy is transformed by the organization and then exported back to the external environment in the form of a product or service. This input–transformation–output pattern of energy exchange is cyclical and, therefore, the product or service 'exported into the environment furnishes the sources of energy for the repetition of the cycle of activities. . . . It is events rather than things which are structured so that they comprise a unity in their completion or closure' (pp. 20–21). Note the language used by Katz and Kahn. They depict organizations as structured *events*, as dynamic not static. Capra, you will recall, pictures the subatomic world in much the same way.

It is what an organization does with its energy that counts. And to complicate matters further Katz and Kahn point out that to survive organizations must function to stop the entropic process. But organizations differ from biological systems in that they are capable of living indefinitely *provided* they take from their environment more than they use or consume, i.e. provided they transform the energy effectively. For a business, of course, this means to continue to make a profit or, at least, not to suffer undue costs. Today this principle is even more complicated in that survival of certain industrial organizations is more threatened than in the past due to the organization not only taking from its environment more than it uses but in a literal sense actually damaging (polluting) its environment in the process.

For survival, then, an organization must not only take from its environment more than it uses but it must constantly arrange for accurate feedback from the environment to ensure that the organization's output is accomplishing what the organization intends. This requires energy not only of the kind Katz and Kahn mean but organizational member energy as well. Channelling this energic process for optimal mission attainment is what organizational life is all about.

It may be easier to understand energy as an important human concept in therapy than in an organization, for Katz and Kahn discuss energy in broader terms – money, raw materials, etc. But they also mean human energy in the organization. To survive, an organization must 'draw renewed supplies of energy from other institutions, or people, or the material environment' (p. 20). For my purposes here the key words in that statement in addition to energy are *renewed* and *people*. It could easily be said that for OD to work there must be people who have renewed energy.

In gestalt therapy a major objective is not only to identify how the patient is using his or her energy but to rechannel it for more productive purposes (see the earlier Zinker quote). The same objective should hold for OD consultation. A first diagnostic step in organization development, therefore, should be to determine how and where people in the organization use their energy.

A popular belief is that in matters of change, i.e. organization development, people use their energy in resistance. People naturally resist change, so the belief goes. Interestingly, the classic study of Coch and French (1948) which established a major research and theory base for much of OD was entitled 'Overcoming resistance to change'. And we have been assuming all along that people simply prefer the *status quo*. Recently, however, a piece of atypical advice was given for OD practitioners by Jerry Harvey (1975). His advice is *not* to make this assumption. Moreover, he insists that resistance to change is a myth. Harvey goes on to state that for one to hold this assumption or belief, one must then explain why some people resist change while others seek it; 'because for resistance to occur, others have to want change to take place. In addition, the concept would have to explain why some of us want to change on some days and resist it on others' (p. 3). Logical, right? Yes, but two additional points of clarification are in order.

First, while people in an organization may not naturally resist change, they do express resistant behaviour from time to time. I think that even though people may not resist change *per se* they do relatively naturally resist the *imposition* of change. In other words, in this age of systems and in these times of 'quality of work life' and 'human dignity and rights', people are not as receptive to unilateral decision making, especially when it affects them directly, and are not as blindly obedient to arbitrary uses of authority as people were during the Machine Age and before.

Thus, resistance in organizations may indeed be found but can be adequately managed. Thus, my second point is that resistance requires energy. Have you ever considered how much energy you use when you wish to be stubborn? Calories burn like August brush fires. Even your jaws and muscles may ache afterwards. From an OD standpoint, therefore, it is a matter of attempting to redirect or rechannel this energy.

It may not be safe to assume that people resist change but it is safe to assume that people in organizations have energy. It may not at times look like it, especially when apathy and lethargy seem to characterize much of organizational behaviour. Unless one is ill, lethargy can last only so long. To expend energy is a natural process. Where does it go is the question. Perhaps it is spent at home, at play, or at a hobby rather than on the job. This direction of one's energy is normal and perhaps beneficial, but is it being directed to other places because the work situation is so boring or frustrating? The recent quality of work life impetus is, of course, directed at alleviating some of these problems.

One final point about resistance. A rather prevalent form resistance can take in an organization is through attempts to 'beat the system'. Beating the system is almost synonymous with 'the American way'. I have heard veterans declare that if GIs on many occasions had not ignored the system, World War II would have lasted much longer. I practised some of this 'American way' myself during my two years in the Army, considerably after World War II, I might add. In such a huge and bureaucratic system, it is not only tempting to see what you can get away with, this deviant behaviour also at times seems necessary when tasks need to be accomplished rapidly. Again, from an OD perspective, it is a matter of mobilizing people's energy from defeating the system to changing it. That is, changing it so that energy is channeled more directly towards task accomplishment rather than towards task accomplishment *plus* the invention of some new, temporary system to get around the existing one. It is interesting to note, incidentally, that in the name of OD some temporary and 'collateral' systems have been established to accomplish work the permanent system could not apparently handle (Alderfer, 1977; Zand, 1974).

Integration v. *disintegration*

When all of an organization's subparts are *integrated* within the whole in such a way that the energy used by each is in the direction of total organizational efficiency and effectiveness, then survival is not only more assured but we shall have what might be called a *healthy* organization. And where poor health or illness exists therapy is in order. A major purpose of gestalt therapy is to put together in an 'organized' way those parts of a person that are not integrated. Accomplishing this purpose often takes the form of confronting the patient with pieces of self which he or she wishes to avoid, reject, suppress, or deny but which are in the final analysis a real part of the person. This part could be a physical feature which the person considers unbecoming or a personality characteristic which the person simply wishes did not exist. Helping the person to accept and integrate these unwanted and/or undesirable parts is therefore the therapeutic goal.

The therapeutic goal of integration and the general systems theory notions of interrelated parts making a whole (a gestalt) have helped me to be clearer about my objectives as a consultant to an organization. I want to see how and if all parts fit the total organized effort, and if some do not, I want to know why not. Unlike a person, it may be relatively easy for an organization to eliminate undesirable parts when they are not contributing to the total effort. Assuming the effort is towards making a profit, then unprofitable parts may, of course, be discarded.

More importantly, however, the consultation in this context is likely to be structural in nature. That is, disintegrated parts (departments, functions, businesses) may be integrated by reorganization. The work of Lawrence and Lorsch (1967) readily comes to mind. Their theory of differentiation and integration is most useful in providing a more detailed framework for this broader system dimension of integration–disintegration.

Summary and conclusion

To be an effective OD practitioner, if not to survive as a consultant to organizations, one must diagnostically view the client organization as an open system which has interdependent subsystems, which depends on and interacts with its environment, and which naturally moves towards its own demise. For survival and for growth, however growth for the organization may be defined, energy and the exchange thereof is required. From an OD perspective this exchange of energy can be viewed as taking three forms for an organization:

(1) the exchange of money and/or materials via an input–throughput–output process, such that more energy is taken in or used than is returned to the environment;
(2) the nature of how organizational members expend their personal energies during the transformation of throughput phase of the open system; and
(3) the exchange of energy between the consultant and the client.

It is important for the OD consultant/practitioner intellectually to understand (1), to diagnose the quantity and quality of (2), and to learn how to practise (3). With respect to this third form, a final word is in order.

Not only must an OD consultant/practitioner provide expertise to the client in the form of (a) accurate assessments of what's right, wrong, and in need of improvement, (b) alternatives for action, (c) help with action steps, and (d) appropriate evaluation, but *energy* in the relationship is expected as well. In other words, a client wants to believe that the consultant can help. Well, at least most of the time. Games are sometimes played by clients, but that's another chapter. With this desire to believe goes expectations that the consultant will *do something*. In OD consultation, especially at the outset, the client may be confused because the consultant wants to talk with a bunch of people before 'taking any action'. The client wants action, the consultant wants more information. For the consultant the energy is in the information, for the client it is in doing something – now. So, in addition to using intellectual energy in trying to understand the information being gathered, the consultant must also provide energy to the client in the form of emotional support. To oversimplify, the exchange is support for information. Being empathic is, of course, one way of providing support. Also telling the client that you are beginning to make some sense out of the information you are gathering is another.

This exchange of energy between consultant and client may also determine a major part of the system diagnosis. As a consultant I have at times felt drained after only a day of work. This has been especially true at the beginning of an OD effort for I am working hard to (a) understand what makes the client system tick, and (b) establish rapport with and support for the people with whom I'm interacting. And it feels as if people in the system are either resisting me or draining me of information, i.e. my having to respond to a myriad of questions. My providing energy to the system in this way is to be expected. But if this is the form the exchange is taking then that tells me something about how energy is used in the client organization itself. In other words, members of the organization may feel as if considerable time is wasted in resistance to new ideas or in too many questions being asked with too few answers. How the energy exchange feels to you the consultant will often reflect how it feels to members of the organization.

In conclusion I shall state perhaps the obvious: There are many ways of looking at organizations. And there are no doubt other relationships among general systems theory, gestalt therapy and organization development. The five dimensions I covered in this chapter, however, have helped me to understand organizations a bit better, and they have given me a different way of diagnosing organizations so that, hopefully, I as a consultant will not make some of the same 'system mistakes' I've made in the past.

References

Ackoff, R. L. (1974) *Redesigning the Future.* New York: Wiley.
Alderfer, C. P. (1977) Improving organization communication through long-term intergroup intervention. *Journal of Applied Behavioral Science*, **13**, 193–210.
Bertalanffy, L. von (1956) General systems theory. *General Systems.* Yearbook of the Society of the Advancement of General System Theory, **1**, 1–10.
Capra, F. (1977) The Tao of physics: Reflections on the cosmic dance. *Saturday Review*, **5** (6), 21–23, 28.
Coch, L., and French, J. R. P. (1948) Overcoming resistance to change. *Human Relations*, **1**, 512–532.
Emery, F. E., and Trist, E. L. (1960) Sociotechnical systems. In C. W. Churchman and M. Verhulst (eds) *Management Sciences: Models and Techniques*, vol. 2. London: Pergamon.
Harvey, J. B. (1975) Eight myths OD consultants believe in ... and die by! *OD Practitioner*, **7** (1), 1–5.
Herman, S. M., and Korenich, M. (1977) *Authentic Management: A Gestalt Orientation to Organizations and Their Development.* Reading, Mass.: Addison-Wesley.
Katz, D., and Kahn, R. L. (1966) *The Social Psychology of Organizations.* New York: Wiley.
Lawrence, P. R., and Lorsch, J. W. (1967) *Organization and Environment: Managing Differentiation and Integration.* Boston: Division of Research, Harvard Business School.
Leavitt, H. (1965) Applied organizational change in industry. In J. March (ed.) *Handbook of Organizations.* Chicago: Rand McNally.
Margulies, N. (1978) Perspectives on the marginality of the consultant's role. In W. W. Burke (ed.) *The Cutting Edge: Current Theory and Practice in Organization Development.* La Jolla, Calif.: University Associates.
Perls, F., Hefferline, R. F., and Goodman, P. (1951) *Gestalt Therapy.* New York: Dell.
Seiler, J. (1967) *Systems Analysis in Organization Behavior.* Homewood, Ill.: Irwin.
Shepard, H. A. (1975) Rules of thumb for change agents. *OD Practitioner*, **7** (3), 1–5.
Zand, D. E. (1974) Collateral organization: A new change strategy. *Journal of Applied Behavioral Science*, **10**, 63–89.
Zinker, J. (1977) *Creative Process in Gestalt Therapy.* New York: Brunner/Mazel.

Systems Theory for Organization Development
Edited by T. G. Cummings
© 1980 John Wiley & Sons Ltd.

Chapter **10**

Organization Development: Structures, Processes, or Systems?

Carson K. Eoyang

OD and systems theory

System approaches and systems theories have been so fashionable among social and behavioural scientists that it is almost as if no text, elementary or advanced, is considered respectable without at least passing acknowledgement to the idea of systems. Yet references to systems concepts (e.g. equilibrium) and use of systems jargon (e.g. entropy) are often metaphorical or illusionary rather than clear statements of logical propositions. Many books or articles about organization development appear to be especially vulnerable to such pretensions. If the behavioural sciences in general and organization development in particular are less than faithful to the more rigorous traditions of systems science, the reasons may lie not only in the ambiguity and imprecision of OD but also in the confusion of what systems theory is or is not.

Kahn (1974) has argued persuasively that organization development, while it may be an art, is certainly not a science. While this tension is most obvious in the writings of the more humanistic OD proponents (e.g. Bennis, 1969; Tannenbaum and Davis, 1969), it is also implicit in virtually every published work on organization development (see Friedlander and Brown, 1974; Alderfer, 1977). Despite the numerous and persistent references to 'systems theory' in assorted texts (e.g. Huse, 1975; French and Bell, 1978), OD is more accurately characterized as eclectic, heuristic, and microscopic rather than truly systemic. OD is eclectic in that a variety of disparate conceptual domains called the behavioural sciences are taken as its intellectual foundation. Unfortunately, the absence of any integrative constructs precludes the coherence and integrity one associates with either systems or theory. This is a fault that OD shares with 'contingency theory' among others (see Longenecker and Pringle, 1978). OD is heuristic in the sense that it includes prescriptions that have reputedly enjoyed success in the experience of prominent OD consultants. Yet the distilled wisdom of however many distinguished practitioners without coherent integration hardly constitutes a unified, orderly discipline. Finally, OD is microscopic in its focus since its traditional orientation has been on the social or interpersonal dimensions, thus slighting other relevant dimensions of organizational systems such as economics (see Beer and Huse, 1972, p. 151).

To be fair, however, the abuse and misuse of the systems paradigm is due not only to OD's primitive theoretical development (Alderfer, 1977, p. 218) but also to the confusion surrounding systems theory. Unlike classical unitary theories of science (e.g. number theory, quantum theory, thermo-dynamics, genetic theory, etc.), systems theory has not achieved the status of an intellectual discipline with well-defined boundaries and an articulated, logical structure. While various techniques of systems analysis are practised by economists, engineers, physicists, operations researchers, cyberneticists, etc., the underlying conceptual core has not been established definitively (Churchman, 1968), although the prospects of such an evolution are promising (Boulding, 1956). Thus, without the existence of clearly developed foundations and boundaries, 'systems theory' is susceptive to naïve interpretaiton by those who believe input, throughput, output, and feedback are the total sum and substance of systems. Unfortunately, such naïvety is not narrowly distributed among OD scholars and practitioners who try to cloak what are essentially intuition and experience with the respectability of systems vocabulary. Although the intentions may be honourable, the resulting contributions may not always be constructive.

After these general criticisms about OD literature and its abuse of systems theory, the responsibility remains to offer constructive suggestions as to how systems notions might be applied fruitfully to the study and practice of OD. In an attempt to do so, it is necessary to begin by addressing two questions.

(1) Is OD a systems approach?

As is probably obvious, the view taken here is that OD has not been notably successful in using true systems approaches. The failures are most prevalent in the practice of OD, while system deficiencies of OD theory are somewhat less serious. In particular the major systems errors of OD practice and theory include:

(1) failure to identify the appropriate system;
(2) underspecification of system dimensions and variables;
(3) limited, narrowly focused interventions; and
(4) imprecise, irregular, and unreliable measurement.

For many OD consultants, both internal and external, the client system is almost always defined by the initial contact within an organization and whomever else the consultant can arrange to meet during the course of the relationship. In short, the boundaries of the system are typically determined on the basis of availability and accessibility. If parts of the organization are not accessible to the consultant, then more often than not they are ignored or neglected in the subsequent interventions. While this may be an eminently practical position (after all, how can you influence that which is inaccessible), it is not a particularly scientific or systematic approach to defining boundaries. To be specific, parts of the client organization may not be open because of geographic, temporal, economic or, most commonly, political constraints. Yet, however relevant they may be to the performance and health of the client, they rarely receive the requisite attention or energies of the consultants. Instead consultants focus their efforts and those of their clients on those people and issues which are available. To be sure, there may be benefits to such an approach; for example, a psychologist may alleviate the anxieties of a client who is suffering from a shrinking market. However, there are also serious risks, such as job enrichment specialists who seek to reduce personnel turnover caused by external competitive pressures. In organizations as in medicine, the right solution to the wrong problem could be disastrous (Drucker, 1967). How much better would clients be if consultants referred them to others with more relevant expertise as is the custom among physicians? Ideally intervention methods should be determined by the objective needs of the client and not by the biases and strengths of the consultant (Dale, 1972). As an illustration, a common omission from many published reports of OD is references to unions however significant they may be. Notable exceptions include instances involving the Scanlon Plan (Lesieur, 1958) or quality of work life experiments (e.g. Meyers, 1971). Of course, many client systems may not have unions, or may be using OD to keep out unions, thus explaining the neglect of unions as an important system component. Alternatively OD consultants may be more attracted to settings consistent with their preconceived notions of what constitutes appropriate client systems. The point of this example is not to castigate OD consultants as antiunion however pro-management they may be, but to illustrate how frequently systems boundaries can be defined as a matter of convenience rather than determined on the basis of what is most relevant.

OD theory and research are somewhat more careful in identifying systems and their boundaries (e.g. Beer and Huse, 1972). Probably because of scholarly training and academic traditions, theorists and researchers tend to pay more attention to issues of system identity and boundary distinctions (e.g. Cummings, 1977). However, it is not uncommon that system boundaries are so broadly drawn that, while little of relevance is excluded, much that is irrelevant is included (Eoyang and Haga, 1977). Thus, OD *practice* is often characterized by deficiencies of systems omission, and OD *theory* by excesses of systems inclusion. As the two converge, perhaps an appropriate balance may be found.

A second common system error of OD is underspecification of dimensions and variables. OD practitioners, as distinct from OD researchers, typically adopt clinical approaches based largely upon intuitive and subjective diagnostic and intervention methods. The ability to articulate explicitly what system variables and relationships obtain in any client organization is not characteristic of many OD interventions. Although many OD consultants can be quite successful without explicit analytic constructs, it would be a gross exaggeration to claim that such approaches are rigorously systematic. In contrast, recent research in OD has conscientiously attempted to specify the most significant variables that distinguish successful from unsuccessful interventions (Alderfer, 1977). Unfortunately the list of variables is often long, the number of cases often small, and the analyses typically weak (White and Mitchell, 1976). Thus, these efforts have not yet developed sufficiently clear knowledge that would intelligently inform the practice of OD in actual situations (Porras and Berg, 1978).

A third problem is that many OD interventions are narrowly focused and rarely affect the entire client system as a whole. This obviously follows from underidentification of the appropriate systems, but in addition many popular OD interventions and techniques are simply quite limited in scope and impact. One of the earliest methods of OD, laboratory training, focuses almost exclusively on the attitudes and behaviours of individuals who may or may not be members of the same organization. Campbell and Dunnette (1968) have argued convincingly that such interventions have little or no impact on back home systems. Although other intervention methods may not be quite so narrow, they are frequently directed at only limited parts of the total system, e.g. process consultation, team development, third party consultation, etc. There is no dispute that specific OD methods, however limited, may have their value in many situations. Yet such techniques can hardly be construed as systems approaches in the context of the whole organization.

A fourth system deficiency of OD is that in the vast majority of cases measurement and evaluation of processes and outcomes are typically weak or non-existent (Alderfer, 1977). Rigorous attempts to assess the efficiency or effectiveness of organizational change are the exception rather than the rule, despite the frequent and compelling encouragement of OD researchers (Porras and Berg, 1978). The measurement problem is consistent with the previously mentioned problems of poor identification of system boundaries and underspecification of system variables. Measurement is exceedingly difficult when either or both conditions exist. Nevertheless, without some reasonable determination of the pre-change client state coupled with an assessment of the post-change client state, any claims to systemic change are pure conjecture. It is perhaps this particular weakness of OD practice that OD theory can most immediately improve. By illuminating the goals, strategies, and methods of organizational evaluation, OD theory could greatly enhance the future evolution of OD practice as well as its current application (White and Mitchell, 1976).

In short, the answer to the question 'Is OD a systems approach?' is 'Not yet'. In practice, OD rarely if ever satisfies the requirements of rigorous systems theory. In principle, OD has the potential for being both systemic and systematic as OD theory, research, and practice develop synergistically to create a true technology of change for organizations. However, it may not be true that development along these lines is either feasible or desirable.

(2) Should OD be a systems approach?

The answer to this question is somewhat easier to frame, since contingency theories have argued that there is no single universally appropriate appraoch for managing or changing organizations. The implication for OD is that organizational change should not be based upon systems concepts in all situations. There are occasions when a systems perspective may be ideal and others when it may not. To illustrate the situational contingencies of when systems approaches may not be helpful, let us consider the systems deficiencies of OD previously discussed.

Identification of system boundaries may not only be helpful in terms of clarifying domains of diagnosis and action, but also may be limiting by introducing artificial constraints. For example, in the classic case of the Hovey and Beard Company (Lawrence *et al.*, 1961), defining the client system at the level of the work group resulted in dysfunctional consequences at the level of the company. However, initially defining the client system as the whole company probably would not have alleviated the immediate technical or managerial problems of the work group. A more fruitful approach might have been a flexible specification of system boundaries that was contingent upon the experiences and outcomes of the diagnoses and interventions carried out. In the case of the Hovey and Beard Company, a shift over time in the definition of what constituted the appropriate system would have been superior to fixing the systems boundaries at either the work group or company level.

Underspecification of system variables and dimensions similarly is not always dysfunctional. Although rigorous application of systems theories would hardly omit this step, it may not be appropriate in all OD settings. Again, this is because many organizations are so incredibly complex and dynamic that the most significant system variables are unknown, unmanageable, immeasurable, or subject to rapid obsolescence. In such cases, rational action logically derived from *a priori* means–ends analyses may simply be unfeasible. There may not be sufficient information, intelligence, or time to generate optimal solutions that satisfy the demands for action by management. Indeed, there are risks that inordinate attention to differentiating system variables and dimensions may result in myopic perspectives that distort or ignore completely the integrated essence or organizational gestalt of the client. For example, early experiments in socio-technical systems (Trist and Blamforth, 1951) illustrated the disadvantages of considering only the quantifiable facets of organizational change and ignoring the qualitative.

It is important to clarify that the issue here is not mis-specification of system variables, e.g. identifying the wrong ones, which is obviously dysfunctional; rather the issue is whether to engage in precise specification of variables at all. Reicken (1978) has indicated that it is not necessarily desirable in all instances, since it may oversimplify the full complexity of everyday life. Some of the dangers have been described by Anatol Rappaport, the eminent mathematician and general system theorist:

Too strong confidence in mathematical general system theory, therefore, may have one of two unfortunate consequences. First, far from adequate models may be taken too seriously, for want of better models which remain tractable. Second, effort may be wasted in trying to subject to mathematical analysis systems so complex that they cannot possibly yield to such analyses, with the consequent neglect of other approaches, for example, the purely organismic approach which, after all, has been considerably successful in classical biology. It would be wise, therefore, to consider mathematical general system theory as an important addition to the conceptual repertoire of the scientist rather than a method destined to drive all the older methods into obscurity. (Rapport, 1969, p. 97.)

In criticizing many OD interventions as narrowly focused and non-systemic in impact, it should be stated that the objections are in the context of whether OD practice is systems-based and not whether limited interventions are efficacious or appropriate. In terms of these latter criteria, strong arguments can be made for narrowly focused change attempts, such as gestalt approaches (Herman, 1972), transactional analysis (Rush and McGrath, 1973), team building (Dyer, 1977), etc. Clearly there are numerous organizational maladies which can be treated without affecting the entire client system. Indeed, there are situations in which narrowly focused interventions are more appropriate and efficient than attempts to bring about system wide changes. Examples include clients who are not yet ready for large-scale change, problems whose complexity requires decomposition (Simon, 1962) and incremental approaches (Lindbloom, 1959), and organizations which lack the resources or time to engage in systemic interventions. In short, systems OD is not for everybody.

As the last qualification of systems approaches, it is not always useful to undertake precise, regular, and reliable evaluation in conjunction with OD efforts. The primary reason which moderates the absolute utility of evaluation is that measurement processes inevitably involve significant costs as well as benefits. Moreover, often the most significant costs are not the direct costs of measurement (e.g. time, money, energy) which may be substantial, but the indirect costs of perturbing the client system. Social phenomena, even more than physical phenomena, are subject to the uncertainty principle which states that measurement itself influences the system and the more accurate the measurement process, the greater the effects on the system (McKnight, 1959). As an illustration of this principle, the Hawthorne effect is a classic example of how organizations can react in unpredictable ways to confound the intentions of practitioners and researchers alike when subjected to outside observation and measurement (Roethlisberger and Dickson, 1939).

Although not all measurement effects are disruptive (see Webb et al., 1966), the problem is to minimize the adverse consequences of assessment while maximizing the positive value of the information obtained. There may well be situations in which favourable tradeoffs are not available, and no evaluation is the preferred alternative. For example, in highly sensitive situations confidentiality and security may be so crucial that no objective assessment is possible without jeopardizing the client's acceptance of the proposed intervention. In these settings, the OD consultant faces the choices of refusing to participate without assessment or engaging in action without objective knowledge of the consequences. Although some consultants may enjoy the luxury of the first choice, many managers and some consultants are compelled to accept the second.

The problem is further compounded by the crude level of evaluation methodology in OD (Porras and Berg, 1978; White and Mitchell 1976). With imperfect and imprecise measurement theories and methods, it is often unclear what immediate client benefits are to be gained from rigorous attempts to evaluate, especially in organizations that are exceedingly complex and dynamic. Results are often ambiguous, inconclusive, or obsolete. However, in the long run careful measurement is absolutely essential to the healthy evolution of OD practice and theory (see Reicken, 1978). In summary, systematic evaluation in OD is not a recommended choice in all organizational contexts. There are occasions when only subjective, impressionistic assessment is applicable, if even that. Nevertheless, where objective measurement is neither feasible nor practicable, consultants and managers cannot always escape the responsibility for action (Babad and Solomon, 1978).

To conclude this discussion of whether OD should be a systems approach, the brief answer is yes in most instances. However, the systems approach is hardly a panacea for the limitations and weaknesses of OD or management. OD consultants and managers must often 'muddle through' (Lindbloom, 1959) in coping with organizational problems whose complexity far exceeds even the most powerful methods of systems analysis. In short, while there may be many OD opportunities in which systems approaches may yield positive results, there are other situations in which systems techniques are simply inadequate, and heuristic and perhaps even intuitive approaches may succeed.

If systems approaches are in fact severely limited in coping with the inherent complexity of many real organizations, two additional questions then arise. First, what alternatives to systems approaches are available to OD practitioners? Second, how are choices to be made among various approaches, given the variety of situations in which OD is applied?

OD: structures, processes, systems

Given the wide variety of methods and techniques associated with organization development, there are numerous and sundry alternatives to rigorous systems approaches. Almost any basic text on OD furnishes a comprehensive inventory of methods (see Huse, 1975; French and Bell, 1978). Although it is not possible to reiterate all of them here, a brief survey may serve to illustrate the conceptual contrasts between the various methods and the more systems-based OD approaches.

A convenient if somewhat overworked basis of classification is the distinction between structure and process. Although Kahn (1974) has argued that the two are often inextricably related in actual practice, it is still useful to differentiate the formal relationships among roles in organizations (structures) from the patterns of interpersonal behaviour among individuals in the same organization (process). In the present context, OD interventions aimed primarily at changing the former are designated *structural approaches* while interventions aimed primarily at affecting the latter are *process methods*.

The general purpose of structural approaches is to clarify, strengthen, and elaborate the formal expectations that bind people together in organizations. Examples of structural approaches include role analysis technique (Dayal and Thomas, 1964), role negotiations (Harrison, 1973), responsibility charting (Galbraith, 1973), creation of temporary task forces (Beer, 1976), and revising structures and roles (Lawrence and Lorsch, 1967). In addition, the rapidly growing area of job design (Beer, 1976) can be regarded as essentially structural in nature, since it is concerned with changing the task characteristics and demands of various work roles. Another related set of structural interventions focuses upon personnel policies. Examples here include changing the pay and compensation policies, such as in the Scanlon Plan (Lesieur, 1958), opening the staffing and hiring policies (Alfred, 1967), and experimenting with human asset accounting (Brummet *et al.*, 1969). What these have in common is an emphasis on the relatively formal aspects of organizations, and a belief that the structural changes may be enduring if they become institutionalized.

In contrast, process interventions tend to focus on the more informal aspects of organization, i.e. the social and interpersonal dimensions of human relationships. These are more difficult to institutionalize, since the personal motivation and commitment required for continued success are almost impossible to legislate. Examples of popular process interventions are counselling, such as gestalt (Herman, 1972) and transactional analysis (Rush and McGrath, 1973) approaches, process consultation (Schein, 1969), third party consultation (Walton, 1969), interpersonal laboratories (Argyris, 1962), team building (Dyer, 1977), goal setting (Beckhard, 1969), and facilitating group meetings (Schein, 1969). More extensive process interventions, such as grid development (Blake and Mouton, 1964) and survey guided development (Likert, 1967), attempt to improve processes on a larger scale by directing attention towards the social climate of organizations.

As true systems approaches, all of these examples are deficient to one degree or another in terms of at least one of the four systems criteria discussed earlier. It might be possible to combine a number of approaches with complementary strengths and weaknesses, but it is likely that such an amalgamation would be cumbersome and lack the integrated coherence of a real system. Until OD theory, research, and practice have evolved sufficiently to create a meaningful systems foundation, perhaps the best that can be hoped for is a variety of heuristic concepts that would enable practitioners and managers to choose more intelligently from among the vast number of OD techniques available. If a few of these concepts are proven by experience and research to be more powerful and accurate than the others, then these may constitute a starting place for the development of OD as a systems science.

A conceptual heuristic for OD choice

An essential requirement for rational choice is some understanding, albeit incomplete, of the likely consequences associated with alternatives available. In the context of organization development, it is important to anticipate the possible effects of any intervention upon the client system. Because most organizations are rather complex and the number of direct and indirect change effects is virtually infinite, it is not practicable to predict with certainty all of the potential or even only the important consequences. Still it is necessary to develop some expectations of the positive and negative reactions of the client system to any intervention if the consultant is to choose intelligently. In order to sort out the more significant results from the myriad possibilities, it would be useful to establish a conceptual framework that would organize the consultant's and client's expectations over time.

There are at least three levels of analysis in theories of organizational development: individuals, groups, and the total organization (Beer, 1976; White and Mitchell, 1976). Each level reflects different perspectives on various system dynamics and may highlight dimensions and variables that are not obvious from the other analytic points of view. For example, the concept of *goals* takes on very different meanings depending upon whether the referent is the individual member, the primary work group, or the formal organization. Indeed, the issue of goal congruence across these various levels represents one of the most common challenges in modern organizations. Yet this has not always been recognized. Several traditional schools of management thought have presumed that goal attainment at one level would naturally lead to goal attainment at another. In particular, scientific management assumed that increased organizational welfare through higher productivity would directly improve individual welfare through greater wages. Similarly, human relations approaches assumed that stronger social cohesion within work groups would generate more collaboration and superior problem solving. Finally, management science assumed that more sophisticated and effective decision making would enhance the welfare of the entire organization and, concomitantly, the welfare of everyone in it. However desirable these correlations may be in principle, it remains an empirical question as to how strong they may be in reality (Nord and Durand, 1978).

In other words, it may not be reasonable to assume that the welfare of the individual, of the group, and of the organization are positively related in all situations. It may be more useful to consider the three welfare functions as independent dimensions of managerial action. Thus, some OD interventions would ideally increase welfare at all three levels, while others may have positive effects at one level and negative effects at others. As a way of visualizing this concept, Figure 1 represents the domain of OD interventions as an action space characterized by the three orthogonal dimensions of individual welfare, group welfare, and organization welfare. Any given intervention would be represented by a trajectory through the welfare states experienced during the change attempt. The ideal OD intervention would maximize welfare along all three dimensions simultaneously and would be depicted as a vector emanating from the origin in a positive direction equidistant from all axes. Unfortunately, the real world is not always benign and the ideal is seldom if ever achieved, at least in the short run. There are frequent instances when the welfare of the organization can only be increased at the temporary expense of the welfare of the individual or of the group (e.g. industry during recession and the military during war).

Typical OD interventions usually entail some initial costs along at least one of the welfare dimensions before long-term benefits can be realized. For example, laboratory training for managers may involve a high degree of anxiety and stress for individual participants, although it may eventually result in a more cohesive and supportive work group. It remains to be seen whether the organization itself receives any tangible benefits from such an exercise (Campbell and Dunnette, 1968). This particular intervention could be illustrated in our conceptual framework as in Figure 2. There is initially a loss in individual equanimity and confidence as the T-group breaks down interpersonal defences and shares critical feedback. As the group begins to build trust, openness, and mutual support, the welfare functions at both the individual and group level start to grow positively. Yet the experience may be neutral as far as the company is concerned, and may even be detrimental if underwritten by company resources with no demonstrable return.

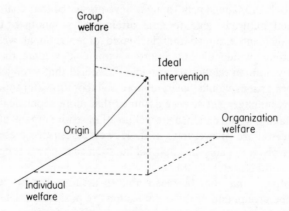

Figure 1   Organization development action space

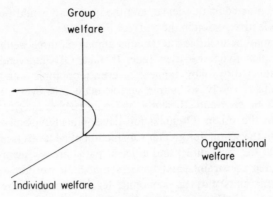

Figure 2   Laboratory training intervention

The interaction between group welfare and organizational welfare can be illustrated by the method of the confrontation meeting (Beckhard, 1967). At first, as conflicts and disagreements are identified and aired, group cohesiveness may decrease and defensiveness may increase, but as the issues become resolved and constructive decisions are made, both the group's welfare and the organization's are expected to improve. Failures in confrontation may not be able to turn the corner (see Figure 3).

The interaction between individual welfare and organizational welfare can be illustrated by two simple examples. In the first instance, the company may ask for a personal sacrifice from the individual employee, such as more challenging objectives, in return for some compensation, such as a promotion. Obviously neither would agree to such an exchange unless both stood to gain in the long run. In the second instance, the employee may ask for a personal consideration from

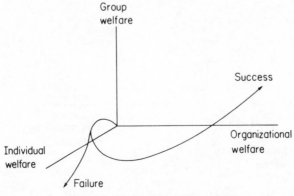

Figure 3   Confrontation meeting

the company, such as education leave, and the company would expect to gain a more loyal and effective person in the end (see Figure 4).

Finally, there may be multiple interactions among all three welfare dimensions that exhibit complex dynamics over time. In fact, OD interventions generally should not be expected to follow a linear or even monotonic course of progress. Organizational life is rarely so simple or fortunate that everyone's welfare is maximized simultaneously and efficiently, as would be characterized by a positive straight line from the origin. Organization development typically follows more circuitous paths in the search for greater satisfaction at all levels (see Figure 5).

The reason that the most direct and efficient paths are not always available is that there are often constraints and barriers that limit freedom of action. The nature of the constraints may be economic, legal, cultural, technological, psychological, physical, etc. For example, the welfare of individuals may be bounded at lower levels by minimum wage laws, union contracts, Occupational Safety and Health Act requirements, employment legislation, and prevailing social norms. At the upper end, individual welfare may be constrained by the economic resources of the organization, other psychological commitments external to the organization, and the personal ability and ambition of the individual to succeed. Similarly, the welfare of the work group may have upper and lower bounds determined by the physical environment, the technology of work, and the customs and mores of the local culture. Organizational welfare may be constrained by economic competition, governmental regulation, and the quality of management. In short, constraints may arise from factors in the external environment or from internal characteristics of the organization. Although the latter tend to be more amenable to OD interventions than the former, the central point is that neither consultants nor managers can act with total freedom in promoting individual, group, or organizational welfare. There are limits that circumscribe the feasibility of OD

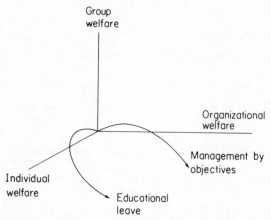

Figure 4   Individual–organization interactions

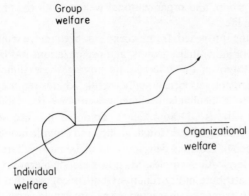

Figure 5   Dynamic organization development

action. They may not be as clear and simple as illustrated in Figure 6, but they are real constraints nevertheless.

The extent to which OD practice explicitly recognizes and accommodates the limits of the feasible solution space pertaining to any given client system will largely determine the absolute and relative success of the OD intervention. In absolute terms, the probability of failure will be reduced by ruling out unfeasible alternatives. In relative terms, the expectation of the likely outcomes on the part of both the client and the consultant will be moderated to be consistent with organizational realities, thus reducing the likelihood of gross disappointment. One of the greatest advantages of an external OD consultant is his objective ability to test and disconfirm the subjective perceptions of imaginary constraints on the part of the client. However, in this strength may also lie the risk of assuming anything is possible, thereby encouraging clients to engage in futile change attempts. It is one of the major challenges of OD to balance the ambitious aspirations to

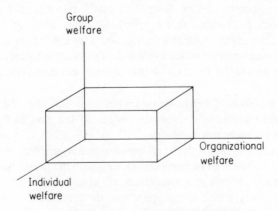

Figure 6   Systemic OD constraints

maximize individual, group, and organizational welfare with the practical limitations of organizational life.

Up to this point the proposed framework has been more conceptual than heuristic. The welfare of individuals, groups, and organizations has been discussed in abstract terms. Moreover the interactions among these dimensions, while analytically graphic, are not yet operationally useful. What is required is a translation of these ideas into a mechanism which will enhance the choice process in selecting from among various OD approaches. To do so, it is necessary to define more specifically the meaning of individual, group, and organizational welfare.

It has long been recognized that determinants of human welfare are complex and numerous at any level. As examples, Maslow's classic hierarchy of needs and the economists' multi-attribute utility functions both recognize that improvement in the human condition cannot be characterized by any single-variable model. The problem becomes even more complicated when the level of analysis moves beyond the individual to groups, organizations, and society at large. However, it is neither possible nor necessary in the present context to develop general and comprehensive welfare functions for all three levels of analysis. What is more appropriate is to provide an outline of potential welfare factors which may suggest salient aspects of OD consequences. The ultimate choice of which factors obtain in any given situation depends upon assessment by the consultant and client together of the relative importance of each factor. Because every organization is unique, it is not possible to specify *a priori* which welfare considerations will be dominant in a given circumstance. However, an essential component of organizational diagnosis should be the deliberate assessment of which aspects will be important at various points in time for a particular client system. The following outline of welfare considerations is not exhaustive but is illustrative of the range of issues that merit the attention of the OD consultant.

(1) Individual welfare considerations

(a) Stress, anxiety, comfort levels. Some OD methods, such as T-groups, confrontation meetings, conflict management, etc., may generate high levels of stress that are not always tolerable or functional for the individuals involved.

(b) Job security. Interventions which involve the risk of termination, demotion, or transfers are bound to be seen as threatening by members of the client organization.

(c) Career opportunities. Change programmes that increase the chances of upward mobility are usually regarded favourably but may be threatening to those not seeking more responsibility.

(d) Job satisfaction. The major thrust of job enrichment, job redesign, and sociotechnical approaches is to increase satisfaction with the performance of work.

(e) Personal growth. Sometimes the result of gestalt methods, transactional analysis, laboratory training, and leadership development can be substantial growth along interpersonal, emotional, and psychological dimensions.

(f)   Financial compensation. Change attempts that may involve significant shifts in income (e.g. the Scanlon Plan) will inevitably arouse intense scrutiny by all parties affected.

(g)   Time and energy demands. As more demands are made for individual time and energy, as in management by objectives and team building interventions, less time is available for other pursuits.

(h)   Interpersonal relations. The intent of many kinds of human relations training is to strengthen the working relations between people. However, some methods – e.g. encounter groups and confrontation meetings – also run the risk of making social interactions worse.

(i)   Learning. Most OD techniques intend to facilitate the acquisition and development of new ways of behaving, thinking, feeling, and knowing. Ideally this learning results in people who are more effective and productive in a wider variety of situations.

(j)   Status and prestige. For many, personal image is extremely important and therefore they may be very cautious about programmes – e.g. T-groups – that may jeopardize their self-concept or others' perception of them.

(k)   Power. Everyone is likely to resist circumstances in which their power may be eroded. Consequently, power equalization tactics (e.g. participative management) are not universally welcome.

(l)   Motivation. A variety of methods (job enrichment, management by objectives, Scanlon plan, etc.) are designed to increase motivation explicitly. But there are others, such as confrontation meetings and process consultation, that may have adverse effects on motivation through the intense frustration and hostility that may be aroused.

(2) Group welfare considerations

(a)   Social cohesion, mutual support. Interventions such as team building, family laboratory training, and participative management, contribute to the development of more supportive relations within work groups. It is presumed that the more cooperative the members are, the more effective the group as a unit will be.

(b)   Trust. There should be a foundation of shared attitudes and feelings of interdependence if intragroup collaboration is to be an enduring group characteristic. Many OD techniques have direct or indirect consequences on the level of group trust.

(c)   Openness. The ultimate indicator of trust is the amount of open behaviour exhibited by the group. It is believed that healthy groups are able to raise public feelings, issues, and conflicts more frequently and constructively than ineffective groups. However, there is some question about how much openness is functional in the long run.

(d)   Stability of norms. The degree to which common expectations are known and predictable reduces uncertainty in the social interactions within the group.

While the absence of shared expectations may weaken group functions, the other extreme of rigid norms may also be dysfunctional in terms of flexibility and change.

(e) Communication. A very common challenge to OD consultants is to improve communications. The free flow of accurate and timely information along formal and informal channels is another index of healthy groups.

(f) Collaboration, cooperation. If groups are high on the five previous criteria, then the probability is high that numerous instances of mutual help and support will be reflected in the actual performance of tasks.

(g) Decision making. An important function of many groups is making decisions. Healthy groups are characterized not only by superior decisions but also by flexible decision processes that match the varying situational and temporal requirements of different decisions (Vroom and Yetton, 1973).

(h) Flexibility of roles. As groups are able to modify and interchange their task and maintenance roles over time, the more effective they are likely to be across a variety of situations and as members of the group change.

(i) Adaptability. Change and occasional crisis are inevitable group experiences. Successful groups adapt to both the revolutionary and evolutionary demands that may be placed upon them.

(j) Resolution of conflict. Another key function of groups is the management of conflict. Inferior groups ignore, suppress, gloss over, or otherwise fail to resolve task and interpersonal conflicts. Superior groups are able to confront conflict directly and seek constructive approaches to resolution.

(k) Group status. A frequently important consideration is the prestige and image of the group in the eyes of its members. When group status is low it may be difficult to effect improvements along the other dimensions of group health.

(l) Power. The ability to command influence or resources in the larger organization can often be a crucial determinant of the group's long-term survival. In classic bureaucracies, formal power may be tightly circumscribed, but informal power may be substantial.

(3) Organizational welfare considerations

(a) Performance. The ultimate criterion for success (commonly refered to as the 'bottom line') may differ from organization to organization. For commercial firms it may be profit, for hospitals the number of patients treated, for schools the number of students enrolled and so forth. However, for some organizations objective success criteria may be unclear or undefined, such as for government agencies and public sector organizations (e.g. churches). Although the measurement of organizational effectiveness may often be problematic (Campbell, 1975), the welfare of any organization is intimately tied to its formal task performance however it is determined. For many client systems the concern for productivity, efficiency, quantity and quality of production, etc., are paramount management concerns.

(b) Growth. A pervasive welfare concern typical of most organizations is the expansion of resources, membership, markets, product lines, assets, etc. Indeed, for many industrial concerns the most important measure of organizational health is the rate of growth over time. However, recently there have been numerous challenges to the imperatives for growth, especially in government and multi-national corporations.

(c) Costs. In the absence of hard output measures, measures of economic input begin to assume even greater importance in determining organizational welfare. Costs and growth in costs are expected to remain within certain standards if organizations are to be regarded as economically sound.

(d) Control. As purposive systems, organizations have a fundamental need for control over the behaviour of their members. Although this control need not be – indeed cannot be – absolute, the degree to which management can direct internal and external activities in conformance with established objectives largely affects organizational success.

(e) Innovation and creativity. Because environments are dynamic and often turbulent, organizations rarely can afford the luxury of maintaining the *status quo*. They will become stagnant or obsolete unless they are able to renew themselves with fresh ideas, opportunities, and capabilities.

(f) Adaptation. What is important at the group level becomes essential at the level of the organization. There must be an openness to the environment so that the organization can develop a robustness across a wide variety of circumstances and opportunities.

(g) Structural flexibility. Occasionally, effective adaptation requires modification of internal structure, e.g. hierarchical and horizonal relations. Rigid, inflexible organizations with great inertia are at a competitive disadvantage with respect to those that are morphogenic in response to external demands.

(h) Climate. The social and psychological ambience of an organization contributes strongly to the motivation and commitment that members are willing to exhibit in the pursuit of collective goals.

(i) Personnel stability. Although certain amounts of employee turnover may be advantageous in terms of renewing membership, low personnel retention may entail severe penalties in performance and cost, especially in scarce labour markets.

(j) Managerial competence. The collective ability of managers to perform all the operational and strategic functions required in modern organizations is a corner-stone upon which future success depends. Without a wide distribution of competence, an organization is extremely vulnerable when key individuals are suddenly lost.

(k) Organizational loyalty. Though an intangible and sometimes rare commodity, loyalty can nevertheless be extremely significant in periods of crisis as well as over long periods of adversity. The dedication and faithfulness of employees are invaluable assets which may pay incalculable dividends.

(l) Integrity. American industry in the past decade has witnessed an unfortunately large number of instances in which organizations failed to exhibit the ethical and moral character expected by society at large. Without a deep and abiding commitment to human and social values, organizations may easily drift towards states of illegitimacy and decay.

In presenting this list of three dozen welfare considerations, I do not pretend that these variables are definitive or that the list is complete. These are only examples which serve to illustrate the range of concerns generally relevant to organizational change. Practitioners should add other considerations that may be pertinent to the specific organization of interest. In addition to lengthening each of the dimensions of individual, group, and organizational welfare functions, it is possible to add dimensions, such as for society at large or even higher levels of analysis. However, for reasons of practicality if not simplicity it is prudent to limit the conceptual framework to three levels at a time.

Now that the concept of welfare functions has been illustrated, it remains for me to suggest a method for using this concept to aid the OD choice process. First, this framework can be used as a point of departure for a comprehensive diagnosis of any particular client system. The consultant may begin by developing a list of welfare considerations of greatest importance to the specific client. Then, as impressions and data are collected, diagnosis along the three dimensions of welfare may be conducted to determine the client's state of health in specific terms. It is important to identify the strengths as well as the weaknesses in any organization, as a narrow focus on pathology will be misleading and may generate inappropriate remedies. In short, the welfare concept may be used to develop a checklist to assess organizational health at a given point in time.

In addition to describing the *status quo*, the framework could also be used to develop a longitudinal prognosis of the client's health in the absence of any outside intervention. In organizations as in medicine, many pathologies are self-limiting – i.e. they disappear without treatment – and therefore it is not always necessary or advisable to act in situations of distress. However, the choice between action and postponement is made more intelligently when there is some reasonably sound expectation of how the client's health and welfare will develop over time. The accuracy of the prognosis is a function not only of the consultant's competence but also of the experienced intuition of the client who is most familiar with the organization and its history.

The third and most extensive use of this framework is to estimate the short- and long-term consequences of alternative OD interventions. As discussed earlier, rational choices in OD require some judgement of the likely effects of any feasible course of action. While these judgements may be subjective, or uncertain, biased and hence imperfect, they are the essential basis for rational action. Of course, the more objective data and reliable theory can inform these judgements, the more accurate they are likely to be. Although OD, like management, is more art than science, these judgements can be improved by recognizing explicitly the temporal nature of organizational change and the inherent tradeoffs associated with available alternatives.

Figure 7 shows a method for the qualitative assessment of the impact of alternative OD interventions. It incorporates in a two-dimensional display the major features of the concepts presented here. The method highlights the qualitative impact of a given intervention on any number of welfare variables over time. The table in Figure 7 illustrates the expected consequences of laboratory training on a hypothetical organization. The OD consultant, in conjunction with the principal client, predicts the most likely effects of the proposed intervention on the organization over four different time periods. The table entries are coded as to whether the predicted outcomes are positive, neutral, negative, or unknown. Another possibility is that a variable may be constrained and not susceptible to attempts at improvement.

The value of this assessment exercise is that it permits the comparison of alternative OD techniques in terms of the anticipated consequences for a specific client system. Once this has been accomplished for the major interventions under consideration, a final choice can be made with a clearer understanding of the benefits

Intervention method: Laboratory training

	Predicted impact of intervention			
Welfare considerations	Immediate (one week)	Short term (one month)	Intermediate (one year)	Long term (after one year)
I. Individual				
A. Stress	–	0	+	?
B. Job security	–	?	+	+
C. Job satisfaction	0	0	0	0
D. Personal growth	+	+	?	?
II. Group				
A. Social cohesion	+	+	0	?
B. Trust	+	+	0	?
C. Openness	+	?	0	?
D. Stability of norms	+	+	+	?
III. Organization				
A. Performance	0	?	?	?
B. Growth	0	?	?	?
C. Costs	–	?	?	?
D. Control	X	X	X	X

Key to table entries: + Positive impact
0 Neutral impact
– Negative impact
? Impact unknown
X Constrained variable

Figure 7   Qualitative intervention assessment

and costs of each of the alternatives. After the choice has been decided and implemented, follow-up assessments can be repeated to determine the actual progress relative to initial expectations.

The basic method can be modified in several ways. First, the list of welfare considerations can be tailored to match the most important concerns of the client. Second, if individuals within groups or groups within organizations are not homogeneous enough to permit meaningful generalizations, then it is possible to specify welfare functions for each principal individual or group. Third, the time horizons can be lengthened or shortened to accommodate the rates of change for different organizations. Fourth, the assessment entries in the table may be more detailed than the simple notation allows. Short written descriptions could replace the symbols. In addition it is possible to attempt quantitative assessments if there are reliable and accurate measures of change. For example, there may be quantitative indices available for performance (e.g. profit), social cohesion (e.g. sociometric tests), and satisfaction (e.g. surveys). Although it is probably prudent not to make the method more elaborate than the competence of the consultant allows, the method can become more sophisticated as the practitioner and client gain more experience and insight regarding the dynamics of the organization of interest.

In summary, the method of qualitative intervention assessment consists of the following steps.

(1) Determination by the client and consultant together of the most important welfare considerations for the given organization.
(2) Evaluation of the current strengths and weaknesses of the welfare variables previously identified.
(3) Prognosis of the likely development of the client's health in the absence of any deliberate change programme.
(4) Assessment of the relevant OD alternatives in terms of the likely impact on the client's health.
(5) Selection of the strategy that maximizes health over the long run.
(6) Implementation of the chosen strategy.
(7) Measurement of the client's progress in terms of established criteria.

Conclusion

In the best of all possible worlds, OD consultants should be able to maximize the welfare of any organization and all groups and individuals in them. But the real world is not utopian and OD practitioners can ill afford to be unrealistic. There will be inevitable tradeoffs among the welfare functions of organizations, groups, and individuals (Nord and Durand, 1978) which need to be recognized by practitioners and researchers alike if OD is to succeed to any kind of managerial or scientific maturity.

The foregoing conceptual framework is a partial attempt to formulate a more comprehensive and potentially more rigorous perspective on the design and management of organizational change. In a limited way it tries to ameliorate the four system deficiencies of other OD approaches. First, the issue of systems identification is highlighted by calling attention to the interactive dynamics of individual, group, and organization welfare functions. Second, the problem of specifying systems variables is treated explicitly by operationalizing the significant components of welfare functions. Third, the tendency to focus interventions narrowly is moderated by the recognition of multiple consequences at numerous levels of organizations. Fourth, the need for measurement and evaluation is accommodated through follow-up assessments in terms of specified criteria.

A final desideratum for a meaningful conceptual framework is that it be intellectually interesting. If it can generate accurate hypotheses, provocative propositions, and challenging questions it may provide the motivation for others to test, modify, and elaborate the concepts in the continuing evolution of organization development as an applied behavioural science. As a measure of this last quality, the following propositions are offered as untested conjectures stimulated by this analytic perspective.

A1. A straight line is not always the shortest distance between two points.

A2. You cannot always get there from here.

B1. In organizations you rarely do just one thing.

B2. Important activities almost always have multiple consequences.

C1. You do not have to do everything simultaneously.

C2. You might be able to do many things sequentially.

D. Since not all problems are equally important, it is not crucial to optimize all solutions.

E1. It is more important where you wind up than how you got there.

E2. There is more than one road to Rome, but many lead to hell.

References

Alderfer, Clayton P. (1976) Boundary relations and organizational diagnosis. In L. Meitzer and F. Wickert (eds) *Humanizing Organizational Behavior*. Springfield. Ill.: Thomas.

Alderfer, Clayton P. (1977) Organization development. *Annual Review of Psychology*, **28**, 197–223.

Alfred, T. M. (1967) Checkers or choice in manpower management. *Harvard Business Review*, **45**, (1), 157–167.

Argyris, C. (1962) *Interpersonal Competence and Organizational Behavior*. Homewood, Ill.: Irwin.

Badad, Elisha Y., and Solomon, Gavriel (1978) Professional dilemmas of the psychologist in an organizational emergency. *American Psychologist*, September, 840–846.

Beckhard, R. (1967) The confrontation meeting. *Harvard Business Review*, **45** (2), 149–155.

Beckhard, R., (1969) *Organization Development: Strategies and Models*. Reading, Mass.: Addison-Wesley.

Beer, Michael, (1976) The technology of organization development. In Marvin D. Dunnette (ed.) *The Handbook of Industrial and Organizational Psychology*. Chicago: Rand McNally, 937–993.

Beer, Michael, and Huse, Edgar F. (1972) A system approach to organization development. *Journal of Applied Behavioral Science*, **8** (1), 79–101. Also in Newton Marqulies and Anthony P. Raia, *Conceptual Foundations of Organization Development*. New York: McGraw-Hill, 1978, 151–167.

Bennis, Warren, (1969) *Organization Development: Its Nature, Origin, and Prospects*, Reading, Mass.: Addison-Wesley.

Blake, R., and Mouton, J. S. (1964) *The Managerial Grid*, Houston, Texas: Gulf.

Boulding, Kenneth E. (1956) General systems theory – the skeleton of a science. *Management Science*, **2**, 197–208.

Bowers, David G., Franklin, Jerome L. and Pecorella, Patricia A. (1975) Matching problems, precursors, and interventions in OD: A systemic approach. *Journal of Applied Behavioral Science*, **11** (4), 391–409. Also in Newton Margulies and Anthony P. Raia, *Conceptual Foundations of Organization Development*. New York: McGraw-Hill, 1978, 151–167.

Brummet, R. L., Pyle, W. C., and Flamholtz, E. G. (1969) Human resource accounting in industry. *Personnel Administration*, **32** (4), 34–46.

Campbell, J. P. (1975) Contributions research can make in understanding organizational effectiveness. *Organizational and Administrative Sciences*, **1975**, pp. 29–45.

Campbell, J. P., and Dunnette, M. D. (1968) Effectiviness of T-group experiences in managerial training and development. *Psychological Bulletin*, August, **70** (2), 73–104.

Churchman, C. W. (1968) *The Systems Approach*. New York: Dell.

Cummings, T. G. (1977) Sociotechnical systems: An intervention strategy. In W. W. Burke (ed.) *Current Issues and Strategies in Organization Development*. New York: Human Sciences Press, 187–215.

Dale, Alan J. (1972) A systemic approach to organizational development. *Journal of Management Studies*, February, **9** (1), 75–83.

Dayal, I., and Thomas, J. M. (1964) Operation KPE: Developing a new organization. *Journal of Applied Behavioral Science*, **1964**, 473–506.

Drucker, Peter F. (1967) *The Effective Executive*. New York: Harper & Row.

Dyer, W. G. (1977) *Team Building: Issues and Alternatives*. Reading, Mass.: Addison-Wesley.

Eoyang, Carson K., and Haga, William J. (1977) Old wine in new bottles. *Behavioral Science*, **22**, 53–55.

French, Wendell L., and Bell, Cecil H., jun. (1978) *Organization Development: Behavioral Science Interventions for Organization Improvement*, 2nd ed. Englewood Cliffs, NJ: Prentice-Hall.

Friedlander, Frank, and Brown, L. David (1974) Organization development. *Annual Review of Psychology*, **24**, 219–341.

Galbraith, J. (1973) *Designing Organizations*. Reading, Mass.: Addison-Wesley.

Harrison, T. (1973) Role negotiation: A tough-minded approach to team development. In W. G. Bennis, E. D. Berlew, E. H. Schien, and F. J. Steele (eds) *Interpersonal Dynamics*, 3rd ed. Homewood, Ill.: Dorsey.

Herman, Stanley M. (1972) A gestalt orientation to organization development. In W. W. Burke (ed.) *Contemporary Organization Development: Conceptual Orientations and Interventions*. Arlington, Va.: NTL Institute, 64–89.

Huse, Edgar F. (1975) *Organization Development and Change*. New York: West.

Kahn, Robert (1974) Organizational development: Some problems and proposals. *Journal of Applied Behavioral Science*, **1974**, 485–502.

Lawrence, P. R., Bailey, J. C., Katz, R. L., Seiler, J. A., Orth, C. D., III, Clark, J. V., Barnes, L. B., and Turner, A. N. (1961) *Organizational Behavior and Administration.* Homewood Ill.: Irwin & Dorsey.

Lawrence, P. R., and Lorsch, Jay W. (1967) *Organization and Environment.* Cambridge, Mass.: Harvard University.

Lesieur, Frederick G. (ed.) (1958) *The Scanlon Plan.* Cambridge, Mass.: Technology Press and Wiley.

Likert, R. (1967) *The Human Organization.* New York: McGraw-Hill.

Lindbloom, Charles E. (1959) The science of 'Muddling Through'. *Public Administration Review,* Spring, 79–88.

Longenecker, Justin G., and Pringle, Charles D. (1978) The illusion of contingency theory as a general theory. *Academy of Management Review,* July, **3** (3), 674–683.

McKnight, John L. (1959) The quantum theoretical concept of measurement. In C. W. Churchman and P. Ratoosh (eds) *Measurement: Definition and Theories.* New York: Wiley, 192–203.

Myers, M. Scott (1971) Overcoming union opposition to job enrichment. *Harvard Business Review,* May–June, 37–49.

Nord, W. R., and Durand, D. E. (1978) What's wrong with the human resources approach to management? *Organizational Dynamics,* American Management Association, Winter, 13–25.

Porras, Jerry I., and Berg, P. O. (1978) The impact of organization development. *Academy of Management Review,* April, **3** (3), 249–266.

Rappaport, Anatol (1969) Mathematical aspects of general systems analysis. In J. A. Litterer, *Organizations: Systems, Control and Adaption,* 2nd ed., vol. 2. New York: Wiley.

Reicken, Henry W. (1978) Memorandum on program evaluation. In W. L. French, C. H. Bell, and R. A. Zawacki (eds). *Organization Development: Theory, Practice and Research.* Dallas, Texas: Business Publications, 413–423.

Roethlisberger, F. J., and Dickson, W. J. (1939) *Management and the Worker.* Cambridge, Mass.: Harvard University Press.

Rush, H. M. F., and McGrath, P. S. (1973) Transactional analysis moves into corporate training: A new theory of interpersonal relations becomes a tool for personnel development. *Conference Board Record,* July, **10** (7), 38–44.

Schein, E. H. (1969) *Process Consultation: Its Role in Organization Development,* Reading, Mass.: Addison-Wesley.

Simon, H. A. (1962) The architecture of complexity. *Proceedings of the American Philosophical Society,* **106,** 467–482.

Tannenbaum, Robert, and Davis, Sheldon A. (1969) Values, man, organization. *Industrial Management Review,* Winter, **10** (2), 67–83.

Trist, E L., and Bamforth, K. W., (1951) Selections from social and psychological consequences of the longwall method of goal-getting. *Human Relations,* **4** (1), 6–38. Also in J. A. Litterer, *Organizations: Systems, Control and Adaptation,* 2nd ed., vol. 2. New York: Wiley, 263–275.

Vroom, V. H., and Yetton, P. W. (1973) *Leadership and Decision Making.* University of Pittsburgh Press.

Walton, T. E. (1969) *Interpersonal Peacemaking: Confrontation and Third-Party Consultation.* Reading, Mass.: Addison-Wesley.

Webb, E. J., Campbell, D. T., Schwartz, R. D., and Schrest, L. (1966) *Unobtrusive Measures.* Chicago: Rand McNally.

White, Samuel E., and Mitchell, Terence R. (1976) Organization development: A review of research design. *Academy of Management Review,* April, **1** (2), 57–73.

Systems Theory for Organizational Development
Edited by T. G. Cummings
© 1980 John Wiley & Sons Ltd.

Chapter 11

On Organization Development Interventions: A General Systems–Cybernetic Perspective

Craig C. Lundberg

Perhaps no other applied field lives up to its central phenomena as much as organization change and development. The practices and knowledge in this field have not only proliferated extensively, but have been elaborated dramatically right from its beginning a few short decades ago. The early value infused injunctions of the field's spokesmen (e.g. Bennis, 1963; Mann and Neff, 1961; Argyris, 1962, among others) were quickly replaced by many more or less descriptive cases of organizational change efforts; these included Partin (1973), the Conference Board (1973), and the early issues of the *Journal of Applied Behavioral Science*. Following the lead provided by Lewin (1947), the first general model of change appeared (Lippitt, Watson, and Westley 1958), and it did not take long for the first tentative models of organization development (OD) to appear (e.g. Shepard, 1960; Fordyce and Weil, 1971; Kolb and Frohman, 1970). The early descriptive cases and impressionist evaluations, however, soon gave way to an increasingly empirical research literature: first, studies of particular interventions and strategies (e.g. Zand, Steele, and Zalkind, 1962; Hand, Estafan, and Sims, 1975; Golembiewski and Munzenrider, 1973); then the beginning of studies of change effectiveness (e.g. Nielson and Kimberly, 1973; Golembiewski and Munzenrider, 1972); and more recently, models of consultancy (e.g. Blake and Mouton, 1976; Lippitt and Lippitt, 1978) and reviews of organization development research (e.g. Bowers, 1973; Porras, 1978a; Margulies, Wright, and Scholl, in press).

The cumulative record of OD, however, remains notably uneven and is quite sparse, in fact, in a number of areas of central importance, especially the conceptual development of intervening practices and interventions. Argyris (1970), of course, represents the notable exception. This relative void is surprising, given the existing plethora of descriptive reports of interventional practice. These descriptions, however, seldom indicate the interventional model utilized. After reading a series of such reports, it appears to me that different models underlie different classes of interventions, or even the same intervention when used in alternative organizational contexts. This chapter blithely attempts to fill this void. The intent here is to explicate a general framework for understanding all or most OD interventions. The perspective offered is that of general systems theory (GST) and its associated discipline, cybernetics; both seem to provide a rationale and language for comprehending OD interventions.

The significance of this effort is more than simply filling a void in the OD literature. The development of a general framework is a timely endeavour given the contemporary conceptual developments in OD, such as the work on grounded theory (Dunn and Swierczek, 1977), the measurement of change (Golembiewski, Billingsley and Yeager, 1976), and efforts to adopt more macro theories (e.g. Bigelow, 1978a). Further, it relates to a wide set of pragmatic OD practices in a way that may enhance the classification of interventions which are central to OD. If a general framework of the functioning of OD interventions can be successfully elaborated, it would enhance OD practice in several ways. First, by explicating its underlying assumptions and by providing a common framework, contemporary intervention practice could be more adequately understood as well as assessed. Second, present interventions might be extended in their application and new interventions created, what Brown (1973) has termed 'creative perversity'. Third, a framework that increases our understanding of what interventions are and what they can do may also eventually contribute towards the meta-model of organizational change and development that has so far eluded OD theoreticians.

The chapter is presented in five parts. The first, relying on a general systems theory–cybernetic perspective, reviews the systems concepts relevant to OD interventions, focusing attention on open, adaptive systems and feedback loops. The second section attempts to show the applicability of GST to organization development by translating interventional 'targets', or so-called client systems, into systems terminology, and shows how this perspective points to the inadequacy of the currently predominant OD strategy – planned change. The third part focuses upon interventions directly. It shows how the cybernetic ideas of negative and positive feedback affect organization change and stability. The section ends with a framework for the analysis of interventions in which the design and management of feedback loops related to the processes of target systems are central. In the fourth section the interventional framework is applied to a sample of familiar interventions and to several descriptive cases, thereby illustrating the conceptual centrality of feedback. The final section summarizes the text and suggests directions in which further inquiry might be fruitfully directed.

The relevancy of general systems theory

As indicated above, general systems theory is the perspective from which we wish to examine OD interventions. Thus, GST becomes the 'language' for discussing organizations and their component subunits and processes which are nominally the targets of change endeavours. Let us begin by recalling the *raison d'être* of GST. Von Bertalanffy (1968, p. 34) states it succinctly: 'It seems, therefore, that a general theory of systems would be a useful tool providing, on the one hand, models that can be used in, and transferred to, different fields, and safeguarding, on the other hand, from vague analogies which often have marred the progress in these fields.'

General systems theory comes about as a consequence of noting the existence of general systems properties appearing in the pattern of similarities and functional isomorphisms found in many different fields, especially those fields studying organized complexity common in the biological, social, and behavioural sciences; that is, fields whose phenomena are not easily explained by mechanical and probabilistic approaches. GST, therefore, offers the promise, already partially kept, of a general science of 'wholeness' – 'taking over the duty of the overworked and perhaps retiring concept of the "organic"' (Buckley, 1967, p. 43) – providing the basis for synthesis as well as discovery, two aims consistent with the thrust of this chapter.

In what follows we shall briefly note how GST is applicable to organization development, and in this way proceed towards the definition of those key terms needed in comprehending intentional change efforts in those complex social systems we call organizations.

What are the motives and hopes for GST? How well has it lived up to its initial promise? In answering these questions, its origins and history are sidestepped, for these are discussed elsewhere (e.g. Bertalanffy, 1971; Miller, 1955; Bertalanffy, 1968; Berrien, 1968; and Laszlo, 1975), and are not directly relevant. Above, GST was characterized as a general science of 'wholeness', where isomorphic laws discovered in different fields were eventually seen as applying to systems of a certain type irrespective of the particular properties of the system and the elements involved. General systems theory's aims, therefore, were to capitalize on the natural tendency towards integration in the various sciences and thereby develop unifying principles running 'vertically' through the universe of the individual sciences.[1] Outcomes of this would be several (as suggested by Buckley, 1967, p. 39): a common vocabulary unifying disciplines; a more synthetic, as opposed to a purely analytic, approach which incorporates a concern for contexts; a viewpoint which emphasizes relations, especially informational flows, as processes; and a non-anthropomorphic view of purposiveness, among others. These are bold aims indeed!

The impact and developmental progress of GST are substantial and well documented elsewhere (e.g. Miller, 1978; the yearbooks of the Society for General Systems Research; and the journal *Behavioral Science*, among other sources). To be fair, any set of ideas as 'sematically rich' as GST over time evolves both empirically sophisticated as well as naïve proponents. Klir (1972, p. 13) cautions that 'the fixed idea of powerful systems theorists, who can solve almost all problems for almost all disciplines, should be recognized as a myth and treated accordingly'. The aims of general systems theory appear to be particularly relevant to the social sciences which may be characterized as (a) tending conceptually to lag behind the natural and physical sciences, (b) tending towards ever more discipline fragmentation, and (c) tending to be relatively under-conceptualized and the captive of simplistic paradigms.

In the social sciences, GST has stimulated both considerable philosophic comment (e.g. Boulding, 1956), and contributed to the development of such reasonably defined offspring as cybernetics (Beer, 1959; Ashby, 1956), information theory (Rapoport, 1956), hierarchy theory (Pattee, 1973), and living systems (Miller, 1965). In addition, a number of applied fields derive, more or less, from GST; these 'systems science/systems design' fields include human engineering, operations research, systems engineering, and socio-technical systems and their spin-offs such as work design. In the fields of management and organization, the 'systems' approach is currently dominant (e.g. Kast and Rosenzweig, 1970; Miner, 1978; Thompson, 1967; and Katz and Kahn, 1966). As Perrow (1973, p. 11) eloquently summarizes: 'But on one thing all the varied schools of organizational analysis now seem to be agreed: organizations are systems – indeed, they are open systems.'

This applied use, however, tends to focus on systems as clockwork (Boulding, 1956) and simple control devices (Pondy, 1976). The attractiveness of general systems thinking cannot be questioned; yet, it has seldom gone beyond its analogic potential. This is especially true for the field of OD contemporary texts; for example, Huse (1975), French and Bell (1973), and Margulies and Raia (1978) tend to insert a rudimentary discussion of systems theory, but leave it unrelated to any models of change or development. Most typically, systems theory is used to map diagnostic endeavours in the change process (e.g. Kotter, 1978; Beckhard and Harris, 1977).

'System' is surely the leading candidate for the most seductive term of contemporary times. Definitions of systems abound. Connotations range widely: a set of interdependent, interacting elements; a set of units so combined as to form an organized whole whose output is greater than the output of its constituent units; a set of objects together with relationships between the objects and between their attributes; a set of components interacting with each other and a boundary which possess the property of filtering both the kind and rate of inputs and outputs to and from the system. These definitions embrace both what nominally is termed a 'closed system' (a set of interrelated parts which are assumed to function within themselves and independently of their context), an 'open system' (a set of interdependent parts which accepts from, responds to, and exports matter, information, and energy to its environment), and an 'adaptive system' (an open system whose parts exhibit an ordered pattern of activity which is congruent with certain system ends). Open, adaptive systems (OAS), therefore, not only exchange matter and energy with their environment, but also information which may serve as feedback. Open, adaptive systems are subject to entropy and this natural process is arrested by importing and storing energy beyond export requirements (Katz and

Kahn, 1978). The active character of OAS gives them a dynamic structure which is more or less homeostatic, and tends towards elaboration and differentiation (Khandwalla, 1977).

Let us more closely examine the characteristics of OAS that have relevance for this essay. Such systems require minimal maintenance of structure. Energy imported is partially devoted to this. When some semblance of a steady structure is achieved, however, the balance of this acquired energy can be devoted to 'work'. OAS, therefore, tend towards a constancy of components and relationships in spite of continuous irreversible processes, such as import and export, building up and breaking down. Over time, considerable component autonomy may occur, even when there is intercomponent interaction, e.g. Weick's (1976) 'loosely coupled' educational systems. The feature just noted is the result of 'codes' developed in the system as to what constitutes appropriate feedback information. Feedback codes that relate directly to desired system states thus 'control' the system and we speak of goal directed action. Where feedback codes are either less closely related to system states or where the states themselves are not well specified, we can speak of goal-oriented action. Learning is an example, for the feedback changes the channels and even sometimes the codes themselves. Note that feedback can affect how the system relates to its environment or its internal structural-processual arrangements. In those OAS which are social systems, some components function to designate feedback codes for goal direction or orientation. Thus, some components, due not only to their connectedness but also because they 'design' and 'monitor' feedback, become relatively influential. Management, loosely conceived, is an example. Changes in system performance and system change, therefore, seem to be controlled by those components that receive or code or design external and internal feedback processes. Consequently, 'Pareto's Law', i.e. that a relatively small percentage of inputs creates a large percentage of outcomes, seems to hold for OAS.

The emphasis of OAS outlined above raises the issue of why systems theory has not made more of an impact in the social sciences and their applied fields. The root ideas of structure and function which have been predominant in the social sciences provide cues here. Structure has been conceived primarily as a static or mechanical construct. A mechanical structure is intrinsically equilibrium seeking, and equilibrium theories are based on a very restricted field of steady state dynamics which are not able to predict sudden change largely because they assume no overall goal as the driving force. As Deutsch (1951, p. 198) points out, 'Altogether, in the world of equilibrium theory, there is no growth, no evolution, no sudden changes, no efficient prediction of the consequences of "friction" over time.' The idea of function in the social sciences went beyond its mathematical connotation to mean that socio-cultural items, e.g. taboos, myths, warfare, functioned to perpetuate the society in which they are found by ensuring its solidarity and harmony. Here, function means how a component positively contributes to the whole of which it is a part. Thus, functional explanations assume that a social system has a goal, e.g. harmony, self-perpetuation, etc. When goals or some other driving force are not assumed, mechanical theories of equilibrium are sought. These mechanical theories seek an understanding of the nature of social systems by exploring cause and effect relationships among component parts. Unfortunately, such theories do not tend to consider the process by which entities are determined. In short, the dominant theories in the social sciences are largely equilibrium and synchronic, where the passage of time is not integral.

In contrast to the above, OAS strongly suggest not only a diachronic model, but perhaps a dialectical model as well (Galt and Smith, 1976) where processes dominate and sources of change are inherent to the system (Benson, 1977). Certainly these seem to be necessary for OD, for all conceptions of OD imply not only the passage of time, but the notion that potential sources of change are inherent in a social system as well as the consequence of environmental press. We come to believe, therefore, in some level of tension as characteristic of and vital to OAS, especially those with more than a minimal complexity. The idea of feedback information in systems, which suggests other than perfect component functioning, confirms this belief – tension thus becomes any uncorrected difference between actual system functioning and that which is called for.

Inevitably this discussion points to feedback information as a pivotable idea. Now, feedback has come to have two connotations. One is the technical meaning whereby a system's actual performance is compared with a predetermined state and information about any deviation between the two directs the system into closer correspondence. The other meaning is a simplification of the first, and feedback becomes any reciprocal interaction between variables. The latter meaning is so general as to be useless, for impact and influence are not registered, while the former meaning is restricted to rather simple steady-state situations. Feedback which counteracts deviation is called negative feedback. It is easily seen that negative feedback is conceptually similar to equilibrium (bringing the system further back or closer to a predetermined state of harmony, form, etc. – sometimes referred to as a morphostatic process). Similarly, negative feedback is conceptually related to function, when components are seen as contributing to the system in some stabilizing way (bringing the system components closer to a predetermined total system state). If we are correct in the dominance of the ideas of structure, function, and equilibrium in the social sciences, then the popularity of negative feedback is understood because of its conceptual consistency with those concepts. At the same time, the more or less exclusive use of the idea of negative feedback constrains us from theorizing about change and development except in a simplistic way, namely achieving only preconceived states.

Our discussion has not been entirely fair, however, for the literature also holds the idea of positive feedback. Positive feedback is information about a system's actions that increases the deviation of the system from its predetermined goal-state. How OD becomes part of an organization's culture may be understood this way. Commonly, an organization with a training department exists, and is relatively homogeneous in its potential for specialization. By some chance one member learns of OD and initiates a modest application. Then typically an external OD consultant is employed, training staff are retrained in OD, and multiple OD projects come into being. One or more staff members become mentors and/or coordinators for OD work and an OD staff is legitimized. This staff facilitates more projects, change management becomes part of all training, and change flourishes and necessitates OD eventually becoming a feature of the firm's culture. Maruyama (1963) has termed this deviation amplifying process the 'second cybernetics', while others more generally refer to it as morphogenesis. In the literature to date, positive feedback has been cast in relatively negative terms, primarily because, unless it is fettered by paralleling negative feedback, systems would build up from some initial 'kick' towards self-destruction.

A discussion of change and development in OAS seems to centre on feedback. OAS of the sort we are concerned with in this essay – e.g. business, public, and voluntary organizations – require many types of changes. Aiding such a system to 'change', that is, to achieve more of its goals and better to adjust itself to its environment, appears to require the use of negative feedback processes. For a system to 'develop', that is, to move into unanticipated new environments or states, or to reorganize its components for better goal seeking or better design of negative feedback, seems to require at least some positive feedback as well.

In this section we have focused on systems of an open, adaptive type. We have seen that they are characterized as having components, and an environment; that they transact energy and information with their environment as well as between components; and that at least some information is needed to guide the system or its components. Feedback processes were identified as either negative or positive. The mutual causal processes of morphostasis and morphogenesis were seen to enable change and development, respectively, to be made. It was also noted that the equilibrium biased theories of a mechanical or functional type have not encouraged examination of positive feedback processes. A general systems perspective, however, goes beyond these previous restrictions and suggests that system change is the result of positive feedback processes, and development most probably is the result of a combination of both negative and positive feedback processes. It is just this premise towards which the remainder of the essay develops.

Organizational change: a systems view

The history of organizational development to date holds three prominent, intertwined trends. One trend stems from OD's origins in T-groups and laboratory training, as well as survey research and feedback, and then adds new change technologies and foci, until today we actively work with total organizations, the organization–environment interface (Beckhard and Harris, 1977), and transorganizational development. A second trend began with the 'image' and 'meta-style' promulgated by the early spokesmen for the field and captured by the metaphor of a 'gardener' (Lundberg, 1973) where a nature-oriented facilitation towards organizational health is the essence. This is OD which facilitates an organization reaching its own unique potentials and beyond. Over time, the field of OD's focal image has seemed to shift more towards that of a 'sculptor' – a more direct creation of one's intention. This is exemplifed by most management consultants. A third trend began with 'action-research', the application of scientific methodology to practical problems with successive action planning and evaluation cycles. Again, there has been a shift towards a long-term, lineal set of stages designed to move an organization towards a preconceived end state – so-called planned change. While OD is undoubtedly multi-faceted, a venerable hydra in fact, the emphasis on the managed, planned change of large units is undeniable. These trends just sketched beg assessment, but before doing so, let us attend to the focus of change directly. The OD literature offers two labels for the focus of change efforts in organizations. From the earliest model is the phrase 'target of change'; subsequent change agents use the term 'client system'. Both of these labels, targets and clients, reflect a crude system's consciousness, but invariably refer to a social unit of analysis along the continuum from individuals to societies. Thus, some social unit, understood to be a 'system', has become the focus of change efforts. Teams are a prominent example (French and Bell, 1973). The point here is a subtle but nevertheless crucial one: the structure and functioning of change targets or clients have captured our attention more than the processes by which they operate, which have become secondary. To be sure, change agents view processes as the means for change – so-called OD technologies primarily impact target or client processes – but seldom view target or client processes themselves as the focus.

The point just made suggests a criticism of managed, planned change. If there is a desired structure and functioning for a larger social unit, and the change agent has the means to achieve it, then there will be an emphasis on reestablishing a new stability and hence on negative feedback. Most of the information useful to such a project will relate to the question: How much closer to our desired end state will we be if we do X? This patently is a deviation counteracting issue. Interestingly, it is also one captive of a managerial point of view, one that assumes that managers know best what the desired state should be. Here we are not simply arguing against the 'establishment' or underrating the vision and wisdom of managers, but merely noting that, from the perspective of general systems theory, present-day OD is perhaps mistakenly focusing on the appropriate targets of change and under-utilizing a repertoire of means. Perhaps client system informational processes are the more fruitful targets of change, where some combination of negative and positive feedback will enhance change efforts; also perhaps change and development, when not entirely captive of preconceived end states, will be equally positive – in sum, an alternative, systems perspective of organization change and development may enhance change practices.

Recall that general systems theory conceptually embraces both negative and positive feedback. Recall, too, that feedback loops control or guide open systems and their components in importing, transforming, and exporting energy, hence providing for adaption. At this point, let us point out some of the 'realities' of organizations in the modern world. Most have multiple goals, many of which may not be clear (Pfeffer, 1978). Most have changing, complex environments which implies that organizations live with considerable uncertainty. Most organizations are not specified completely which suggests that some components and processes are not under direct control. For example, the socialization of members is typically more extensive than formal orientation and training programmes accomplish. While a listing of organizational realities might be easily continued, these will suffice to remind us that not only are organizations open, adaptive systems, but that a managed, planned change strategy may only deal with the tip of the organizational iceberg, that is, those change endeavours that are managed from the top will of necessity focus on some things and not others simply because of the perceptual set of which management is captive.

A general systems view of organizational change minimally suggests a conception of organization patterning that includes multiple, linked components, with component specialization of process and function; and multiple purposes, in a complex, uncertain environment, characterized by a dynamic equilibrium at best, hence embodying inherent conflicts. A general systems view of organizational change must also incorporate a conception of organizational processes that includes energy flows, under the control of information flows, which vary in type and function and are sometimes multiplicative and have time lags, 'within and between' components, and the environment. Note that the conventional wisdom of organizations and their management has been altered. This assumes, more realistically, that organizations have the potential for multiple, quasi-stable states. It further assumes that organizations use negative feedback to maintain a particular quasi-stable state and positive feedback (although infrequently to be sure) to drive the organization towards alternative states or patterns and new environments. Organization changes aimed at efficiency and effectiveness rely on designing and managing negative feedback loops, while systemic organizational development requires attention to the design, installation, and monitoring of positive feedback loops.

This section has showed how general systems theory and cybernetics prompt a reconceptualization of organizations and change. Processes now become the targets of change, not the system or component structures. Energy and transformation processes, when altered, will give not only enhanced goal achievement and efficiencies, but will transform the patterning of the organization itself. The key to such alteration and transformation lies in the balance between negative and positive feedback, hence the creation, utilization, and extinction of feedback loops become the crux of managing both change and development.

Intervention: a cybernetic approach

The practices whereby organizational change and development are effected represent the pragmatic side of OD. This 'tool kit' of OD technologies seems to grow exponentially. The techniques for noticing opportunities and preparing for change, generating data, diagnosis, making strategies and action planning, implementing, assessing, and institutionalizing changes are collectively termed 'interventions' (some, however, would limit intervention to just implementation). The relevant literature (Argyris, 1970; Hornstein *et al.*, 1971) proposes that interventions are defined by their purpose – 'helping' a social system to alter its behaviour and functioning. Clearly such a general meaning encompasses much of what managers do every day as well as what OD specialists do. Classifications of OD interventions, therefore, have posited several dimensions to bring order to the array of interventions available (French, Bell, and Zawacki, 1978). Interventions have been classified by type of causal mechanism, e.g. educative, confrontive, increased interaction, etc.; depth of intervention, e.g. degree of self-exposure involved; underlying theme, e.g. dilemma, procedural, structural, etc.; time and comprehensiveness; and the size and complexity of the client group. To date a cybernetic definition of OD intervention has not been offered. Yet, if interventions are what persons do to effect change and development, the previous discussion suggests a definition of interventions in terms of altering feedback loops both within and between components and systems.

As discussed above, feedback loops carry information which, when perceived by the appropriately coded component, guides performance by amplifying or counteracting mutual causal processes – i.e. feedback loops function to stabilize or provide variation in the activities by means of which energy flows and transformations occur. OD interventionists have focused almost exclusively on negative feedback processes. Influential organization and organizational change writers probably account for this (as well as a prevailing 'managerial' philosophy which emphasizes control). Katz and Kahn (1962, p. 22) say it directly: 'the simplist type of information input found in all systems is negative feedback. Information feedback of a negative kind enables the system to correct is deviations from course.' Chin (1976, p. 95) likewise alludes to negative feedback mechanisms: 'improving the feedback process of a client will allow for self-steering or corrective action to be taken by him or it.' Mann (1963, p. 324) defines the elements of a feedback process as '(1) the orderly collection of information about the function of the organization, and (2) the reporting of this information into the system for (3) its use in making further adjustment.' In his study, Mann fed back a variety of perceptions and attitudes of employees regarding work, supervisors, peers, etc., helping to clarify the expectations among members of an organizational family and between organizational families. With the expectations clear, any deviations in fulfilling expectations could be identified and minimized. Although the effectiveness of existing relations was improved, no systemic changes occurred.

Regardless of prior emphasis on negative feedback alone, an enlarged perspective is advocated here. Altering feedback loops – adding, subtracting, and modifying – within and between components and at the system/environment interface is viewed here as the practice that induces change and development. And yet intervening is more complex if we posit first and second order interventions. A first order intervention alters directly client system feedback loops such as when regular appraisal is instituted or a report format is redesigned. Indirectly altering feedback loops which in turn alters the loops that guide system activities represents second order interventions. Examples of second order interventions might be the establishment of an OD group in an organization, an organizational ombudsman, and the organizational mirror intervention (Fordyce and Weil, 1971). The distinctions noted – targets which are relational processes *within* or *between* systems/components, intentions of increasing *stability* or *variation* in processes, and modifying feedback loops by *adding, subtracting,* or *altering* existing loops – may be combined to offer a new and quite different classification of interventions. Figure 1 presents this classification scheme.

Applying this classification to a pair of well-known interventions may aid its comprehension. Process consultation (Schein, 1969), for example, typically encompasses (a) improvements in a team's decision making procedures (cells 9 or 11) and (b) better agenda formulation and attention (cells 5 or 7), and (c) legitimizes the expression and use of data on team members' feelings (cells 1 or 3). Intergroup team building (Blake and Mouton, 1965), by contrast, focuses on two

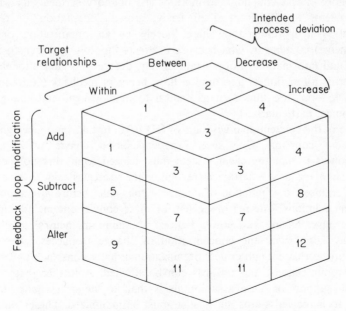

Figure 1   A cybernetic classification of interventions

groups, typically modifying their relationship by decreasing the misconceptions each has about the other as well as decreasing extraneous, non-functional intergroup behaviours. This intervention, therefore, modifies feedback loops within cells 2, 6, and 10.

Although this classification is illustrated more fully in the next section of this chapter, its congruence with present-day ideas is noteworthy. Central to the discussion has been a view of system–environment and system–component relationships as differing in their degree of 'coupling' (Weick, 1976; Glassman, 1973), i.e. the amount of dependence and interaction that exists. Whereas older prescriptions of organizations consciously or unconsciously advocated tightly coupled (bureaucratic) structures and strong managerial controls (negative feedback dominated), these have, under the banner of 'contingency' thinking (Lawrence and Lorsch, 1967), given way to the view that the degree of tightness of and number of links appropriate between organizational units is a function of numerous factors, e.g. the degree of environmental turbulence, the nature of technology and personnel. Recently, organizational boundaries have been reconceptualized in terms of their permeability (Alderfer, 1976). Organizations are now seen not as simple open systems, but ones of more or less openness. Similarly, the preferable style of managing is now seen as one that is consistent with the state of coupling of the organization. Managers of tightly coupled systems are oriented more inwardly than managers of loosely coupled systems. OD intervention technologies, therefore, must examine, affect, and institutionalize either more or less coupling and more or less boundry permeability where there are problems in effectiveness, efficiency, growth, adaptation, or redirection. Inter/intrasystem (understood here loosely as an organization or its subcomponents) coupling is vital because it affects the flow and transformation of energy and information in organizations. The degree of organizational coupling, however, is a function of information flow, hence of feedback (Galbraith, 1973). Feedback loops are thus seen as central to management and change, and to development particularly.

Some of the conventional wisdoms of OD begin to take on a new light in terms of system coupling. One such experience-based conviction held by OD practitioners is that the client system must exceed some threshold of stability before change can be entertained (revolutionary strategies aside).[2] A second conviction counsels the initiation of change within units before attempting to alter inter-unit relations. The reasons given for these convictions include achieving a critical mass; having key power figures, at minimum, neutral to change but hopefully supportive; the concentration of change resources and reasonable autonomy so that enough critical organizational dimensions such as job structuring, communications, and rewards can be affected. A further reason typically given in support of these assumptions is that, to avoid resistance to change, threats to perceived status and justice must be minimized. These commonsense convictions suggest that a minimum of certainty is requisite for readiness for change, and that readiness is a requisite for awareness of issues or new possibilities – understood here as goals for coupling. The exception to the above is when instability/uncertainty is so high that members view change as essentially riskless; these are the conditions for revolutionary change. Revolutions are rare in work organizations, and interventions for them will not be considered here.

The conventional wisdoms introduced above suggest the beginnings of a strategic model of interventions. These convictions suggest the following intervention sequence under more or less typical OD circumstances: first, intervene to enhance the stability of relationships within an organizational unit; second, intervene to effect inter-unit changes; repeat the cycle. The unit (person, team, department, and so on) must, according to this strategy, be in sufficient condition to be able to deal with other units at the same or a greater level. When the target unit is seen as either an organization or its components, this sequence apparently covers all types of possible changes and development. The classification portrayed in Figure 1 can be 'mapped' onto this intervention strategy as follows: interventions falling in cells 1, 5, and 9 precede those falling in cells 3, 7, and 11, which in turn precede interventions falling in cells 2, 6, and 10, which in turn precede those in cells 4, 8 and 12. Of course, particular circumstances encountered in an organization may dictate a different sequence, especially since this strategic model assumes the weakest point of departure. For example, sometimes units are so incapable that the investment in intra-unit works makes no sense.

This conceptual discussion of intervention type and strategy has suggested a new view of organizational change and development. Organizational change may now be seen as the management of negative feedback loops, where management implies the design and use of such loops. Organizational development then becomes the management of an appropriate combination of both negative and positive feedback loops.

This section has offered a cybernetic definition of intervention, a classification of intervention types consistent with an open, adaptive social system conception of organizations, and a rudimentary strategic intervention model. So far the level of discourse has been rather abstract in order to avoid the conceptual quagmire and gaps which now characterize the OD literature on interventions, and to retain a reasonable fidelity to the language of general systems theory and cybernetics. However, illustration of what we have developed thus far now seems in order.

OD interventions: illustration and application of feedback loops

This section shows how the classification and model presented above can be used to understand OD interventional practice. The reader can readily anticipate that negative feedback can be portrayed by reference to a sampling of well-known OD change interventions. To illustrate what we now term organizational development, OD case studies are examined as well as the organic use of interventions.

OD change technologies

Five 'classical' OD interventions have been chosen to illustrate negative feed-back loops and their consequences: (1) the job expectation technique (Huse, 1975), (2) the family group diagnostic meeting (French and Bell, 1973), (3) the confrontation meeting (Beckhard, 1967), (4) the third phase of the managerial grid (Blake and Mouton, 1964), and (5) open systems planning (Krone, 1974; Beckhard and Harris, 1977). Each is described briefly and then analysed in terms of feedback loops.

Job expectation technique (JET) is an intervention at the individual/organization interface. It has been used to develop a new team, to reduce role conflict and ambiguity in an established team, and for bringing a new member into a team quickly. JET proceeds quite simply. Members take turns listing their perceived job duties and responsibilities; others comment until a consensus job definition is reached, and so on until the whole team has developed an understanding and agreement of each member's prescribed and discretionary role space. The process of JET opens channels of information about jobs among employees. JET informs the focal person of how relevant others believe he should and should not behave – providing norms or standards for performance and, hence, feedback for dampening behavioural variation. Given the team as the target, JET is an intervention that falls within cells 1, 5, and especially 9 of Figure 1. While JET may be used only once, periodic reviews are recommended, and hence recurrent negative feedback loops are created.

The family group diagnostic meeting (FGDM) focuses on the personal work style of a group. Its purpose is to identify where the group is going and how it is doing. Typically, a leader initiates the meeting by requesting members to consider the group's problem individually, whether task, relationship, or process oriented. After initial consideration, the group is reassembled and, either by pairing, job grouping, or total group discussion, diagnostic data are shared. The next step is to classify issues, grouping them into themes and ordering them by priority. Action steps are then planned before the meeting is over. The FGDM legitimates group self-diagnosis. As an intervention, it resembles JET in that it opens information channels which provide feedback to group members on group related issues. When used repeatedly, it is another illustration of the creation of negative feedback loops. Even with one meeting, however, there is modification of loops within the group via self-diagnosis. The FGDM as an intervention falls into the same cells of Figure 1 as did JET.

Beckhard's (1967) 'confrontation meeting' provides a third illustrative intervention. Like the previous two discussed, it is a short-term intervention typically conducted in one day. A confrontation meeting is a system-wide intervention designed for the entire management of an organization to assess their own organization's health. The meeting involves a series of steps: climate setting by the top manager; subgroups composed of managers from different functional areas then meet to list obstacles that exist as well as desired conditions; reporters from each subgroup then report to the entire meeting, and this information is circulated; following this, functional subgroups identify issues from the overall list related to their area, order these by priority from the organization's point of view, and design action steps and how they will communicate the results of the confrontation meeting to their subordinates; top management then meets to plan a follow-up meeting and, later, a group progress review session. This description of the confrontation meeting has both within and between target aspects (cells 1 and 2), given that the whole organization is represented, as are department units. It appears to represent a modification of information flow because of the meeting of all managers. The follow-up and progress review stages are examples of the establishment of negative feedback loops; indeed, the total intervention may be seen as one too, in that the issues generated and actions planned are those that are supposedly impeding the organization from fully achieving its goals.

The next intervention is the third phase of the managerial grid which focuses on intergroup development. This phase follows team development – an example of the progression of our strategic intervention model. Huse (1975, p. 156) describes the process of improving intergroup relations as following four steps: (1) prior to the sessions, each person prepares a written description of the actual working relationships as contrasted with the ideal relationships; (2) each group, in relative isolation, summarizes its perceptions of the actual and ideal relationships; (3) the two groups meet and, using a spokesman, compare their perceptions; (4) the two groups then work on making the relationship more productive. This action phase is completed when both groups have a clear understanding of the specific actions each will take and how they will be followed up.

This intervention is designed to open channels of information between groups or focus interaction on relational improvement. It constitutes a reciprocal feedback process between the two groups; the goal of making the relationship 'more productive' implies that closer conformity to preestablished goals is desired and hence negative feedback is the essence. Outcomes of the process would seem to suggest that the intervention potentially falls into cells 2, 6, and 10 of Figure 1.

The final intervention is focused on the organization – environment interface – open systems planning. It assumes that since organizations have permeable boundaries, interaction with the environment is a significant force in determining how the organization functions and changes. The technique involves several steps: determine the 'core mission' of the organization; map the environmental demand forces; map the current response practices; project the probable demand forces in three to five years, assuming there is no change in the organization's response pattern; identify the desired environmental conditions in three years; list activities necessary to achieve the desired conditions; and analyse the social and economic costs of the action alternatives. Open systems planning is intended to lead to strategic planning, the planning for where and how an organization will manifest its unique mission. Examining this intervention, we see the first step as goal or standard setting and resulting steps as information processing to test present and possible actions against the goals, i.e. the establishment and use of negative feedback loops.

In each of the above illustrations, there has been information generation or gathering supposedly relevant to individual (JET), group (FGDM), organization (confrontation meeting), intergroup (grid phase III), or organization–environment (open systems planning) functioning. These illustrations, of course, only begin to sample the vast array of intervention technologies available. The point, however, is that all the interventions mentioned, and probably those most currently available, involve modification of negative feedback loops. The prior discussion of the cybernetic differentiation between change and development suggests that the bulk of OD interventions, if utilized as mechanistically as presented, are really organizational change devices. Argyris (1970), in fact, claims that the generation and use of valid data about organizational functioning is the central, defining characteristic of OD. Nadler (1977, p. 8) agrees: 'Data and data feedback will be considered tools to be used for bringing about organizational change.' (We note that Nadler's use of change has the same meanings we have given to change – although Nadler actually uses change and development synonymously.)

The above description of interventions has implied a mechanical or programmed application. The sensitivity and style of an interventionist, however, sometimes permits the interjection of positive feedback loops. For example, one consultant, because of some impressions he had picked up in the interviewing step of FGDM, opened up the second phase by asking each team member to take a turn at being silent while his cohorts told the consultant about him. Ostensibly this was to better acquaint the consultant with the team members; however, as the process unfolded, team members began to say things to the silent member that had been unexpressed previously. Thus the consultant had initiated a feedback opportunity which was positive in that almost every kind of comment imaginable eventually was expressed – a clear increase over the strict task communications that had characterized the team.

Positive feedback can be illustrated by those interventions that produce some kind of disconfirmation situation, where established practice is suddenly met with failure. What happens at the beginning of an encounter group is a familiar example; the norms for leader and for agenda dependent behaviour that most persons adhere to do not apply. The behaviour resulting when the trainer does not rescue the initial confusion is clearly the first kick of a positive feedback loop.

In the earlier examples, change defined as improved goal achievement was the outcome of intervening so that negative feedback loops were modified. In the last two illustrations of interventional practice, at least some positive feedback existed in addition to the negative, hence these, by our prior definition, represent development. The following OD cases further illustrate feedback applied to development.

The first case concerns a residential school for mentally disturbed children. The school administration comprised a white male director, two female associate directors, one white, the other black, fourteen professional teacher-counsellors of varying ages, genders and of both races, and several support personnel, including secretaries, cooks, housekeepers, and janitors. The school ran on a 'new' model of treatment and as such was unique. It was related to state mental health bodies and the public school system, and was financed by both federal and state funds. The white associate director was acquainted with a consultant whom she called one day to express some vague sense of dissatisfaction with the 'climate' of the school. The consultant was sympathetic, but asked for a conference call between him and the director and associate directors. During this call no specific problems were cited, although there was agreement that 'somehow, things could be better'. A one-day diagnostic visit by the consultant was then planned. He would casually observe and interview members of the school, and at the end of the day offer his impressions to the administration and professionals.

At the end of the visit, the consultant 'reported' that in his opinion the organization seemed to be remarkably effective and, in fact, felt like a good place to work. At the end of these remarks, which were quite laudatory, the consultant pointed out that he had noticed some 'polite' behaviour among some personnel which seemed at variance with the general culture of the school. The group quickly voiced agreement and hypothesized that the quality of their professional relations probably affected the quality of teacher–child relations. Hence, they reasoned, improving professional relations was highly desirable. They asked the consultant what to do. He offered to return and conduct a one-day workshop in which the staff could actively discover what the quality of their relationships actually was and what, if anything, they wanted to do about them. This proposal was accepted.

The workshop was designed as a series of experiential activities in which trust, influence, communications, and similar relational dimensions were explored. The staff entered into the workshop with considerable energy. The consultant soon observed that when some minor difficulties were discovered, the staff quickly set about 'contracting' a way to improve them. By early afternoon, the consultant felt pleased; he had structured opportunities for the staff which they had used energetically and positively. At that point, the consultant asked whether the workshop was meeting participant expectations. There ensued a veritable barrage of positive response. One black male professional 'appeared' hesitant to speak, however. The consultant asked: 'What is it you want to say?' The man made a rambling speech touching on several topics. The consultant listened carefully and restated what he believed to be the two issues encased in the speech: the possibility of both racism and sexism among the staff.

A hush fell swiftly upon the group. The consultant asked the black professional to verify his understanding with some specifics. At that point, the black turned to the director and claimed that he had acted with racial prejudice. Simultaneously, one woman professional charged one of the associate directors with sexism. The air became electric. The consultant asked the two pairs just noted to sit facing each other and talk. The other staff were asked to cluster around the pair of their choosing and help them to talk 'descriptively and fully'. For the next hour the pairs continued, being replaced over and over again as other staff voluntarily took turns 'in the barrel'. The consultant observed a series of caring confrontations as well as support from clusters. The topics of racism and sexism soon expanded to include a variety of grievance and bias topics, such as single parenting, old age, and mental health. At approximately 4 p.m. the consultant interrupted and asked the staff to summarize their learnings. Everyone took a turn, mentioning both positive and negative insights into themselves and their relationships. After everyone had had a chance to speak, the consultants then asked the director to lead a discussion utilizing wall charts in which preferred staff behaviour were listed. This he did. The consultant then asked the staff to form natural work groups and negotiate interpersonal 'contracts' in line with the listing of preferred behaviours. After subgroups had done this, the consultant asked the staff to similarly contract with anyone else present whom they worked with; this occurred. (This concluded the workshop except for a short discussion of how the day had been and an appointment for a follow-up visit by the consultant several weeks later.)

This case suggests that feedback loops had been stable prior to the consultant's visits; that informal norms as well as school rules and procedures had established some standards; that social and work related conversations provided negative feedback to reinforce these standards, though, as the end of the meeting on the diagnostic day showed, the quality of staff relationships was somewhat lower than generally desired. The workshop was ostensibly intended as a way for the staff to receive information that would enhance their behaviour, and hence improve the quality of their relationships. The workshop, prior to the racism and sexism topics, illustrates the adding of negative feedback loops on relational dimensions that were not previously legitimate. The consultant's interventions to pair and cluster, however, brought many more 'heavy' topics to the fore. The events of that period appear to illustrate positive feedback – e.g. greater variation in topics as well as more styles of confrontation. The consultant's intervention of asking the director to list 'preferred' behaviours and the group work that followed seem to represent the enactment of negative feedback loops which stabilized relations at a new state. This case also illustrates a major premise of the strategic model of intervention developed earlier – the workshop began by focusing on intraschool relations, then, stability accomplished, it was able to move to relations between individuals at a more intensive level, then it focused on intrateam work which, when solidified, permitted a final round between individuals at a rather deep level. Hence, we see a cycling of 'within then between' interventions, with the two phases of work constituting a first cycle which utilized negative feedback loops; the next two phases constitute the second cycle using a combination of positive and negative feedback loops.

The Peace Corps provides two nice case examples (Bigelow, 1978a). In the first example, the Corps in its early period held a growth policy. Initial growth led to an excitement that kept the Peace Corps in the public eye and attracted people to the organization. During this period, growth produced results which encouraged further growth, i.e. it was producing negative feedback. About 1965, poorly programmed positions led to increasing numbers of unhappy volunteers as well as dissatisfaction by host countries. The unhappiness and dissatisfaction were being communicated to potential applicants at American universities which diminished the flow of applicants. At this point the growth policy was producing positive feedback, i.e. growth produced results which discouraged further growth.

The second Peace Corps example involved their way of training volunteers. In Bigelow's (1978b, pp. 241–242) words:

The Peace Corps began with a university model of training and it quickly became apparent that this was not a satisfactory model. Some felt that training in-country would be better but early attempts to do so failed; training was not yet to the point where it worked in-country. The Peace Corps then took an intermediate step. It moved off-campus but stayed in the U.S. in surrogate cultures. This was not an entirely satisfactory alternative but in this environment which was intermediate between the campus and the host country, the Peace Corps developed training technologies which would work in host countries. Soon after, the Peace Corps began increasingly to train in host countries.

Maruyama (1963, p. 168) gives a similar example to this, of an organism successively moving to and adapting to colder climates, and concludes: 'Thus the selection of, or accidental wandering into, a certain type of environment and the direction of survivable mutations amplify each other.'

Similarly, by selecting the off-campus training environment, the Peace Corps was able to develop training techniques which would work in them. This, in turn, made possible a move to in-country training which had previously not been possible. To paraphrase Maruyama, deviations in training location and training techniques amplified each other.

Let us now turn to a more complex case (Torbert, 1976). A small professional school of low quality (a subpart of a large, urban university) had a conservative administration. The underpaid staff tended to meet their teaching responsibilities minimally and spent most of their time acting as consultants to organizations. There had not been any curriculum changes or research in years. A group of concerned alumni decided to support improvement in the school. They provided large sums of money and forced a replacement of the dean. The man selected as the new dean was known nationally, was highly energetic, and professed a vision of a different form of school, one where teaching, research, and service are integrated and students learn by doing in a self-starting manner. The new dean quickly employed a few highly-qualified teachers who were attracted to his vision. Within a year or so, these new members of staff were appointed to the key administrative positions of a totally new school structure. These newer staff members actively recruited other qualified colleagues who were attracted to the dean's vision, the financial resources for improvement, and the excitement of making something important happen. At the time of the school's restructuring, the reward system was changed by fiat. Whereas seniority had been the prior consideration for salary and promotion, the new procedure clearly and solely rewarded performance in scholarship and instruction, especially innovation in the latter. The newly recruited teachers invented and adopted modern pedagogies, worked hard, and soon attracted and stimulated an eager student body. The original staff tried to behave as before, but soon began to embark on political strategies intended to discredit the new dean and staff in the eyes of the rest of the somewhat conservative university and business community. This came to little avail, and over time the original staff either left the school or joined the 'Dean's Team', with a few tenured staff holding-out for the 'good old days'. About five years after the new dean had begun the school's improvement programme, three of his original nucleus of teachers resigned – to take up high positions or new challenges. Privately, however, they confessed to the strain that the school's new culture placed on them. Turnover of newer teachers continued at a modest rate over the next few years. More conventional reward practices were then slowly reintroduced. The school had in this period attained national recognition for its accomplishments but began more and more to resemble other professional schools.

This case begins with the organization stabilized, presumably under the control of conventional, negative feedback processes. The major inputs of new leadership, finances, staff, and so forth permitted the setting of different goals (the dean's vision). The shift to a merit reward procedure emphasizing innovation and the recruitment of quality staff were crucial changes. On the one hand, they appear to represent different standards for negative feedback control. On the other hand, the key terms (innovation and quality) are so vague that goal-oriented as opposed to goal-directed behaviour occurred. Since these were heavily rewarded, they increased the variation in activities within the school immensely. Some of the new norms and procedures appeared to act as positive feedback loops – e.g. the innovative practices led to rewards which lead to more innovation, etc – while others, related to the on-going administration of the school, were negative feedback loops. The eventual turnover of staff may be interpreted as an unanticipated cost of the increased deviations that emerged – staff eventually became exhausted with the multiple demands from increased variation. This turnover reestablished more negative feedback. Thus, the school developed from primarily negative feedback to a combination of negative and positive feedback, and finally appeared to be once more dominated by negative feedback. As a postscript to the case, two further aspects are noteworthy. At about the time the case ended, there was an incident that prompted the school to attend to their external relationships with the original alumni group and the university administration. This is consistent with the proposed strategic model in that it is the first 'within then between' pattern. The second aspect concerns events in the few years since the case. Faculty concern with accreditation prompted a change in many of the school's policies, resulting in stabilization of practices as well as minor regressing to some more conventional school practices. Development was over, at least for a while.

The interventions and cases presented above provide examples of the cybernetically derived classification of interventions and indicate tentative consistency between OD practices and the intervention model. The abstractness of the idea of feedback loops makes it difficult to provide empirical examples. Similarly, the abstract nature of the notion of an open, adaptive system is not translated easily into the realities of organizations. Given these difficulties, however, this section has provided preliminary confirmation for a general systems–cybernetic perspective on interventions.

Summary and concluding commentary

In this chapter, the task of reconceptualizing OD intervening was begun. By adopting the concepts of general systems theory, it was possible to specify organizations as open, adaptive systems and further note the necessity of feedback loops for altering organizational processes. This perspective suggested that the traditional conception of OD as managed, planned change is limited to equilibrium/synchronic models of organizations. By utilizing general systems theory, organizations may be viewed as potentially having both goal-directed and goal-oriented potentialities. This, in turn, enabled us to apply the ideas of negative and positive feedback and posit new definitions of change and development: *change* being the outcome of negative feedback loops used to better achieve system states, and *development* being the result of both negative and positive feedback loops where the latter are oriented to goals of changing system states. This line of reasoning prompted a classification of interventions which, when linked to two experience-based convictions, resulted in the designation of a strategic model of interventionism: intervene within units first, if necessary, and then tackle inter-unit relations. The classification and more diachronic and dialectical model were then illustrated with reference to a variety of well-known OD interventions and three descriptive cases.

The line of reasoning presented in this essay seems promising. As a rudimentary beginning, it leaves much to be developed on at least two fronts. Conceptually, the ideas need considerable elaboration and refinement. Both the classification and the model are relatively crude. Empirically, the ideas in this essay require operationalizing. More importantly, OD practitioners need consciously to design and manage positive feedback loops so that experience with them can occur. Lewin has been credited with the dictum that the best way to learn about something is to change it. Perhaps this advice is especially vital to intervention practice. With more experience, the nature and appropriate ratios between positive and negative feedback, or what here has been defined as developmental processes, should permit further reconceptualization. The promise is great. The need for more adequate change and development practices is unquestioned.

Acknowledgement

The author wishes to acknowledge the bibliographic assistance of Lisbeth S. Brody in the preparation of this essay, and especially the critical commentary of John Bigelow, Tom Cummings, Kurt Motamedi, and A. P. (Tony) Raia on an earlier draft of this essay.

Notes

1. General systems theory quite clearly has contributed to a science of uniformities. Interestingly, 'systematics' is the label given to the science of diversity (McKelvey, 1978).
2. Typically this conviction is stated in the revise, i.e. 'people in the organizations must feel pressure in order to be ready for change' (Beer and Driscoll, 1977, p. 366).

References

Alderfer, Clayton (1976) Boundary relations and organizational diagnosis. In H. Meltzer and F. R. Wickert (eds) *Humanizing Organizational Behavior*. Springfield, Ill.: Thomas.

Argyris, Chris (1962) *Interpersonal Competence and Organizational Effectiveness*. Homewood, Ill.: Irwin-Dorsey.

Argyris, Chris (1970) *Intervention Theory and Method*. Reading, Mass.: Addison-Wesley.

Ashby, W. Ross (1965) *An Introduction to Cybernetics*. New York: Wiley.

Beckhard, Richard (1967) The confrontation meeting. *Harvard Business Review*, **45**, 149–155.

Beckhard, R., and Harris, R. T. (1977) *Organization Transitions: Managing Complex Change*. Reading, Mass.: Addison-Wesley.

Beer, Michael, and Driscoll, J. W. (1977) Strategies for change. In J. R. Hackman and J. L. Suttle (eds) *Improving Life at Work*. Santa Monica, Calif.: Goodyear.

Beer, Stafford (1959) *Cybernetics and Management*. London: English University Press.

Bennis, Warren G. (1963) A new role for the behavioral sciences: Effecting organizational change. *Administrative Science Quarterly*, **8** (2), 125–165.

Benson, J. Kenneth (1977) Organizations: A dialectical view, *Administrative Science Quarterly*, **22** (1), 1–22.

Berrien, F. Kenneth (1968) *General and Social Systems*. New Brunswick, NJ: Rutgers University Press.

Bertalanffy, Ludwig von (1968) *General System Theory*. New York: Braziller.

Bertalanffy, Ludwig von (1971) The history and state of general systems theory. In George Klir (ed.) *Trends in General Systems Theory*. New York: Wiley–Interscience, 21–41.

Bigelow, John (1978a) Approaching the organization Navel: An evolutionary perspective of organizational development. Working paper, School of Business, Oregon State University.

Bigelow, John (1978b) *Evolution in organization*. Ph.D. dissertation, Department of Organizational Behavior, Case Western Reserve University.

Blake, Robert, and Mouton, J. S. (1964) *The Managerial Grid*. Houston, Texas: Gulf.

Blake, Robert, and Mouton, J. S. (1965) *Managing Intergroup Conflict in Industry*. Houston, Texas: Gulf.

Blake, Robert, and Mouton, J. S. (1976) *Consultation*. Reading, Mass.: Addison-Wesley.

Boulding, Kenneth (1956) General systems theory – the skeleton of science. *Management Science*, 2, 197–208.

Bowers, David (1973) O.D. techniques and their results in 23 organizations: The Michigan ICL study. *Journal of Applied Behavioral Science*, 9 (1), 21–43.

Brown, Dave (1973) Action research: Hard-boiled eggs out of eggheads and hardhats? Paper presented at the Annual meeting of the Academy of Management, Boston.

Buckley, Walter (1967) *Sociology and Modern Systems Theory*. Englewood Cliffs, NJ: Prentice-Hall.

Chin, Robert (1976) The utility of system models and developmental models for practitioners. In W. G. Bennis, K. D. Benne, R. Chin, and K. E. Corey (eds) *The Planning of Change*. New York: Holt, Rhinehart & Winston.

Conference Board (1973) *Organization Development: A Reconnaissance*. New York: Conference Board.

Deutsch, Karl (1951) Mechanism, teleology and mind. *Philosophy and Phenomenological Research*, 12, 185–222.

Dunn, William, and Swierczck, F. W. (1977) Planned organizational change: Toward grounded theory. *Journal of Applied Behavioral Science*, 13 (2), 135–157.

Fordyce, Jack, and Weil, R. (1971) *Managing with People*. Reading, Mass.: Addison-Wesley.

French, Wendell, and Bell, C. (1973) *Organizational Development*. Englewood Cliffs, NJ: Prentice-Hall.

French, W. L., Bell, C. H., jun., and Zawacki, R. A. (1978) *Organization Development: Theory, Research and Practice*. Dallas Texas: Business Publications.

Galbraith, Jay (1973) *Designing Complex Organizations*. Reading, Mass.: Addison-Wesley.

Galt, Anthony, and Smith, L. J. (1976) *Models and Study of Social Change*. New York: Schenkman.

Glassman, R. B. (1973) Persistence and loose coupling in living systems. *Behavioral Science*, 18, 83–98.

Golembiewski, Robert, Billingsley, K. and Yeager, S. (1976) Measuring change and persistence in human affairs: Types of change generated by OD designs. *Journal of Applied Behavioral Science*, 12 (2), 133–157.

Golembiewski, Robert, and Munzenrider, R. (1972) Persistence and change: A note on the long-term effects of an organization development program. *Academy of Management Journal*, 5 (4), 149–153.

Golembiewski, Robert, and Munzenrider, R. F. (1973) Social desirability as an intervening variable in interpreting OD effects. *Academy of Management Proceedings*, 534–542.

Hand, Herbert, Estafan, D., and Sims, H. P. (1975) How effective is data survey and feedback as a technique of organization development: An experiment. *Journal of Applied Behavioral Science*, 11 (3).

Hornstein, H. A., Bunker, D. B., Burke, W. W., Gindes, M. and Lewicki, R. J. (1971) *Social Intervention*. New York: Free Press.

Huse, Edgar (1975) *Organization Development and Change*. New York: West.

Kast, Fremont, and Rosenzweig, J. E. (1970) *Organization and Management*. New York: McGraw-Hill.

Katz, Daniel, and Kahn, R. L. (1966) *The Social Psychology of Organizations*. New York: Wiley.

Katz, Daniel, and Kahn, R. L. (1978) *The Social Psychology of Organizations*, 2nd ed. New York: Wiley.

Khandwalla, Pradip (1977) *The Design of Organizations.* New York: Harcourt Brace Jovanovich.

Klir, George (1972) The polyphonic general system theory. In G. L. Klir (ed.) *Trends in General Systems Theory.* New York: Wiley–Interscience, 1–18.

Kolb, David, and Frohman, A. (1970) An organizational development approach to consulting. *Sloan Management Review,* **12** (1), 51–65.

Kotter, John (1978) *Organizational Dynamics: Diagnosis and Intervention.* Reading, Mass.: Addison-Wesley.

Krone, C. (1974) Open systems redesign. In J. D. Adams (ed.) *New Technologies in Organization Development 2.* La Jolla, Calif.: University Associates.

Laszlo, E. (1975) The meaning and significance of general systems theory. *Behavioral Science,* **20,** 9–24.

Lawrence, Paul, and Lorsch, J. (1967) *Organization and Environment.* Division of Research, Graduate School of Business, Harvard University.

Lewin, Kurt (1974) Frontiers in group dynamics. *Human Relations,* **1947,** 5–41.

Lippitt, Ron, Watson, J. and Westley, B. (1958) *The Dynamics of Planned Change.* New York: Harcourt Brace & World.

Lippitt, Gordon, and Lippitt, R. (1978) *The Consulting Process in Action.* La Jolla, Calif.: University Associates.

Lundberg, Craig (1973) Images and meta-styles of change agents. *Interpersonal Development,* **4,** 69–76.

McKelvey, Bill (1978) Organizational systematics: Taxonomic lessons from biology. Working paper no. 78–7, Human Systems Development Study Center, UCLA.

Mann, Floyd C. (1963) Studying and creating change: A means to social organizations In T. W. Costello and S. S. Zalkind (eds) *Psychology in Administration.* Englewood Cliffs, NJ: Prentice-Hall.

Mann, Floyd, C., and Neff, F. W. (1961) *Managing Major Change in Organizations.* Ann Arbor, Mich.: Foundation for Research on Human Behavior.

Margulies, Newton, and Raia, A. P. (1972) *Organization Development: Values, Process and Technology.* New York: McGraw-Hill.

Margulies, Newton and Raia, A. P. (1978) *Conceptual Foundation of Organizational Development.* New York: McGraw-Hill.

Margulies, Newton, Wright, P. L., and School, R. W. (in press) Organizational development techniques: Their impact on change. *Group and Organization Studies.*

Maruyama, Magoroh (1963) The second cybernetics: Deviation amplifying mutual causal processes. *American Scientist,* **51,** 164–179.

Miller, James G. (1955) Toward a general theory for the behavioral sciences. *American Psychologist,* **10,** 513–531.

Miller, James G. (1965) Living systems: Basic concepts; structure and process; cross-level hypotheses. *Behavioral Science,* **10,** 193–237, 337–379, 380–411.

Miller, James G. (1978) *Living Systems.* New York: McGraw-Hill.

Miner, John (1978) *The Management Process.* New York: Macmillan.

Nadler, David (1977) *Feedback and Organization Development: Using Data-Based Methods.* Reading, Mass.: Addison-Wesley.

Nielson, Warren, and Kimberly, J. K. (1973) The impact of OD on the quality of organizational outputs. *Academy of Management Proceedings,* **1973,** 527–542.

Partin, J. Jennings (1973) *Current Perspectives in Organization in Development.* Reading, Mass.: Addison-Wesley.

Pattee, Howard (1973) *Hierarchy theory: The challenge of complex systems.* New York: Braziller.

Perrow, Charles (1973) The short and glorious history of organizational theory. *Organizational Dynamics*, **2** (1).

Pfeffer, Jeffrey (1978) *Organizational Design*. Arlington Heights, Ill.: AHM Publishing.

Pondy, Louis (1976) Beyond open system models of organization. Working paper, Organizational Behavior Group, University of Illinois.

Porras, Jerry (1978a) The current state of research in OD. Paper presented at the Annual meeting of the Academy of Management, San Francisco.

Porras, Jerry (1978b) The impact of organizational development. *Academy of Management Review*, **3** (2), 249–266.

Rapoport, Anatol (1956) The promise and pitfalls of information theory. *Behavioral Science*, **1**, 303–309.

Schein, Edgar (1969) *Process Consultation: Its Role in Organization Development*. Reading, Mass.: Addison-Wesley.

Shepard, Herbert A. (1969) An action research model. In *An Action Research Program on Human Behavior*. Ann Arbor, Mich.: Foundation for Research on Human Behavior, 33–34.

Thompson, James (1967) *Organizations in Action*. New York: McGraw-Hill.

Torbert, William R. (1976) Learning, loving and organizing: The politics of higher education. Unpublished manuscript, Graduate School of Education, Harvard University.

Weick, Karl (1976) Educational organizations as loosely coupled systems. *Administrative Science Quarterly*, **21**, 1–19.

Zand, Dale, Steele, F. I. and Zalkind, S. (1967) The impact of an organizational development program on perceptions of interpersonal, group and organizational functioning. *Journal of Applied Behavioral Science*, **5** (3), 393–410.

Systems Theory for Organization Development
Edited by T. G. Cummings
© 1980 John Wiley & Sons Ltd.

Chapter 12

Paedogenesis and Other Modes of Design

Will McWhinney

> *You see how it is; the method must be absolutely practical, reasonable, realistic, the aim, the whole, the conception is an eternal poem.*
>
> *Thomas Massaryk*

Design concretizes intention. It is a conscious process of making choices directed towards a purpose. Designing, in concept and execution, postulates a denial: it marks off durations and assigns resources. Every artifact we design as architects, statesmen, educators, or entrepreneurs is a violation of the primordial integrity of time, space, and psyche. Design can also be a high art in which every act of demarcation generates awareness of the encompassing universe. Then, designing becomes the poetry of which Massaryk speaks, a life fomenting thrust towards wholeness.

This chapter is about the processes of design, viewed as general processes applicable in any field of human creative effort. Examples are drawn from a variety of fields, but special focus is placed on organizational design and development. The design processes are seen to be related, both by the conceptual scheme presented here and by the recognition that they are elements of a *cycle of design*, one that can be recognized in the styles of behaviour typical of different historical eras.

We can also experience the cycle in the design activity of everyday events. The entrepreneur aboard his executive jet designs quite differently from the expert, consultant, senator, or Buddhist monk. Each works out of a different perception of reality and each evolves from different sets of assumptions. The stereotypical approach associated with the administrator, scientist, architect, or engineer is basically a developmental model, designing forward from preestablished goals to completed outputs. This mode is *progressive*. On the other hand, the world of the senator, manager, and therapist calls for a *selective model*, an approach which designs from the premise that the outcome must be responsive to differing, conflicting sets of values: those of the users and producers, of the Californian and Nebraskan, of the quarterbacks and the coaches, for example.

The design process of the artist comes from a totally different viewpoint, one that lets the viewer see anew what was always there. The artist, sometimes in the guise of scientist or entrepreneur, *transforms* our reality in a mode I call *paedogenic*. And the Buddhist creates a world in which that which happens is that which was intended to have happened. His ideal is the conjunction of the 'no design' with total design, a process referred to as *lotal* design.

Each of these major types of design process is valid, each serves specific intentionalities, each flows from distinctive ways of perceiving what is real. Utilizing one or another is parallel to the artist choosing a dominant mode from among exaggeration, selection, and abstraction. The emphasis the artist places on one or the other depends on the match of the topic, the artist's personality and skills, and the environment in which he or she works. So also, the designer or developer of organizations, of social institutions in general, chooses his or her approach to forming or reforming an organization according to personal and situational variables.

The approaches can be classified according to the elements which are being dealt with: (1) the premises (or constraints), (2) the criteria (or goals), and (3) the solutions. This scheme identifies three major design classes, each based on the three variables:

Progressive This mode assumes the constraints and the goals of the situation to be given and searches for a solution which fits.

Selective This mode works within a set of given constraints, goals, and solutions. The task is to identify a solution (or a combination of partial solutions) which satisfies some accepted goals within the established constraints.

Paedogenic This mode assumes neither constraints nor goals but creates a new reality which contains solutions to be discovered. This is one form of a more general class of transformative modes.

The progressive and selective modes are familiar, for they include the common practices of scientific management and organizational development respectively. The paedogenic mode is less familiar, in part because we have less experience with it, in part because we have not recognized that many practitioners do work which so transforms the systems and their members as to create new worlds and fundamentally new understandings. Neither this nor other transforming methodologies have been developed into rich strategic approaches common to the first two. Some contemporary investigations have been made to create a dialectic method out of Hegel's paradigm (e.g. Churchman, 1971; Grabow and Haskin, 1973) and more extensive work has been done under the label of creative problem solving. In some cases detailed methods have been worked out: Gordon's *Synetics* (1961) is a pivotal contribution and catalogues a variety of tools. The logosynthesis mode developed by Ted Matchett, a British consultant little known in the USA, produces deeply transforming outcomes (Matchett, 1973). The effects of his processes are similar to those of the approach to be discussed in this chapter: *paedogenesis*.

Paedogenesis is literally 'child formed', but more generally, *generated out of a non-mature form of the system*. This model implies a retreat from the mature form to that of the child; a retreat from the acquired habits, assumptions, and old learnings to a stage when systems were flexible, unencrusted, and uninvested in the present reality. We move towards this mode when we talk about getting away from the daily pressure to get perspective, about 'sleeping on an issue', about going back to examine first principles. Dreams, fantasies, and retreats are examples of 'going back for a better start'.

Paedogenic processes are among the most ancient of design modes, yet either they have fallen into disrepute or their role has been simply overlooked in the rational and industrial eras by the experts in planning and design. And this is to be expected, for the transformational approaches are not in keeping with the scientific or competitive models we have been using to conceptualize our world during the last few centuries. But now we are presented with such a cacophony of new technologies, new political and cultural events, new societal and ecological problems that the users of the other design modalities find themselves overwhelmed. Their solutions now are more likely to be the source of new problems than resolutions of the old. The time is appropriate for an exploration of design processes appropriate to a world seen to be unendingly turbulent, processes which are paedogenic.

Three modes of design

Progressive, selective, and paedogenic design processes comprise a natural developmental series – elements of a spiral of ascending power-to-create-new-designs. Figure 1 shows this progression and suggests that as the individual, institution, or society that has been designing predominantly out of one mode evolves to the next mode, the results become more powerful.

Each mode arises out of the prior one, yet none is strictly fundamental to the others. Thus, there is not a natural point from which to start the discussion of the different design processes. It is our Western convention to begin the description of a cycle with the birth (with spring), continuing through with the development, maturation, decay, and ending with death or, if appropriate, with rebirth. I will follow this convention, though there is much to be said for beginning with the death of the old or the conception of the new. Thus I begin this discourse with the progressive, followed by the selective mode. The majority of the chapter is dedicated to the transforming mode, and in particular to the paedogenic process as this is by far the least familiar.

In the penultimate section I introduce a fourth mode, the *lotal*, the way of the lotus. This appears to be a mode unrelated to the first three. Perhaps it is a mode

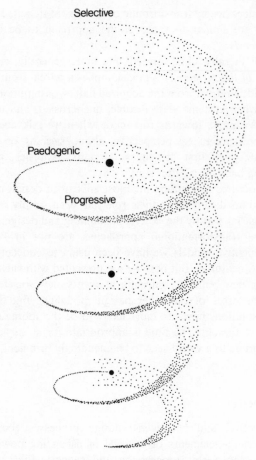

Figure 1   The cycle of design modalities

into which the others converge as the designer lets go of attachment to his creations, allowing the design, designing, and designer to become one.

Progressive designing

Progressive designing is a filling out, a hypo-deductive unfolding of an idea into an environment. It assumes the major structural elements, values, and images of the present environment. A progressive design statement begins with preestablished goals and from these searches for aspects and functions which can be organized and adapted to produce an overall solution effective for the established purpose. This mode assumes a sense of confidence: confidence that the world is well (enough) defined and that the goals for the design are uncontested.

We can see such a circumstance in the classic design problem of engineering a road or similar earth work. The task of engineering a highway appears (to a non-engineer at least) to perfectly fit this concept. The fundamentals of mechanics and the properties of materials are held to be fixed and knowable. If an unexpected phenomenon is encountered, all the relevant information is accessible, and an explanation can be located, given sufficient time and resources. Similarly, the social constraints are well established. The work has to be done with integrity, with concern for the safety of the workers, with honesty towards suppliers and government, and with respect for those people encountered along the way. The goal is well defined: completion of the highway to specification within limits of time and resources. The design is *progressive*; it is a step-by-step process leading to a preestablished goal. It is forward-oriented, making choices towards achievement of an objective. We often think of it as a *linear* progression.

Almost all physical and social artifacts result from progressive design, some by using it as the basic process, others using it in a secondary relationship to one of the other modalities. Industrial plants, educational systems, families, administrations, legal codes, and towns all are built upon existing structures and precedents, more or less creatively working together in a progressive mode. This mode of design is explicitly called for in most contracts and instructions that go along with the expression of need for some new system or product. However, products we call style goods tend to be designed selectively. More on this mode below.

The term *designing* is typically associated with activities which are, by the definition I have introduced, primarily progressive. Appropriately, much of what has been written about design processes focuses on the progressive search for a solution to problems in which there is little argument about the goals or about the definition of reality within which a solution will be valid. The sequence laid out in Figure 2 can usually be found in most books on design methodology (see Jones, 1977). Many similar descriptions could be selected from the fields of scientific research, architecture, manufacturing, or even the advice given on how one should design one's life.

In organizational development work, progressive design is the mode we associate with the work of *expert consultants*. Their mode is to proceed from analysis to create a structure, a method or strategy which is to be 'sold' to the client system. Working in this mode, the consultant assumes the organization's goals (such as higher production, a fairer pay system, or a new research organization) and searches for a procedure which will attain those goals.

The cultural assumption underlying the progressive mode is that the environment is benign and that the desired outcomes can be achieved by clear thinking and hard work. The engagement is assumed to be with nature, not a battle against men who have values and/or world views. The viewpoint of the designer is objective; he is working out of a given set of rules and values. In the setting of the organization his style may appear to be autocratic or paternalistic, but not participative or democratic. The criteria are given; the design energy is devoted to finding the solution(s).

Cumulative stages

(1) Identify the critical aims: i.e. those that must be achieved if the design is to be acceptable to the sponsor, to the users, and to others affected.

(2) Define external factors that could prevent the achievement of any critical aim.

(3) Define unambiguous criteria by which unacceptable solutions can be recognized.

(4) Devise a test situation for each criterion. Tests should be

(a) no more precise than is necessary to discriminate between acceptable and unacceptable solutions;

(b) such that tests affecting many alternative solutions are applied before tests that affect only a few;

(c) such that the permissible design–cost/artefact–cost ratio for the thing being designed is not exceeded.

Non-cumulative stages

(5) Collect a wide variety of alternative subsolutions for each critical criterion and make rough models of extreme solutions.

(6) Apply the sequence of tests to the models, discarding those that fail at each stage, until there is clear evidence of convergence on to one set of sub-solutions.

(7) Deal with design conflicts

(a) by further tests designed to show the *simultaneous* effects of several criteria (recycling as necessary);

or

(b) by seeking ways of combining subsolutions to eliminate conflicts.

(8) Settle on one outline solution that satisfies all critical criteria *before* dealing with details and refinements.

Figure 2   Cumulative strategy of design

The world view which accompanies a progressive effort is the type II environment of the Emery and Trist (1965) classification. The world is assumed to be *placid* in the sense that the valued and disvalued states stay put. What is perceived as good at one point in time keeps its value and vice versa. Further, the environment is viewed as being *clustered* or comprehendable. The objects and values of our world are so clustered that a rational search will find positive solutions in the neighbourhood of others and negative ones associated with other negatives. The common term for this environment is 'scientific'.

The above description of progressive design applies to the common situation of a preestablished reality; it begins long after the conception of that reality. The initial conditions for progressive designing arise from a seemingly opposite condition in which the individual or the society create a new world and explore this new creation in grand isolation from the reality and concerns of the surrounding populations. This designing process produces a progressive thrust but its source is a fundamental creative transformation which is the central event in the paedogenic process which must precede it.

The spiral evolution of designing continues as the progressive mode provides the base for selective design. The findings and solutions of progressive work become the elements out of which the selective designs are composed. The richer the variety of solutions which have been developed under a progressive regime, the greater is the power of the selective designs which follow.

Selective designing

To design by selection is to make judgements among alternatives, allocating resources to some alternatives while rejecting others. This mode is more a valuing process than a creating process. The extreme form of this mode is selecting itself, for example, by purchasing the whole product or service from among proffered alternatives. Such designing is simply a matching of a solution to a set of needs, values, or constraints. The more typical application involves selecting *and* organizing components in a way which combines the selective and progressive modes. Putting together a computer system, planning a library, appointing a staff, and writing tax legislation are pure selective examples. Decorating a home, planning a meal, and playing a football game are combinations which depend strongly on the selective activity.

The design of houses on a housing estate or tract is a typically selective process in that it develops out of an awareness of the values of potential purchasers. The tract or estate designer must have his ear to the market, being sensitive to what the buyer wants. He must be aware of what else is being offered, of what combinations will be most attractive at what prices, and how he can best differentiate his design from the competitor's. He will also know that the buyer is looking for what will serve his need best now *and* when it is time to move on. Housing is a typical and particularly complex example but most style goods, such as clothes, furniture, cinema productions, popular music, and so on, emerge through similar processes.

Selective designs are combinations of familiar elements satisfying varying sets of goals. With time and repeated use, the small adaptations can accumulate to such an extent that we recognize the selective design as being so significantly novel as to label it a new product. The changes which have accumulated in the design of the motor car over 90 years illustrate well the Lamarckian nature of selective design.

Selective designing is fundamentally done in the context of people; it is a *game* (in the theoretic sense). Playing it depends on an awareness of the values of those who may be involved in the designing or in the use of the designed. Selective design is participative, either overtly out of the recognition that we need to incorporate the perspectives of others, or covertly in that we are always 'testing the market'.

Selection is the prominent design process in any situation where there are a number of visible and understood alternatives; an assumption that resources are scarce; and a multiplicity of potential 'buyers' who differ either in their assessment of the environment or in their valuations which lead them to compete in a varied market. Emery and Trist label this environment *disturbed reactive* (type III). It is an environment which they describe as including more than one system and having therefore multiple and conflicting sets of purposes. Such a world appears disturbed because it has multiple directions and it is reactive in the interplay of tactics designed to counter the purposes of the other systems competing for the scarce resources. The disturbed reactive environment calls for strategic development to anticipate systematically and to respond to the reaction of the other systems to one's choice of actions. In this sense the design is not a straightforward or linear evolution as is the progressive path, but a circuitous and often hidden calculation of what might work. Hence, a typical selective design activity moves back and forth among attempts to identify solutions which fit one set of goals, recognizing that the found solution fits a different set of goals even better than the initial target; exploring for the population to which the new set of goals is most relevant; finally searching again for solutions which may fit even better the new goal configuration.

The selective sequence has a homogenizing effect on the population which uses it. As the mode is exercised the alternatives and values become bland and the outcomes settle into cycles of styles such as we experience in contemporary architecture and fashions. Designing in the selective mode tends towards a survival of the fittest. Without mutations – the old term 'sports' captures the connotation better – selective environments lose energy and direction.

Selection is common in designing style goods. It is also the traditional mode for organizational development (OD) in this era. The organization is a disturbed and reactive environment fraught with varied needs, limited in resources, and lacking in shared information. The designer/developer must confront a diversity of purpose at every level from the individual up to the interorganizational field and attempt to reduce the conflict so that some one solution set will become acceptable. To create the acceptance requires a value synthesis among the members. Without such synthesis the circuitous game continues with increasing predictability into an enervating bureaucracy. Such a weakened state is the precursor of the turbulence from which paedogenic design emerges.

Paedogenic designing

> *Almost all the men who come to see me have strange imaginings about man. The strangest of these is the belief that they can progress only by development. Those who will understand me are those who realize that man is just as much in need of stripping off rigid accretions to reveal the knowing essence, as he is of adding anything.*
>
> The sufi, Rais El-Aflak

Paedogenic design begins with stepping back from the available technology and social institutions, stepping back to more fundamental levels of the central processes in the design activity. It moves inward in a search for deeper awareness of meaning and of the environment in which one exists. Over the centuries this designing process often has been described in terms of a person who would redesign his own life engagements.

Teilhard de Chardin, in the *The Divine Milieu*, describes his experiencing of this 'passivity of growth':

And so, for the first time in life perhaps (although I am supposed to meditate every day!), I took the lamp and, leaving the zone of everyday occupations and relationships where everything is clear, I went down into my inmost self, to the deep abyss whence I feel dimly that my power of action emanates. But as I moved further and further away from the conventional certainties by which social life is superficially illuminated, I became aware that I was losing contact with myself. At each step of the descent a new person was disclosed within me of whose name I was no longer sure, and who no longer obeyed me. And when I had to stop my exploration because the path faded from beneath my steps, I found a bottomless abyss at my feet, and out of it came – arising I know not from where – the current which I dare to call *my* life.

Stirred by my discovery, I then wanted to return to the light of day and forget the disturbing enigma in the comfortable surroundings of familiar things – to begin living again at the surface without imprudently plumbing the depths of the abyss. But then, beneath this very spectacle of the turmoil of life, there re-appeared, before my newly opened eyes, the unknown that I wanted to escape. This time it was not hiding at the bottom of an abyss; it was concealed beneath the inumerable strands which form the web of chance, the very stuff of which the universe and my own small individuality are woven.

Such a process has been labelled *regression* (by Freud and later Kurt Lewin (1951)). In the context of psychology, regression has been considered to be a defensive retreat aimed at preserving the ego. The present view is that regression also serves as the precursor to a creative 'rebirth' and that it is a very general psychic and social process. In its deepest forms the paedogenic regression is a *night* journey:

a regression of the integrative tendencies, a crisis in which the mind undergoes an atavistic relapse – to return refreshed and ready for a higher form of synthesis. It is once more the process of regenerative equilibrium, of a return for a better start; the integrative drive, having lost its bearing in trivial entanglements, has gone back towards its origins to recover its vigor. (Koestler, 1949, p. 373)

Paedogenic designing takes the form of a cycle: a *disequilibrating event*, a *retreat* for a better start, a *founding* or a reassertion of identity and, finally, a *return* which produces the forward designing. Each of these phases is complex. The conditions under which the forces combine to knock a system off its path, and which set the depth and direction of retreat, the mode of recomposure from which to start again, and the technical processes of design, are complex. Each involves basic human processes of self-doubt, identity searching, self-assertiveness, and appreciating anew and creating from a point of great uncertainty. The cycle moves away from intellectualization and emotional expression into an intuitive sensing mode and out again to reengage in the practical world. It is a non-linear process, full of approaches and retreats.

Paedogenesis is the design mode of revolution. It begins with a breaking. The process is fundamentally a personal process which can occur at all stages of a society's history. But it will be supported and encouraged by an environment which is experiencing broad disequilibration. It will be supported in a time when the fundamental fabric of the society is decaying, in which the rules of conduct are in question, in which established values are no longer to be relied upon. Such an environment Emery and Trist call *turbulent* (type IV).

Disequilibration   The disequilibrating event is a visible, often dramatic turning-point in an on-going process; sometimes a spectacular failure, sometimes a quiet fear, sometimes a self-observation of what one has known but not articulated. It may be the first overt step in coming to terms with a loss of thrust or connection with one's environment, the first overt act of accepting a new goal or concept which diverts one from one's present course. The event might be as mundane as the loss of a source of raw material critical to a manufacturing activity or a long overdue awareness of a potential shortage as with the contemporary energy 'crisis' which has disequilibrated the entire world. It might be the existential confrontation with meaninglessness that up-ends so many at mid-life, or a personal rejection, a long illness, or a confinement in a wartime prison camp. The loss of a leader, the shock of a competitor making a great jump ahead, the realization that one has attained one's goal (a world championship, a doctorate, or one's first million dollars) bespeak the variety of events which disorganize a person or a system's connection with its environment. A major research laboratory, for example, fell into deep retreat when its satellite failed to go into orbit in the panic after Sputnik was launched. The lab had experienced years of unbroken success; its failure was that of one who was 'riding for a fall'.

The disequilibration can also be viewed as the final step in an evolution of forces which have weakened the system's integration. Figure 3, derived from Kurt Lewin's model of change, itself a paedogenic model, illustrates the process, identifying the increasing divergence between the overt response to the world and the internal organizational state.

The variable represented in Figure 3 is the degree (or perhaps maturity) of organization in the system's behaviour over time. The two lines indicate the amount of divergence between internal and external thrusts, illustrating the proposition that the period preceding the visible disequilibration may be one of increasing disparity between the need to hold onto external symbols and the integrating need for self-acceptance. Married couples, for example, have been observed to involve themselves deeply together in buying a new home – increasing

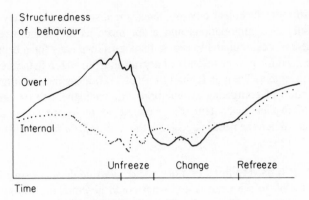

Figure 3   Paedogenic cycle over time

the degree of the marriage's organization – just as the forces for separation are about to surface. And, conversely, in later stages, the graph indicates that there is often a rise of internal integration in advance of the overt behaviour.

The phenomena of disequilibration affect whole societies as well as persons and organizations. Anthony Wallace (1961) identified a variety of ways in which the integration of societal structures fails:

The severe disorganization of a socio-cultural system may be caused by the impact of any one or combination of a variety of forces which push the system beyond the limits of equilibrium. Some of these forces are: climatic or faunal changes which destroy the economic basis of its existence; epidemic disease which grossly alters the population structure; wars which exhaust the society's resources of manpower or result in defeat or invasion; internal conflict among interest groups which results in extreme disadvantage to at least one group; and very commonly a position of perceived subordination and inferiority with respect to an adjacent society.

Wallace's list applies equally well to a single organization, to which the last force listed is particularly pertinent. The presence of an invidious comparison is often destructive of a system when its resources, particularly its people, are mobile. One of the major pressures for an organization to review its policies is its awareness of a competitor who is markedly more successful. We call it envy, jealousy, or shame when the pressure is recognized in a person.

An important variation of the disequilibrium phenomena is the 'revolution of rising expectations'. It is recognized that many political revolutions emerge from the frustration of a population which has been rising from oppression and suddenly finds its rise blocked.

Frequently systems, be they individuals, organizations, or whole cultures, adapt continuously so that the stresses mentioned are accommodated through established mechanisms, such as scapegoating and treating the deviant as comic or 'mad'. In relatively placid environments such containments can be socially functional. In more turbulent environments, the disequilibration may exceed the powers of such accommodations and erupt more as an earthquake does in a sudden release of accumulated tensions. Its occurrence calls for a broader recognition of the need for new positions of integration from which the system can confront its environment. Thomas Kuhn (1970, p. 91) notices that such times include 'the proliferation of competing articulations, the willingness to try anything, the expression of explicit discontent, the recourse to philosophy and debate over fundamentals'. When the need is accepted, the *retreat for a better start* can begin.

The retreat   It is hard to think of a design activity that does not start by stepping back at least a bit to see what is and what could be done and to loosen existing constraints and notice what is not right. Almost every design begins with an act that is at least divergent from the main line of thrust. The divergence may take any of a variety of forms – exploring one's assumptions, rejecting traditional modes, searching for new materials and sources, brainstorming to relax one's critical facilities, and so on. Each of these active processes strips away accrued goals, attitudes, structures, and acceptances of the beliefs with which one goes into designing. The retreat becomes a more potent precursor for creative work when the active stripping gives way to a passive letting go, the mode Chardin called the *passivity of growth*. Hence, letting go of familiar forms applied in familiar ways is a necessary condition for the direct experiencing which is the base from which creative designing flows.

Inasmuch as the retreat is a letting go, actively or passively, it often begins as a search, as an attempt to find a more integrative or whole answer to our existence. The retreat might begin with some general quest, like 'Why am I doing what I'm doing?' Or it may begin with some mundane questions, such as 'What business are we really in?' or 'Why is it that the children should be learning all this school work?' or 'Why am I maintaining this big house and fancy car?' But equally, a retreat may begin with less articulation, seen only as a deep malaise left over from the disequilibrating events. It may also begin with anger, guilt, or a growing sense that we are not properly equipped to deal with the situation that brought about the crisis. Almost of necessity, the retreat begins with detachment and a wandering about looking for an entry to a path that will go somewhere not too strange. We sometimes enter this path through humour – through holes in our defences opened by deep laughter.

A retreat can proceed along a variety of routes that lead to letting go of different aspects of one's own or one's system's structuring and thus to obtaining different freedoms for new integrations and redesigns. Since the differing routes exact different tolls in terms of time, effort, and psychic risk, it is of value to have a sense of the available alternatives.

Three major routes of retreat are discussed below. Each involves a form of letting go: in one case, of one's history; in another, of social identity; in a third, of the cohesiveness of one's current mode of operation. Any actual retreat will involve each of these to some degree.

Rejuvenilization is the archetypal route, appearing in myths of creation and reports of the most seminal of discoveries. It produces religious conversions and revolutions and is an essential step in founding new genetic orders; that is, it is a source of biological, social, and technical 'sports'. Rejuvenilization is an explicit retreat to an immature form of the species; a retreat to a youthful stage in which the organism had a different form, usually one less channelized in its response to the environment. This form could be far more complex than the adult form, but the essential quality is that it be more flexible in reference to its ecological challenges, less specialized in the use of its resources.

A highly significant biological example of this process is represented in the life cycle of the sea urchin and its echinoderm relatives. As a larval creature, the sea urchin is free-swimming. It is bilaterally symmetrical, with calciferous supports for its four 'arms'; it has a multipart alimentary canal and the first stages of a nervous system. As its metamorphoses into its adult form, the structure literally oozes away; the arms are replaced by a myriad of spines, the alimentary canal disappears and a new mouth is opened to the digestive sac. The swimming body becomes a formless sedentary disc anchored to a rock. It has lost its mobility, as well as its need to move, settling into an environment in which the ever-moving tides bring food as they have continued to do for thousands of years. The adult is simpler and less flexible than its immature form, but evidently well adapted to its enduring ocean medium. It is an efficient and economic organism. The adult spawns larvae which begin anew the creature's natural life cycle. Occasionally, however, young urchins, still in the larval stage, reproduce without ever having entered the usual adult form. The offspring matures while still in its free swimming form. This ex-sea urchin, now freed of its slovenly adult form, is a likely ancestor of the species out of which developed the kingdom of vertebrates and thus the human race (see Garstang, 1958).

Rejuvenilization is the condition for creation of a new animal, of a new direction; for setting up new criteria for excellence; for demanding new names and new responses from the environment. It releases the child trapped in the mature adult. Of the routes identified, it is the most likely to produce a radical new design.

Rejuvenilization is an uncertain process. A retreat from one's knowledge and skills and from what one is valued for is not always successful. The sloughing of the adult mantle does not always open the organism to renewed development. The computer design story recounted in Figure 4 illustrates both a productive and an ineffective retreat. The first group chose to step back to reconsider the physical design constraints: primarily the idea that the electrical elements had to be physically separate. On gaining this freedom, they quickly searched for ways of combining the physical support system of the various components and selecting those which satisfied the space–weight limitation. The second group took a far deeper route of retreat, questioning the assumptions about switching which

A tale is told that in the late 1950s an Eastern aircraft manufacturer was faced with the need to develop a fire control computer which would fit into a space behind the head of the pilot of a new fighter-bomber that the firm was designing. Contemporary technology had produced a device weighing about 100 pounds and occupying about 5 cubic feet. The requirement was to package it into a 1 cubic foot enclosure and limit the weight to 10 pounds. By some wisdom or accident the task was assigned to two wholly independent groups. One saw the problem as miniaturization and began directly to find components which were compact and light and to redesign in a way to eliminate unnecessary elements. For example, resistors became the forms on which coils were wound, condensers were used as structural supports and electronic shields. Ferrite was substituted for heavier iron. With selectivity, combining functions and structural redesign, this group presented a design which just satisfied the constraints. The second group saw the task as deeper than simply mechanical miniaturization and chose to search for a design philosophy in which size was a natural outcome instead of a problem to be resolved. Their initial search took them back to the question, 'What is a computer?', to which they answered, 'A mechanism for controlling electrons with high reliability.' Adding the compactness criterion led the group to a more specific question: 'What is the smallest number of electrons which can be managed with sufficient reliability?' This led to a new insight as to what a computer could be made of, for the quantity of electrons required was orders of magnitude lower than flowed through contemporary circuits. With this realization they now no longer thought in terms of components called resistors, condensers, coils, etc., but of considering metal films and eventually of printed circuits. These, combined with the far lower power requirements, led to a design which was realized in a computer of less than 5 pounds and smaller than half a cubic foot.

The second group had gone back to 'fundamentals' for a better start, dropping preconceptions which had their origin in electrical design half a century old. They found a new integrating concept which emerged out of the rephrased question and created a whole new technology. They might have gone back even further, as has been done since, but the decision to use films pushed them as far into areas of ignorance as was compatible with their ability to produce a practical design in the allotted time. A deeper dive surely would have pushed the group beyond its ability to solve each of the problems posed by the giant step *back*, or forward, as you may wish to look at it. The choice evidently represented a balance between continuing to deepen the levels of integration and a need for a practical output — which is one of the conditions needed to maintain the group's identity.

Figure 4   Design of a computer

underlie the computer theory. This line of retreat moved them from the science of electricity (as developed between 1800 and 1950) back to questions of electron flows, which are prior both historically and logically. Having redefined the design question to that of electron movement and away from the gross concepts of electricity, the team could begin a search for a suitable technology (a progressive mode) and then select among various paths to concretize a design. Much of the genius displayed in paedogenic exploration is finding what is essential and relaxing the constraints which prevent the designing from flowing out of the essential property. The first group failed by choosing a constraint incidental to the computer which it was designing.

A second kind of failure in rejuvenilization is what Kurt Lewin called retrogression. He used this term to identify refocusing backward to an earlier state of the system. It is symbolized in the return to the honeymoon cottage or, equally, in the re-creation of a cottage industry to avoid the complexities of modern industry. Retrogression finds its success in recreating the old. Rejuvenilization finds success in 'growing up' again to reengage with or transcend present reality.

Relaxation is a route characterized as a loosening rather than a letting go. It 'unfreezes', in Kurt Lewin's terminology, the forces which hold the system in its present configuration. Relaxation proceeds by reducing tension, communications, time pressures, physical proximity, and any of the other ways in which we interrelate. Such conditions are created in return to play, to acknowledging *homo ludens*. A vivid example in the recent decade has been the relaxation of the pressure for an individual to conform to the traditional middle-class values which are imposed through family and social institutions. There has been a marked drop in the pressure on the maturing person to follow what seemed to be an inexorable march from infancy through the schools and immediately on to the responsibility of employment, spouse, and family. Relaxation could also come through deprivation and isolation in a prison or insane asylum, or through therapeutically breaking a faulty integration in one's personality.

Alternatively, relaxation is produced by pulling out the *intrusions* the whole makes into the parts. The supervisor intrudes into the work rhythm of the subordinate; the parent and teacher into the psyche of the child; our super-egos into the ego or self; and so on. The term 'retreat' is used, particularly in a religious context, to identify a place where one goes to avoid intrusions. Such a place has strong boundaries to keep out the confusions of the work-a-day world and social relations to allow a reconnection with those essential elements of ourselves as individuals or systems.

Dissolution is the extreme of relaxation; it is the dissolution of the central organizing force of the system. Examples are immediate: a divorce, a failure of a business, school, or other social organization, and political anarchy. The process begins with the sloughing of the system-wide constraints, such as would occur when an enemy lifts a siege. The momentary community that is formed by disaster fails when the storm passes and help arrives. The focus of a group of students reverts from the class back to the individual at graduation, that Janus-like event which is also called 'commencement'. Dissolution leaves the components operative, the ex-members are still alive and functioning, the companies of the dissolved conglomerate still in business. Of course, if the components fail we are dealing with death not redesign.

Dissolution continues with a redirection of issues at the level of the whole to those of the parts, or with grouping to rebuild a system at the original level. With

the dissolution, the parts, be they individuals, corporate entities, or whole communities, find themselves in newly defined environments faced with one of two
design questions: design at the level of the part or redesign at the original level.
Design at the level of the part is encountered in the design for single life of a
divorced man or woman, also in the creation of separate governments as was
required when French Indochina dissolved into Laos, Cambodia, and Vietnam,
and in the new life formed by the slave freed at the end of the Confederacy.
Redesign of the whole is encountered in the return to married life, or in the formation of a new government as was done by the former colonies in the founding of
the United States. Dissolution provides the occasion for the deepest reexamination
of meaning for it confronts us with questions of identity; dissolution presents the
question of whether we alone define our identity or make it the decision of a
group.

These routes compromise a spectrum of possible paths we take back from the
present condition, paths taken in order to free a system for redesigning. Initially,
they seem to lead away from design; they take us away from accepted constraints
and direction. Formation of a new base and a sense of thrust are required to begin
anew the designing. Such a formation 'founds' the new effort, starting the
individual or society on a new upward turn of the spiral.

Founding

> And when I stopped my exploration because the path faded beneath
> my steps, I found a bottomless abyss at my feet, and out of it came,
> – arising I know not from where – the current which I dare to call
> my life.
>
> Teilhard de Chardin

The founding event creates a base from which to return from the deep experience
of retreat. It is a point of turn around out of which is created new integrations, a
new idea, art style, social institution, physical plant, or scientific creation. The
turning around is a process of uncovering, or revelation, an 'Aha!' It is preceded,
as the quotation from Chardin indicates, by a sense of loss, confusion, and a lack
of energy to continue on. The deeper the journey of retreat has been, the more
likely it will end at a point of despair or in some more or less veiled sense of terror.
The emotion can be expressed simply as blocking the continuation along a line of
search; we feel we can no longer manage what we might be getting into. In a
group, a person may repeatedly take over the conversation, diverting it to trivia or
to an immediately practical issue. The individual will do the same to himself,
involuntarily interrupting himself with diversions. The deepest expression may be
a break into schizoid behaviour, followed by deep withdrawal from any
engagement. Ronald Laing documents such responses in his *Politics of
Experience* (1967).

In the awareness of a new synthesis, feelings we experience are quite the opposite of despair: at the very least, a release from tension; at most, exhilaration and seemingly boundless energy. A creative storm spreads into the newly opened space as automatically as the fertilized ovum takes over the whole space within the egg shell. The events described in the caterer's tale in Figure 5 present such a fertilization in an organizational context. It is a mini-example of the whole cycle of rejuvenilization. The disequilibration came through the organization's loss of a number of catering contracts. The retreat began in six days of self-exploration of the management group, learning the paedogenic methods at the level of the individual; that is, for themselves. This was followed by five days of focusing on the company's direction. The group's mood followed the expected cycle of depression, withdrawal (and anger), and then explosive highs expressed in creative 'dumps' when the participants 'founded' their enterprise anew in the deep human experience of nourishment and celebration. Back home they continued the process of return by developing with the kitchen staff and students the dining experience which captured the wholeness of the experience in economically viable ways.

Return   The caterer's tale is not so much one of designing as of anti-design. The 'design' event metaphorically moved the management out of the kitchen to join the students' experience. In that act, it destroyed the managers' accepted world, replacing it with one which was not yet articulated with procedures, designed objects, criteria of judgement, etc. For those managers it created *a new reality*. For the computer group described in Figure 4, the founding was the move back from the limiting assumptions of electricity to the broader field of fundamental electronics. The retreat created a whole new context for exploration.

The paedogenic mode is anti-design; it does not concretize out of an intention, a designed object, a social structure, a procedure, etc. It is a process which creates *what is*. The source of energy that leads to the creation is varied. For some people, it may be to achieve simplicity; for the theory builder, it may be understanding; for the religious, it may be the movement towards divine unity. Paedogenic design, at its highest level, is inarticulate, uncommunicable, and so the product cannot be concretized. It just is.

The Impressionists created a new world of light with pointillistic technique. The painter Duchamp created art works everywhere by labelling 'found objects' art. Similarly and explicitly, the appearance of non-Euclidean geometry broadened the boundary of Western thinking to a universe far beyond that which we had seen. Freud spent his lifetime in exploring the unconscious world and still left most of a universe still to be articulated. It is design as a high art which generates awareness of the encompassing universe. Such foundings accumulate to produce the deepest societal recontexting, an outcome Thumas Kuhn called *paradigm shifts*. The same process of recontexting appears in more mundane daily events. Many airline companies recently came to recognize that the protective walls they had built to assure their profits excluded much of the traffic they could serve. The new reality

A few years ago we were working with a company which caters meals for universities and colleges as well as to other institutions. They were a bit unhappy about their success at being able to put on meals that anybody liked. We asked them to tell us what it was they did, what was their view of putting on a meal in a university restaurant? They told us their story by drawing pictures following a technique we use often to let people connect with themselves. And so they start off, drawing pictures: a truck, the loading dock and a

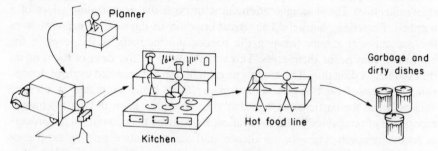

door through which they brought in the supplies, then a planner/manager in his office. They had a kitchen with people preparing meals and then a little further over they had a counter with people serving meals, with people picking up their trays of food. The last scene was the students dumping the trays at a garbage pail. That was their view of serving meals.

Now, it wasn't until they stood back from the pictures that they recognized they had omitted the people who were eating the meals – totally left out the eating. At the first level of consciousness this business was all about serving meals and not about eating meals. One person suddenly lit up and emitted, 'Aha, our business is converting food into garbage.' When this unpleasant revelation had settled in, we asked them to enter into the student role and imagine the whole process of eating a meal. 'Close your eyes, settle back into yourself as a twenty-year-old student and fantasize what it is to eat a meal.'

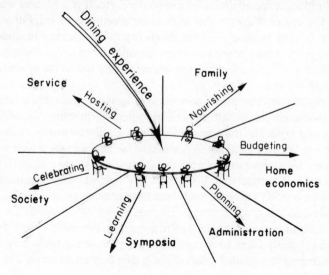

And, within a few moments, fantasies began popping up; of loneliness from home, of friends, of bantering with servers, of long conversations with a boy-friend over coffee, of good food and bad. What emerged was a 'dining experience'. With the imagining of a dining experience, they saw themselves sitting in the middle of a hall at a university becoming aware of all the great things it means to dine. Ideas flowed out. 'Let's see, Socrates was having dinner at a symposium. A symposium starts with food.' And then they thought about homes, what does home mean. Home often meant warmth and celebration, preparing meals and choosing and buying (ah, home economics). Dining, instead of being something peripheral, like transforming food into garbage, now can be seen as at the centre of the college. From this, all manner of pro-cesses can emanate. A sense of connectedness, a sense of intellectual dis-course and theatre, a sense of economy, a sense of style and taste. So the caterers came out with a wholly different concept of what it means to serve a meal.

Figure 5   The caterers' tale

is a recognition that they can profitably serve a mass market, not simply the affluent and the desperate.

The paedogenic mode is anti-design which, at the highest level, becomes lotal design. It is the new land discovered by a child. He is the cause of his world. It is unmapped and he enters it without a destination. We tend to label people who make deep paedogenic designs genius, mystic, or lunatic. Freud was certainly such a child-person as were a number of the physicists of the early part of this century. Walt Whitman and Antonia Gaudi further exemplify this world defining type. The inventor Nikola Tesla (1856–1943) is a tragic epitome of one who creates a world so removed from that of his contemporaries that no one can join him. Outsiders called it a fantasy and his fellow scientists described it as unscientific. His 'discoveries', often announced with wit and drama, in the field of alternating current electricity, radio, turbines, fluorescent lighting, and long-range transmission of power, should have gained him fame exceeding that of his some-time friend, Edison. His discoveries were prodigious, yet they came out of a world no one else saw.

Tesla's mode of discovery epitomizes as well the deepest of progressive design. Having *founded* (designed) a new world, he set out to discover its content. While the paedogenic mode culminates in creation, the progressive mode takes a path, choosing a direction for search which expresses the qualities of a person or system operating in the new reality, more or less unencumbered by the preexistent environment with its knowledge, motivations, and resources. Chardin called this direction, in the previous quote, 'the current which I dare to call *my* life'. The concept of the dining experience provided such direction for the caterers. The process of discovery, or search as it may appear, is the *core process*.

At the simplest level the core process of a human being is the life cycle from conception to death, whether we see it genetically driven or as a life force. But more significantly, the core process reflects identity; *my* life, the distinctive path of intention that a person or system takes for its fulfilment. It is being-aware-and-choosing (Bugental, 1965). An art museum gained a sense of itself when its directors came to see its identity in the core process of 'stimulating discovery (via artworks)'. A telephone company gained focus when it saw itself as 'infra-structuring society'.

The core process is the system's guidance mechanism; its entelechy. It is purpo-sive; its motivation is intrinsic and idiosyncratic in the sense that achievements are incomparable. Within the created world of the paedogenic designer, motivation is not separable from action. Our common language of psychological and utilitarian motives fails to give useful information about paedogenic behaviour. When we ask what are the objectives, needs, and goals of the effort flowing from the core process, the typical response is akin to the mountain climber's 'because it is there!' We tend to use terms like 'vision', 'energy', and 'drive' to point to what we do not participate in.

The motivations and environment of paedogenesis as described here are different from those introduced earlier in discussing the progressive mode. The procedures and outcomes are similar, but the progressive design which follows a paedogenic retreat is a private process. The definition of reality is created by the designer(s); whereas the progressive is described as accepting the constraints (which define that reality) as given. The situations may seem to be the same to those variously involved. Tesla and Freud's worlds were seemingly as God-given as that of the civil engineers, but the former are private realities, the latter is shared by all who have been educated into its rules. The motivations at one extreme are the inarticulate need to discover; at the other, the common needs for achievement, success, or survival.

When others beyond the initial designer(s) enter the new reality, they continue to 'discover' with the progressive mode. They may choose the vision of the creator and thus be judged by or judge themselves by the core values of the founder(s), or they may continue to apply the rules of the broader society in their explorations. When the new values are accepted, there is a paradigm shift, grand or small. But more commonly those who have initially accepted the definition of the new reality fail to see its possibilities or flee from its challenges. The need to stay in com-munication with friends and co-workers and to share their reality leads to a rejec-tion of the new values and a return to the accepted calculi of economic and psychological motivations. The new space becomes familiar territory; its potential is ignored and the design mode reverts to the selective.

In summary, there are three design modes in the spiral:

The paedogenic	discovery in the created world
The progressive	the linear search in a publicly accepted space
The selective	the interactive search for an acceptance among alternatives

We do not have a totally free choice among their use – each will work best in its proper 'season' (place in the spiral), each fits particular individuals according to their personal characteristics, and each is differentially applicable to social design.

Social design

In recent decades the dominant mode in social design has been the selective. It is easiest to use in situations characterized by easy movement across organizational boundaries, competing reasons for joining and staying in a social system, and large differences in the values and educational backgrounds of the system members. Its use is supported by theories and training developed in an Emery and Trist (1965) type III environment. These assume vast differences in motivations, values, and information under a condition of scarce resources. The selective mode underlies many of the techniques developed under the labels of behavioural science, human relations, and participative management. Often, the selective mode has been used in combination with the progressive mode to resolve issues created by the entrepreneurs and administrators who, working out of a progressive mode, take no cognizance of the conflicts which arise when systems designed independently are merged.

Prior to 1950 the progressive mode was by far the more prominent. Most organizations were designed out of the unitary model of the founding entrepreneur or the bureaucratic expert coming from a civil service or scientific management orientation.

The paedogenic has never been the prominent mode, but it does come into importance during a period of turbulence, for in the long run paedogenesis (and other transformational modes) provide the foundation for the subsequent era of development (that is, of a type II environment). The decade beginning in the mid-1960s was a period of significant paedogenesis in all manner of social institutions: there was an upsurge in the creation of intentional communities, political and religious groups, and work organizations. They were consequential far beyond their numerical importance *and* so far most have been short-lived; these are both characteristic features of paedogeny.

A central characteristic of paedogenic social design is that it arises out of *a group which created a new social reality*; without the unitary framework which emerges out of the paedogenic work, the process of design reverts to the progressive or selective. The new reality is conceived from the interaction of the whole group during a cycle of disequilibration, retreat and founding. The cycle can vary greatly in its scope. The work can evoke a new reality as trivial as catching a pun or as grand as the transforming religious experience which binds lives together for ever. But what is critical is the shared awareness of the events of the cycle. Community members may pass years together without an awareness of sharing a unique reality. A group may come together briefly to raise a building or start a newspaper and therein form a deep bond through awareness of what they have accomplished. Such awareness can achieve a powerful cohesion among members and a level of trust seldom achieved in ordinary commerce.

It is, I believe, the shared events of the retreat which establish the existential bond. These awarenesses are rare events in most people's lives; they are occasions of great aliveness, of rich awareness of the common core of existence which the members are experiencing. Our tradition is filled with stories of such events occurring at the time of disasters and in wartime, events which confront the members with the fragility of life and of one's self-image. The paedogenic process gains a firmer base for development when it operates in a positive context, such as mountain climbing, putting on a dramatic production, or sharing in the birth of a child. I suspect that constructing the great sacred edifices, such as the cathedral of Chartres, the Pyramids, and the great temples of the East, produced a special reality among the craftsmen and workers involved.

The necessity of *sharing the paedogenic process* produces two impediments to the use of the mode. The first involves the effort necessary for the paedogenic design itself and the second concerns the fact that groups which participate in the cycle tend to become closed to outsiders.

Gaining the commitment to go through a shared experience, such as described in the caterer's tale, is difficult. In part, it is difficult because our experience is uncommon in this area. People are reluctant to join an effort which is bound to evoke discomfort when they have little understanding of the payoffs. External pressure is usually required to get the effort started, such as orders from a common employer or charismatic leader or an emerging awareness of danger on a common path. The use of external pressure is an effective approach but one which creates its own difficulty. The very person or organization that induced the group to go into a retreat is likely to be threatened by or be at odds with the new realities and directions which subsequently emerge. The approach sets up a political dilemma discussed in the following section.

Dependence on a shared awareness requires a visible or articulate focus. Universities have often been the source of such articulate awareness, as evidenced by their suppression in authoritarian states. So, too, common involvement in political campaigns or social service can lead to awareness among members of a group who have observed and felt the same injustices, threats, or opportunities.

The second impediment to using the paedogenic mode in social design is the tendency to produce a closed group. Those who share in a deep retreat often emerge with a shared bond that excludes others. One overt indication of the new privacy is the special vocabularies or shorthand expressions developed by the members. The language excludes others, either blocking their joining or relegating them to second-class membership when they are allowed to join. Whether a small clique or a grand movement, the closed group is typically annoying or threatening to outsiders. This sense of being excluded is a major cause of persecution of religious sects and an inhibitor of social innovation. Exclusion produces such strong feelings that most paedogenic designs are either suppressed or destroyed by people in the surrounding society. The very words used to describe the biological paedogenic, 'mutant', and the social paedogenic, 'revolution', connote danger to most people much of the time. Those 'sports' that do survive, do so because they have been able to grow in isolation or hide their specialness until they have sufficient strength to surface.

Overcoming the barriers to acceptance is a two-way problem, both that of acceptance of the sport by society and that of entry for new members into the paedogenic organization.

Overcoming demands a systematic procedure which will routinely incorporate new members. The classic acceptance procedure is the *initiation rite*. The purpose of the rite is to give the initiate the same social reality as that of the members of the paedogenic organization. He or she gains entry through experiencing, in a ritualized setting, the pain and joy of the retreat and founding events in the company of the members. Membership is founded in the shared responsibility for maintaining the values and images; the created world would collapse without these beliefs. The initiate gains values not available outside; there is no trade in the coin of belief.

A powerful initiation process enables organizations to be perpetually paedogenic. One enters as a child or novice and remains in the unitary organization, accepting its created world, yet as an insider having the right to search for new solutions, new designs. The power of organizations that have maintained their created realities is apparent throughout history. Religious and secret societies are the most dramatic examples, but the professions, science, medicine, and law, and so on, also have extended membership only to those who have been initiated via deep training and certification processes. The vitality of all these organizations wanes as membership comes to be a matter of utility – of using the coin of society-at-large. The acceptance of coin, of any mechanism for comparing values, moves the design process to the selective mode. With this transition, the paedogenically founded organization joins the open commerce of society, members coming and going as the momentary balance of utilities favours one or another membership.

The special qualities of paedogenic organizations create considerable difficulties for their survival in cultures to which they are alien, which they are, by definition. Their presence adds a dimension inconsistent with the competitive and turbulent arena. It introduces new rules into the games of power which lead us to recognize that design must deal with questions of politics.

The politics of design

> *Every act of creation, by its mere existence, denies the world of master and slave.*
>
> *A. Camus*

Designing, in concept and execution, delimits energy flows, postulates denial, demands durations, and assigns resources. It is a political process. Our choices as designers of social organizations are political ones.

Choosing a progressive mode avoids political engagement, for one stands outside the on-going social processes. The progressive route in social design is that of the expert, as consultant, bureaucrat, or other agent of the system. The expert creates an 'as-if' world at a distance from the social reality. We usually call such creations 'plans'. Such plans do not bear on organizations until they have been accepted by the established sources of power. When they are in concurrence with the sources, they are usually accepted and made ready for installation. The installation is essentially an autocratic process. If any attempt is made to introduce the designs without acceptance of the authorities, the designs are often perceived as challenges. The history of consulting is full of such confrontations. The typical outcome is that the consultant and his design are simply ignored.

Choosing a selective mode is to engage with the allocation of power. Every act can be seen as competitive or participative. Each step requires managerial decisions; the evolution of a selective design implies the allocation of resources all along the way. The involvement calls for a continuing negotiation, a continuing probing, testing, and integrating of design ideas with the existing power structure. The tests can come on issues of technical and economic feasibility or on interpersonal relations. A fundamental question in selective design is the degree and timing of integration of the members of the system. And this is, of course, the central political issue: how much participation will be allowed in each of the two roles of selecting the alternatives and weighing them against the multiple valuing systems of the members?

Clearly the vast majority of work in organizational development is carried out within these political issues. Most of the questions of responsibility, leadership, intergroup relations, training and promotion, and motivation are answered as a function of the existing power relations and the variety of members who are involved in the design process. In organizations that have great central power, held either through the strength of the shared beliefs or through the autocratic power of the leadership, participation is easy. It deals only with means, not with goals. There is no fear of participants generating ideas which will challenge the existing order. The practice of organizational development (OD) would be very easy in such a secure organization. In an organization in which the central thrust is not so well shared, where alternative value systems are in contention, power issues arise with various design alternatives. It is in such environments that the present forms of OD are both appropriate *and* most difficult to exercise. Here the emphasis has moved from the design of alternatives to the design of implementations, i.e. to accommodation of power centres. (Perhaps one of the major causes of the failure of academic training in OD is the misplaced emphasis on technique and the avoidance of the political aspects of the work.)

A deeply transforming design process produces a new class of political issues.

Whereas the progressive joins with power and the selective contends, the paedogenic and dialectic destroys the bases of power. The transformation destroys the reality on which the power has been founded as Camus's epigram indicates. In destroying the social power base, the individual's basis of *meaning* is exposed to question. And the deeper the implied redirection, the more likely it is that the central belief system on which people have built their lives will be seen as unnecessary, as devoid of value. What follows from such a loss is predictable in view of historic changes, such as the Protestant Revolution, the emergence of modern science, or, more immediately, the response of the capitalistic world to the appearance of Marxist doctrine.

Paedogenic changes at a societal level or in the mundane events of everyday life may appear as attacks. Contemporary experience with paedogenic changes in an organizational setting reproduces the chain of effects seen in social revolution. The chain is evident in mini-revolutions of technological change. A poignant example is that of the craftsman experiencing the development of machinery which renders his lifetime of skill building useless; for example, the steelmakers in Pittsburgh who judged the readiness of a batch of steel by the qualities of the flames at first could not give credence to the possibility that a colorimeter could do his job. When the colorimeter did test out, the anxiety changed to anger and continued into deep depression for many, followed by early retirement and early death. Similarly, a deep erosion of personal meaning follows from the possibility that we can create effective organizations in which supervision (like parenting) is but a temporary aspect of training. The response across the range of employees is not to question how or why but simply to deny. The denial is initially directed to the possibility: 'Since it cannot be, don't discuss it.' This is the response that Galileo was said to have received when he invited the astronomers to see Jupiter's moons through the new telescope. As the possibility becomes undeniable, the response moves to anxiety and finally anger. The anger surfaces with the awareness that the new reality undermines the old and produces an attack which goes beyond the threatened person's base of wealth and social position to the very survival of the systems which justify one's ego and the roles through which it is expressed.

There is a valid basis for this response to a paedogenic 'attack', for the result of an attack is a new configuration of reality. There is empirical evidence as well as theory to indicate that a new species is extremely energetic. The newly fertilized ovum consumes energy at a rate 1000 times an adult's rate. The rejuvenilized species, which sharply redefines reality (e.g. by making use of a new fuel), can be many orders of magnitude more energy consuming that its predecessor, as science fiction writers continually remind us. (One of the roles of science fiction writers is to desensitize us to the possibility of being overwhelmed by 'giants' who might arise to consume our habitats.) The new species present threats that go beyond the languages and logics of the existing values. Cultural examples are easy to locate in the successive conquests that moved us progressively from copper and bronze to iron and steel, from hunting to agriculture, from wood and coal to gas engines, electricity, and atom power. Since the new powers debase the currency of the existing ones, it is not surprising that the established powers typically reject the new sports on 'illogical' grounds.

This illogical rejection has been the fate of the vast number of paedogenic creations. A case of particular interest to social designers at the moment is the resistance by industry and labour to the new socio-technical and open systems work designs that have developed over the past two decades. These highly efficient operations have repeatedly met with denial, anxiety, anger, and passive avoidance. In almost every case they have been squashed. There are a number of visible examples that have emerged in major corporations and that have since been phased out; the most publicized of these are the General Foods plant in Topeka, Kansas, the machinists' group working in a General Electric plant at Lynn, Massachusetts, and the coal mine experiment in Rushton, Pennsylvania. Apparently the anxiety produced by these experiments outweighs their system-wide advantages. The presence of these new social designs suggests that a paradigm shift is under way but is not yet strong enough to disequilibrate the present industrial order. Perhaps when large numbers of individuals have themselves experienced rejuvenilization and a new founding, the possibilities implied in the new work designs will not induce such overwhelming anxiety. The present conservative swing could, in fact, be the visible rigidification that hints at a readiness for the disequilibration accompanying a paradigm shift.

Lotal design

Design concretizes intention; it violates the primordial integrity of time, space, and psyche. Like economics, it can be a dismal science. Design can also be a high art in which every act is holographic; that is, within every demarcation, there is reflection of the totality.

Lotal design is one approach to creating the holistic design. It is an emergent process that creates by allowing integrated images to arise out of the unconscious. The process is basically a meditative evocation around a focal idea, problem, or image. Its origin is in Eastern meditation. (It was popularized in the 'Kung Fu' television series as a problem solving device.) The lotal mode proceeds in a manner free of the constraints defining the three modes described above; it does not depend on an articulated logic, nor is it limited by established judgements, boundaries, or goals. It is as likely to find serendipitous solutions as that which was searched for. Like the paedogenic, the lotal mode may produce elegant solutions that need to be developed via progressive search and be integrated into the practical world selectively. It is also the mode least used of the four. Until recently, we had no vocabulary for describing the approach, although it may have been used without recognition.

Lotal designing flows from meditation on a focal concept. The concept can be any object or process or institution to be designed. I have used the word 'service' to explore the service aspects of work in a public utility company. Other examples are: objects, such as 'chair'; events, such as 'Ann's 60th birthday'; institutions, such as 'marriage'; processes, such as 'maintenance' (as required for a chemical refinery); 'dining' as used in the caterer's tale; or 'desalination of sea water'. Any word or image related to the design objective can be selected. The process will be more efficient if the word is essential to the problem and has positive connotations, for example, 'maintenance' rather than 'breakdown'.

The process for using the lotal mode is simple and follows LeShan's procedure for meditation (LeShan, 1974). Once the focal image is selected, the designer settles into a meditative state. Then the selected image is brought into focus and the designer waits for another image to come into mind. When it does, it is held for a few seconds and quietly observed as one might scan titles in a second-hand book store. The image is played with, examined, and released. Attention is returned to the focal concept and the designer waits for a new image, letting it unfold as a petal from a lotus blossom centre. The process continues until either excitement or a sense of completion takes over. Often there is an 'Aha!' signalling that an image has integrated all aspects of the focal issue. But sometimes the aconscious exploration is off target and no image resolves the issue. Then it is necessary to find a new focal concept and, after another meditative period, begin again.

As practised initially the lotal process is similar to brainstorming and it is easy to lose the focal image, wandering off on free association. As one's skills improve in selecting images, concentrating on the focal point, and letting images float up, the outcomes increasingly express the whole situation. Perhaps the clearest example of producing such outcomes is musical composition, particularly in the creating of themes and melodies.

The lotal process, like the paedogenic, can create the basis for a design to be developed progressively, as one would build on a musical theme to produce a full composition. It can also provide insights which constitute a design without further elaboration. The exploration of 'service' exemplifies the latter. In this exercise a number of the early 'petals' clustered around the image of servant, subordinate, service as tableware, and service as copulation of animals. All these were related to the way in which service work was viewed by the public utility employees. Another group clustered around service in a religious context, as in the performing of the sacraments. Through a variety of images, this idea of service led to the concept of service to God, to the God-within, and finally to service to oneself as a developmental process. The design is complete in this insight, the concept of service is transformed from a demeaning and alienating activity to one central to the employee's life. When such a design effort is conducted by the employee (the client) nothing more need be done. But the developmental image can also serve as a base for creating a new work environment through training and job redesign.

The lotal processes are distinct from those of the other three design modes.

Whereas the paedogenic design backs away from the constraints and reality of the existing world, the lotal designer is unattached from the beginning. Reality is but a convention, loosely assumed at a point in time, to be dropped or modified at will. The lotal does not use the logical premises of the progressive mode; neither that of the association of valued and disvalued elements nor their cause-and-effect connections. The selective mode might be seen as a sort of external version of what goes on within the psyche during the lotal evocations, paralleling the relation of an informal discussion in groups to the tacit thinking within the individual. But the deeper the lotal mode is experienced, the more it becomes a process of creating resonance among the parts of the environment. The *design* becomes not a design but an evoking reflection of the whole, and not the product of the designer but of the designer's recognition that he is but a channel; and thus the designing becomes the eternal poem of which Massaryk wrote.

Why a model of designing

What is the value of a model of designing, of an articulation of the types, and a structure through which to relate them? One answer is simply to express my delight in creating such a conceptualization and watching myself in each of the various modes as the ideas emerge – a narcissistic romp through a whole turn of the spiral. A second answer is that it provides a tool to sharpen our appreciation of the process of design. I have presented one model out of many possible ones; if it is set in counterpoint to others it may prove evocative to the reader.

A third rationale which emerged for me as I worked on this model is the recognition that it provides a basis for a strategy of design. The strategy of design is a fundamental tool for anyone involved in questions of social change and the management of resources which are used in supporting design work. Such a model can provide a guidance system to select from among the variety of alternative ways to approach a design question.

For example, do we write social tracts, which was a major alternative of the nineteenth century? Do we evolve participative engagements in the manner of Saul Alinsky's work in Chicago during the 1950s and 1960s? Do we join with disequilibrating forces to aid a client system on a paedogenic plunge into the dark night of the soul? Or do we convince organizations that a paradigm shift is under way and that we should all join the post-industrial society?

The routes we have taken in organizational and social design have typically been due to inessential accidents, chosen because of the skills and experience of the experts and the proclivities of the leadership, taking little account of the social environment, the resources available, or the political climate. The choices could be made strategically; planned change could be planned and designing could be designed. The Appendix provides an aid to organizing our approach to these choices.

On reflection, this paper is a proposal for approaching a strategy of design. It

Appendix: Characteristics of design modes

Design mode		Elemental design act	Associated environment	Historical era (in Western world)
Name	Discriminator			
Progressive	Linear search in a well-defined space	Identifying the core process	II – placid clustered	Sixteenth century–1930s
Selective	Strategic (gaming) in field populated with alternatives and competitors	Value synergizing	III – Disturbed reactive	Tenth century–1960s
Transformative	Redefinition of possibility space (of reality)		IV – Turbulent	Twentieth Century →
Dialectic	– with a new solution	Synthesizing		
Paedogenic	– with new direction	Reconstructing		
Lotal	Flowing with: creating resonance	Non-attaching	Independent of environment	←——→

introduces an organic model having representations at the level of the individual, of the organization, and of the culture. As an individual model, it deals with the processes of maturation; at the organizational level, it deals primarily with issues of direction and purpose; at the societal level, the model is reflective of the energy and integrative forces which, over time, call for a return-for-a-better-start, then for a progressive development, a selective exchange and, with the inevitable loss of cohesive direction, the chaos that is the womb of a new paedogeny.

References

Bugental, J. F. T. (1965) *The Search for Authenticity*. New York: Holt, Rinehart, Winston.

Camus, Albert (1956) *The Rebel*. New York: Knopf.

Churchman, C. West (1971) *The Design of Inquiring Systems*. New York: Basic Books.

Emery, F. E., and Trist, E. L. (1965) The causal texture of organizational environments, *Human Relations*, **18**, 21–32.

Emery, F. E., and Trist, E. L., (1973) *Toward a Social Ecology*. New York: Plenum Press.

Garstang, W. (1958) *Larval Forms and Other Zoological Verses*. Oxford: Oxford University Press.

Gordon, William J. J. (1961) *Synetics*. New York: Harper & Row.

Grabow, Stephen, and Haskin, Allen (1973) Foundations for a radical concept of planning. *Journal of the Institute of American Planners*, **39**, March.

Jones, J. C. (1970) *Design Methods*. London: Wiley.

Koestler, Arthur (1949) *Insight and Outlook*. New York: Macmillan.

Kuhn, Thomas (1970) *The Structure of Scientific Revolutions*. Chicago: University of Chicago Press.

Laing, Ronald (1967) *Politics of Experience*. New York: Ballantine Books.

LeShan, Lawrence (1974) *How to Meditate*. Boston, Mass.: Little, Brown.

Lewin, Kurt (1951) *Field Theory in Social Science*. New York: Harper & Row.

Matchett, E. (1973) Logosynthesis; a meta-controlled design discipline. *Systematics*, September.

Suzuki, Shunryu (1970) *Zen Mind, Beginner's Mind*. San Francisco: Weatherhill.

Teilhard de Chardin, Pierre (1960) *The Divine Milieu*. New York: Harper & Row.

Wallace, A. F. C. (1961) *Culture and Personality*. New York: Random House.

Beyond Systems: Expanding the Boundaries of Organization Development

Introduction

So far the major focus of this book has been to clarify the systems approach and to explore its applications to organization development. The basic point of reference has been the organization, its interrelated parts, and its relationship with the wider environment. The three chapters in Part IV extend this orientation to consider organizations from ecological, interorganizational, and evolutionary perspectives. These conceptual frameworks move the system or organization boundary both *upward* to sets of organizations or interorganizational systems and *backward* to the historical processes giving rise to existing organizational structures and practices. This expands the traditional domain of OD to higher-level and longer-term organizational phenomena, directions conspicuously missing in current OD practice.

Stratton and Flynn apply ecological theory to OD. They provide a brief history of this perspective and relate its concepts to organization structures and behavioural processes. This serves to explain the theory and to raise issues typically neglected in OD. The authors make a strong argument that as organizations face increasingly complex or turbulent environments, their problems become ecological; this calls for an interorganizational focus where dissimilar organizations learn to manage their interdependence because their fates are positively correlated. Stratton and Flynn suggest an ecological approach to OD and review recent attempts to apply the strategy to interorganizational systems.

Congruent with Stratton and Flynn's ecological stance, Cummings develops a conceptual framework for diagnosing and changing interorganizational relationships. He describes several conditions leading organizations to experience problems managing dependency upon other organizations, and shows how the two dominant theories of interorganizational relations – exchange and power/dependency – account for interaction and coordination among organizations. Based on these perspectives, Cummings develops a diagnostic strategy for assessing interaction and coordination between and among organizations and raises significant issues for intervention. He argues that OD is ill-equipped to deal with many interorganizational problems, especially those involving power/dependency. Cummings suggests several directions for developing organizations in an interorganizational context.

Bigelow completes the book with a provocative and insightful account of OD from an evolutionary perspective. He draws on his recent theoretical work and research to clarify how evolutionary thought can be applied in an organizational context. This provides the necessary groundwork for classifying OD in terms of intervening in three evolutionary processes in organizations: (1) intervention in evolutionary content – i.e. changing specific organizational practices; (2) first order intervention in evolutionary mechanisms – i.e. changing the methods which generate practices; and (3) second order intervention in evolutionary mechanisms – i.e. changing the way in which mechanisms are themselves generated. Throughout the discussion, Bigelow relates organizational behaviour and OD to the evolutionary processes of variation, selection, and retention, and shows how these concepts account for organizational adaptation as a process rather than an outcome. His model of different orders of organizational evolution raises the issue of how OD practitioners evolve their own practice. Bigelow offers three possibilities, each presenting a dilemma that few of us are likely to resolve.

Systems Theory for Organization Development
Edited by T. G. Cummings
© 1980 John Wiley & sons Ltd

Chapter 13

Ecological Theory and Organization Development

William E. Stratton
and
Warren R. Flynn

Introduction

Traditional approaches to organization development (OD) originate primarily in theories first advanced in the fields of social psychology and sociology. While the value of these behavioural science contributions is hardly a subject of debate, this historical development of the field has resulted in its 'overpreoccupation with the human and social dynamics of organizations to the detriment of attending to the task, technical, and structural aspects and their interdependencies' (French and Bell, 1978, p. 257). Thus, while the behavioural sciences have made a necessary contribution, it has not necessarily been a sufficient one.

Among researchers and practitioners there has been a growing awareness that the theoretical base underlying OD has been somewhat limited in scope. At the same time, the range of factors considered important to the success of increasingly complex strategies of organizational change has been growing (Emery and Trist, 1973; Kahn, 1974; Burke, 1976; Pfeffer and Salancik, 1978). As a result new approaches and concepts which reflect the expanded knowledge base are being introduced from widely diverse fields. Examples of the growing array of methodology include

socio-technical systems (Trist, 1969), job design and job enlargement (Alderfer, 1969), job enrichment (Ford, 1969; Paul, Robertson, and Herzberg, 1969), intergroup conflict management (Burke, 1974), agreement management (Harvey, 1974), sociophysical arrangements (Steele, 1973), management by objectives (Beck & Hillmar, 1972), recruitment (King, 1972), motivation and career development (Brynildsen, 1974), and open systems planning (Krone, 1974). (Burke, 1976, p. 27.)

Reference to various definitions of OD (Lawrence and Lorsch, 1969a; Argyris, 1970; Beckhard, 1969; Margulies and Raia, 1972) and to the numerous subjects (listed above) falling under the rubric of OD lead to the observation that OD should not be viewed as a unified concept in the scientific sense of the word, but rather as an umbrella encompassing an array of ideas and approaches. Kahn (1974, p. 491) describes OD as 'a convenient label for a variety of activities'. In order to be precisely defined, OD must have a 'prescribed and verifiable place in a network of logically related concepts, a theory' (Kahn, 1974, p. 490). To the extent that any such theory will draw from a variety of disciplines, it is desirable to explore potential contributors. The purpose of this paper is to examine one such contributor, ecological theory, and its potential to offer valuable new insights to the OD field.

The development of ecological theory

Ecology is the field of study concerned with the relationship between living organisms and their environment (Knight, 1965, p. 2). The primary vehicle through which such study is effected is ecological analysis, the study of inter-species interactions and species–environment interactions using a systems approach (Hawley, 1973). Historically, man's awareness of his interdependence with the rest of nature can be traced back at least to the early Greek writers who emphasized the importance of environmental studies (Knight, 1965, p. 4). Later, more formal approaches to such studies resulted in the introduction of the term 'oekologie' (derived from the Greek words for 'home' and 'study') by Reiter in 1868. The British Ecological Society and the Ecological Society of America were established in 1913 and 1916 respectively, attesting to the considerable duration of time that ecological concepts and approaches have been of interest in the natural sciences.

The term 'ecosystem' was first proposed by the British ecologist, A. G. Tansley in 1935 as a name designating the interaction system consisting of living things together with their non-living habitat (Odum, 1972, p. 66; Tansley, 1935). The ecosystem is the basic unit of ecology, including not only the organism complex, but also the complex of physical factors forming the surrounding environment, and involving the circulation, transformation, and accumulation of energy and matter and further characterized by a multiplicity of regulatory mechanisms (Evans, 1965, p. 166).

The use of the word 'ecology' has, in recent years, spread beyond scientific circles to become something of a household expression. It has even come to be regarded as a political movement, to the dismay of some scientists (Calder, 1973, p. 277). To some extent this growing popularity coincides with the realization that civilization has begun to approach some of its environmental limits. Concurrently, the awareness of the average person of underlying problems of interdependence has increased. Man has now come to the realization that his existence depends, as does all of nature's, upon complex systems of mutual interaction and support. These are the ecosystems that interest ecologists and biologists, and considerable progress has been achieved in developing concepts and methodologies necessary to their study.

In the social sciences, and particularly the fields of sociology and anthropology, ecological terminology and concepts are being applied under the banner of 'human ecology'. However, in the field of organization theory and behaviour this development is, at best, only beginning. The first listings in *Sociological Abstracts* dealing with ecology in an organizational context appear in the 1970s. The *Business Periodicals Index* did not index the word 'Ecology' until 1967 when the first entry appeared under 'human ecology'. A review of *Dissertation Abstracts* in the social sciences and business turned up only two dissertations utilizing ecological concepts (as designated in their titles) between 1967 and 1975.

However, many of the concepts of general systems theory, a subject which is closely related to ecology, have been adopted. Evidence can be found in the titles of many recent works in the field of organization theory (Carzo and Yanouzas, 1967; Kast and Rosenzweig, 1970; Evan, 1976; Hellriegel and Slocum, 1976; Melcher, 1976; Galbraith, 1977). These theorists, utilizing systems concepts and contingency approaches in their work, are beginning to develop what could for the first time be considered a science of organizations (Khandwalla, 1977, p. 249). For the OD specialist, this presents a promising opportunity to use enhanced analytical tools in the diagnosis and treatment of organization problems.

Although the process has only just begun, the implications of viewing organizations and OD from an ecological perspective are impressive. The ecologist has developed a number of elaborate concepts and procedures for studying the entire 'pattern of life in some defined habitat, in the belief that it constitutes one system' (Emery and Trist, 1973, p. vii). The assumption is that this system is a field of multiple, mutual influences constantly at work, and not merely a series of causal chains of influence. Margalef has developed a general mathematical model of the ecosystem as a cybernetic system (Margalef, 1968, pp. 1–25), although he and others have noted that 'even the simplest system displays features incompatible with the usual matrix formulations in terms of links which may exist between parts of the system' (Steele, 1976, p. 451), and that 'competing species may in fact interact in numerous and often counteracting ways' (Levine, 1977).

As the developed nations of the world enter the economic stage of post-industrialism and a new industrial revolution based on information technology emerges, organizations are faced with increasing levels of complexity and uncertainty. Changes affecting these social systems are taking place in the contextual as well as the task environment. As a result, organizations must adapt to what Emery and Trist (1965) call 'turbulent environments', or fields of constantly interfacing, multiple, mutual influences. These are the same types of systems studied by the ecologist and this parallelism gives impetus to an attempt to apply ecological concepts to organization theory and to OD.

The implications of looking at organizations from an ecological point of view can be considered from at least three separate perspectives: (1) the study of

organizations from a descriptive standpoint; (2) the application of ecological concepts to the study of on-going processes within organizations; and (3) the application of ecological concepts to the analysis of organization behaviour at the
interorganizational level. In each case, an attempt is made to relate on-going work
in organization theory and behaviour to the ecological concepts presented.

Ecological description at the organizational level

Ecology is *defined* as the

integrated study of *populations, communities,* and *ecosystems* . . . *Populations* can be
regarded as groups of organisms having a common origin, form and function. They are
generally treated as identical with *species. Communities* are associations of populations
linked by some interdependent function. *Ecosystems* are conceptual systems formed by
relating a community or communities with the totality of prevailing environmental factors.
(Boughey, 1971, p. 2, emphasis in original.)

The organizational correlates of each of these terms are readily apparent. The
organization can be viewed as an ecological community, operating within its
greater environment or ecosystem. Internally it is composed of a series of
mutually dependent, relatively homogeneous subgroups or departments, conceptually similar to populations or species. Those who view organizations as
coalitions will find remarkable similarities in this approach.

Much of the terminology employed by organization theorists has its ecological
counterparts. Concepts such as differentiation and integration are well developed:

The importance of the community (organization) concept, however, lies not so much in
the populations (subgroups) themselves, as in the set of functional interactions between
them . . . Different populations (subgroups) have different functions in any community
(organization). The term most commonly used to describe the total role of any species
(subgroup) in the community (organization) is the ecological niche . . . Every population
(subgroup) has an ecological niche, and this niche is the major determinant of the
structural, physical, and behavioral adaptation of that population (subgroup). (Clapham,
1973, p. 103.)

Additionally, the notion that vastly different organizations are often
structurally similar has an ecological equivalent, as described in the following
paragraph:

Different communities (organizations) in ecosystems characterized by similar environments are often exceedingly similar in their structure, and they may contain one or more
niches that are essentially identical. The adaptations of populations (subgroups) inhabiting
these niches may also be exceedingly similar even though they are totally unrelated . . .
This phenomenon . . . is called ecological equivalence. (Clapham, 1973, p. 103.)

As numerous studies by the contingency theorists have shown, organizations also have their 'ecological equivalence'. Woodward (1965) found, for instance, that organization structure was dependent on the technological environment of the organization and that similar structures developed as a result of similar technologies. Lawrence and Lorsch (1969b) found the degree of centralization or decentralization in organizations to be dependent on the type of environmental uncertainty faced by the organization. Additionally, the organizational notions of variations in hierarchy, differentiation, and integration have a functional counterpart in the ecological concept that 'no two species populations (subgroups) can occupy precisely the same niche in a single community (organization)' (Clapham, 1973, p. 104).

Ecologists have developed a number of additional concepts for describing systems which appear to be of potential use to the organization analyst, but which have not yet been formalized in organization theory. As an example, the term 'niche space', or the relative position and overlap in n-dimensional space of the responses of two subgroups to various environmental factors, appears to offer some potential for the study of conflict as the following statement would imply:

If the amount of overlap is very small then the two populations (subgroups) can exist simultaneously in essentially separate niches. If the overlap is virtually complete, then the population (subgroup) that is more successful in exploiting the environment will drive the less successful population (subgroup) into extinction. The problem is to determine when niche overlap is sufficiently small that coexistence is possible and when it is sufficiently large that only one population (subgroup) can survive. In other words, the number of potential niches in the community (organization) is a function of the degree to which the development of the community (organization) under a given environmental regime leads to a separation of partially overlapping niches. (Clapham, 1973, p. 107.)

Ecologists have also developed other useful concepts, such as *niche divergence*, the process by which populations become more specialized to avoid competition for the same niche; *richness*, the number of species in a community; *equitability*, the degree to which different populations approach equality in their relative abundance in the community; *diversity*, a measure of the integration of a biological community; and *dominance*, a measure of the impact of a given population on the community (Clapham, 1973, pp. 107–112). In short, ecologists have devised a logical and systematic framework which permits them to study and describe populations and communities in precise, unambiguous ways. This same system, with only minor modification, appears to have excellent potential when applied to the study of organizations.

Ecologists have expended considerable effort in identifying and classifying the various types of interaction between populations. Table 1 describes eight of these interaction types.

The table points out graphically the degree to which ecologists have categorized and labelled the logical possibilities for subgroup interactions. It is possible that the adaptation of such terminology to the OD setting would permit much clearer

Table 1   Types of subgroup interactions*

| Type of interaction | Effect on growth and survival of two subgroups, A and B | | | | General results of interaction |
| | When not interacting | | When interacting | | |
	A	B	A	B	
1. Neutralism	0	0	0	0	Neither group affects the other
2. Competition	0	0	−	−	Subgroup most affected eliminated from niche
3. Mutualism	−	−	+	+	Interaction obligatory for both
4. Protocooperation	0	0	+	+	Interaction favourable to both, but not obligatory
5. Commensalism	−	0	+	0	Obligatory for A; B not affected
6. Amensalism	0	0	−	0	A inhibited; B not affected
7. Parasitism	−	0	+	−	Obligatory for A; B inhibited
8. Predation	−	0	+	−	Obligatory for A; B inhibited

*Adapted with permission of the publisher from W. B. Clapham, Jun., *Natural Eco-systems*, New York: Macmillan, 1973, p. 65.

explication of the on-going relationships and processes existing between and among the many subgroups that constitute the organizational community.

Ecologists have also studied the progression of ecological succession in a community, particularly that which follows a major disturbance. In the process they note such things as the total mass of the system, system production, and species diversity. Similar studies in organizations might lead to additional insight concerning the dynamics of intergroup behaviour. As an example, Likert's (1967) work in which he monitors changes in various factors in an organization over time, as management changes from System 1 to System 4, is analogous to this. Additionally there have been studies of the changes taking place as bureaucratic systems develop over time (Downs, 1967).

One final example of a concept that has been quite useful to ecologists is that of 'limiting factors'. It involves a situation in which the production or output of a system becomes dependent on that factor which is present in the least quantity. When this occurs, other factors begin to interact and form new combinations which, together, tend to offset the effects of the limiting factors. Similarly, the statistical techniques of multivariate analysis have been developed to calculate the effects of individual factors when acting in combination with others (Pielou, 1969). These techniques are particularly useful in situations, such as organizational settings, where many variables interact in complex ways and are not experimentally controllable.

As this brief review suggests, biologists have developed many concepts which are useful in describing ecological systems and analysing processes of interaction within them. The selection here of a number of these concepts in order to show their applicability to the study of organizations has been intended as a sample of what is potentially available. Many of the concepts have been previously applied under differing terminology in the social or organization sciences, but always eclectically and never within an encompassing framework, such as that provided by the ecological approach. Currently, however, progress is being made as these concepts are expanded and as new terminologies and methodologies are applied to organizations (Pfeffer, 1972; Garvey, 1975; Hannan and Freeman, 1977; Kasarda and Bidwell, 1977). As modern societies become increasingly characterized by what Trist calls type 4 (turbulent) environments, organizations begin to take on more of the characteristics of ecosystems. In short, we have reached the point where theorists and practitioners alike can profit from the concepts and approaches already developed by the ecologists. This in turn will demand that the organization analysts create more complex, multidimensional models to which multivariate techniques can be applied.

When fully developed, the ecological approach offers a unifying concept for the integration of systems approaches and contingency approaches to organization theory. It also offers the OD practitioner an expanded and integrated model from which to view organizations, a model which is capable of dealing systematically with the evolution of organizational climates. Finally, it offers the OD analyst the basis for applying a more comprehensive approach to organization change and development than that provided by the current eclectic collection of techniques.

Ecological analysis of organization behaviour

To study the organization from an ecological perspective, it is necessary to consider the organization in conjunction with its external environment. Pfeffer (1972) has argued that 'susceptibility to external interorganizational influence is a central problem for organizations'. Organizations, in order to survive, must effectively maintain some form of homeostatic balance. Effectiveness, in turn, is related to the ability to acquire, process, and distribute resources, all of which creates a complex system of interdependence between the organization and its environment.

Recognition of these dependency relationships with various elements of the task environment is not new. Thompson (1967) described the nature of contingencies and constraints imposed by the environment and described the competitive and cooperative strategies that could be employed as coping devices. These strategies incorporated the structure of boundary spanning units created within the organization specifically to deal with external issues. Dill, as early as 1958, also wrote of the nature of the constraints imposed by the task environment. What is new is that writers are now beginning to give more than perfunctory attention to the influences of the environment upon the organization (see Evan, 1976; Pfeffer and Salancik, 1978). This is in sharp contrast to past practices in which most authors dealt thoroughly and almost entirely with the internal, efficient disposition of resources *once acquired*.

As an example of this trend, Pfeffer and Salancik (1978) have recently expressed an ecological view of organizations with the observation that 'a good deal of organizational behavior, the actions taken by organizations, can be understood only by knowing something about the organization's environment and the problems it creates for obtaining resources'. They go on to state that 'it is not likely administrators would have a large effect on the outcomes of most organizations' (Pfeffer and Salancik, 1978, pp. 3, 10). This basic theme is then developed into a detailed explication of the nature of environmental contingencies and constraints, the ways in which the organization becomes aware of them, and the means of coping with them. This approach to studying organizations is clearly ecological in nature.

Since viewing organizations from an ecological perspective leads to an increased emphasis concerning the role external factors play in organization behaviour, a number of implications for relating the practice and forms of OD in organizations arise.

First, if the critical contingencies for an organization lie in the external environment, then the OD practitioner must develop a heightened awareness of these contingencies as well as their potential impact. This, in turn, will lead to a shift in strategies from concentration on internal concerns (interdepartmental cooperation, decision making, etc.) to enhancing the organizational ability to deal with the environmental constraints. French and Bell (1978) summarize this need as follows:

In the future, organization development specialists must know much more about such matters as goal setting and structural changes and must establish linkages with practitioners in such fields as management science, personnel and industrial psychology, operations research, and industrial engineering in order to provide a broader range of options for organizational intervention. (French and Bell, 1978, p. 257.)

Fortunately, many of the skills needed in these endeavours may already be part of the repertoire of OD. Much is known, for instance, about the development of key boundary spanning roles, the principles of effective bargaining strategies, and the means of coping with conflict. Other skills will have to be learned, however. If the OD consultant is attempting to improve an organization's adaptive ability by affecting change in its relationships with external factors, new talents may be called for. Examples might include legal expertise to create or change contractual arrangements; political talents to influence legislative or regulatory decisions; managerial or professional knowledge of the raw materials, technologies, and product markets of the organization in order to promote advantageous mergers or coalitions.

Taken together, these activities sound more like the concerns of strategic decision makers than those of the traditional OD practitioner. But this is precisely the point. If external contingencies are crucial to an organization's existence, then change and development efforts relating to these contingencies will be necessary. Undoubtedly, internal approaches concerned with the efficient operation of the organization will continue to be vitally important. This perspective needs to be balanced, however, by a greater external awareness. Conceivably, the OD expert of the future may be well-versed in the processes of internal and external change, and might direct and coordinate the efforts of a group of specialists in an attempt to alter the relations between the organization and its various environments.

An increased appreciation of the external influences on an organization should have an additional payoff for the OD practitioner in terms of an improved ability to predict the likely outcomes of changing situations or change efforts. To be sure, there are interested external parties who will be affected by such changes, and certainly they will react in terms of the meaning change has for them. An ecological perspective will afford a greater insight into the potential effects of change and a greater ability to predict the sources and strengths of resistance.

Natural scientists have found that 'every environment is different and inconsistent, and that complex systems can be understood only by meticulous data-collection, logical analysis, and repeated ... investigation to identify the governing factor in each real situation. Neglect of any part of this combination leads quickly to nonsense' (Calder, 1973, p. 280). Or, stated more simply, 'All points in an ecosystem have unique properties' (Margalef, 1968, p. 20).

The same observation applies to organizations. To assume an ecological perspective requires an analytical approach and an awareness of a broad range of phenomena within the organization, such as the flows of energy, material, and information that may be pertinent in any change context. One is less likely to ignore or simply be unaware of important interdependencies within the system.

Viewing the organization as an ecosystem also enhances the appreciation of the interdependence of the internal parts of the system. Many OD efforts, like most mutations in natural systems, fail because systems reinforce the *status quo* in a myriad of ways through interdependencies that have developed over time. Although the climate for change can evolve over time, it tends to do so slowly. Current OD practitioners have come to realize this more and more as they now call for integrated, long-range programmes of change to replace isolated efforts which often do not endure.

By way of summary, adopting an ecological perspective of organizations and dealing with them as parts of ecosystems implies the need for an increased knowledge of and focus on the specifics of the surrounding external environment and their possible implications for the focal organization, and may call for a number of skills that are typically outside the repertoire of the traditional OD practitioner. Along with the expanded knowledge base comes a broader perspective, an improved ability to foresee the consequences of change by calling attention to processes and interdependencies that might otherwise be neglected.

Ecological analysis at the interorganizational level

Even though organizations take on an ecological perspective with regard to their external task environments, that alone may not be enough to guarantee continued effectiveness and viability. The developed nations of the world are entering what has been termed by Daniel Bell the post-industrial society (Bell, 1965). One characteristic of this development is the 'increased interdependence of the parts and the unpredictable connections which arise between them as a result of the accelerating but uneven change rate' (Emery and Trist, 1973, p. 122). This condition is described as a turbulent field or type 4 environment in which the organization acting alone is incapable of dealing with environmental contingencies. Not surprisingly, the major problems of type 4 environments are, from an organizational point of view, ecological. Dissimilar organizations must learn to cooperate because their fates are positively correlated owing to the interconnectedness of their environments. In the absence of cooperation, autoregulative processes are in danger of breaking down (Crozier, 1964), leading to the possibility of societies falling into what Vickers (1968) terms 'ecological traps', or developmental dead-ends. If autoregulative social processes cannot be depended upon to result in the coordinated interaction of organizational ecosystems some alternative must be found.

To overcome these coordination problems, Lawrence K. Frank (1967) has suggested that a new, more complex intervention strategy is needed to cope with the emerging conditions brought on by post-industrialism. Emery and Trist have developed an approach that may be used to implement such a strategy. Basically they argue that an adaptive, self-regulating system must have built-in redundancy or else have a limited repertoire of responses capable only of dealing with a fixed set of environmental conditions. Since such a limitation is obviously insufficient for dealing with turbulent environments, redundancy is needed. It can be based either on redundant *parts* organized for any particular adaptive response, which entails higher and higher orders of special control mechanisms, or on redundant *functions* of the individual parts. Redundancy of function 'does not entail a pressure toward higher and higher orders of special control mechanisms, but it does entail effective mechanisms within the part for setting and resetting its function – for human beings, shared values are the most significant of these self-regulating devices' (Emery and Trist, 1973, p. 131).

Operationally, 'the choice is between whether a population seeks to enhance its chances of survival by strengthening and elaborating special social mechanisms of control or by increasing the adaptiveness of its individual members' while utilizing values as the coordinating mechanism. 'Values have the conceptual character of 'power fields' and act as guides to behavior' (Emery and Trist, 1973, pp. 69–71).

During a time of social transition as great as the present, there is a need to create new institutions and to renew old ones. Government is now involved in societal activities to an extent previously unknown. By either direct intervention and control, by means of specific regulations, or by establishing the basic ground rules for interaction, the government has alternative strategies for developing the mechanisms of social and organizational regulation. This increased governmental activity, while perhaps reducing uncertainty in some areas, creates additional constraints and contingencies for organizations in others.

Emery and Trist (1973, p. 184) call for a new method of social regulation involving a negotiated order based on mutual accommodation of legitimate interests in the place of an order based on the competitive challenge of superior power. For them, the surrender of power is necessary for survival in a type 4 environment. In this manner of thinking, they advance the hypothesis that:

The planning process (not the plan) can become the basis for a new 'culture' of politics. This new political culture will involve continuous dialogue, painful confrontation, . . . hard bargaining and multiple interest group accommodation. But these are the processes which can lead to innovative joint problem-solving as experience is gained and greater trust is established. (Emery and Trist, 1973, pp. 205–206.)

Such informed social action will demand the collaboration of scientists, professionals, administrators, and politicians in an atmosphere of mutual respect. Unfortunately, what has yet to occur, 'and what is not occurring at the pace required, is any corresponding change in our cultural values, organization philosophies, or ecological strategies'. Until this is recognized 'we cannot develop the capability, though we have the resources, to shape our future to good advantage' (Emery and Trist, 1973, pp. 153–158).

This scenario of change and adaptation at the interorganizational level has some rather staggering implications for the practice of OD. It is obvious that potentially crucial contingencies for organizations exist within this environment and that some means of coordination or articulation among sets of organizations, which are interdependent in complex ways must be developed.

There is some evidence that a broadening of interest in the practice of OD is taking place. During the 1950s, collaborative studies focused on the single organization, omitting the broader contextual element. However, as Emery and Trist (1973, pp. 113–114) point out, 'the path-finding projects for the next few years are likely to be characterized both by a greater social extensiveness and a greater psychological intensiveness than the major collaborative studies of the "fifties".' In short, OD will expand both the breadth and depth of its efforts.

Researchers at the Tavistock Institute have for some time undertaken projects dealing with multi-organizational clusters rather than with single organizations, with a major commitment of resources over an increased time scale, and with the involvement of an extended mix of disciplines.

When dealing with a set of organizations, the problem of clearly identifying the client becomes far more difficult than is typically the case in the single organization. Perhaps the allegiance of the change agent will adhere to certain values rather than to any particular individual or organization.

The ecological niche that any particular organization occupies is a complex result of many factors, such as its ability to compete, to bargain, or to receive the benefits of favourable legislation. Currently, many interorganizational differences are adjudicated via the mechanism of law, planning bodies, regulatory entities, or even at times by the mobilizing of public opinion. To the extent that these autoregulative social mechanisms can, and often do, fail, it is possible that additional mechanisms need to be developed to deal more effectively with the complex problems involving sets of organizations. What these mechanisms will be, and what role OD will play in them, is at present highly speculative. It is quite conceivable, however, that scientists who are trained in and adept at following the potential effects of systems changes through the web of an organizational ecosystem may have an important function to perform. Due to the increasing complexity of interdependencies, OD involvement may tend to be at the level of planning *programmes* as compared with involvement solely or primarily at the *project* level.

As OD practitioners become increasingly involved in a wider range of organizations and organizational settings they may find many of their tools are insufficient or inappropriate. Until recently, OD has been involved primarily at the project level within a single organization or subunit of an organization. The result has been the development of strategies appropriate to such activities. Taking a more ecological view of organizations places relatively greater importance on the external factors which influence organizations. The result is both a need and an opportunity to think in broader terms. This, in turn, will undoubtedly lead to the development of new tools and the adaptation of older techniques to new organization cultures and situations.

Opportunity exists for OD involvement at a higher level than has typically been the case so far. At this level, overriding values must be developed to form the basis for interorganizational coordination in a turbulent environment. Just how such roles will be developed and how acceptance and legitimacy will be achieved are hard to surmise at this time.

If adaptation to the environment is to be achieved through the utilization of new approaches, leading to a more organic society rather than a more engineered and controlled society, the need will increase for individuals trained in the social sciences and skilled in fostering collaborative interaction in highly complex settings involving linked sets of organizations. There will be a strong demand for people capable of conducting experiments or trials, and evaluating the consequences of such programmes and their attendant policies. The OD practitioner may find additional opportunities in newly created, special roles in key boundary spanning positions both within and among organizations. The various roles played in these positions will be an important determinant of the adaptability of organizations and society to the turbulent conditions brought about by the transition to post-industrialism.

Summary and conclusion

Any attempt to approach the subject of OD from an ecological perspective must, of necessity, range far afield. This paper is no exception. Many concepts and approaches utilized by ecologists in their study of ecosystems have their correlates or analogues in the study of organizations by theorists or OD specialists. In some potentially relevant areas, ecologists have succeeded in systematizing concepts and synthesizing theory to a greater extent than organization theorists. Ecology may, in fact, present a model for organization theory that could serve to organize and unify many of the presently dissociated themes, while simultaneously providing a structure within which much of the disparate research data can be integrated. For the OD practitioner, it offers the tempting possibility of an integrated model within which to view his activities.

Moving from ecological views of the organization along to an expanded perspective in which the organization is seen as part of a larger system, the organization must be viewed as one member of an interrelated set of organizations interacting in complex ways, as part of an ecological system. The need for adaptation is clearly implied in the trend towards post-industrialism with its increasing organizational complexity and mutual interdependence. New approaches will develop based on collaboration and cooperation in a negotiated order dependent upon the emergence of values that have an overriding significance for members of the field. The opportunities and challenges are immense for the social scientist capable of working in these new settings and aiding diverse organizations and interests in the process of developing the values by which they will live. The task involves dealing not only with the climate within the organization, a difficult enough problem in itself, but also fostering the cultural change that will permit the move to these new adaptive processes.

References

Alderfer, C. P. (1969) Job enlargement and the organizational context, *Personnel Psychology*, **22**, 418–426.

Argyris, C. (1970) *Intervention Theory and Methods*. Reading, Mass.: Addison-Wesley.

Beck, A. C., jun., and Hillmar, E. D. (eds) (1972) *A Practical Approach to Organization Development Through MBO*. Reading, Mass.: Addison-Wesley.

Beckhard, R. (1969) *Organizational Development: Strategies and Models*. Reading, Mass.: Addison-Wesley.

320 SYSTEMS THEORY FOR ORGANIZATION DEVELOPMENT

Bell, D. (1965) Twelve modes of prediction. In J. Gould (ed.) *Penguin Survey of the Social Sciences*. Harmondsworth, Middx.: Penguin.

Boughey, Arthur S. (1971) *Fundamental Ecology*. Scranton, Pa.: Intext Educational.

Brynildsen, R. D. (1974) Motivation and individual career achievement. In J. D. Adams (ed.) *Theory and Method in Organization Development: An Evolutionary Process*. Arlington, VA.: NTL Institute, 159–180.

Burke, W. W. (1974) Managing conflict between groups. In J. D. Adams (ed.) *Theory and Method in Organization Development: An Evolutionary Process*. Arlington, Va.: NTL Institute, 255–268.

Burke, W. Warner (1976) Organization development in transition. *Journal of Applied Behavioral Science*, **12** (1), 22–43.

Calder, Nigel (1973) The future of environmental science: Et cetera. In Nigel Calder (ed.) *Nature in the Round*. New York: Viking, 277–285.

Carzo, Rocco, jun., and Yanouzas, John N. (1967) *Formal Organization: A Systems Approach*. Homewood, Ill.: Irwin.

Clapham, W. B., jun. (1973) *Natural Ecosystems*. New York: Macmillan.

Crozier, M. (1964) *The Bureaucratic Phenomenon*. London: Tavistock; Chicago: University of Chicago Press.

Dill, William R. (1958) Environment as an influence on managerial autonomy. *Administrative Science Quarterly*, **2**, 409–443.

Downs, Anthony (1967) *Inside Bureaucracy*. New York: Little, Brown.

Emery, F. E., and Trist, E. L. (1965) The causal texture of organizational environments. *Human Relations*, **18**, 21–32.

Emery, F. E., and Trist, E. L. (1973) *Towards a Social Ecology*. New York: Plenum.

Evans, W. M. (1966) The organization set: Toward a theory of inter-organizational relations. In J. D. Thompson (ed.) *Approaches to Organizational Design*. University of Pittsburgh Press.

Evan, W. M. (1976) *Organization Theory: Structures, Systems, and Environments*. New York: Wiley.

Evans, Francis C. (1965) Ecosystem as the basic unit in ecology. In Edward J. Kormondy (ed.) *Readings in Ecology*. Englewood Cliffs, NJ: Prentice-Hall, 166–167.

Ford, R. N. (1969) *Motivation Through Work Itself*. New York: American Management Association.

Frank, L. K. (1967) The need for a new political theory. *Journal of the American Academy of Arts and Sciences*, **96**, 809–816.

French, Wendell L., and Bell, Cecil H., jun. (1978) *Organization Development*, 2nd ed., Englewood Cliffs, NJ: Prentice-Hall.

Galbraith, Jay R. (1977) *Organization Design*, Reading, Mass.: Addison-Wesley.

Garvey, Lou Ann Benshoof (1975) *Ecological theory and international relations: The case of wheat*. Ph.D. dissertation, The American University.

Hannan, Michael T., and Freeman, John (1977) The population ecology of organizations. *American Journal of Sociology*, **82** (5), 929–964.

Harvey, J. B. (1974) The Abilene Paradox: The management of agreement. *Organizational Dynamics*, **3**, 63–80.

Hawley, Amos H. (1973) Ecology and population. *Science*, **179**, 1196–1201.

Hellriegel, Don, and Slocum, John W. jun., (1976) *Organizational Behavior: Contingency Views*. New York: West.

Kahn, Robert L. (1974) Organization development: Some problems and proposals. *Journal of Applied Behavioral Science*, **10** (4), 485–502.

Kasarada, John D., and Bidwell, Charles E. (1977) The organization as an ecosystem. Paper presented at the annual meeting of the American Sociological Association.

Kast, Fremont E., and Rosenzweig, James E. (1970) *Organization and Management: A Systems Approach*, New York: McGraw-Hill.

Khandwalla, Pradip N. (1977) *The Design of Organizations*. New York: Harcourt Brace Jovanovich.

King, D. C. (1972) Selecting personnel for a system 4 organization. In W. W. Burke (ed.) *Contemporary Organization Development: Conceptual Orientations and Interventions.* Washington, DC: NTL Institute, 201–211.

Knight, Clifford B. (1965) *Basic Concepts of Ecology.* New York: Macmillan.

Krone, C. E. (1974) Open systems redesign. In J. D. Adams (ed.) *Theory and Method in Organization Development: An Evolutionary Process.* Arlington, Va.: NTL Institute, 364–391.

Lawrence, P. R., and Lorsch, J. W. (1969a) *Developing Organizations: Diagnosis and Action.* Reading, Mass.: Addison-Wesley.

Lawrence, Paul R., and Lorsch, Jay W. (1969b) *Organization and Environment.* Homewood, Ill.: Irwin.

Levine, Stephen H. (1977) Exploitation interactions and the structure of ecosystems. *Journal of Theoretical Biology*, **69** (2), 345–355.

Likert, Rensis (1967) *The Human Organization: Its Management and Value.* New York: McGraw-Hill.

March, James G., and Simon, Herbert A. (1958) *Organizations.* New York: Wiley.

Margalef, Ramon (1968) *Perspectives in Ecological Theory.* University of Chicago Press.

Margulies, N., and Raia, A. P. (1972) *Organization Development: Values, Process, and Technology.* New York: McGraw-Hill.

Melcher, Arlyn J. (1976) *Structure and Process of Organizations: A Systems Approach.* Englewood Cliffs, NJ: Prentice-Hall.

Odum, Eugene P. (1972) Ecosystems. In William White, jun., and Frank J. Little, jun. (eds) *Ecology and Pollution.* Philadelphia, Pa.: North American Publishing Company, 66–69.

Paul, W. J., Robertson, K. B. and Herzberg, F. (1969) Job enrichment pays off. *Harvard Business Review*, **47** (2), 61–78.

Pfeffer, Jeffrey (1972) Organizational ecology: A system resource approach. Ph.D. dissertation, Stanford University.

Pfeffer, Jeffrey, and Salancik, Gerald R. (1978) *The External Control of Organizations: A Resource Dependence Approach.* New York: Harper & Row.

Pielou, E. C. (1969) *An Introduction to Mathematical Ecology.* New York: Wiley.

Steele, F. I. (1973) *Physical Settings and Organization Development.* Reading, Mass.: Addison-Wesley.

Steele, John (1976) Application of theoretical models in ecology. *Journal of Theoretical Biology*, **63** (2), 443–451.

Tansley, A. G. (1935) The use and abuse of vegetational concepts and terms. *Ecology*, **16**, 284ff.

Thompson, James D. (1967) *Organizations in Action.* New York: McGraw-Hill.

Trist, E. L. (1969) On socio-technical systems. In W. G. Bennis, K. D. Benne, and R. Chin (eds) *The Planning of Change*, 2nd ed. New York: Holt, Rinehart & Winston, 269–282.

Vickers, Sir Geoffrey (1968) *Value Systems and Social Process.* London: Tavistock; New York: Basic Books.

Woodward, Joan (1965) *Industrial Organization: Theory and Practice.* London: Oxford University Press.

Systems Theory for Organization Development
Edited by T. G. Cummings
© 1980 John Wiley & Sons Ltd.

Chapter **14**

Interorganization Theory and Organization Development

Thomas G. Cummings

In the past two decades organization development (OD) has expanded gradually from individual and group approaches to planned change to more comprehensive strategies encompassing the whole organization and its relevant environment. Movement in this direction has extended the domain of OD to wider aspects of the organization including planning and strategy, organization design, and environmental management. Attempts to deal with these more macro issues have frequently pushed OD beyond the organization's boundaries to diverse segments of its environment. This open systems orientation is evident in the recent OD literature (Alderfer, 1977; Galbraith, 1977; French and Bell, 1978; Margulies and Raia, 1978) and in the growing number of projects involving organization and environment interfaces (Trist, 1967; Culbert *et al.*, 1972; Tichy, 1977; Motamedi, 1978).

Application of OD to organization and environment issues invariably leads to consideration of interorganizational relations. This follows from the simple fact that other organizations are a critical part of the environment of any organization. Since organizations frequently have problems establishing and maintaining necessary linkages with other organizations, there is a practical need to develop diagnostic and intervention strategies appropriate to interorganizational relations. Unfortunately, OD practice in this area often proceeds with little theoretical or empirical direction. Relevant interorganizational theory and research are currently not applied systematically to planned change making it difficult to diagnose interorganizational problems and to generate specific solutions to resolve them.

The purpose of this chapter is to apply in a preliminary manner interorganizational theory and research to OD. The paper discusses (1) the need for OD to address interorganizational issues; (2) a research-based framework for understanding interorganizational relations; and (3) the implications of this perspective for OD.

The need to apply OD to interorganizational relations

The major argument for applying OD to interorganizational relations rests on an assessment of whether such linkages are problematic to the organization's effectiveness. This issue may be addressed by considering interorganizational relations in the context of the organization's need to manage environmental dependency. This perspective rests on the premise that organizations are open systems, dependent on their environments for resource exchange, yet requiring independence to operate rationally (Thompson, 1967; Jacobs, 1974; Aldrich, 1976; Pfeffer, 1978). Since environmental dependency places constraints on the organization's ability to function autonomously, it must manage such dependency to survive as an independent entity (Kotter, 1979). Organizations typically manage environmental dependency by establishing and maintaining resource exchanges with other organizations (Levine and White, 1961). To the extent that such exchanges allow the organization sufficient autonomy to operate rationally, the organization is in harmony or balance with its environment. Conversely, to the extent that they jeopardize the organization's independence, problems of survival arise.

Current theory suggests that the nature of the organization's environment affects its ability to manage environmental dependency (Emery and Trist, 1965; Thompson, 1967; Terreberry, 1968; Aldrich, 1975). Specifically, Aldrich (1975) identifies seven dimensions of the environment as important determinates of interorganizational exchange:

(1) *Stability* refers to the degree of organization turnover in the environment. The more stable the environment, the more organizations can develop formalized exchanges with other organizations.

(2) *Homogeneity* represents the degree of similarity among the organizations in the environment. Like stability, the more homogeneous the environment, the more organizations can establish standardized relationships.

(3) *Concentration* involves the degree to which resources are evenly distributed among the organizations in the environment. To the extent that resources are concentrated in a few organizations, organizations can exploit their positions in the environment by developing appropriate exchange strategies.

(4) *Capacity* refers to the relative level of resources available from organizations in the environment. The richer the environment, the more intense and reciprocal interactions between organizations are likely to be.

(5) *Domain consensus* represents the degree to which the organization's claim to a specific environmental niche is disputed or recognized by other organizations. The more there is domain consensus among organizations, the more cooperative their exchanges tend to be.

(6) *Turbulence* involves the extent to which organizations in the environment are undergoing change. The greater the turbulence, the less organizations are able to formalize exchanges and plan for future relationships.

(7) *Mutability* refers to the extent to which other organizations in the environment are manipulable. The higher the mutability, the more there is leverage for influencing exchange processes.

The above mentioned factors provide a preliminary indication of whether interorganizational relations are likely to be problematic. When viewed as continuous variables, the environmental dimensions suggest that interorganizational exchanges are more difficult to establish and maintain to the extent that the organization's environment is unstable, or heterogeneous, or dispersed, or lean, or domain conflicted, or turbulent, or immutable. Given each or a combination of these conditions, the organization is likely to experience problems in managing environmental dependency, hence maintaining its autonomy.

The need to apply OD to interorganizational relations arises in precisely these circumstances. When the organization's ability to manage environmental dependency is problematic, issues of development (or even survival) are likely to emerge in the context of interorganizational relations. This may explain the growing movement of OD towards organization and environment issues. There is considerable speculation that contemporary organizations are facing increasing amounts of environmental complexity and change (Emery and Trist, 1965; Terreberry, 1968). If so, traditional attention to internal organization problems is likely to shift towards external demands, especially those from the more organized parts of the environment.

A framework for understanding interorganizational relations

Interorganizational theory and research are still in a formative stage. Current studies focus on the nature and consequences of interorganizational exchange, especially among social service organizations (Zeitz, 1974). Although existing research does not form a coherent body of knowledge, attempts to provide integration seem promising. Specifically, two recent studies conceptualize and empirically examine motivations for and patterns of interorganizational relations (Hall *et al.*, 1977; Schmidt and Kochan, 1977). When taken together, they provide a conceptual framework for explaining the development and consequences of interorganizatinal linkages.

Motivation to interact

A first step in understanding interorganizational relations is to explain the motivational basis underlying interaction. Presumably, the basis of motivation affects the nature of subsequent interaction. Schmidt and Kochan (1977) address this issue using two competing approaches to interaction: exchange and power/dependency. They argue that the exchange perspective accounts for *symmetrical* linkages where both organizations are motivated to interact in order to maximize their joint benefits (Levine and White, 1961). Since both organizations perceive mutual benefits from interacting, such exchanges are characterized by a high degree of cooperation and problem solving. The power/dependency approach, on the other hand, accounts for *asymmetrical* linkages where one organization is motivated to interact but the other is not (Benson, 1975; Schmidt and Kochan, 1976). Here relationships form when the motivated party is powerful enough to induce the other to interact. Since motivation to interact is externally generated for at least one of the organizations, such linkages are characterized by a high degree of bargaining and conflict.

Schmidt and Kochan (1977) suggest that interorganizational relations are based on either symmetrical or asymmetrical motives, the former resulting in complementary exchanges and the latter in power/dependency linkages. Moreover, they argue that an organization can enter into both types of relationships with different organizations in its environment, and that a given relationship may shift from one basis to another over time.

Based on exchange and power/dependency approaches to interorganizational linkage, Schmidt and Kochan (1977) develop hypotheses relating motivation to interact with frequency of interaction. In a symmetrical situation, frequency of interaction is purported to be high when both organizations perceive benefits from interaction; conversely, frequency of interaction is hypothesized to be low when neither organization perceives benefits. In an asymmetrical relationship, frequency of interaction is purported to be high when the organization perceiving low benefits from interaction sees the motivated organization as (1) having goals which are compatible with its own; (2) being important to its functioning; (3) having greater influence over it; and (4) acting aggressively in pursuing its interests by using bargaining and conflict-oriented strategies of influence.

The hypothesis involving asymmetrical relations focuses on concepts central to power/dependency theories. Compatible goals reduce the likelihood that the organization perceiving low benefits will resist interaction because such situations pose little threat to the organization (Evan, 1966; Gutzkow, 1966). Importance, influence, and aggressiveness affect the balance of power between organizations, hence the organization perceiving low benefits may be forced to interact because it is dependent on the more important, influential, and aggressive organization.

Schmidt and Kochan (1977) present evidence to support these hypotheses. Although the data are cross-sectional, they suggest that the motivational basis for interaction affects the nature of relations between organizations. If this view is correct, attempts to understand interorganizational relations must start from a motivational base. Since this assumes that organizations interrelate to maximize their self-interests, interaction is likely to be high either when both organizations perceive benefits from the relationship (symmetrical situation) or when one organization is induced by the other to relate because it is dependent on the other (asymmetrical situation).

Whereas Schmidt and Kochan (1977) focus on the motivational antecedents of interorganizational relations, it is also necessary to understand the consequences of interaction. Here the major issue is whether interaction leads to coordination or conflict between the organizations.

Mechanisms for coordination

Hall and his colleagues (Hall *et al.*, 1977) propose that different mechanisms promote interorganizational coordination (rather than conflict) depending on the basis of the relationship. Specifically, three bases of interaction are identified: voluntary, standardized-voluntary, and mandated. *Voluntary* exchanges arise when organizations perceive mutual benefits from interacting. This is similar to Schmidt and Kochan's (1977) symmetrical exchange. *Standardized-voluntary* relations emerge when organizations enter into formal agreements to structure the exchange. Like voluntary interactions, these exchanges are symmetrical yet formalized. *Mandated* relationships arise when laws or outside agencies govern the interaction. Aldrich (1976) suggests that these exchanges tend to be more intense, imbalanced in favour of one of the organizations, and associated with lower cooperation, and hence are similar to Schmidt and Kochan's (1977) asymmetrical interaction.

Hall and his co-workers (Hall *et al.*, 1977) hypothesize specific mechanisms likely to promote coordination under each type of exchange. In voluntary interactions, domain consensus and positive evaluations of each organization's performance are purported to lead to coordination, even though attempts to exert power may still occur. In standardized-voluntary exchanges, issues of domain consensus and power relationships are likely to be resolved in formalizing the interaction; hence, mutual recognition of good performance is hypothesized to promote coordination. In mandated relations, domain consensus and power relations are likely to be controlled by legal statutes; hence positive performance evaluations are purported to facilitate coordination.

Hall and his colleagues (Hall *et al.*, 1977) present considerable evidence to test these assumptions. Their findings support the contention that coordination is achieved through different means depending upon the basis for interaction. When exchange was voluntary, the data showed that positive evaluations (i.e. positive assessments of performance, competence of personnel, and compatibility of philosophy), frequency of contact, and person-to-person contact were significant predictors of coordination. When interaction was standardized-voluntary, the findings revealed that power relationships, frequency of contact, and importance of contact were important contributors to coordination. When exchange was mandated, the data showed that positive evaluations (minus compatibility of philosophy), frequency of contact, and quality of communications were significantly related to coordination. Although the data generally support the authors' hypotheses, the presence of power relations and the absence of positive performance evaluations as predictors of coordination in the standardized-voluntary situation were contrary to expectation.

Interorganization framework

The above mentioned studies (Hall *et al.*, 1977; Schmidt and Kochan, 1977) may be integrated into a comprehensive framework for understanding interorganizational relations. Schmidt and Kochan explain the motivational antecedents for interaction; Hall and his colleagues account for mechanisms that determine whether such interaction results in coordination rather than conflict. When taken together, the two studies provide preliminary knowledge of the motivational antecedents and coordinative consequences of interorganizational relations.

The interorganizational framework is summarized in Figure 1. It starts with the fundamental issue of why organizations are initially motivated to interact.

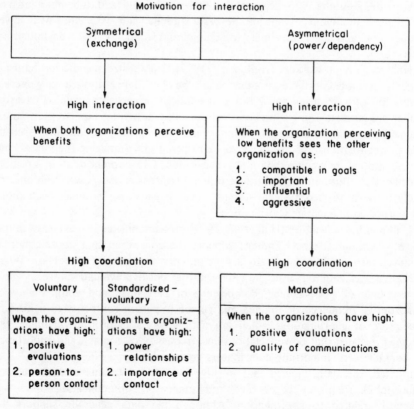

Figure 1   A framework for understanding interorganizational relations

Depending on the motivational basis for interaction, symmetrical or asymmetrical, the model suggests that high interaction is likely to occur either when both organizations perceive mutual benefits from interacting or when one organization is induced to interact by the other organization because it is dependent on the other – i.e. it sees the other as compatible in goals, important, influential, and aggressive. Given high interaction, the framework specifies mechanisms likely to lead to high coordination. It is important to note that the mechanism 'frequency of contact' is related to high coordination in all three situations studied by Hall and his colleagues (Hall *et al.*, 1977). Since this variable appears to be a measure of interaction, it is deleted from the framework to avoid redundancy with the 'interaction' variable of the model. In the symmetrical situation, the model suggests that high coordination is achieved by different means depending on whether interaction is voluntary or standardized-voluntary. In the voluntary case, high coordination depends on high positive evaluations and high person-to-person contact; high coordination is achieved in the standardized-voluntary situation when power relations and importance of contacts are both high. In the asymmetrical situation as exemplified by mandated exchanges, high coordination results from high positive evaluations and high quality of communications.

In its present state the framework is only a crude representation of interorganizational relations. Further theory and research are needed to refine and extend the conditions affecting interaction and coordination. Most relations are neither purely symmetrical nor asymmetrical. Additional research is necessary to define these mixed-motive exchanges and to specify the factors likely to affect interaction. Similarly, more refined categories of exchange are necessary for more precise specification of the mechanisms for coordination. This is especially needed in respect of asymmetrical relationships. The present model is limited to mechanisms appropriate to mandated types of asymmetrical exchange. Research into other forms of asymmetrical linkage, such as protest groups seeking to influence corporate decisions, is needed to extend understanding of the coordinative mechanisms. Since the framework is based on cross-sectional research, longitudinal studies are needed to test the causal linkages implied in the model – i.e. the motivation–interaction–coordination premise. Such research is likely to uncover significant feedback relationships among the variables (e.g. the effects of coordination on subsequent motivation to interact), hence providing a more dynamic explanation of interorganizational relations.

Implications for OD

Based on the premise that OD needs to attend to interorganizational relations when the organization's ability to manage environmental dependency is problematic, the foregoing framework suggests a number of implications for applying OD to interorganizational issues. These are addressed in the context of two major stages of OD practice: diagnosis and intervention. To provide a clear reference point for discussion, diagnosis and intervention are treated from the perspective of a focal organization attempting to establish or improve relations with other organizations.

Interorganizational diagnosis

Diagnosis invariably involves judgements about relevant organizational variables and their interrelationships. The framework developed here guides such judgements by specifying factors likely to affect interaction and coordination between organizations. Application of the model to an actual situation, however, requires a prior step of identifying the other organizations that relate directly to the focal organization. Since this provides an initial map of the interorganizational terrain, it seems necessary to formalize this process as much as possible.

Evan (1966) provides a useful concept for environmental mapping: the *organization-set*. This refers to those organizations that interact directly with the focal organization. Evan suggests that an organization has both an input and output organization-set. The former set comprises those organizations providing the focal organization with various types of resources, such as materials, personnel, and legitimacy; the latter includes organizations in the market of the focal organization, such as customers and competitors. Mapping the organization's environment in terms of its input and output organization-sets is useful for identifying relevant interorganizational linkages. It structures the environment analysis into categories, input and output sets, likely to be meaningful to boundary spanning personnel who deal predominantly with organizations on either the input or output sides of the focal organization. This helps to identify individuals who possess relevant knowledge of interorganizational relations and to focus their information on coherent segments of the environment. Moreover, differentiation of the organization's environment into input and output organization-sets permits potentially useful comparisons between the two sets on certain common dimensions, such as size, concentration, and overlap in membership and goals (Evan, 1966). Such comparisons may indicate whether the diagnosis should treat each set similarly or differently.

Once the relevant organizations relating directly to the focal organization are identified, diagnosis of interorganizational relations proceeds. The framework suggests a number of interorganizational issues requiring analysis. To simplify somewhat the discussion, diagnosis is treated as though the focal organization is interacting with only one other organization, though in reality it may be necessary to examine a number of problematic exchanges as well as possible interactions among them.

Diagnosis begins with the fundamental issue of whether interaction between the organizations is needed and, if so, whether it is problematic. If interaction is desired yet not achieved, it is necessary to analyse each organization's motivation for interaction with the other. This requires an evaluation of the costs and benefits to interaction in terms of each organization's specific goals. This reveals the extent to which the relationship is based on symmetrical or asymmetrical motives as well as the extent to which each organization sees benefits as outweighing costs. If the analysis shows that the relationship is symmetrical yet both organizations perceive low benefits to interaction, motivation for exchange is likely to be low. If the data reveal that the relationship is asymmetrical, further diagnosis is needed to assess whether other factors are hindering interaction. Specifically, it is necessary to evaluate the extent to which the organization perceiving low benefits sees the other organization (i.e. the organization perceiving high benefits) as compatible in goals, important, influential, and aggressive in its bargaining strategy. If these conditions are found to be low, motivation for interaction is likely to be low.

A second diagnostic issue arises when preliminary analysis reveals that desired interaction between the organizations exists. Now attention is focused on whether coordination is problematic. If coordination is desired yet not achieved, mechanisms for coordination between the organizations need to be analysed. This proceeds in two stages. First, it is necessary to determine the basis of interaction. Rather than assess only the symmetry (or asymmetry) of motives between the organizations, it is necessary to extend the above mentioned motivational analysis to account for different types of symmetrical and asymmetrical exchange: voluntary, standardized-voluntary, and mandated. Like the previous analysis, diagnosis begins with an assessment of the costs and benefits to interaction in terms of each organization's goals. This shows the extent to which interaction is based on symmetrical or asymmetrical motives, and is hence an indication of whether linkage is of the voluntary or mandated type. If the data reveal that interaction is symmetrical, it is necessary to evaluate further whether it is voluntary or standardized-voluntary. This may be determined by examining the extent to which the relationship is guided by formal agreements, usually in contractual form. On the other hand, if the analysis shows the interaction to be asymmetrical, it is likely to be mandated by laws or regulations specifying areas of domain, information flows, and financial obligations. Since asymmetrical exchange may be other than mandated (e.g. forced by a pressure group), it seems necessary to assess whether these conditions are indeed present.

Once the specific basis of interaction is identified, the second stage of this diagnosis analyses the extent to which particular coordinative mechanisms are operative. In the voluntary situation, this requires an assessment of each organization's evaluations of the other in terms of performance, competence of personnel, and compatibility of operating philosophies. The extent to which the relationship is based on person-to-person contacts also needs to be determined. If these factors are found to be low, coordination is likely to be low. In the standardized-voluntary case, diagnosis addresses the extent to which interactions are based on power relationships – i.e. the extent to which one organization affects the other. It is also necessary to determine the extent to which contacts between the organizations are important to the work of each. If the data show these mechanisms to be inoperative (or low), coordination is likely to be low. In the mandated situation, analysis focuses on each organization's evaluations of the other with reference to performance and competence of personnel. The quality of interorganizational communications also needs to be evaluated. If the analysis reveals these dimensions to be low, coordination is likely to be low.

The diagnostic strategy discussed above is summarized as an algorithm in Figure 2. This provides a logical set of rules for analysing interorganizational rela-

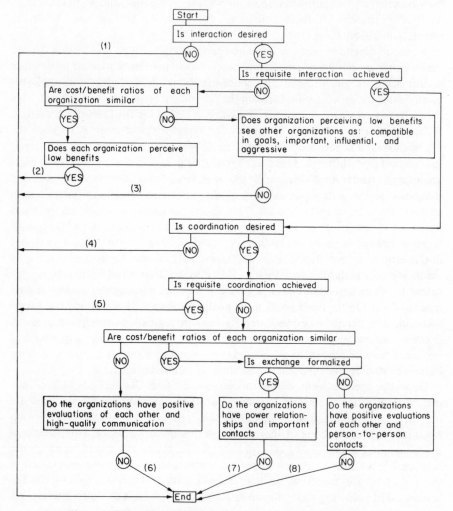

Figure 2   Algorithm for diagnosing interorganizational relations

tions. The rules derive from the interorganizational framework and specify whether interaction or coordination is problematic and, if so, the likely causes of the problem. The steps of the algorithm lead to eight possible diagnostic conclusions (the numbers correspond to those in Figure 2):

(1) Interaction is not desired, suggesting the absence of an interorganizational problem.
(2) Requisite interaction is not achieved and the problem is probably caused by factors specific to symmetrical exchange.
(3) Required interaction is not accomplished and the problem is probably attributable to variables related to asymmetrical linkage.
(4) Requisite interaction is achieved yet coordination is not desired, implying no interorganizational problem.
(5) Both required interaction and coordination are achieved, suggesting the absence of problems in these areas.
(6) Requisite interaction is accomplished but coordination is not; the problem is probably caused by factors specific to mandated exchange.
(7) Required interaction is achieved but coordination is not; the problem is probably attributable to variables related to standardized-voluntary relations.
(8) Requisite interaction is accomplished but coordination is not; the problem is probably caused by factors specific to voluntary exchange.

The diagnostic strategy, like the framework upon which it is based, represents an introductory outline for assessing interorganizational relations. Its major value at this stage of development is clarifying diagnostic issues derived from interorganizational research. Although this provides a much needed conceptual base for analysing interorganizational linkages, the strategy requires considerable refinement. Specifically, the diagnostic variables need to be operationalized and measured systematically across different organizations. Methods for gathering and analysing relevant data need to be developed and tested in different interorganizational contexts. Finally, the model needs to be integrated into an action-research perspective appropriate to planned interorganizational change.

Interorganizational intervention

The interorganizational framework also suggests implications for OD intervention. Starting with the initial issue of improving or developing desired interaction, the model implies that different intervention strategies are required, depending on the motivational basis of linkage: symmetrical or asymmetrical. In the symmetrical situation, interaction is likely to be problematic because each organization perceives low benefits from interaction. Here the task is to establish mutual dependence between the organizations.

Kotter (1979) provides a framework appropriate to this purpose. He describes five strategies used by organizations to form favourable relationships with other organizations. These range on a continuum with respect to the degree of dependence incurred and include (in order of increasing dependence):

(1) Advertising and public relations in order to create favourable attitudes towards the organization.
(2) Creation of boundary spanning roles to increase personal linkages with outside organizations.
(3) Contracting in order to legalize or formalize relationships with other organizations.
(4) Co-opting members from outside organizations usually through advisory boards or directorships.
(5) Forming coalitions or other joint ventures with other organizations.

Although these methods for establishing mutual dependence between organizations are not typically considered to be OD interventions, they seem congruent with traditional planned changed strategies emphasizing perceptual change, role negotiation, and intergroup relations. This suggests that such OD techniques may augment the interorganizational strategies by facilitating their implementation. For example, changing the perceptions of key employees who manage the organization's boundary exchanges may help to identify and negotiate points of mutual dependency with other organizations. Since this may include such strategies as contracting, co-opting, and coalescing, OD techniques appropriate to these issues need development.

In the asymmetrical situation, linkage is likely to be problematic because the motivated organization does not have the requisite power to compel the organization perceiving low benefits to interact. Here the task is to increase the power of the motivated party relative to the other organization, hence inducing the other to interact. Although the following discussion is limited to strategies for establishing power/dependency relations between organizations, an equally important issue for future study is how OD applies to organizations seeking to ward off external attempts to force linkage.

The interorganizational framework suggests that an organization can improve its power over another organization by appearing to be more goal compatible, important, influential, and aggressive to the other. Presumably, the resistant organization will be forced to interact because it is dependent upon the more powerful organization. At least two strategies seem relevant to forming power/dependency relationships between organizations:

(1) The motivated party can deceive the resistant organization by appearing to be more powerful than it actually is. Public relations and rumour initiation are often used to gain power over others deceptively.
(2) The motivated organization can achieve 'real' power over the resistant organization either directly by changing its own goals and strategies, or indirectly by exploiting its leverage over third parties which hold power over

the resistant organization in order to coerce them to induce the resistant organization to interact with the motivated party. A common example of the direct method is the expansion of an organization's resources in order to increase its power over other organizations which value or need the resources (Lehman, 1975). The indirect strategy is typically used by pressure groups which seek to influence resistant organizations by bargaining with powerful third parties to intervene on their behalf.

Current OD techniques seem least applicable to increasing one organization's power over another. Traditionally, OD has emphasized power equalization or collaborative methods rather than those involving power, coercion, and competition (French and Bell, 1978; Margulies and Raia, 1978). This suggests that attempts to induce power/dependency between organizations may conflict with OD assumptions and values. This appears particularly troublesome when desired interaction requires the motivated party to deceive or indirectly coerce the resistant organization. Although it is beyond the scope of this chapter to resolve this dilemma, OD practitioners may need to confront and expand their value premises before interventions appropriate to power/dependency relations are developed (Thomas, 1977).

Turning to problems of coordination, the framework suggests that OD interventions need to focus on different coordinative mechanisms depending on the basis of the relationship. If interaction is either voluntary or mandated, coordination is likely to be problematic because one or both organizations evaluates the other poorly or because person-to-person contacts and quality of communications between the organizations are poor. Since these conditions are likely to result in conflict between the organizations, OD strategies appropriate to conflict resolution seem relevant. Before discussing such methods, however, it is important to note that interorganizational conflict is not necessarily bad or destructive (Assael, 1969); conflict is problematic to the extent that it is dysfunctional for achieving desired coordination.

The current organizational conflict literature is rather diverse, comprising a variety of descriptive theories and normative recommendations. Although most of the relevant material focuses on conflict within rather than between organizations, Kilmann and Thomas (1978) provide a meta-model of conflict management useful for developing interorganizational strategies. Their framework identifies key assumptions underlying current approaches to conflict diagnosis and intervention, and categorizes the different strategies according to these premises. Since the model explicates the existing alternatives for conflict resolution, such as 'interaction management', 'contextual modification', and 'consciousness raising', it provides a practical checklist of the full range of possibilities. This seems a useful starting-point for developing OD interventions applicable to interorganizational conflict. Moreover, it suggests that many of the existing methods for conflict resolution may be extended to interorganizational phenomena with relatively little modification. For example, each of the conflict perspectives identified by Kilmann and Thomas includes assumptions about the causes of conflict behaviour similar to those discussed above for voluntary and mandated exchanges. Given this conceptual congruence, extension of current methods of conflict management to interorganizational relations seems promising.

In the final case of standardized-voluntary relations, coordination is likely to be problematic because power relationships and importance of contact between the organizations are poor. This suggests that despite a formal agreement between the organizations, coordination may be troublesome because power relations are still unresolved or one or both organizations has lowered its evaluation of the importance of the linkage. Here the task is to reestablish stable power/dependency relations between the organizations in respect of issues that each perceives as important to its goals. Although interventions applicable to power/dependency linkages have been discussed previously, their relevance to standardized-voluntary relations may be overlooked. Since such linkages are voluntary and formalized, it is logical to assume that the power relations involved in formulating the initial agreement have been resolved, hence the exercise of power is no longer important. Indeed, Hall and his colleagues originally made this assumption (Hall *et al.*, 1977); their subsequent research showed, however, that power relations rather than positive evaluations predicted coordination in the standardized-voluntary situation. This suggests that attention to power relations is necessary even after agreements between the organizations are reached. To the extent that such relations are problematic, strategies relevant to establishing power/dependency between the organizations seem appropriate.

Whereas interorganizational theory provides a necessary conceptual base for interorganizational diagnosis and intervention, application of this knowledge requires appropriate consultation methods for translating it into specific OD practice. Among the practical issues requiring further conceptualization and research are:

(1) The role of the interorganizational consultant – e.g. appropriate training and skills; expert *v.* process orientation; internal *v.* external base.
(2) Relevant unit of analysis and change – e.g. the conditions under which interorganizational change is most appropriate at the level of the organizational subunit, the total organization, or the set of interacting organizations.
(3) Entry into the client system – this includes such questions as who the client is (e.g. the organizational subunit, the whole organization, or the set of interacting organizations); where in the organization entry is most advantageous (e.g. at the institutional level where strategy and policy are formulated or at lower boundary spanning levels where more standard exchanges are carried out); when to enter the organization (e.g. at the time initial linkage is being established or when on-going relations become problematic).

(4) Approaches to interorganizational change – e.g. collaboration *v.* non-collaboration in goal setting; unilateral *v.* shared power in implementing change.

(5) Action-levers for interorganizational change – e.g. structural, process, and strategy variables likely to impact relations with other organizations.

Conclusion

Increases in the complexity and turbulence of contemporary organization environments are likely to make interorganizational relations problematic. OD must attend to such issues if it is to remain a viable strategy for organization effectiveness and growth. Current interorganizational theory and research provide preliminary understanding of this area; yet, such knowledge has not been applied systematically to planned change. The framework developed here is a needed step in this direction. It integrates recent interorganizational research into a comprehensive model that accounts for both interaction and coordination between organizations. Explication of the variables that affect these interorganizational outcomes raises specific implications for OD diagnosis and intervention. Hopefully, this application of interorganization theory to OD will generate further attempts to integrate these so far separate fields.

References

Alderfer, C. (1977) Organization development. In *Annual Review of Psychology*, **20**, 197–223. Palo Alto, Calif.: Annual Reviews.

Aldrich, H. (1975) An organization–environment perspective on cooperation and conflict between organizations in the manpower training system. In A. Negandhi (ed.) *Interorganization Theory*. Kent, Ohio: Comparative Administration Research Institute, 49–70.

Aldrich, H. (1976) Resource dependence and interorganizational relations: Local employment service offices and social services sector organizations. *Administration and Society*, **7**, 419–454.

Assael, H. (1969) Constructive role of interorganizational conflict. *Administrative Science Quarterly*, **14**, 573–582.

Benson, K. (1975) The interorganizational network as a political economy. *Administrative Science Quarterly*, **20**, 229–249.

Culbert, S. Elden, J., McWhinney, W., Schmidt, W., and Tannenbaum, R. (1972) Transorganizational praxis: A search beyond organization development. In *International Associations*, **24**, 200–205. Santa Barbara, Calif.: Center for the Study of Democratic Institutions.

Emery, F., and Trist, E. (1965) The causal texture of organizational environments. *Human Relations*, **18**, 21–32.

Evan, W. (1966) The organization-set. In J. Thompson (ed.) *Approaches to Organizational Design*. University of Pittsburgh Press, 173–191.

French, W., and Bell, C. (1978) *Organization Development*. Englewood Cliffs, NJ: Prentice-Hall.

Galbraith, J. (1977) *Organization Design*. Reading, Mass.: Addison-Wesley.

Gutzkow, H. (1966) Relations among organizations. In R. Bowers (ed.) *Studies on Behavior in Organizations*. Athens, Ga.: University of Georgia Press, 13–44.

Hall, R., Clark, J., Giordano, P., Johnson, P., and Roekel, M. van (1977) Patterns of interorganizational relationships. *Administrative Science Quarterly*, 22, 457–474.

Jacobs, D. (1974) Dependence and vulnerability: An exchange approach to the control of organizations. *Administrative Science Quarterly*, 19, 45–59.

Kilmann, R., and Thomas, K. (1978) Four perspectives on conflict management: An attributional framework for organizing descriptive and normative theory. *Academy of Management Review*, 3, 59–68.

Kotter, J. (1979) Managing external dependence. *Academy of Management Review*, 4, 87–92.

Lehman, E. (1975) *Coordinating Health Care: Explorations in Interorganizational Relations*. Beverly Hills, Calif.: Sage.

Levine, S., and White, P. (1961) Exchange as a conceptual framework for the study of interorganization relations. *Administrative Science Quarterly*, 5, 583–601.

Margulies, N., and Raia, A. (1978) *Conceptual Foundations of Organizational Development*. New York: McGraw-Hill.

Motamedi, K. (1978) The evolution from interorganizational design to transorganizational development. Paper presented at the National Academy of Management Annual Meeting, San Francisco, Calif., 9–12 August.

Pfeffer, J. (1978) *Organizational Design*. Arlington Heights, Ill.: AHM Publishing.

Schmidt, S., and Kochan, T. (1976) An application of a political economy approach to effectiveness: Employment service–employer exchanges. *Administration and Society*, 7, 455–473.

Schmidt, S., and Kochan, T. (1977) Interorganizational relationships: Patterns and motivations. *Administrative Science Quarterly*, 22, 220–234.

Terreberry, S. (1968) The evolution of organizational environments. *Administrative Science Quarterly*, 12, 590–613.

Thomas, K. (1977) Towards multi-dimensional values in teaching: The example of conflict behaviors. *Academy of Management Review*, 2, 484–490.

Thompson, J. D. (1967) *Organizations in Action*. New York: McGraw-Hill.

Tichy, N. (1977) *Organization Design for Primary Health Care*. New York: Praeger.

Trist, E. (1967) Engaging with large-scale systems. A paper contributed to the McGregor Conference on Organization Development, Endicott House, Endicott, Mass.

Walton, R. (1969) *Interpersonal Peacemaking: Confrontation and Third Party Consultation*. Reading, Mass.: Addison-Wesley.

Zeitz, G. (1974) Interorganization relationships and social structure: A critique of some aspects of the literature. *Organization and Administrative Sciences*, 5, 131–139.

Systems Theory for Organization Development
Edited by T. G. Cummings
© 1980 John Wiley & Sons Ltd.

Chapter **15**

Approaching the Organizational Navel: An Evolutionary Perspective of Organization Development

John D. Bigelow

As a profession, organization development (OD) has been known primarily through its practices, and less so through its theory. This is probably not a desirable state of affairs, since it is through theory that practices can be communicated, tested, and developed. In this chapter an evolutionary perspective of organizations is presented, which the author believes is congruent with the practices and intuitive concepts of many OD practitioners. Such a perspective can potentially serve a valuable function in OD by providing a theoretical underpinning (or at least the beginnings of one) for many concepts in OD which have hitherto gained acceptance only through their intuitive value to OD practitioners.

Since there already exist a number of theories of organizations, it seems pertinent to begin by discussing why it is necessary to add another in order to achieve relevance for practice. Following this, some central premises of an evolutionary perspective of organizations are presented. This perspective is then related to current concepts of OD, and some implications of the theory which go beyond present practice are raised.

Qualities of practice-relevant theory

Although nearly two decades old, OD has yet to benefit extensively from organizational theories (OT). As Friedlander and Brown (1974) state: 'With a few major exceptions, contemporary organizational theory has not yet contributed heavily to the field of organization development. Its prime concern is in describing, analysing, and theorizing about the status quo of the organization rather than the planned change process which might improve its condition' (pp. 313–314).

A low level of linkage between practice and theory is also seen in the persistent inability of OD practitioners and recipients to describe exactly what OD is. OD tends to be described more in terms of its qualities and techniques, and less in terms of underlying theory (e.g. Bennis, 1969; French and Bell, 1973; Kahn, 1974; Burke, 1976).

Why have OT and OD remained so distinct from one another? A major reason lies in the tendency of most current theories of organizations to be ahistorical in their perspective. Current organizational theories may be quite extensive, encompassing an organization's relation to its environment, or even to its 'ecology' of organizations, but they tend to do so in a framework of the present or near present. While the broader present context of an organization is undoubtedly important in understanding the organization's current state, such a perspective must inevitably neglect the historical processes by which the organization came to this state, and by which the organization may be proceeding to some different future state (Benson, 1977).

The importance of historical processes in an organization has been pointed out in the recent literature by a number of scholars (e.g. Starbuck, 1971; Clark, 1972; Greiner, 1972; Stratton, 1974; Strauss, 1974; Pettigrew, 1976). This literature suggests that one reason why OT and OD have remained distinct from one another is that OT tends not to consider historical processes of change; these, however, are the very processes in which OD practitioners are most interested.

At the same time, a reason why an evolutionary perspective may be of interest to OD practitioners is indicated: evolutionary theory concerns the historical process by which living systems take form. Thus, an evolutionary viewpoint may be pertinent to OD practitioners, who are specifically concerned with this process in organizations. Evolution, however, means different things to different people. Over the last 150 years, evolution has been applied to a number of entities. The best known of these, of course, is its application in biology, where the 'modern synthesis' has become dominant in most biological fields. However, evolutionary theory has also been applied to social systems, such as societies (Campbell, 1965) and individuals (Pringle, 1951). Thus, in developing an evolutionary perspective of organizations, it is first necessary to clarify in what sense evolution is to be applied. This is done in the next section.

Premises of an evolutionary perspective of organizations

Application of evolution to a particular entity requires explication of which evolutionary constructs are to be used, and how these relate to the entity in question. These issues were addressed by the author in an earlier work (Bigelow, 1977) in which current streams of evolutionary thought were analysed, and a particular ('process-centred') approach was investigated in an organizational context. The major conclusions of that investigation were as follows:

(1) 'Social' evolution is the central process by which organizational change occurs.

Here, a distinction is made between biological and social evolution. While a number of authors have considered effects of biological evolution on social and organizational systems (e.g. Adrian, 1970; Eibl-Eibesfeldt, 1970; Maclay and Knipe, 1972; Trivers, 1977; Wilson, 1975), these effects are essentially static in a practitioner's time frame, and relatively immune to change by the tools at present available to him/her. Social evolutionary processes, on the other hand, are likely to be in a more rapid state of change, and the process is more accessible to change efforts.

(2) Organizations exist in environments, and must adapt – reactively and proactively – to them in order to survive.

This statement is consistent with contingency and open system perspectives of organizations (see Thompson, 1967). It is important to note that 'adaptation' is not necessarily a reactive process, but can be proactive as well: that is, an organization may adapt by acting on and changing its environment, as well as by changing itself to fit its environment. In this respect, adaptation, as used here, has much the same meaning as Summerhoff's (1950) 'directive correlation'. It should also be noted that in some instances an organization's survival is not necessarily independent of societal survival at some higher level. For example, a poorly operating school system may be prevented from failing (unlike a poorly operating private enterprise) by the governmental system. In such instances, the higher-level system is an appropriate unit of evolutionary analysis.

(3) Organizational practices are a principal means of adaptation.

While evolutionary theory shows that more than one kind of entity may be evolving in organizations (e.g. knowledge systems, kinds of people included, and physical artifacts of the organization), it appears that organizational practices are the central means of adaptation. Other kinds of evolution are pertinent to organizational adaptation, but tend to follow, rather than lead, organizational practices (cf. Weick, 1969). For example, the type of person included in an organization may tend to 'evolve' through discriminatory appointment, but consequent tendencies towards racism, sexism, and nepotism may be countered by changes in organizational practices, such as recruiting, screening, and interviewing.

(4) Adaptation is a process involving (a) development of a selective process by which successful and unsuccessful practices can be recognized; (b) generation of a variety of practices; and (c) continuation or discontinuation of practices based on selection.

Here, evolutionary theory goes beyond open systems and contingency perspectives of adaptation by defining adaptation as a process of variation, selection, and retention. Adaptation is not simply an outcome of the process: it is the process. The following paragraphs briefly describe the nature of organizational variation, selection, and retention.

Selection occurs through the application of indicators predictive of survival, rather than through actual survival. An important distinction is made between 'natural' selection, or survival of the fittest, and 'vicarious' selection (Campbell, 1965) which takes place prior to, and acts to forestall, natural selection. Natural selection is active in biological evolution and in ecologies of competing organizations, but is rarely seen within organizations. Here, indicators of organizational success, such as profit, productivity, job satisfaction, withdrawal, etc., are identified and monitored. Practices which appear to enhance the indicators are continued, while others are discontinued.

Organizations generate variations in practices by borrowing from other organizations, making incremental variations in existing practices, creating original variations, and adopting 'blind' variations. Organizations typically monitor the practices of other, similar organizations, and will try out practices which appear to be more successful than their own. Organizations also try out minor variations of their own on-going practices in attempts to boost their indicators. 'Original' variations are sometimes generated (e.g. through a suggestion box) and tried out. Finally, random variations in practices sometimes lead to improvements, and if this is noticed the variation may be institutionalized.

Retention of practices occurs through translation into memories and records, and through systems which ensure appropriate translation back into practice. 'Practices' have no intrinsic existence apart from their doing. Thus, retention must involve translation of practice into some more durable media. This in itself is no assurance of retention (i.e. continuation of practice, as opposed to mere storage). Consequently, organizations devise policies, rules, regulations, training programmes, reward systems, etc., which regulate retranslation into practice.

(5) Organizational evolution does not occur in a vacuum: organizations develop concrete, enduring mechanisms through which evolutionary process occurs.

While organizational members may not be explicitly following an evolutionary model, organizations do develop and institutionalize mechanisms for variation (e.g. creativity training, R & D units, norms encouraging innovation), selection (e.g. economic and social indicators, assessment centres), and retention (e.g. policies, rules, regulations, guidelines, training). Through these mechanisms, organizations seek out, identify, and retain organizational practices adaptive to their current situation.

(6) Evolutionary mechanisms themselves evolve.

It was stated above that evolutionary process is implemented through concrete mechanisms existing in the organization. Since the organization evolves, it follows that mechanisms are also capable of evolving. The evolution of evolutionary mechanisms, however, appears to occur through a process somewhat different from the evolution of organizational practices. Selection of selection mechanisms may be self-consistent (e.g. is assessment of cost-effectiveness itself cost-effective? Are measures of efficiency applied efficiently?), but unique selection criteria may be used as well. For example, it is important that selection criteria be applicable, and adequate to assess all variations which may arise. Retention processes should be reliable, and not subject to loss through aging of records or turnover of knowledgeable members. Further, short-term and long-term selection criteria should be consistent with one another (e.g. do high quarterly profits predict long-term financial stability?). Using these criteria, evolutionary mechanisms can be assessed, and if current practices are found wanting, alternatives may be tried and retained.

Evolution of evolutionary mechanisms is a reflexive notion, which brings to mind an infinite order of mechanisms evolving mechanisms, *ad infinitum*. This does not appear to be the case in actual organizations, since the evolutionary rate becomes progressively slower as one moves to higher orders of process; in order to assess a mechanism, it is necessary to try it out for a while. Thus, while an organization may have fairly well-defined 'first order' evolutionary mechanisms, its 'second order' mechanisms (i.e. mechanisms which evolve first order mechanisms) must be less well defined, since a longer period is involved in their confirmation. Thus, as one moves to progressively higher orders, focus is rapidly lost, and third or fourth order mechanisms may be entirely missing, since the time required for the confirmation may exceed the life span of the organization. An important implication is that higher order mechanisms are more likely to be out of phase with current adaptive requirements, because of the relative slowness of their evolutionary processes.

This section has briefly overviewed some premises of an evolutionary perspective as applied to organizations. It is seen that this is a dynamic view in which organizations develop mechanisms which regulate the process of variation, selection, and retention, and thereby adapt to their situation. Let us now turn to how this perspective of organizations may be useful in OD.

Evolution and organization development

In relating the evolutionary perspective described above to OD, a question immediately arises: why is OD needed? In an evolutionary perspective, organizations are seen as adapting on their own,[1] without planned intervention. The answer to this question must be this: while it is true that organizations develop adaptive mechanisms, these are not always appropriate to or effective in achieving required adaptations.[2] This can be for a number of reasons. First, if an organization is confronted by the need for rapid and unexpected change, the magnitude of the change required may simply overtax the organization's adaptive resources (Bennis, 1969).

Second, the design of an organization's evolutionary mechanisms may not be entirely appropriate for its circumstances. For example, an organization which has existed in a stable environment for some time is likely to have developed a satisfactory set of practices for its circumstances, and thereafter to be concerned primarily with retention of these practices. Thus, the organization's evolutionary design would emphasize rules and regulations, and explicit reward systems, to ensure that practices which proved satisfactory in the past continue to be carried out. Such a design is likely also to discourage organizational innovations, since the payoff is likely to be low. If, however, this organization's environment becomes less stable and more dynamic, this design is apt to become inappropriate. Since no set of practices is likely to remain adaptive for long in a dynamic environment, a more appropriate evolutionary design would give greater emphasis to variation (in an on-going search for satisfactory practices), and place less emphasis on a reliable retention system (cf. Burns and Stalker's (1961) concepts of mechanistic and organic organizations). However, an organization may be slow in changing its evolutionary design, since, as noted earlier, processes of change at this level are relatively slow.

Another example of inappropriate evolutionary design has to do with adequate linkages between variation, selection, and retention. Adaptation is contingent not only on the existence of the three types of mechanisms, but also on their effective linkage to form a complete evolutionary cycle. However, it is sometimes found that evolutionary mechanisms exist, but are not adequately linked. For example, the US Peace Corps had a well-developed programme selection process in its research and evaluation division, but the findings of the division had little impact on actual programme practices (Bigelow, 1977). Similarly, Alexander (1978) reviewed the uses made of a number of organizational assessment centres (which serve a selection function), and found that the findings of these centres often received little use. Other examples of possible problems of evolutionary design include unreliable retention systems due to high turnover of skilled staff, bounding of variations in ways excluding potentially successful variations, and over-emphasis on 'objective' short-term success indicators, without checking to see if they reliably predict long-term success.

A third type of problem which may exist in relation to organizational evolution concerns the organization's ability to design appropriate evolutionary mechanisms. It was suggested earlier that such 'second order' processes may lack definition. Operationally, this may mean that individuals in the organization have hazy criteria for recognizing successful mechanisms; ideas about evolutionary designing may be arbitrary, and unrelated to how well current mechanisms are actually working. Additionally, knowledge of alternative designs may be lacking. If this is the case, the organization may be unable to design effective evolutionary mechanisms or, if changes in the environment take place, to redesign mechanisms accordingly.

In sum, three possible reasons why organizational evolutionary processes may be inappropriate or ineffective in achieving organizational adaptation have been discussed. First, the magnitude of change required may overload the organization's adaptive resources; second, current design of evolutionary mechanisms may be inadequate; third, the organization may lack the ability to develop effective evolutionary mechanisms.

Three points of evolutionary intervention

These three types of problems with evolutionary processes are fundamentally different from one another, and constitute three distinct foci for organizational change efforts. Correspondingly, three types of organizational consultancies have developed, each with its own change targets, methods, and problems. These are discussed below:

(1) Intervention into evolutionary content   The point of intervention here is organizational practices, apart from the organization's evolutionary processes which normally produce them. There are a number of technical and structural consulting firms which will simply design and install a set of practices for a particular organization. This may be worthwhile for the organization when complex and/or technical changes are required which are beyond the organization's resources to devise on their own. There are advantages to intervention at this point: results are rapid and relatively easy to evaluate. However, intervention here leaves unchanged an organization's higher order evolutionary processes, raising the possibility that practices may not fit the organization's success criteria, and will eventually be nullified or dismantled. Here, Bennis's (1969) analogy of this kind of consultancy as a 'doctor–patient' relation is apt; while the doctor has the capability to transplant a set of practices, the patient may thereafter reject the transplant.

(2) 'First order' intervention concerning evolutionary mechanisms   Here the consultant designs and installs evolutionary mechanisms. This may involve variation (e.g. training in creativity or entrepreneurship, suggestion system), selection processes (e.g. assessment centres, social accounting), and/or retention (e.g. reward systems, record keeping procedures, training programmes). Argyris and Schon (1978) refer to this point of intervention as 'double-loop' learning, in which governing variables for identifying successful organizational practices are the focus apart from the actual practices they lead to, or how these governing variables are derived. Interventions at this point may persist longer than the previous type, and may eventually have beneficial consequences for organizational practices; however, they are still potentially subject to second order effects which could nullify them.

(3) 'Second order' intervention, into evolution of evolutionary mechanisms   Here, the consultant is concerned with how successful mechanisms are identified, possible alternatives, and means by which mechanisms are retained. This point of intervention appears to correspond with Bateson's (1972) 'deutero-learning', or learning how to learn. Here, the concern is not with organizational practices or the mechanisms which produce them. Rather, it is with ways by which organizations generate these evolutionary mechanisms. The following consultancy approaches appear to place much of their emphasis here: participative job design, action-research, process consultation, team building, socio-technical systems, and job enlargement. Interventions at this point may persist for some time, and should have amplified first order and evolutionary content effects. These

effects, however, may be a long time in coming; moreover, their relation to the intervention may be indirect and difficult to assess.

One could conceivably go into 'third order' and higher order points, and the complexity of organizations may eventually reach the point where these orders are relevant. Currently, however, third and above orders are so ill-defined as to be operationally non-existent. It is evident that the above classification of consultancies according to intervention points is not necessarily 'clean'. While a particular consultative approach may tend to place the bulk of its effort at one point, there may be variations in how the approach is actually implemented: for example, socio-technical design may be conducted unilaterally by an outside expert and then 'installed' (a content and first order intervention), or may be conducted participatively with the people involved (a second order intervention).

Relation of evolution to contemporary OD practices

Practitioners reading this paper may by now have made some connections between the evolutionary concepts presented above and their own, perhaps intuitive, orientation to OD. This perspective views OD as one of a number of types of consultancies concerned with aspects of organizational adaptation. OD is distinguished from other types of consultancies in that its characteristic domain is second order evolutionary processes; that is, the means by which organizations develop evolutionary mechanisms. In OD interventions, first order processes (the actual design of mechanisms) and evolutionary content are more under the control of the organization itself.

This viewpoint also provides insight into the longstanding issue of facilitation v. directiveness as the preferred mode of OD (Burke, 1976). In an evolutionary perspective, the OD consultant is highly directive in second order matters, even standing in temporarily in place of second order process. For example, the consultant might press his/her views and values about criteria for effective evolutionary design, or define possible alternatives to current second order mechanisms. However, by being directive at the second order, the consultant is at the same time facilitative at the first order; to guide a process by which others make their own decision is the meaning of facilitation. The same reasoning applies to the issue of OD as process or outcome. OD specifies second order outcomes (i.e. design of second order mechanisms) which set the processes affecting first order outcomes. Thus, OD is outcome-oriented at the second order, but process-oriented at the first order.

Beyond current OD

We have touched on some ways in which evolutionary ideas may be related to current OD. In addition, it is possible to make some preliminary comments on a specifically evolutionary conception of OD. From this viewpoint, OD activities are appropriate when an organization is having difficulties in adaptation (i.e. when the consequences of its practices do not meet its success criteria), and when this is largely due to its difficulty in evolving effective evolutionary mechanisms. It must also be assumed that the organization is not on the brink of disaster, and has time to engage in this relatively time consuming process. If not, a lower order intervention may be more appropriate, at least in the short term.

The task of the consultant is to develop effective second order mechanisms by strengthening existing mechanisms, nullifying factors inhibiting second order processes, and standing in as a second order mechanism where required. Carrying out this task implies at least three steps: (1) identification of existing second order mechanisms and their effects on first order mechanisms; (2) assumption of and reshaping of second order mechanisms, and (3) evolution of first order mechanisms via the second order process. Each of these steps is discussed below.

Identification of existing second order mechanisms

The first step is for the consultant to attempt to find out about the nature of existing second order mechanisms. For example, what criteria does the organization use for recognizing successful first order mechanisms? How does the organization generate variations in first order mechanisms? How does the organization retain and continue to use first order mechanisms? As was suggested earlier, these second order mechanisms may not exist with the same degree of clarity as do first order mechanisms. They may be more *ad hoc* than institutionalized, and organizational members may not have a clear idea as to when or how they are used. Second order mechanisms may be episodic, coming into use only after important chronic problems have been in existence for some time, and lower order efforts have not been sufficient.

It is also possible for second order mechanisms to exist outside the awareness of organizational members. Campbell (1965) suggests that social evolution may proceed on the basis of blind variation, and consequently that such systems may be wiser than their members. Similarly, it is conceivable that an organization could irrationally evolve second order mechanisms without being explicitly aware of them, or at least of their function. To the extent that organizational members are aware of them, practices evolved in such a way may be thought of as tradition, ritual, or red tape, or may be rationalized in terms of some other (non-evolutionary) function.

This raises a potential problem for the consultant in finding out about second order mechanisms. If the consultant relies on members' understanding of the organization, it is still possible for existing, but unrecognized, second order mechanisms to later emerge, and possibly interfere with the consultant's second order activities. This suggests that in finding out about such mechanisms, the consultant should go beyond the views of individuals, and look at the the actual behaviour of the organization. This may be done in a number of ways. For example, one can examine the organization's actions in historical situations to see if second order mechanisms were in evidence then. This is consistent with Argyris and Schon's (1978) method of having managers write case studies of critical past situations, and using these to gain insight into higher order processes. Another possibility is that the consultant may be in a position whereby he/she can create situations evocative of organizational second order response, and observe what happens. This might be done, for example, by assembling top managers, and running a simulation of a near future organizational crisis. This type of approach, of course, is a longstanding technique of ethnomethodology. More recently, Salancik (1978) has advocated a similar approach, of 'tickling' the organization in the course of organizational research.

Assumption of second order processes

In the course of the above step, the consultant is gaining knowledge of how second order mechanisms of the organization currently function. The next step is for the consultant to move to a position in the organization where he/she can effectively take over and/or reshape parts of these mechanisms.

The consultant can generally expect that this step will not be easy. Argyris and Schon (1978) propose that most organizations are 'model one' in design, in which second order changes are resisted. One can see reasons why this may be so: changes in second order processes are likely to have multiplier effects as first order and content changes follow. In complex organizations, it may take some time for consequent adjustments to take place. In the meantime, it is difficult for the organization to develop adaptive responses to its situation, since its criteria for success and its range of possible alternatives (i.e. first order evolution) are in a state of flux. Consequently, we would expect organizations to develop a conservative stance with relation to second order mechanisms. This works well as long as these mechanisms are working well, but becomes a disadvantage if they are not.

This touches on the well-recognized OD issue of 'entry', in which the consultant marshals forces contributing to attaining this position (e.g. his/her own personal force and reputation, support of critical members, pressures on the organization), and pits them against the counterforces indicated above. It would appear that one tactic currently used is for the consultant to offer novel OD approaches. Many organizations seem persistently open to novel variation in OD. Unfortunately, these are all too often tried, perhaps superficially, and then abandoned. It may be that many OD consultants are taking advantage of a widespread second order selection criterion which favours novelty, but unless this leads to a sufficient degree of success, this criterion may eventually shift in a more conservative direction.

First order evolution via second order process

Assuming that the consultant has to some extent gained a position of influence over second order processes, the next step is to enact these processes, thereby evolving first order mechanisms. Specifically, this involves (1) acting as a selector of effective first order mechanism designs, (2) stimulating variations in first order mechanisms, and (3) seeing that effective first order mechanisms are retained:

(1) Selector of first order designs   The consultant should be knowledgeable about the appropriate design of first order mechanisms for given environmental circumstances, and be able to recognize effective or ineffective designs. Some examples of design issues follow:

Selection – Are the selection criteria of the organization compatible with one another? For example, an organization cannot have the goals of both maximizing profit and maximizing satisfaction, or of both developing a secure market niche and innovative product lines. The issue of aligning short-term and long-term goals, mentioned earlier, is also relevant here.

Variation – To what extent do the boundaries placed around potential variations exclude potential improvements in first order mechanisms? Conversely, to what extent are variations accepted uncritically, even when the likelihood of their constituting an improvement is low?

Retention – Is retention of first order mechanisms reliable? Or are mechanisms lost through turnover of skilled employees and loss of critical records? Are reward systems effective in inducing accurate translation of records into practice?

Interactions – Given the level of uncertainty of the organization's environment, is the rate of variation sufficient to keep the organization adapted? Is the retention system permeable enough to allow this rate of variation? Are variation, selection, and retention adequately linked to one another? Or are there variations which are not assessed, successful variations which are not retained, etc.?

(2) Stimulator of first order variations   The consultant should be aware of different ways that first order mechanisms can be designed, and be able to stimulate thinking about alternatives to current first order mechanisms. For example, how is first order selection currently done? What other ways might be tried? What ways exist to create first order variation? In what different ways can first order retention be achieved?

(3) Retention of first order mechanisms   The consultant must ask how first order mechanisms are currently retained, and how this affects changing these mechanisms. Clearly, of all the second order processes discussed, second order retention is the one most necessarily delegated to the organization. While it may be possible for the consultant to stand in for second order variation and selection, if he/she intends to end the consulting relationship and wants the effects of consulting to endure, retention must be delegated.

Above, second order processes and some related issues are discussed. This discussion has been necessarily sketchy, not only because organizational evolutionary thinking is at an early stage, but also because these issues are broad, encompassing much of the field of OD. Nonetheless, it may be that consultants reading this paper will find the framework congenial to their own thinking, and will be able to flesh it out with their own experiences.

In the view of consultancies presented above, a consultancy can itself be seen as a multi-ordered evolutionary process external to the organization, which can be hooked up to the organization at one of the three points identified. Thus, a technical consultancy might be seen as having its own first and second order evolutionary mechanisms, which are harnessed in the service of organizational practices. Consultants typically draw on physical or behavioural sciences, which can also be viewed as a fairly formalized process of knowledge evolution (Campbell, 1960; Notz, 1978). This, however, raises an important question concerning OD consultancy, which is considered in the next section.

The organization's navel

A model of evolutionary 'orders' was presented earlier, in which a potentially infinite regression of orders was raised, but limited in fact to about two. It was also suggested that, by intervening at the second order, the OD practitioner sits on 'top' of the existing regression. If so, and if higher order mechanisms are missing, how does the OD practitioner evolve his/her practice?

One can argue that a practitioner's preparation is in fact a kind of 'third order' training. The applied behavioural scientist attains a broader and more in-depth orientation, which may make resolution at second and third orders more attainable than might data from a single organization. This, however, is only postponing the inevitable: how about the $(n + 1)$th order? At some point we have to admit that this order is so abstruse, and takes so long to confirm (perhaps longer than the history of civilization), that it is not effective in determining lower orders.

At this point we are very close to the 'OD is a fad' viewpoint. One might postulate that OD in fact has no solid basis, and is wandering blindly from one technique to another as fashion dictates. This, however, may be too pessimistic a view, since there appear to be other resources OD can draw on in establishing valid practices. One possibility is that higher orders can to some extent be deduced from lower orders. For example, an OD practitioner can evaluate the validity of his/her practice in terms of its consequences for job satisfaction and productivity. The danger in doing this, of course, is that a circular process is developed, which tends to justify the *status quo*. Notz (1978) suggests that this is in fact the case with much social research, which picks up administrators' lay theories and feeds them back as social science fact.

A second possibility is that philosophical bases can be drawn on. At some point, the OD practitioner has to stop and say, 'These are my starting assumptions.' These assumptions are difficult to confirm or disconfirm, and are therefore more a matter of belief than of learning. Here, the practitioner is usually drawn into one or another philosophical stance: e.g. humanism, behaviourism, or existentialism (cf. Hainer, 1964; Friedlander, 1976; Motamedi, 1977).

A third possibility might be referred to as passing through the organization's navel. The OD practitioner attains a fundamental appreciation of the basic uncertainty underlying human endeavour and approaches a 'no method' method of OD, similar to the Zen concept of enlightenment (thus the metaphor – the navel is a place where physiological transforms lead outside the body). This method is similar to the 'here and now' used in sensitivity and gestalt approaches, although truly enlightened OD practitioners are undoubtedly scarce, if they exist at all at present. There is evidence of a certain dropout (fall through?) rate among practitioners, possibly related to the effects of this appreciation. People visited by this insight often do not remain in practice, and may be severely jarred in the course of their career.

Conclusion

Some concepts of an evolutionary perspective of organizations, as well as some of their implications for OD, have been discussed. OD is portrayed as a consultancy directed at second order organizational processes. The task of the OD consultant is to link with the organization at this point, and to a large extent stand in as a second order mechanism. The steps of diagnosis (of second order mechanisms), entry, and second order action on first order mechanisms are suggested as parts of the OD process. Finally, the issue of how OD evolves is raised, and some alternatives to an infinite regress are pointed out.

It is seen that an evolutionary theory of organizations is complex, and its manifestations have yet to be fully explored. However, it is the author's belief that these concepts correspond in large degree to what experienced practitioners already intuitively know. Evolutionary concepts get away from the time limited view of organizations which currently predominates in OT, and which is of marginal relevance for OD practitioners. Evolution provides a historical perspective of organizations which hopefully can serve as a theoretical framework in which the practitioner's knowledge can be organized, expressed, and itself evolved.

Notes

1. Even if they do not, ineffective organizations may be removed from the population of organizations by 'natural' selection. Thus, an implicit value of 'organizational' development is that evolution at the organizational level is preferable to evolution at the interorganizational level.
2. It is possible to use evolutionary theory to analyse such circumstances as changes in environmental stability and organizational growth, and to predict the types of adaptive problems which organizations will encounter. This, however, is beyond the scope of this chapter; see Bigelow (1977).

References

Adrian, C. (1970) Ethology and bureaucracy. Paper read at the Eigth World Congress of the International Political Science Association, held at Munich.

Alexander, L. D. (1978) An exploratory study of the utilization of assessment center results. California: UCLA Graduate School of Management working paper.

Argyris, C., and Schon, D. (1978) *Organizational Learning: A Theory of Action Perspective.* Reading Mass.: Addison-Wesley.

Bateson, G. (1972) *Steps to an Ecology of the Mind.* San Francisco: Chandler.

Bennis, W. G. (1969) Organizational Development: *Its Nature, Origins, and Prospects.* Reading, Mass.: Addison-Wesley.

Benson, J. K. (1977) Organizations: A dialectical view. *Administrative Science Quarterly*, **22** (1), 1–21.

Bigelow, J. (1977) Evolution in organizations. Dissertation, Case Western Reserve University, Cleveland.

Burke, W. W. (1976) Organization development in transition. *Journal of Applied Behavioral Science*, **12** (1), 23–43.

Burns, T., and Stalker, G. (1961) *The Management of Innovation.* Chicago: Quadrangle.

Campbell, D. T. (1960) Blind variation and selective retention in creative thought as in other knowledge processes. *Psychological Review*, **67** (6) 380–400.

Campbell, D. T. (1965) Variation and selective retention in socio-cultural evolution. In H. R. Parringer, G. T. Blankston, and R. W. Mack, (eds) *Social Change in Developing Areas.* Cambridge, Mass.: Schenkman.

Clark, B. R. (1972) The organizational saga in higher education. *Administrative Science Quarterly*, **17**, 178–184.

Eibl-Eibesfeldt, I. (1970) *Ethology: The Biology of Behavior.* New York: Holt, Rinehart, & Winston.

French, W. L., and Bell, C. H. (1973) *Organizational Development: Behavioral Science Interventions for Organizational Improvement.* Englewood Cliffs, NJ: Prentice-Hall.

Friedlander, F. (1976) Organizational development reaches adolescence: An exploration of underlying values. *Journal of Applied Behavioral Science*, **12** (1), 7–21.

Friedlander, F., and Brown, L. D. (1974) Organization development. *Annual Review of Psychology*, **25**, 313–341.

Greiner, L. E. (1972) Evolution and revolution as organizations grow. *Harvard Business Review*, July–August, 37–46.

Hainer, R. (1964) Rationalism, pragmatism, and existentialism: Perceived but undiscovered multicultural problems. In P. Glatt and L. Shelly (eds) *The Research Society.* Washington, D.C.: Office of Naval Research.

Hirschman, A. O., and Lindblom, C. E. (1962) Economic development, research and development, policymaking: Some converging views. *Behavioral Science*, **7**, 211–222.

Kahn, R. L. (1974) Organizational development: Some problems and proposals. *Journal of Applied Behavioral Science*, **10**, 485–502.

Maclay, G., and Knipe, H. (1972) *The Dominant Man: The Pecking Order in Human Society.* New York: Dell.

Motamedi, K. (1977) Toward explicating philosophical orientations in OB. Oregon State University School of Business working paper, February.

Notz, W. (1978) Some factors necessitating the experimenting organization. Paper presented at the convention of the American Institute for Decision Science.

Peterson, R. A., and Berger, D. G. (1971) Entrepreneurship in organizations: Evidence from the popular music industry. *Administrative Science Quarterly*, **16** (1), 97–106.

Pettigrew, A. M. (1976) The creation of organisational cultures. Paper presented to the joint EIASM-Dansk Management Center Research Seminary on Entrepreneurs and the Process of Institution Building, Copenhagen, 18–20 May.

Pringle, J. W. S. (1951) On the parallel between learning and evolution. *Behavior*, **3**, 174–215.

Salancik, G. (1978) Field stimulation. Paper presented at the 38th Academy of Management Annual Meeting, San Francisco, 9–13 August.

Starbuck, W. H. (ed.) (1971) *Organizational Growth and Development*. Harmondsworth, Middx.: Penguin.

Stratton, W. E. (1974) Organizations and environment: A case study in adaptation to change. Dissertation, Case Western Reserve University, Cleveland.

Strauss, G. (1974) Adolescence in organization growth. *Organization Dynamics*, Spring, 3–17.

Summerhoff, G. (1950) *Analytical Biology*. London: Oxford University Press.

Thompson, J. D. (1967) *Organizations in Action*. New York: McGraw-Hill.

Trivers, R.L. (1977) The evolution of altruism. *Quarterly Review of Biology*, **46** (4), 35–57.

Weick, K. (1969) *The Social Psychology of Organizing*. Reading, Mass.: Addison-Wesley.

Wilson, E. O. (1975) *Sociobiology: The New Synthesis*. Cambridge, Mass.: Belknap.

Index

355